ADDITIONAL ADV

SPY SITES OF ̶ ̶ ̶ ̶ ̶

"The history is extraordinary and, until now, never told in this way. This is a must read for anyone interested in the ins and outs of espionage, and they will discover that, once again, New York City plays center stage."

—**DAVID COHEN,** CIA Deputy Director for Operations (1995–97); NYPD Deputy Commissioner, Intelligence (2002–14)

"Melton and Wallace are like having a CIA historian at your elbow. If you loved their book *Spycraft* on the intricate world of espionage tradecraft, you will find this guide an essential roadmap to the intelligence landmarks in and around New York."

—**DAVID HOFFMAN,** author of *The Billion Dollar Spy: A True Story of Cold War Espionage and Betrayal*

"*Spy Sites of New York City* is an indispensable guide to the back alleys of American intelligence in the city that never sleeps, . . . reveal[ing] New York's secrets to both casual and serious students of espionage."

—**COL. CHRISTOPHER P. COSTA,** US Army (Ret.), former special assistant to the president, career intelligence officer, and executive director, International Spy Museum, Washington, DC

"The amount of research that went into this book is remarkable. It turns out that wherever you are in New York, you are near a place where spy history was made."

—**MARK STOUT,** former historian for the International Spy Museum, Washington, DC

SPY SITES

OF NEW YORK CITY

SPY SITES

OF NEW YORK CITY

A GUIDE TO THE REGION'S SECRET HISTORY

H. KEITH MELTON AND ROBERT WALLACE

WITH HENRY R. SCHLESINGER

FOREWORD BY
JOSEPH WEISBERG AND JOEL FIELDS

GEORGETOWN UNIVERSITY PRESS
WASHINGTON, D.C

Library of Congress Cataloging-in-Publication Data

Names: Melton, H. Keith (Harold Keith), 1944- author. | Wallace, Robert (Retired intelligence officer), author. | Schlesinger, Henry R., author.
Title: Spy Sites of New York City : A Guide to the Region's Secret History by H. Keith Melton and Robert Wallace ; with Henry R. Schlesinger ; foreword by Joseph Weisberg and Joel Fields.
Description: Washington, DC : Georgetown University Press, 2020. | Includes bibliographical references and index.
Identifiers: LCCN 2019004746 (print) | LCCN 2019007748 (ebook) | ISBN 9781626167100 (ebook) | ISBN 9781626167094 | ISBN 9781626167094 (pbk.: alk. paper)
Subjects: LCSH: Espionage--New York (State)--New York--Guidebooks. | Espionage--New York (State)--New York--History. | Spies--New York (State)--New York. | LCGFT: Guidebooks.
Classification: LCC UB271.U5 (ebook) | LCC UB271.U5 M46 2020 (print) | DDC 327.1209747/1--dc23
LC record available at https://lccn.loc.gov/2019004746

This book is printed on acid-free paper meeting the requirements of the American National Standard for Permanence in Paper for Printed Library Materials.

21 20   9 8 7 6 5 4 3 2 First printing

Printed in the United States of America.

Cover designer, Tim Green, Faceout Studio.
Cover images courtesy of Getty Images: "Run For Your Life!" By Donald G. Jean and "Below Highland Park" by ©fitopardo.com
Text designer, Paul Nielsen, Faceout Studio.
Cartographer, Chris Robinson.
Acquisitions assistant, Juliette Leader.
Production assistant, Rachel McCarthy.

CONTENTS

FOREWORD

Imagine yourself as a spy in New York City. You don't know if you're being watched. Where can you leave a package for your agent to pick up? If anyone sees you leave it, your agent could be arrested when he or she comes to pick it up. What about meeting your source in person? Where can you have a talk without worrying that you might be seen by someone who knows either of you?

Spies are always looking for these locations—places to leave dead drops, make brush passes, have clandestine meetings. Think about how hard it would be to find spots to do any of these things in a tiny village. But a big city—that would provide limitless spaces for these clandestine acts, wouldn't it? The problem is, spies have to evade the host country's secret police, which makes it all very difficult.

When we were filming the television series *The Americans* in New York City, our world converged with the spy's world. We spent a lot of our time looking for locations too—locations to film scenes where these same types of clandestine activities could take place: dead drops, brush passes, secret meetings between officers and their sources.

We had a few enormous advantages over real-world spies: We didn't have the secret police following us (just the occasional regular police officer if our location van made an illegal turn). And we had the benefit of controlling crowds when we filmed, so our intelligence officers only had to worry when we wanted them to. On the other hand, we had different kinds of problems. Our show was set in Washington, DC, in the 1980s, so we had to find locations that could pass for a different city in a different time than the one we were shooting in—not easy! But also not dangerous.

For us, it was all make-believe. But it was exciting to think about what really happened on the streets, in the parks, and in all the hidden byways of New York City. Over many decades, spies from all over the world had converged on New York City to ply their trade. Some of them got caught; most of them didn't. Agents of the Federal Bureau of Investigation followed them when they knew who they were, but most of the meetings, brush passes, and dead drops were undetected and live on only in the dusty files of secret police agencies of foreign countries, never to be seen or heard of by anyone again.

Fortunately we do know about some of them. H. Keith Melton and Robert Wallace, along with Henry Schlesinger, have put together an amazing compendium of some of the most notorious and fascinating spycraft encounters ever to take place in New York City and the surrounding area. And they pinpoint the exact place and moment that these incidents took place. Having scoured the same city in search of these same locations, we can tell you that fact is even better than fiction.

Whether you are an espionage aficionado or someone with a new interest in this strange world, there is no better way to see how spycraft really works than to immerse yourself in the real places, in the real moments of these spies' lives.

Spy Sites of New York City takes you there.

—Joseph Weisberg and Joel Fields
Showrunners and Executive Producers of *The Americans*

PREFACE

There is seemingly no end to construction and reconstruction in New York—a nice town once they get done building it. In a city that relishes and rejoices in the new and novel, buildings rise and fall with unfailing regularity. An innovative grid system developed in 1811 that divided part of the city into regular blocks with little concern for topography, to ease the way for development between 14th Street and Upper Manhattan, did not include a large section of Lower Manhattan. Consequently, 18th-century addresses are frequently tricky and may not correspond exactly to those of the present day but rather offer approximate locations.

The resulting ambiguity of exact coordinates of some operations described in this work is consistent with the spy's profession, where intrigue often masquerades as the mundane. Who could believe that a coffee-shop conversation is really a plot to overthrow a government or that a clothing store is the cover for a spy ring? Is the chalk mark on a mailbox graffiti or a signal that a nearby dead drop has been loaded? Are all the moviegoers really interested in the feature film, or are some looking for a dark location to exchange briefcases loaded with secrets?

Working together on other intelligence history books during the past two decades, we developed an extensive database of espionage-related locations in the United States. We found that many locations scattered throughout intelligence literature are often presented as a footnote or minor detail. Others appeared in official documents such as government reports, affidavits, and indictments. The resources of both the Library of Congress and the National Archives and Records Administration were readily accessible and invaluable. Newspaper accounts of spy arrests and trials sometimes mentioned locations of arrests, residences, or places of birth. We received gracious assistance from several research libraries that held collections of the papers of prominent individuals who had worked in intelligence. Finally, we were particularly fortunate to be offered private assistance from family members of now-deceased relatives who were central to many of the cases.

Combined, these sources provided a wealth of new operational information as well as numerous sites and images that were either obscure or previously unpublished. A selected bibliography is included for readers whose interests extend to greater detail on stories behind sites presented.

In researching New York locations with ties to intelligence operations, we discovered spy sites in homes, hotels, restaurants, parks, brothels, bars, and governmental offices. We found them at monuments, street corners, under bridges, and on utility poles. Some of these historic sites remain; others have been demolished and redeveloped. Addresses change over centuries, and buildings are rebranded or repurposed, while private homes where spies once lived are purchased by new owners who may be unaware their residence occupies a place in America's clandestine history. As you visit any nonpublic place we describe, please respect the property rights and personal privacy of present-day owners.

We recognize that no book about spy sites is complete, as many operations remain unknown except to the participants or those authorized to read secret files. Some well-known spies such as Sidney Reilly, Jacob Golos, Rudolph Abel, and Anna Chapman used dozens of operational sites for their espionage. Therefore, the number of locations alone presents a limiting factor for any book that has the good fortune to draw upon such a richness of material. Since not every interesting site can be included, we selected more than 400 addresses and 350 images to accompany 233 spy stories to capture the history of espionage and clandestine operations in New York City and the surrounding area, especially on Long Island and in northern New Jersey.

Each entry pairs a primary location that the reader can visit with an associated spy story. When only a street address is provided, the location is in Manhattan. Sites in the other New York City boroughs include the name of the borough and street address. Sites beyond the city on Long Island and in New Jersey are clearly identified as such. The narrative proceeds chronologically and includes surprising, glorious, and notorious episodes in New York's intelligence history.

Many entries also contain additional sites related to the primary story for readers interested in visiting additional locations where spies lived and operated. An appendix of maps shows sites by neighborhood, city, or county, and pinpoint numbers on the maps correspond to entry numbers in the text. Readers are encouraged to customize their own itinerary for a spy tour.

We attempted to write each entry with sufficient fullness to convey a concise but stand-alone story about the site, individual, or operation. To do so, we were required, in a few instances, to repeat certain details that appear elsewhere, but we have attempted to keep this to a minimum. We appreciate the reader's patience with this necessary redundancy.

Today, with more spies likely operating in New York than ever before, the need for new signal sites, places for clandestine meetings, and covert communication locations continues to expand. As you explore more than two centuries of New York's clandestine history, remember that while the buildings, streets, subways, apartment houses, businesses, alleys, and hotels may have changed, the excitement, intrigue and danger of espionage surrounds you—in fact, the unknown person standing next to you could be a spy on a mission.

Finally, if you know of a spy story and a site not included in this book, we would love to hear about it. Thank you for joining us in these espionage adventures.

ACKNOWLEDGMENTS

This was not a book we planned to write until encouraged to do so by Don Jacobs, senior acquisitions editor of Georgetown University Press. In 2014, Don recognized the value of capturing stories about historical locations of espionage operations in Washington, DC, and supported our research that led to publication in 2017 of *Spy Sites of Washington, DC*. Based on the immediate positive response to that book, it seemed that a companion volume centered on New York, a city where spies directed by Gen. George Washington contributed directly to the outcome of the Revolutionary War, would more fully capture the significance of intelligence operations in America. These two cities, one the political capital and the other a symbol of America's financial and industrial power and seat of the United Nations, are centers of a largely secret history of spies who, on behalf of governments, friendly or hostile to the interests of the United States, influenced the course of world affairs. That we should write stories of one but not the other seemed like painting only half a picture.

We extend our appreciation to Don, Juliette Leader, and Glenn Saltzman from the Georgetown University Press staff for their helpful recommendations on style and substance. Don McKeon applied superb copyediting skills to our manuscript to assure accuracy of names, places, and dates and, when necessary, gently reminded us that proper grammar is never out of style. We especially acknowledge the contributions of Gerald Goodwin and two other outside readers who fact-checked our research based on their personal awareness of New York's neighborhoods, streets, and social history. The Georgetown University Press design and production team made the book a handsome reality. Our agent, Dan Mandel of New York's Sanford J. Greenburger Associates, artfully managed the necessary contract and business elements.

Presenting this number of intelligence organizations, spy cases, and operational sites in New York required substantial assistance from historians and photographers, government as well as private. Intelligence bibliographer Hayden Peake and FBI historian John Fox pointed us to lesser-known New York sites documented in 20th-century espionage literature and cases. Bill Kline, Alan Kohler, Keith Clark, Paul Cook, David Robarge, Mr. T, Ms. S, and Jerry Richards contributed significant insights into specific operations. Mark Stout's research on John "Frenchy" Grombach revealed a forgotten and colorful chapter in New York's espionage history.

Our education in New York's history was sharpened by John Glass's expansive knowledge of New York's iconic buildings. Allison Chomet, adjunct assistant curator in the New York University Archives, and Emily Johnson, graduate archives assistant, clarified the historical record of early Cold War spy Valeri Makayev. Timothy Phillips, author of *The Secret Twenties: British Intelligence, the Russians and the Jazz Age,* shared some finer points of early Soviet intrigue with us. Alexandra Levy of the Atomic Heritage Foundation added little-known details about New York's role in the Manhattan Project, and the helpful staff at the New York Yacht Club brought to our attention the club's important role in World War I.

The majority of the nonpublic images in the book were made available either through the courtesy of the Melton Archives or from the many hours Henry R. Schlesinger, Maxwell Schlesinger, and William Schlesinger devoted to photographing buildings and sites throughout the city. The contributions of their efforts cannot be overstated. Perhaps they received a small reward by acquiring broader area familiarity as they took the subway to explore neighborhoods throughout the five boroughs. An adventurous Ben Wargo volunteered to photograph several less accessible sites outside the city. Gary Kern, Jack Barsky, and Pete Earley were generous in allowing us to use several images from their personal collections.

Other images, published here for the first time or rarely seen, were provided by the Office of Public Affairs of the US embassy in Lisbon; by Beth Amorosi, granddaughter of attorney James B. Donovan; by Jessica Pearl, who assisted in acquiring images from the Raynham Hall Museum; by Maria Raitik at the St. Regis Hotel; and by Avery Fletcher of the 21 Club. We extend special appreciation to Bruce White, inveterate photographer of works of art and architecture for cultural institutions such as the Metropolitan Museum of Art, the J. Paul Getty Museum, and the Curators Office of the White House for his image of the sculpture of Albert Einstein by Sergey Konenkov.

Melissa Walker-Schlesinger and Mary Margaret Wallace read many drafts and properly insisted that confusing government acronyms be deleted or explained, spy jargon exiled, and wordiness eliminated. We thank them for making the book more reader-friendly. Any remaining errors are those of the authors.

To our readers: We are deeply appreciative of your interest and trust this volume will enliven your exploration of New York City's secret intelligence history.

ABBREVIATIONS

APL	American Protective League
BOI	US Bureau of Investigation
BSC	British Security Coordination
CIA	Central Intelligence Agency
COMINTERN	Communist International
COI	Office of the Coordinator of Information
CPUSA	Communist Party of the United States of America
DCI	director of Central Intelligence
FBI	Federal Bureau of Investigation
GRU	Glavnoye Razvedyvatel'noye Upravleniye (Soviet military intelligence service)
HUAC	House Un-American Activities Committee
KGB	Komitet Gosudarstvennoy Bezopasnosti (Soviet intelligence agency)
MGB	Ministry of State Security (USSR)
MI5	British internal security service
MI6	British foreign intelligence service
MI-8	Military Intelligence Division, Section No. 8 (US Army)
MSS	Ministry for State Security (People's Republic of China)
NKVD	Narodnyy Komissariat Vnutrennikh Del (Soviet intelligence agency)
NSA	National Security Agency
NYPD	New York Police Department
OGPU	Joint State Political Directorate (Soviet secret police)
ONI	Office of Naval Intelligence
OPC	Office of Policy Coordination

ABBREVIATIONS

OSS	Office of Strategic Services
OWI	Office of War Information
SOE	Special Operations Executive
SVR	Sluzhba Vneshney Razvedki [Russian intelligence agency]
SWP	Socialist Workers Party
UN	United Nations
USSR	Union of Soviet Socialist Republics

SPIES OF THE AMERICAN REVOLUTION

(1775–1783)

The population of New York City during the Revolutionary War was in a state of dramatic flux. Apprehension about the future initially caused the city, home to some 25,000 civilians, to empty except for a few thousand packed into the southern tip of Manhattan. That changed under British occupation as Tory refugees flooded into the city, swelling its population to what is estimated at more than 30,000. New York City experienced few battles, yet as a major port, center of commerce, and foundation of British governance in the colonies, the city was a hub of espionage by both patriot and Tory spies.

Gen. George Washington learned the consequences of intelligence failure early in the war when patriot spy Nathan Hale was caught and executed by the British. Hale's death served as both a cautionary tale and an inspiration for Washington's army. Even if a suspected patriot spy managed to escape the hangman, British prison ships anchored in New York Harbor and makeshift prisons of converted sugar warehouses often amounted to a death sentence from disease or privation.

Despite such enormous risks, Washington, as America's first spymaster, understood that winning the war depended on secret intelligence. His agents, called confidential correspondents, operated clandestinely inside British-occupied New York City as well as throughout the colonies by applying the tools of classic tradecraft, such as dead drops, signal sites, commercial covers, invisible ink, ciphers, numbered code names, and aliases. So good were their covers and tradecraft that the identities of some of the most valued spies remained secret well into the 20th century.

Brooklyn native Frederick William MacMonnies sculpted the 13-foot-tall Nathan Hale statue unveiled November 25, 1893—Evacuation Day— commemorating the last British soldier leaving the colonies in 1783.

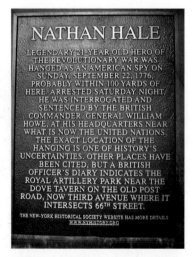

The Nathan Hale plaque on Third Avenue between East 65th and 66th Streets offers a vivid reminder of the sacrifices made for freedom.

■ 1. PATRIOTIC SPY

MAP I ➤ **Nathan Hale statue:** City Hall Park at Broadway, Park Row, and Chambers Street

Nathan Hale was untrained, ill equipped, and by many accounts particularly unsuited for espionage. He was too tall and easily recognizable by powder burns on his face, and his cover as a schoolteacher could not withstand close scrutiny. According to one witness, Hale was tricked into confessing his mission when questioned by a wily British officer, Robert Rogers. Still, the young patriot achieved American hero status after the British hanged him without benefit of trial or clergy on September 22, 1776. More than two centuries later, the specifics of his short-lived secret mission have long been forgotten by most Americans, yet the failed Revolutionary War spy is known to every schoolchild for his last words, "I only regret that I have but one life to give for my country."

Unfortunately, history has obscured the precise location of his execution site. A plaque adorns the Yale Club, 50 Vanderbilt Avenue near the intersection with East 44th Street, proclaiming it near the site of the execution. In fact, Hale was a Yale graduate (class of 1773), but the location is less than precise. The Yale Club plaque was transplanted from its original location on East 46th Street and First Avenue in 1948 after the slaughterhouse on which it was mounted was torn down to make way for the United Nations headquarters complex. More likely Hale was hanged near East 66th Street and Third Avenue at what was then the Royal Artillery Park. Another plaque is on the western side of Third Avenue between East 65th and 66th Streets. A statue depicting a stoic Hale facing execution stands in City Hall Park at Broadway, Park Row, and Chambers Street.

> "I wish to be useful, and every kind of service necessary to the public good becomes honorable by being necessary. If the exigencies of my country demand a peculiar service, its claim to perform that service are imperious."
>
> —**Nathan Hale, as quoted in memoirs of Capt. William Hall**

■ 2. SERVING UP DECEPTION

MAP 5 ➤ **Mary Lindley Murray commemorative plaque:** Southwest corner of East 35th Street and Park Avenue

According to New York folklore, in the opening weeks of the Revolutionary War, Mary Lindley Murray, the wife of wealthy Quaker landowner Robert Murray, prevented a defeat of patriot forces. On September 15, 1776, as Gen. Israel Putnam was retreating from advancing British troops, Murray and her daughters invited British general William Howe and his officers into their home for cake and wine. Reportedly the delay enabled Putnam's army to avoid capture. However, Murray's motives remain the subject of debate. Her husband, a well-known loyalist, was absent at the time, and some speculate

Mary Lindley Murray is said to have delayed the advance of British troops during the Revolutionary War by offering them lunch. This plaque notes the location of the once sprawling Murray estate in what is now the Murray Hill neighborhood.

INSPIRING HOSPITALITY

Fact or fiction, the story of Mary Murray's hospitality delaying British troops inspired two Broadway plays, including 1925's *Dearest Enemy*. The hit musical, which featured music and lyrics by Lorenz Hart and Richard Rodgers, ran for nearly 300 performances. A less successful dramatic production, *A Small War in Murray Hill*, by Robert E. Sherwood, was staged in 1957.

his wife was only trying to curry favor with Howe in anticipation of the inevitable British occupation of New York City.

The neighborhood of the Murray estate, originally called Inclenberg, eventually became known as Murray Hill. A plaque on the southwestern corner of East 35th Street and Park Avenue is said to be near the center of Murray's estate. Another plaque is located on the southern tip of the traffic island at Park Avenue and East 37th Street. Mary Lindley Murray is also the namesake of Public School 116, 210 East 33rd Street.

■ 3. REVOLUTIONARY WAR SPECIAL OPS

MAP 8 ➤ **Columbia University mathematics building:** 2990 Broadway, between West 117th and 118th Streets

Lt. Col. Thomas Knowlton, a native of Connecticut and veteran of the French and Indian War, was selected by George Washington in August 1776 to form Knowlton's Rangers, an elite company for conducting reconnaissance missions behind enemy lines. A month later, on September 16, 1776, the British discovered Knowlton's scouting party. Badly outnumbered, the Rangers at first retreated through what is now Upper Manhattan. However, they regrouped to fight valiantly after becoming enraged when a British bugler rallied his troops by mockingly sounding the fox-hunting call "Gone Away," traditionally used to signal a fox in full flight. Washington ordered reinforcements that eventually succeeded in pushing the British troops back. Known as the Battle of Harlem Heights, this first victory under Washington's command in the war proved costly as Colonel Knowlton was killed.

This illustration by A. R. Waud depicts the Continental Army driving back the British at the Battle of Harlem Heights on September 16, 1776. It was a morale-building early victory for George Washington's troops.

According to the Connecticut Society of the Sons of the American Revolution, Knowlton was buried with full military honors in an unmarked grave at what is now West 143rd Street and St. Nicholas Avenue. Plaques commemorate the battle throughout the area, including one on Columbia University's mathematics building at 2990 Broadway, between West 117th and 118th Streets, and another in the small park at 122nd Street across from Riverside Church.

■ 4. TURTLE ATTACK

MAP | ➤ **America's first attack submarine:** Western side of the Battery in Lower Manhattan

Designed and built by Connecticut inventor David Bushnell, the *American Turtle* was the new nation's first combat submersible. Constructed from oak, the spherical one-man vessel featured a small conning tower and was powered by a hand crank and screw propeller. The only navigation was by way of a small porthole and compass.

On the night of September 6, 1776, Sgt. Ezra Lee boarded the *Turtle* on the western side of the Battery in Lower Manhattan with

REENACTMENT SCARE

The *American Turtle* reappeared in New York during the summer of 2007 when a Brooklyn performance artist launched a plywood-and-fiberglass replica of the submersible toward the *Queen Mary 2*. Apprehended by New York police within 200 feet of the cruise ship, the artist emerged smiling from the hatch, drinking a can of beer.

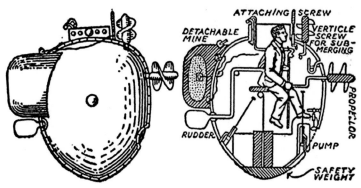

BUSHNELL'S TURTLE

Invented by American patriot David Bushnell, this early submersible was America's first attack submarine.

orders to sink the British warship HMS *Eagle*, anchored in the harbor, and help break the British blockade. Bushnell, who had proved that dynamite could be detonated underwater, designed an explosive device that could be screwed into the hull of the ship from the submerged *Turtle*. However, when Lee reached the *Eagle* and descended beneath the waterline, he was unable to affix the explosive to the metal-clad hull of the warship. Despite the operational failure, New York City can rightly claim honor as the launching site for history's first wartime submarine attack.

■ 5. PRINTER TO THE KING AND MOST EXCELLENT SPY

MAP | ► **James Rivington publishing house**: Northeastern corner of Wall Street and Broadway (site redeveloped)

A bookseller turned newspaper publisher, James Rivington published an unabashedly loyalist newspaper from offices at the foot of Wall Street. Publishing under the motto "Open and Uninfluenced," the *Royal Gazette* billed its owner as "Printer to the King's Most Excellent Majesty" and seemed to go out of its way to taunt New York City patriots. Rivington published rumors, outrageous lies, and open challenges to the Sons of Liberty, a secret organization dedicated to opposing British taxation. The *Royal Gazette* proclaimed that George Washington fathered illegitimate children and was secretly plotting

James Rivington, publisher of the *Royal Gazette*, clandestinely sent a steady stream of intelligence to General Washington from British-occupied New York.

to turn the new nation Roman Catholic. Other stories falsely reported that Benjamin Franklin was on his deathbed and that France's King Louis XVI was destined to be crowned King of America if the Revolution succeeded. Widely mocked and even burned in effigy, Rivington kept printing inflammatory stories. Finally, in May 1775, a mob of enraged patriots gathered outside his office, smashed the printing press, and carried off the lead type to melt down for bullets.

Alexander Hamilton tried, unsuccessfully, to calm the mob while George Washington called for restraint. And, in short order, Rivington was back at the presses, again publishing his incendiary messages. With the British occupying New York, he also opened a coffee shop that sold portraits of the king, stationery, and writing accessories. The store became a favorite among British troops because, despite wartime privation, Rivington somehow managed to keep it stocked with tempting delicacies.

The secret source of the store's inventory was Rivington's very silent partner, Robert Townsend of the Culper spy ring, and his patriot business contacts who pitched in to keep the coffeehouse well stocked to attract British soldiers. From his military customers, Rivington compiled intelligence tidbits, which he wrote in invisible ink, known as sympathetic stain, on blank pages bound into books or inserted into sheets of writing paper purchased at the store and delivered directly to Washington. So perfect was his cover that for more than a century following the Revolution, he was reviled nearly as much as Benedict Arnold. Rivington's role in the patriot cause remained hidden until historians in the 1950s uncovered his secret role in the Revolution through forensic analysis of his handwriting and paper samples.

After retirement Rivington lived at 114 Pearl Street. He died on July 4, 1802, and was buried at the Middle Dutch Church at Nassau and Cedar Streets, which no longer stands. The spy's remaining monument is Rivington Street, which runs between the Bowery and Pitt Street on the Lower East Side.

■ 6. THE PATRIOT'S MASTER SPY

MAP | ➤ **Culper spy ring headquarters:** Peck Slip, near Pearl Street (site redeveloped)

Following Nathan Hale's execution, Washington knew he needed better spies and more secure tradecraft. He turned to Gen. Charles Scott and Maj. Benjamin Tallmadge for help. A classmate and drinking partner of Hale's from Yale, Tallmadge took the execution of his friend particularly

This once bustling waterfront street was a natural for stores like Robert Townsend's that secretly supported the patriots.

WHO WAS AGENT #355?

A mystery agent, a female member of the Culper spy ring, is mentioned only once in documents from the time. She is known only as "355," and her true identity has been the subject of debate and speculation. One candidate that historians have offered as agent 355 was the mistress of the brooding Robert Townsend. According to legend, she was arrested, put aboard the prison ship HMS *Jersey*, and gave birth to his child yet managed to keep the Culper ring's secrets even as she was dying. Another account holds she was a member of the coterie of women who trailed after the charming British major John André as part of New York City Tory high society. However, it is more likely the elusive agent 355 was Anna Strong, a neighbor of one of the Setauket members of the Culper ring. Recruited to enhance the cover of her partner, the pair would pose as an ordinary married couple to enter and exit New York City without suspicion.

hard and, along with Abraham Cooper Woodhull, a farmer from Setauket, Long Island, formed the Culper spy ring. Culper, according to historians, may have been a shortening of Culpeper County, Virginia, where Washington once worked as a surveyor.

Each member of the ring received aliases as well as code numbers for secrecy and communication. Washington's number was #711, Tallmadge was #721, and communication was based on a code Tallmadge devised himself. Information flowed in a series of relays from New York City through Queens, then across the Long Island Sound by whaleboat to Connecticut and on to Washington's headquarters. Nearly everyone in the ring was either related by blood, marriage, or lifelong friendship. Key to the operation was Robert Townsend, #723, alias Samuel Culper Jr., a New York City merchant. His store was a favorite among British officers who were drawn by its assortment of lemons, rum, and quality dry goods. Although not a patron, General Washington was also fond of the enterprise since it secretly served as a clearinghouse for high-value intelligence dispatched out of New York City.

Townsend's store at Peck Slip near Pearl Street also served as his home, and from there he penned pro-British writings for James Rivington's *Royal Gazette*. General Washington well understood the value of the store's cover. "It is not my opinion that Culper Jr. [Townsend] should be advised to give up his present employment," America's first spymaster wrote to Tallmadge in September 1779. "I would imagine that with a little industry he will be able to carry on his intelligence with greater security to himself, and greater advantages to us—under cover of his usual business, than if he were to dedicate himself wholly to the giving of information."

Using an invisible ink called sympathetic stain or white ink, formulated by James Jay, the physician brother of John Jay, Townsend sent a steady stream of secret intelligence from British-occupied New York to General Washington. As spymaster, Washington showed an intense interest in the smallest elements of tradecraft, providing detailed instructions on how Townsend should write his secret reports: "He should occasionally write his information on the blank leaves of a pamphlet, the first second, and other pages of a common pocket book, or on the blank leaves at each end of registers, almanacs, or any new publication or book of small value. He should be determined in the choice of these books principally by the goodness of the paper, as the ink is not easily legible unless it is on paper of good quality."

Townsend, a secretive man and lifelong bachelor, never spoke or wrote of his role as a spy. His identity as Culper Jr. remained a mystery until the 20th century.

■ 7. LOOSE LIPS AT THE TAILOR SHOP

MAP I ➤ **Mulligan brothers store:** 23 Queen Street (now Pine Street)

Hercules Mulligan, although married to the niece of a Royal Navy admiral, was a staunch patriot, a member of the Sons of Liberty, and an agent of the Culper spy ring. Mulligan operated a clothing shop at 23 Queen Street (now Pine Street), featuring "superfine cloths of the most fashionable colours" and, more significantly, "epaulets for gentlemen of the army and militia." British officers who frequented the shop were measured and fitted for their uniforms by Hercules himself. As they selected material and stood for fittings, Mulligan listened for gossip about troop strengths and movements. In one instance, Mulligan observed British

The brothers Hercules and Hugh Mulligan, who were members of the Sons of Liberty and supported the Culper spy ring, are buried in this vault in Trinity Church's cemetery.

officers ordering particularly heavy clothing, indicating a movement north to a colder climate, which turned out to be Quebec. This vital information was quickly passed to the revolutionaries.

At the end of the war, Washington rewarded Mulligan's loyalty not with a bag of gold—the usual payment for spies—but by buying a full set of clothing from the shop. Thereafter, the business thrived, boasting signs and advertisements that read: "Clothier to Genl Washington." Hercules along with his brother, Hugh, is buried a few yards from the grave of their good friend Alexander Hamilton in the Trinity Church yard, 74 Trinity Place at Wall Street.

ESPIONAGE ARTIST

Patience Wright was among the more intriguing spies of the Revolutionary War. A sculptor by profession, she created full-sized, lifelike wax figures of notables and wealthy clients. Although a resident of Philadelphia, she maintained a gallery on Queen Street (now Pine Street), not far from the Mulligan tailor shop.

Wright went to London in February 1772 with introductions from Benjamin Franklin and there built a client base of British royalty, politicians, and soldiers. Her eccentric and outspoken manners disarmed those sitting for their wax likenesses, enabling her to elicit information about military deployments, shipments, and political topics, which she recorded and sent to Philadelphia concealed in sculpted wax heads.

Wright's ploy had similarities to one used at Mulligan's tailor shop, where information was obtained from talkative British during fittings. Could Mulligan, Wright's New York neighbor, or Franklin, her Philadelphia contemporary, have recruited the artist to spy? Possibly either, given the apparent relationship with the two patriots. Days before leaving on the 1772 voyage to England, she wrote her will, a common practice for those making a hazardous sea journey, which was witnessed by Hercules Mulligan.

Raynham Hall was the home of Robert Townsend, one of the Setauket spies and member of the Culper spy ring.

■ 8. SETAUKET HARBOR SPIES

MAP 12 ➤ Abraham Woodhull grave: Setauket Presbyterian Church cemetery, 5 Caroline Avenue, Setauket, Long Island

Beginning in 1778, Maj. Benjamin Tallmadge, General Washington's chief intelligence officer, organized the Culper spy ring to obtain critically needed intelligence about British troops and fortifications in New York City and on Long Island. The primary members of the ring were Abraham Woodhull (alias Samuel Culper Sr.), Robert Townsend (alias Samuel Culper Jr.), and Caleb Brewster. Tallmadge, using the alias of John Bolton, controlled the ring, but Washington himself tasked the spies with collecting the sensitive information. The ring, which operated until 1783, was particularly effective from 1778 to 1781.

Woodhull typically gathered information in Manhattan, then traveled 55 miles to Setauket on Long Island to pass it to Caleb Brewster, who rowed across Long Island Sound and delivered it to Major Tallmadge. Brewster's family was from Setauket, and his uncle ran a tavern in his farmhouse on

Route 25-A (still in existence), alongside Setauket Harbor. One of the six small coves on the sound that Brewster used to bring his boat ashore was only 150 feet from the house. Later Tallmadge arranged for a series of couriers to make the journey from the city to Setauket to meet Woodhull.

Setauket lore holds that a local woman, Anna Strong, arranged to hang her petticoats out to dry in ways to send coded messages to Woodhull and Brewster. A black petticoat signaled that Brewster had arrived in Long Island via his whaleboat from Connecticut. The number of white handkerchiefs hanging to the side of the petticoat corresponded to one of six prearranged meeting places where Woodhull would pass information to Brewster.

In 1779, the ring was nearly discovered when a Long Island privateer, John Woolsey, was captured and bartered information on Abraham Woodhull to secure his parole from the British. The investigation of Woodhull was assigned to Col. John Graves Simcoe, commander of the Queen's Rangers. When Simcoe visited Setauket, he failed to find Woodhull and instead attacked and beat the spy's father, Judge Richard Woodhull. The original Woodhull home burned down in 1931, but a marker commemorating this site is near the intersection of Bob's Lane and Dyke Road.

Woodhull was in Manhattan at the time of the attack and engaged Townsend, alias Samuel Culper Jr., to remain and gather intelligence while he returned to Setauket. Townsend also created a new courier route for Austin Roe, who carried the information from the city. Upon arriving in Setauket, Roe would dead-drop the information in a box in the middle of a field owned by Woodhull. Woodhull took the secrets to Brewster, who delivered them to Major Tallmadge.

Tallmadge provided each of the Culper spy ring participants with codes, dead drops, and aliases. The identities of the agents were so closely held that even George Washington did not know the true names of some of his most important spies. The spy ring's security held tight for almost 150 years. Only

PATRIOT SPIES ON TELEVISION

Turn: Washington's Spies, a hit AMC series from 2014 to 2017, revealed to a 21st-century audience stirring and treacherous espionage stories from the American Revolutionary War. The show depicted historically accurate tradecraft practices used to evade British spy catchers, such as concealments, invisible inks, and codes and ciphers, including the Cardan grille and the original Culper spy code. Other dramatic elements, however, such as passing messages written in invisible ink on hard-boiled eggs, are not known to have been used by the Culper spy ring. Nor was the John Hawkins letter-writing machine, developed in 1803 after the war, used either to forge documents or as a lie detector.

in the 1930s was Townsend's identity as "Culper Jr." discovered. A scholar examining Townsend's letters in the family archive noticed the similarity of his handwriting to that in letters from "Samuel Culper Jr." in George Washington's collection. Other information eventually confirmed his secret identity.

Both Abraham Woodhull and Robert Townsend survived the war. Woodhull passed away in Setauket in 1826 and Townsend at his home, Raynham Hall, at 20 West Main Street, Oyster Bay, Long Island, in 1838. Woodhull's grave is in the cemetery of the Setauket Presbyterian Church at 5 Caroline Avenue, Setauket. Townsend is interred at the end of Simcoe Street in Fort Hill Burying Ground in Oyster Bay. Maj. Benjamin Tallmadge was promoted to the rank of lieutenant colonel at the end of the war and passed away in 1835. His birthplace and the still-standing Tallmadge family home were the Old Manse, 30 Runs Road, Setauket.

■ 9. THE SONS OF LIBERTY DRANK HERE

MAP I ➤ **Fraunces Tavern:** 54 Pearl Street

Fraunces Tavern was a meeting place for the Sons of Liberty and the site of George Washington's farewell address to his officers on December 4, 1783.

Samuel Fraunces purchased the Queen's Head Tavern at 54 Pearl Street in 1762 and changed its name at the start of the Revolutionary War. The tavern became a regular meeting place for the Sons of Liberty and later served as Gen. George Washington's last residence in New York. In the tavern's Long Room, Washington delivered his farewell address to his officers on December 4, 1783. A short time later, when New York was the nation's capital, the tavern housed the Department of Foreign Affairs, the Department of War, and the Department of Treasury.

Was Samuel Fraunces (called "Black Sam") a spy? Maybe. What's known for certain is Fraunces came from the West Indies and remained loyal to Washington throughout the Revolution. The strongest hint of his role as a spy can be found in the grant voted to him by the New York State Legislature and the US Congress for aiding American prisoners of war and unspecified "other services."

One story of those services involved Fraunces's daughter, Phoebe, who worked as Washington's housekeeper. Phoebe is said to have uncovered a plot by one of Washington's bodyguards, Thomas Hickey, to assassinate the general with a plate of poisoned peas in 1776. In another version,

Samuel, not his daughter, discovered the plot. Regardless of the source, Hickey was executed.

Fraunces Tavern was damaged by fire in 1844, then purchased and renovated by the Sons of the Revolution. Reopened in 1907, the historic landmark became the target of a terrorist bombing by the radical Puerto Rican independence group FALN that killed four people in 1975. Today Fraunces Tavern and four adjacent buildings house a museum of 18th-century New York City exhibits.

■ 10. THE TRAGEDY OF MAJOR ANDRÉ

MAP | ➤ **Kennedy Mansion:** 1 Broadway (no longer standing)

Maj. John André, adjutant-general of the British Army under Gen. Sir Henry Clinton in New York, was described as handsome, witty, charming, poetic, and "possessed of a shining spirit." He selected John or James Anderson for his aliases and directed spy operations from the Kennedy Mansion at 1 Broadway and from the Beekman Mansion (called Mount Pleasant, demolished in the 1870s) at what is approximately First Avenue and East 51st Street today.

André ran a number of successful agents, including Ann Bates, a schoolteacher from Philadelphia. The wife of a British field artillery repairman, Bates knew armaments and military terminology better than most soldiers. Using the alias Mrs. Barnes, she infiltrated American troop encampments disguised as a peddler. For two years, from 1778 to 1780, outfitted with goods and suitably dressed, Bates enjoyed virtually unrestricted movement among the soldiers as she carefully rationed her inventory to acquire as much information as possible to report to André at British headquarters. Her success is apparent in one of her reports: "I had the Opportunity of going through their whole Army Remarking at the same time the

British officers watched from the windows of the old Kennedy Mansion as a mob pulled down the nearby statue of King George at the beginning of the American Revolution. The mansion later became headquarters for both British and Continental Army officers, depending on who held Manhattan.

A depiction of the arrest of Maj. John André (second from the left)

strength & situation of each Brigade, & the number of cannon with their situation and weight of Ball each cannon was charged with." Bates's intelligence, in part, prompted British general Henry Clinton to send reinforcements to Rhode Island and force American and French forces to withdraw following the Battle of Quaker Hill in 1778.

André's operations ended following a secret meeting behind colonial lines with his most important agent, Maj. Gen. Benedict Arnold, commander of the American fortifications at West Point. After a lengthy negotiation, Arnold agreed to surrender West Point, where a great chain restricted British ship movements up and down the Hudson River. In exchange for the traitorous act, Arnold would receive a commission as a British brigadier general, a lifetime pension, and several thousand pounds. However, after their final meeting, André was apprehended out of uniform as he attempted to return to British lines. A search revealed incriminating documents from Arnold hidden in André's boots.

Washington convened a board of seven senior officers to try André on charges of espionage. On September 28, 1780, the board found André guilty and sentenced him to death by hanging, a sentence partially motivated in retaliation for Nathan Hale's execution four years earlier. The decision was controversial because André truthfully claimed he was stranded behind enemy lines when his transport sloop, the *Vulture*, came under fire and left without him. Abandoned in hostile territory, André asserted he was not spying but rather attempting to escape back to British lines and justified in wearing civilian clothes. Washington even proposed a swap of Major André for Benedict Arnold, but General Howe, commander of the British forces, refused the offer and sealed the young British officer's fate.

André appealed to Washington for a soldier's execution by firing squad, but the request was rejected. The 29-year-old André was hanged as a spy on October 2, 1780, in Tappan, New York. Alexander Hamilton wrote of him: "Never perhaps did any man suffer death with more justice, or deserve it less." According to eyewitness accounts, André calmly tied his handkerchief for a blindfold with these last words, "Only this, gentlemen, that you all bear witness that I meet my fate like a brave man." First buried in Tappan near the gallows, his remains were reinterred in the middle of a little-used aisle in London's Westminster Abbey in 1821.

■ 11. CODES, CIPHERS, AND CANNON THEFT

MAP 8 ▶ **Alexander Hamilton residence:** Hamilton Grange National Memorial, 414 West 141st Street between St. Nicholas Avenue and Hamilton Terrace

As General Washington's aide-de-camp, Alexander Hamilton, who would eventually become the first US secretary of the treasury, was responsible for decrypting letters from the Culper spy ring. After arriving from Nevis, West

The only home that Alexander Hamilton ever owned, the Grange, was named after his grandfather's estate in Scotland.

Indies, Hamilton attended the Elizabethtown Academy in Elizabethtown (today Elizabeth), New Jersey, then moved to New York and enrolled at King's College (today Columbia University). Boarding at the Mulligan brothers' home on Water Street (between Burling's Slip and the Fly Market Slip, now part of the South Street Seaport), the three became lasting friends.

In 1775, both the Mulligans and Hamilton were members of a mob that made off with British cannons mounted on the Battery on the southern tip of Manhattan while under fire from the HMS *Asia*, moored in the harbor. Once the Revolution heated up, Hercules had a friend and confidential correspondent close to Washington, while Hamilton knew he could trust Mulligan.

The only home Hamilton ever owned sat on his 32-acre estate at Convent Avenue and West 143rd Street, which his family sold in 1889. The 298-ton structure was moved

A simple monument marks Hamilton's tomb on the southern side of Trinity Church.

HAMILTON V. JEFFERSON

Alexander Hamilton was so closely linked to New York that his adversaries called the city "Hamiltonopolis." They did not intend it as a compliment. Another Founding Father, Thomas Jefferson, hated New York, calling it "a *cloacina* [toilet/sewer] of all the depravities of human nature."

to its present location, 414 West 141st Street at the north end of St. Nicholas Park, in 2008. Now known as the Grange or the Hamilton Grange National Memorial, the site was reopened to visitors in 2011 after undergoing extensive renovation by the National Park Service. A Founding Father, a contributor to the Federalist Papers, a secretary of the treasury, a diplomat, and a congressman, Hamilton is buried at Trinity Church yard at Trinity Place and Wall Street, just a few yards from the Mulligan brothers.

■ 12. WHO CAN BE TRUSTED?

MAP I ➤ **Benedict Arnold residence:** 5 Broadway

Benedict Arnold

Following his treason at West Point, Benedict Arnold fled first to Philadelphia then moved into a New York residence at 5 Broadway. Now a brigadier general in the British Army, he began raising his own troops from among the Continental Army's deserters, offering signing bonuses along with tailored uniforms to those joining what he called the American Legion.

Arnold became the target of one of General Washington's most daring espionage operations in the fall of 1780. Conceived by Maj. Henry "Light-Horse Harry" Lee, father of Civil War general Robert E. Lee, the operation envisioned kidnapping the despised Arnold and bringing him to justice. A Virginian, Sgt. Maj. John Champe, was to fake desertion, join the American Legion, and capture the unsuspecting Arnold as he went on his customary evening walk.

The operation began well. Champe moved freely around New York in his new British uniform and established clandestine contacts with other patriot agents eager to see Arnold hanged. However, the plot collapsed when Arnold's troops unexpectedly sailed for Virginia on the night of the scheduled kidnapping. Champe then deserted a second time, making his way back to General Washington's headquarters.

A year later, Washington sent another agent into New York City pretending to be a deserter. This second spy, Sgt. Daniel Bissell, successfully joined Arnold's American Legion in 1781. For over a year, spending some of that time in an unheated hospital after falling sick, Bissell gathered intelligence on British troop strength, fortifications, and operations. He was the last recipient of

Washington's Badge of Military Merit, receiving one of only three awarded by Washington himself.

Arnold survived the war but among the British never escaped the shadow of the dashing Major André, to whom he was constantly compared and whose death for the Tory cause was viewed as honorable and heroic. One harsh critic of Arnold at the time called him a "mean mercenary, who, having adopted a cause for the sake of plunder, quits it when convicted of that charge." Despised in the new United States, Arnold eventually settled in England, which he disliked, and died in London in 1801. He was buried without the military honors normally befitting a British brigadier general. Still reviled by the country he betrayed, the invocation of Arnold's name remains an insult after more than two centuries.

■ 13. AMERICA'S FIRST SPY CATCHER

MAP | ➤ **John Jay birthplace:** 66 Pearl Street

John Jay

John Jay was born on December 12, 1745, at a no longer identifiable address of 66 Pearl Street on the site of one of New York's earliest landfills, called the Water Lots. The area's construction expanded the buildable area in Lower Manhattan before redevelopment replaced the original structures. He would later reside at 133 Broadway (then between Cedar and Liberty Streets). Jay, who played critical roles in the American Revolution, was a major contributor to the Federalist Papers and became the first chief justice of the United States Supreme Court. Like Alexander Hamilton, Jay recognized the value of intelligence and in Federalist Papers no. 64 promoted the necessity of spies for the executive branch of government.

The noted jurist got his start in counterintelligence as chairman of the New York State Committee and Commission for Detecting and Defeating Conspiracies. In this position, Jay oversaw scores of investigations, including one that uncovered a conspiracy to assassinate General Washington as well as plots to sabotage New York's infrastructure. Through his brother,

James, a physician and chemist in London, American patriots got their first shipments of invisible ink, then called sympathetic stain or white ink.

Jay also ran his own spy networks during the Revolution. One of those involved, Enoch Crosby, operated in what was known as the Neutral Ground. The area, extending from Upper Manhattan to approximately thirty miles north into what is today Westchester County, was neutral only in the sense it was not held consistently by one side or the other.

From Jay's accounts of Crosby's exploits, James Fenimore Cooper gathered ideas for America's first espionage novel, *The Spy*, and its protagonist, Harvey Birch. Crosby later recounted his own espionage adventures in the memorably titled book, *The Spy Unmasked; or, Memoirs of Enoch Crosby, Alias Harvey Birch, the Hero of Mr. Cooper's Tale of the Neutral Ground: Being an Authentic Account of the Secret Services Which He Rendered His Country during the Revolutionary War. (Taken from His Own Lips, in Short Hand), Comprising Many Interesting Facts and Anecdotes) Never before Published.*

The Prison Ship Martyrs' Monument in Brooklyn's Fort Greene Park marks the tomb of soldiers and suspected spies who died while being held aboard British prison ships during the Revolutionary War.

■ 14. PRISON SHIP MARTYRS OF THE REVOLUTION MONUMENT

MAP 10 ➤ **Fort Greene Park:** Between Myrtle and Dekalb Avenues and between St. Edwards and Cumberland Streets, Brooklyn

The Prison Ship Martyrs' Monument, a single Doric column of Deer Isle granite, stands more than 140 feet tall in Fort Greene Park in Brooklyn. Its top is a bronze brazier while its base contains a crypt with the remains of some of the prisoners who died aboard British prison ships anchored in New York Harbor from 1776 to 1783. The remains, which were washed ashore or uncovered from shallow graves along the shoreline following the Revolutionary War, were collected by Brooklynites in hopes a fitting monument would someday be built to lay them to rest. Among the dead were spies, soldiers, and others who fought for liberty from England. Designed by architect

Stanford White of the firm McKim, Mead and White, the monument rises from a terrace approached by a stairway of 100 steps.

The present-day monument is the third resting place for the prison ships' dead. The remains were first interred in a small plot near the Brooklyn Navy Yard waterfront in the early 19th century. When that land was purchased by a private citizen, the remains were moved to their current location and a plain mausoleum constructed. However, by the 1890s, support for constructing a larger, more fitting memorial to the Revolutionary War dead grew. The dedication of new monument on November 15, 1908, was attended by more than 15,000, including President-elect William Howard Taft.

■ 15. ONCE A BRUTAL AND TERRIBLE PLACE

MAP ∣ ➤ **Rhinelander Sugar House prison site:** 1 Centre Street

A structure behind the Municipal Building, 1 Centre Street, holds a small window with centuries-old British prison bars. Once part the Rhinelander Sugar House prison, the bars are embedded in a wall of the shed-like building near the site where the makeshift prison once stood. The bars are a historic architectural detail and reminder of the sacrifices made for freedom during the American Revolution.

The original structure from which the window was salvaged was once part of a five-story sugarhouse at the corner of Duane and Rose (later William) Streets. The structure was demolished in 1892 to make way for the Rhinelander Building, but the window and some of the original bricks were preserved and built into the wall. The Rhinelander building was, in turn, demolished in 1968 to build the New York Police Department (NYPD) headquarters at 1 Police Plaza.

The Rhinelander Sugar House prison (right) is depicted here in an 1857 drawing by Adam Weingartner that was published in *The Manual of the Corporation of the City of New York for 1857.*

A section of the Rhinelander Sugar House preserved as part of a structure behind the Centre Street Municipal Building near 1 Centre Street.

Commerce in sugar with the British West Indies was a major industry in 18th-century New York. The British Army commandeered the hulking warehouses and converted them into prisons during the occupation of New York. Hundreds of American prisoners of war, both soldiers and private citizens accused of being spies, were jailed and died in the hellish conditions of these jails.

Each morning, death carts arrived to collect the bodies of those who had perished overnight. According to some reports, six or more prisoners died each day of hunger, exposure, or disease. Estimates are that more than twice the number of deaths occurred in the sugarhouse prisons and prison ships in New York Harbor than on the battlefields.

A monument to the Revolutionary War heroes who perished as prisoners in the Rhinelander Sugar House prison can be found on the grounds of Trinity Church at Broadway and Wall Street.

■ 16. AMERICA'S FIRST STAY-BEHIND AGENT

MAP I ➤ **Sugar House Prison:** 34 and 36 Liberty Street (then called Crown Street)

Haym Salomon (or Soloman), a Jewish immigrant from Poland, worked for Washington's fledgling intelligence service as a stay-behind agent following the general's retreat from New York in 1776. A member of the Sons of Liberty, Salomon sheltered American spies and escaped prisoners in his New York home. The British arrested Salomon in 1777 and confined him to a makeshift prison in the Livingston's sugar warehouse at 34 and 36 Liberty Street, but he was released by the Hessian

Haym Salomon

commander, Gen. Leopold Philip von Heister, to serve as interpreter. Nevertheless, he continued to spy, was arrested again in 1778, and sentenced to death. Salomon then bribed one of his guards and escaped to Philadelphia, where he became a major financier of the war.

2

CIVIL WAR SPIES

(1861–1865)

Although New York was more than 100 miles from the bloody bat-tlefields of the Civil War, the city felt its effects. Its prominence as a financial and news center in support of the Union attracted spies from the North and South who ran aggressive intelligence operations throughout the hostilities. Counterfeiters, privateers, saboteurs, and celebrities were among the city's Civil War intelligence operatives. In one major plot, a handful of rebel conspirators set fires in hotels up and down Manhattan in an ill-fated effort to throw the city into chaos and possibly change the course of the war.

The Civil War touched every neighborhood of New York, from the rough-and-tumble Five Points in Lower Manhattan to Millionaire Row along Fifth Avenue. Newly arrived immigrants and established families alike lost loved ones in the conflict. Those not directly involved suffered from civil unrest and war profiteering. The prac-tice of legal payment of substitutes to fight eventually led to bloody Draft Riots of 1863. Through it all, New York endured, emerging as the nation's leading city and recognized as one of the world's great metropolitan centers.

The famous Old Grapevine Tavern was a den of spies during the Civil War.

■ 17. SPACE FOR MEN ONLY

MAP 2 ➤ **Old Grapevine Tavern:** West 11th Street and Sixth Avenue (site redeveloped)

Built in the 18th century, the Old Grapevine Tavern was housed in a three-story clapboard house at West 11th Street and Sixth Avenue in Greenwich Village. Originally called the Hawthorne, the tavern later acquired its better-known nickname from an ancient grapevine growing on one side. Popular with actors, writers, artists, politicians, and New York's fashionable men, the Grapevine became a Civil War gathering spot for Union officers as well as Confederate spies.

The common phrase "heard it through the grapevine" is said by some to have originated at the drinking establishment. Alec McClelland, one of its last proprietors, predicted the end of an era when he sold the property in 1912. "The new tenant felt he had [purchased] a mint. But my ways were too old-fashioned and he started to bring the place up to date by putting in a back parlor, where women could sit and drink," McClelland lamented to a *New York Times* reporter. "To me that was the worst of all. Never in my career have I sold a drink to a woman. No women were allowed in the place." The Grapevine was demolished three years later.

■ 18. UNION SPYMASTER

MAP 5 ➤ **George H. Sharpe residence:** 31 East 39th Street (site redeveloped)

George H. Sharpe, head of the Union army's Bureau of Military Information

Lawyer, diplomat, and soldier George Sharpe began the war as a captain, was soon promoted to colonel, and in 1863 was appointed head of the Union army's Bureau of Military Information. Under his direction, the army began the modern practice of intelligence analysis, which included organizing and comparing information from a variety of sources before passing it up the chain of command. Sharpe's system included interviewing prisoners of war and refugees, retrieving papers from Confederate soldiers fallen in battle, and monitoring supply lines with a network of "guides." One of Sharpe's most valuable sources was the Elizabeth Van Lew network in Richmond, Virginia, which successfully penetrated the Confederate White House.

By the war's end, Sharpe was a brigadier general stationed with Gen. Ulysses S. Grant's headquarters at City Point, Virginia. At Appomattox, he oversaw the granting of parole certificates to the soldiers of the Army of Northern Virginia after Gen. Robert E. Lee's surrender.

Following the war, Sharpe was appointed special agent to the US State Department and sent to Europe to investigate Americans connected to President Abraham Lincoln's assassination. He returned to New York and a law practice while holding a number of government jobs, including Surveyor of the Port of New York and US Marshal for the Southern District of New York State. In the latter position, he investigated the corrupt Tweed Ring and Tammany Hall run by William Magear Tweed, a.k.a. Boss Tweed. Sharpe died in 1900 at the Manhattan home of his daughter and son-in-law.

■ 19. HANGED AS A SPY AND PRIVATEER

MAP 10 ➤ **John Yates Beall execution site:** Castle Williams on Governors Island

John Yates Beall joined the Confederate cause as a young man and received wounds that rendered him unable to continue serving in combat. He then turned to privateering, attacking Union ships on the waterways along the Great Lakes, eventually making his way into the Chesapeake Bay, near Washington. Beall was captured by the Union army, then exchanged in a prisoner swap. He wasted no time, however, before returning to privateering and plotting to free Confederate prisoners, only to be recaptured.

Castle Williams, a three-tiered fort constructed in 1811 on Governors Island, was known as the "Cheese Box" because of its nearly circular shape.

Beall was confined to Fort Lafayette on a small island just off Brooklyn's Bay Ridge section (demolished in the 1960s for construction of the Verraz-zano-Narrows Bridge) and tried as a spy and privateer in 1865. Despite the intercession of six US senators and 91 members of Congress on Beall's behalf, the condemned was hanged on Governors Island on February 24, 1865. He was the last man executed there, and Beall's ghost reportedly still haunts Castle Williams.

■ 20. NEW YORK'S FINEST AND PINKERTON'S BEST

MAP 3 ► **New York Crystal Palace:** Bryant Park, West 42nd Street between Fifth and Sixth Avenues

Timothy Webster was a New York City cop before he became a legendary operative of the Pinkerton National Detective Agency. An immigrant from England who arrived at a young age with his parents, Webster was providing security at the New York Crystal Palace on 42nd Street between Fifth and Sixth Avenues (today Bryant Park), which was part of the 1853 Exhibition of the Industry of All Nations.

Webster, a 32-year-old sergeant, so impressed agency head Allan Pinkerton with his efficiency and manners that he was offered a job in Chicago, with paid travel expenses, where the detective agency was then based. Within a few years Webster became one of Pinkerton's most notable agents. He worked undercover to expose a plot by secessionists to assassinate Lincoln on the president-elect's journey from Illinois to Washington for his inauguration. When it was judged that preventative arrests couldn't assure the president-elect's safety, Pinkerton called for a number of security measures to be integrated into the journey and personally accompanied Lincoln to Washington. "He, amongst all the force who went with me, deserves the credit of saving the life of Mr. Lincoln, even more than I do," Pinkerton later wrote in a 40-page pamphlet titled *History and Evidence of the Passage of Abraham Lincoln from Harrisburg, PA. to Washington D.C. on the 22nd and 23rd of February, 1861.*

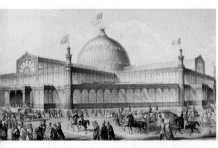

During the Civil War, Webster spied for the Union by infiltrating the Confederate intelligence organization as a courier in Richmond. At one point he was arrested by Union troops and imprisoned as a spy for the Confederacy, necessitating Pinkerton to secure his release without arousing suspicion.

Back spying in Richmond, Webster fell ill in early 1862 and was

One of Allan Pinkerton's most effective agents, Timothy Webster, met Pinkerton while serving as a guard at the New York Crystal Palace in 1853.

bedridden in a hotel there. Two operatives Pinkerton sent to assist him were captured and under interrogation revealed that Webster was a Union spy. Hanged on April 29, 1862, in Richmond's Camp Lee, Webster became the first person executed for espionage in the Civil War. Requests by Pinkerton for Webster's body were denied, and not until the war was over did he recover the remains. Webster is buried in the Pinkerton family plot in Chicago.

Following the Civil War, the Pinkerton National Detective Agency opened a New York City office at 66 Exchange Place.

> "He [Webster], amongst all the force who went with me, deserves the credit of saving the life of Mr. Lincoln, even more than I do."
>
> —From Allan Pinkerton's *History and Evidence of the Passage of Abraham Lincoln from Harrisburg, PA. to Washington D.C. on the 22nd and 23rd of February, 1861*

■ 21. CONFEDERATE CURRENCY COUNTERFEITER

MAP | ➤ **Winthrop Hilton printing plant:** 11 Spruce Street

With the Civil War in progress, New York printer Winthrop Hilton found a profitable sideline in printing high-quality replicas of Confederate currency. Though marketed as novelties, millions of dollars of Hilton's counterfeit Confederate bills, printed at 11 Spruce Street, flowed south, and the genuine Confederate currency was devalued. Hilton promoted his bogus money with ads in popular magazines such as *Harper's*

Confederate currency

Weekly, declaring, "So exactly like the genuine, that where one will pass current the other will go equally well. $500 in Confederate notes of all denominations, sent free by mail on receipt of $5." Anyone reading Hilton's advertisement could reasonably assume the Confederate cash could be safely spent in Southern states.

Two Confederate agents were dispatched to New York, where they forged a letter, written in easily broken code, and saw that it came to the attention of the authorities. The letter cleverly alleged Hilton was in the employ of the Confederacy as a printer of genuine currency. In early 1864, authorities raided the print shop and found millions of dollars in bogus Confederate money. Imprisoned, but finally released, Hilton ceased printing bogus Confederate currency.

■ 22. A SPY ON THE STAGE

MAP I ▶ **Pauline Cushman residence:** Astor House Hotel, west side of Broadway between Vesey and Barclay Streets

After the Civil War, actress and spy Pauline Cushman donned a Union soldier's uniform to recount her exploits before packed theaters in New York, as seen here in a juxtaposition of two portraits by Mathew Brady.

For a brief time in the 1860s, Pauline Cushman dazzled New York as a genuine Civil War hero and spy. Born Harriet Wood in New Orleans, she changed her name and became a stage actress. While performing in Louisville, Kentucky, she volunteered her services to the Union cause. Posing as a Confederate camp follower through Kentucky and Tennessee, Cushman collected information on Confederate troop movements. However, she was arrested in Shelbyville, Tennessee, with sensitive documents in her possession. After Cushman received a death sentence, her execution was postponed because of her ill health, and later she was freed by Union troops.

By 1864, Cushman had become famous in New York, and Lincoln bestowed on her the honorary rank of brevet major, leading many to call her "Miss Major Cushman." At one point a crowd of admirers gathered outside her Astor House Hotel residence on Broadway between Vesey and Barclay Streets to serenade the lady spy with patriotic songs.

The New York Times gushed:

A large number of citizens gathered on the sidewalk in front of the Astor House, about 11 o'clock last evening, to testify their appreciation of the eminent service of Miss Major CUSHMAN, the gallant Union scout and spy, whose daring and skill have elicited the warmest commendations of ROSECRANS, GARFIELD, and other Union officers. A fine band was in attendance and greeted the fair Major with several patriotic airs. Miss CUSHMAN appeared at a window in the second story and was introduced to the assembly by Mr. F. W. B. HIBBARD, Esq., of this City. She was received with three cheers.

A tour followed the war in which she recounted her exploits, some of which may have been embellished for entertainment value, to sold-out theaters. Her biography, published in 1865 and written by a friend, Ferdinand Sarmiento, *Life of Pauline Cushman, the Celebrated Union Spy and Scout: Comprising Her Early History; Her Entry into the Secret Service of the Army of the Cumberland, and Exciting Adventure with the Rebel Chieftains and Others While within the Enemy's Lines; Together with Her Capture and Sentence to Death by General Bragg and Final Rescue by the Union Army under General Rosecrans*, burnished her reputation and caused a sensation. Sarmiento extolled Cushman: "Dashing, charming, fearless, yet lady-like, she combines in herself all the daring of the soldier with the tenderness and modesty of the woman. Not one of the milk-and-water women of the day, whose only thought is of dress and amusement, but one of the women of old, whose soul was in their country's good, and whose fearless, yet womanly, because noble, actions, shall live forever."

Despite fame, Cushman's life following the war was filled with tragedy. She had multiple marriages and experienced the deaths of her children. Eventually Cushman worked as a seamstress and maid but suffered from addiction to opium and is reported to have committed suicide in 1897 in San Francisco. Cushman is buried in the San Francisco National Cemetery under her married name. The tombstone reads, simply, "Pauline C. Fryer Union Spy."

■ 23. "A VAST AND FIENDISH PLOT"

MAP | ➤ **P. T. Barnum's American Museum:** Broadway and Ann Street

As Maj. Gen. William Tecumseh Sherman marched on Atlanta in the fall of 1864, eight Southern agents plotted to set fires in hotels strategically located across New York City in the hope of triggering chaos, which could lead to the seizure of federal buildings and the freeing of Confederate prisoners to overrun the city. "The spirit of revolt was manifest and it only needed a start," wrote one of the conspirators, John W. Headley, in his 1905 book *Confederate Operations in Canada and New York*.

Fortunately for New York, after a Union double agent carrying messages between Richmond and Canada alerted officials, President Lincoln ordered 10,000 troops into

A desperate Confederate terrorist attack on New York sought to create chaos and fear by setting the city ablaze. The badly planned and executed scheme resulted in only minimal damage.

the city under the command of Gen. Benjamin "Beast" Butler. Despite the looming obstacles, the conspirators met in a cottage in the unfinished Central Park and decided to go forward with their plan. Using 12 dozen bottles of "Greek fire," a long-known combustible fluid mixture acquired from an unnamed chemist living west of Washington Square, they began to set the fires.

On November 25, 1864, small blazes erupted around the city, including the St. James Hotel (Broadway and West 25th Street), the Fifth Avenue Hotel (Fifth Avenue and East 24th Street), the Lafarge House (Fulton and Pearl Streets), and the Howard Hotel (Broadway and Maiden Lane). In all, rooms in 19 hotels were set on fire as well as P. T. Barnum's American Museum at Broadway and Ann Street along with some hay barges in the East River. The chemical compound ignited as planned, but the inexperienced arsonists left the hotels' windows closed and the fires were starved of the oxygen they needed to spread. As a result, hotel employees and local fire departments quickly extinguished the fires. The *New York Herald* described the ill-conceived effort as "a vast and fiendish plot to burn down our Empire City" and said that it "gave rise to the most profound excitement among all classes of our citizens."

Not only had the operational security of the Confederate saboteurs been compromised by the double agent—they also picked the wrong targets. Had they attacked Manhattan's gasworks on the city's West Side, much of New York could have burned, possibly altering the course of the war. All the conspirators escaped, except for the unlucky Robert Cobb Kennedy, who was apprehended in Detroit. Tried and sentenced to death, Kennedy was hanged at Fort Lafayette on the island that now serves as a support for the Verrazzano-Narrows Bridge.

■ 24. UNDERCOVER CONFEDERATE SLAVE

MAP 9 ➤ **Former Mary Elizabeth Bowser memorial site:** Old West Farms Soldiers' Cemetery, Bryant Avenue and East 180th Street, Bronx

A tree and a memorial plaque to honor freed slave and Civil War spy Mary Elizabeth Bowser was once situated in the Old West Farms Soldiers' Cemetery, Bryant Avenue and East 180th Street in the Bronx. Formerly owned by the Van Lew family of Richmond, Virginia, Elizabeth Bowser worked with abolitionist Elizabeth Van Lew to provide intelligence about Confederate plans. In this tandem operation, Elizabeth Van Lew assumed an eccentric persona that earned her the nickname "Crazy Bet" within Richmond society, which was unaware of her role as a spy.

Bowser assumed the identity of Ellen Bond, a slow-witted slave generously loaned to Varina Davis, the wife of Jefferson Davis, the Confederate president. When her cover was blown in January 1865, she attempted to set fire to the Confederate White House before fleeing and vanishing from sight. After her grave was discovered in Richmond in 2000, Bowser was inducted into the Military Intelligence Hall of Fame in Fort Huachuca, Arizona.

■ 25. FINAL CHAPTER OF BEST-SELLING SPY

MAP ┃ ➤ **Astor House Hotel:** West side of Broadway between Vesey and Barclay Streets

As a reporter for Horace Greeley's *New York Tribune*, located at what is now 1 Pace Place, Albert D. Richardson went behind Confederate lines during the Civil War ostensibly to cover the war but secretly as an important spy for the Union. Captured and imprisoned, he escaped and returned to New York to write the best-selling books *The Secret Service, the Field, the Dungeon, and the Escape* and *A Personal History of Ulysses S Grant*.

However, Richardson's daring success in the face of the enemy may have only served to embolden his scandalous private life. In November 1869, he was shot by Daniel McFarland, the jealous husband of actress Abby Sage McFarland, in the *Tribune*'s offices. The mortally wounded Richardson was carried to the Astor House Hotel on the western side of Broadway between Vesey and Barclay Streets. As Richardson lingered near death, Mrs. McFarland, who had obtained a divorce, and the journalist spy were married in a dramatic deathbed ceremony. After Richardson died, the murder trial of Daniel McFarland created a 19th-century media frenzy. The politically well-connected defendant was eventually acquitted.

A photograph of journalist-spy Albert D. Richardson from his book *The Secret Service, the Field, the Dungeon, and the Escape.*

3

SPIES AND SABOTEURS OF WORLD WAR I

[1914–1918]

In the second decade of the 20th century, before "the war to end all wars," New York began emerging as a British-German battleground of espionage, sabotage, and propaganda. Although the United States was officially neutral until 1917, trading with America was of vital importance to the European Allies from the beginning of the conflict. German U-boats patrolled the Atlantic in an aggressive strategy to sever supply links to Britain and France, and spying on America's largest port became essential to Germany's war effort. The captains and crews of some ships steaming out of New York Harbor were unaware explosives were concealed within their munitions holds or coal bunkers. The explosives were detonated by devices timed to activate while the ships were at sea. As a likely result, several vessels mysteriously vanished in mid-voyage. Factories producing supplies for the Allies were under constant sabotage threat, while ambitious propaganda campaigns by both British and German operatives attempted to influence American politicians and sway public opinion.

The combatant nations aggressively expanded the reach of their secret operations, adopted new technologies, and formed new intelligence organizations. Just as technology was revolutionizing 20th-century military tactics, new devices and inventions fo communication, transportation, and photography were transforming the tradecraft of spies. "Colorful," "reckless," and "courageous" are all terms that could apply to New York's World War I spies as they blended into the city's crowds. It was the dawn of the modern age of espionage.

The experimental Tesla Tower, built by eccentric genius Nikola Tesla, aroused suspicion at the start of World War I. Amid fears it was being used for communication with German submarines, the 185-foot tower was partially demolished in 1917.

■ 26. SUSPECTED SPY TOWER

MAP 12 ➤ **Wardenclyffe Tower:** 5 Randall Road, Shoreham, Long Island (only base remains)

Wardenclyffe Tower, also known as the Tesla Tower, was constructed in 1901 to support experiments in "wireless power" proposed by scientist Nikola Tesla. He envisioned using the earth as a giant electrical condenser for distributing inexpensive energy without the extensive infrastructure required of a power grid. Tesla also believed the tower, when operational, could compete with Guglielmo Marconi's "wireless telegraph" system.

A 185-foot-tall tower and a 100-foot-deep well were constructed in Shoreham, Long Island, at the cost of $200,000 as Tesla attempted to demonstrate the viability of his experiments using the earth to conduct signals. Unfortunately, his primary financial backer, J. P. Morgan, refused to fund the needed enhancements, and the experiments never progressed beyond their initial stages.

In 1917, as the scourge of U-boat attacks on American shipping along the East Coast increased, suspicious people were seen lurking near the abandoned facility. Authorities suspected it was used for clandestine communication with German spies and submarines. Taking no chances, the federal government ordered the tower destroyed. The top half was blown off with dynamite in August 1917, followed by demolition of the remainder at the end of the year. The debris was sold for scrap to offset Tesla's debts.

Today the tower is gone, but the base remains, as does Tesla's laboratory, a 94-by-94-foot brick building designed by noted architect Stanford White. The site is undergoing environmental cleanup but is viewable from behind a fence.

■ 27. COMMERCE AND SPYING

MAP 12 ➤ **Telefunken transmission tower:** North of the railroad tracks, west of Cherry Avenue, West Sayville, Long Island (only remnants of tower remain)

The 477-foot-high Telefunken transmission tower in West Sayville, Long Island, was one of the most powerful wireless stations in the world before World War I. Built in 1912 by Germany's Telefunken Company on a 102-acre site, the tower was part of a transatlantic communications network for diplomatic and business communication. From the tower, a signal could be transmitted 3,500 miles to a receiver in Nauen, Germany.

In the buildup to World War I, the United States attempted to remain neutral and as early as 1914 cautioned Telefunken against sending secret messages to aid Germany's war effort. The station was allowed to transmit, but outgoing messages were subject to censorship by the US Navy. American officials continued to believe, however, that Germany was secretly sending coded notices of ships departing from US ports. Their concern was justified when two ciphered messages from the site evaded censorship.

The first message advised of the departure from New York City to Britain of the RMS *Lusitania* on May 1, 1915. German submarine warfare was intensifying in the Atlantic, and the area around the British Isles was declared a war zone. Six days later, on May 7, a U-boat torpedoed the *Lusitania* 11 miles off the southwestern coast of Ireland. Nearly 1,200 passengers and crew died in the attack, including 128 American citizens. The deaths helped shift public sentiment in the United States against Germany.

The second message, from German foreign minister Arthur Zimmermann in Berlin, was relayed on January 19, 1917, to Heinrich von Eckhardt, the country's ambassador to Mexico City. The coded message proposed an agreement with Mexico in exchange for an attack on the US southern border. Because Britain had severed the German undersea cable to the Americas, the message was transmitted in German diplomatic code over three routes, one of which went through the Sayville tower. The telegram was intercepted by British intelligence and decoded.

Telefunken's 477-foot high transmission tower in West Sayville, Long Island, was used by German intelligence for sending coded messages prior to America entering World War I.

The United States learned of the message in late February, and Zimmermann admitted its validity weeks later. Known as the Zimmermann Telegram, it inflamed America's passion for entering the war.

German-American relations had so soured by February 1917 that Telefunken wireless workers were ordered off the site, and a month later the station was operating with a US Navy crew. After the United States entered the war on April 6, 1917, US Marine Corps guards protected the Sayville station, which was also secured by an electrified fence and flood lights.

After the war, the tower was taken over by the McKay Radio and Telegraph Company and later by the Federal Aviation Administration. The tall transmission mast was demolished in 1938, but the large concrete anchors for the supporting wires remain in place.

■ 28. GENTLEMEN READING ANOTHER'S MAIL

MAP 5 ➤ **American Black Chamber:** 141 East 37th Street

Herbert O. Yardley

America's World War I code-breaking organization was the US Army's Military Intelligence Division, Section No. 8 (MI-8), based in Washington, DC. After the war, the codes and ciphers function was renamed the Cipher Bureau, nicknamed the Black Chamber, and operated as a joint effort of the State Department and War Department. Because State Department funding could not be expended legally in the District of Columbia, in 1919 the Black Chamber relocated to a New York City townhouse belonging to society figure T. Suffern Tailer at 3 East 38th Street. It moved a year later to 141 East 37th Street and then to 52 Vanderbilt Avenue. Operating under a business cover of the Code Computing Company, the firm could be contacted via letters sent to P.O. Box 354, Grand Central Terminal, or by phone at Vanderbilt 7539.

Code Computing produced codebooks for confidential business communication, including one titled *Universal Trade Code*, which sold well enough to turn a profit. However, its real business was breaking the diplomatic communications of other nations. The successful efforts were led by Herbert O. Yardley, a cryptographer, who lived on the top floor of the 37th Street location. The organization continued until 1929 when Secretary of State Henry L. Stimson is said to have declared, "Gentlemen do not read each other's mail." Soon afterward the State Department, and then the army, withdrew funding.

Two years later, without government sanction, Yardley published an account of the secret operation called *The American Black Chamber*. In it, he recounted multiple cryptographic successes against foreign governments, most notably Japan. The publication caused a sensation and made Yardley a celebrity, but government anger at the unauthorized revelations of such sensitive material earned him an official rebuke.

Nevertheless, Yardley continued writing and produced a book of puzzles called *Yardleygrams*. A radio drama followed, sponsored by Forhan's toothpaste, which offered a vial of secret ink and a decoder to listeners who sent in empty toothpaste boxes. Yardley also wrote

The second location of the Black Chamber, at 141 East 37th Street (door on left). Its ominous-sounding name was derived from the 16th-century French term for secret facility.

fiction, including *The Red Sun of Nippon* and *The Blonde Countess*. The latter became a hit 1935 movie, *Rendezvous*, starring William Powell as a heroic cryptographer and Rosalind Russell as his glamorous love interest. His last book, *The Education of a Poker Player* (1957), remains a classic of the genre.

Stimson's views on the value of code breaking reversed after he became Secretary of War during World War II. As secretary, Stimson relied heavily on decrypted enemy communications for wartime policy decisions. America's ability to secretly read "other gentlemen's mail" provided the Allies with a significant advantage that shortened the war.

Yardley died in 1958 and is buried at Arlington National Cemetery. In 1999, 110 years after his birth, the code breaker received overdue recognition when his name was added to the Hall of Honor at the National Security Agency (NSA), America's present-day code-breaking service.

"ZEST, BLOOD, AND SEX"

Author Ian Fleming, creator of the James Bond novels, was a fan of Herbert Yardley's last published work, *The Education of a Poker Player*. Fleming reportedly championed the book's publication in the United Kingdom after reading the US version and wrote a laudatory introduction to the British edition, proclaiming, "The book had zest, blood, sex, and a tough, wry humour reminiscent of Raymond Chandler."

■ 29. DEN OF SPIES

MAP I ▶ **Office for German sabotage operations:** 60 Broadway

Johann Heinrich von Bernstorff

Nine days after the July 1914 assassination of Archduke Franz Ferdinand in Sarajevo, Count Johann Heinrich von Bernstorff, the German ambassador to the United States, was summoned to Germany to consult with military intelligence, Section 3B of the German General Staff. Bernstorff was informed that no experienced military intelligence officers could be deployed to the United States because all of Germany's best officers and espionage agents were already operating against its current primary enemies in the war, the British Empire, France, and Russia. Further, even if Section 3B could identify a sufficient number of trained agents and mobilize them against the United States, the odds of infiltrating them into America undetected was remote.

Section 3B told Bernstorff that he was to be Germany's chief officer for espionage and sabotage for the Western Hemisphere. To support his effort, he would be assisted by German military attaché Capt. Franz von Papen and Capt. Karl Boy-Ed, a naval attaché, both of whom were accredited to the United States and Mexico. Commercial attaché Dr. Heinrich Albert became the finance officer for the operations, and Capt. Franz von Rintelen later joined the intelligence effort. With this small group of men and a healthy budget, Bernstorff initiated a complex intelligence-and-sabotage offensive against the United States.

With Bernstorff in Washington, the other three officials established their operational base in New York City. Papen operated from an office at 60 Broadway, and Albert operated in the Hamburg-America Line building at 45 Broadway. Boy-Ed used an office in the German consulate at 11 Broadway. The conspirators met at the Deutscher Verein (German Club/Society) at 112 West 59th Street (today 112 Central Park South) and at the Hotel Manhattan at East 42nd Street and Madison Avenue. Rintelen ran operations through several cover companies, such as the Mexican Northwest Railway at 55 Liberty Street and the Transatlantic Trust Company at 57 William Street.

By late January 1915, German spies and saboteurs were also entrenched in boardinghouses in the New Jersey ports and saloons along the waterfronts, but success did not come quickly. A plot to sabotage Canada's Welland Canal represented an early failure, though other plans, such as disrupting the supply line of phenol, a component of high explosives, that supported the British war effort, were more successful. Then a series of some 200 unexplained fires and explosions jolted the New Jersey munitions plants and waterfront and brought the war home to America. In July 1916, the most spectacular attack of all occurred at the Black Tom Island munitions depot, with an estimated $20 million (current value $400–$500 million) of damage inflicted on its structures and equipment.

Plots to attack munitions ships on the high seas after leaving US ports by creating rudder bombs also

> ### THE BUTLER DID IT
>
> Count Johann Heinrich von Bernstorff was rumored to be romantically linked to Mrs. Hugo Reisinger, the widow of a wealthy art collector and daughter of Adolphus Busch, the St. Louis brewer. The German diplomat frequently visited Reisinger's Gilded Age mansion at 993 Fifth Avenue (no longer standing), but the relationship may also have been a cover for intelligence operations. When Secret Service agents raided Reisinger's mansion in 1917, they discovered a sophisticated radio set on the roof. The radio was reported to include state-of-the-art "De Forest Audian Detector" technology capable of sending and receiving transmissions from Germany. Mrs. Reisinger denied knowledge of the rooftop station, claiming it belonged to a butler who had since left the country.

were initially ineffective. However, by 1915, the Germans had successfully developed safe and efficient pencil bombs, a.k.a. cigar bombs. These time-delay explosive devices, placed in a ship's munitions hold or coal bunker before sailing, ignited when the vessels were at sea, causing an explosion powerful enough to sink the vessel. At least 36 ships were successfully attacked, causing loss of life and damages in the millions of dollars. Other ships just disappeared at sea with sabotage suspected. Once the United States entered the war in April 1917, the attacks diminished.

■ 30. A SAFE HOUSE IS NOT A HOME

MAP 2 ➤ **Martha Held "residence":** 123 West 15th Street

Former opera singer Martha Held (a.k.a. Martha Gordon), a buxom lady with dark blue eyes and glossy black hair, ran a safe house for World War I German spies at 123 West 15th Street. Her townhouse included a well-equipped kitchen, wine cellar, and a large first-floor dining room with walls lined with photographs of herself and other performers in opera costumes. Held occupied four floors of the building with the help of two servants.

Neighbors observing the steady stream of male visitors to the house assumed that Held was operating a bordello. This was near the truth, as she was paid by the German government to manage the house as a "recreational facility" for German sailors stranded on interned ships, for reservists, and for dignitaries. It was better, the German high command reasoned, that they eat, drink, and be merry in a German venue rather than run loose in New York where they might spill secrets during a night of carousing.

In addition to providing beer and attractive ladies, the house served German intelligence as a safe house and operational base. Dinner guests often brought samples of new explosive devices that were passed around for examination. These would then be stored in a cupboard by Held until needed. Sometimes blueprints were spread out on the dining table to be examined along with photographs of ships and munitions plants. The basement served as a warehouse for larger quantities of explosives.

Food, drink, beautiful women, spies, and intrigue at Held's house attracted German dignitaries such as German ambassador and spymas-

This safe house at 123 West 15th Street doubled as saloon and social club for German dignitaries and naval officers prior to World War I.

Mena Edwards, a popular model known as "the Eastman Girl," was a hostess at the West 15th Street German safe house.

ter Count Bernstorff and an intelligence officer, Capt. Franz von Papen. Among Papen's favorite girls were a French woman named "Vera," a low-level German agent who resided at the Pasadena Apartments at 10 West 61st Street, and model Mena Edwards. Pretty and vivacious, Edwards was known as "the Eastman Girl" for her ads for the Eastman Kodak company. She lived in a hotel at West 86th Street and Broadway with her roommate, the actress Marie Wells.

■ 31. US PASSPORTS AT BARGAIN PRICES

MAP ı ➤ **Carl Ruroede office:** Maritime Building, 8 Bridge Street (replaced by skyscraper), opposite the Alexander Hamilton US Custom House

Britain severed the undersea communication cable between Germany and America at the beginning of World War I. Although the United States was officially neutral, it forbade use of its wireless transmitters to send ciphered dispatches to Germany. As a result, Capt. Fritz von Papen, the Ger-

man military attaché in New York, realized the need to devise alternative means of secure communication with Berlin. Using trusted couriers to hand-carry dispatches was an option, but Allied warships were searching transatlantic vessels for German citizens. Genuine US passports, with altered photographs and seals to match the bearer's profile, were required to assure the couriers' safe passage.

Carl Ruroede

Papen instructed a German American lawyer, Hans von Wedell, to establish an office at 8 Bridge Street and secretly procure US passports as cheaply as possible. Emissaries were sent to German residents in Hoboken, New Jersey, as well as the Bowery and other locations of "down and out" individuals. The office offered up to $20 to men who would apply for a US passport. Once received, the passports were delivered for payment to German officials at the Deutscher Verein at 112 West 59th or an Elks Club.

Wedell and his successor, Carl Ruroede Sr., working from the 8 Bridge Street office, room 204, used the passports for German officers recalled by the General Staff to Berlin who might otherwise be detained and for spies Papen directed to England, France, Italy, and Russia.

The no-longer-standing Deutscher Verein (German Club/Society) on Central Park South was a clearinghouse for forged passports and other espionage activity.

Wedell and Ruroede's efforts were on such a large scale that they eventually came to the attention of US authorities. A clever Department of Justice special agent, Albert Adams, befriended Ruroede and learned the German had established a secret workshop in his second-floor office to swap photos and alter seals. The process was described in *The German Secret Service in America, 1914–1918*, by John Price Jones and Paul Merrick Hollister:

> We wet the photograph, and then we affix the picture of the man who is to use it. The new photograph also is dampened, but when it is fastened to the passport, there still remains a sort of vacuum in spots between the new picture and the old, because of ridges made by the seal. Well, turn the passport upside down, place it on a soft ground made with a silk hand kerchief, and then, taking a paper cutter with a dull point, just trace the letters on the seal. The result is that the new photograph looks exactly as if it had been stamped by Uncle Sam. You can't tell the difference.

Armed with the information, the US government arrested Ruroede, who pleaded guilty and was sentenced to three years in the Atlanta federal prison. Wedell fled the United States as a passenger aboard the steamer *Bergensfjord*, getting as far as England with an altered passport before he was arrested and imprisoned.

■ 32. DYNAMITERS IN AMERICA

MAP 2 ➤ **Safe house:** 123 West 15th Street

German-born Franz Wachendorf arrived in the United States in 1912 and served briefly in the US Army. He then joined Pancho Villa's revolutionary force in Mexico, adopted the name Horst von der Goltz, and attained the rank of major. After World War I began, Goltz's skill as a saboteur attracted the attention of German diplomat-spy Franz von Papen. The Germans were planning operations in New York City to cripple Canadian and US production and shipping capabilities supporting Germany's enemies. Recruiting a skilled saboteur such as Goltz became essential.

Horst von der Goltz

One of Papen's sabotage targets was the Welland Canal locks, which linked Lake Ontario and Lake Erie on the Canadian side of the border, just west of Buffalo. Shippers of commodities and suppliers of raw materials for munitions companies depended on the canal for transportation. Goltz later described the reasoning for the operation: "Canada was, after all, our principal objective; we could strike a telling blow against it, and at the same time create consternation throughout America by blowing up the canals which connected to the Great Lakes."

With funds from Papen, Goltz began acquiring explosives. He used the pretext of blasting tree stumps on a farm as rationale for tasking German army captain Hans Tauscher, the Krupp representative in New York, to buy dynamite from the Dupont Powder Company. Goltz stored the explosives at a German safe house operated by the former opera singer Martha Held at 123 West 15th Street.

1918 advertisement for the film *The Prussian Cur.*

Goltz, using the alias Bridgeman H. Taylor, recruited several local men to support the operation. The small group left New York for Buffalo by train, unaware they were followed by US Secret Service agents. After surveying the canal and observing the Canadian locks were more heavily guarded than anticipated, the saboteurs got cold feet and abandoned the plan.

Papen reported the failure to Berlin, and Goltz was recalled to Germany but then inexplicably ordered almost immediately back to the United States. When his return ship stopped in England, Goltz contacted Scotland Yard and during his interrogation revealed the sabotage plot against the Welland Canal. He was then returned under guard to New York City to be a principal witness against the plotters.

As a result of Goltz's testimony, Hans Tauscher and Papen's deputy, Wolf von Igel, were arrested. German diplomats Karl Boy-Ed and Carl Lüderitz were also accused of espionage, sabotage, and passport offenses. Goltz pointed Department of Justice officers to the safe house run by Martha Held. When questioned about the dynamite, however, Held avoided charges by asserting she was asked only to hold a suitcase and did not know what it contained.

Goltz was ultimately pardoned and released. In 1917, he published an account of his activities as a spy and saboteur, *My Adventures as a German Secret Service Agent*, and played himself in *The Prussian Cur*, a 1918 silent propaganda film by the US government.

■ 33. IT'S ALWAYS THE DISGRUNTLED

MAP 8 ➤ **George Fuchs residence:** 630 West 139th Street

Paul Koenig, one of German spy-master Franz von Papen's agents, seemed particularly effective at defeating surveillance. A security officer for the Hamburg-America Line, then located at 45 Broadway, Koenig was a street-smart operative who had been stationed in New York for years. He regularly made what appeared to be innocent business visits to German establishments, such as Lüchow's, a restaurant at 110 East 14th Street, and the Pabst Grand Circle Hotel and Restaurant, then on the site of today's Time Warner Building at Columbus Circle. Koenig's tactic to evade surveillance was to transit the hallways of large buildings or crowded subways prior to clandestine meetings with the Abteilung IIIB (Germany's military intelligence service).

Koenig recruited trusted men from the Hamburg-America Line as agents for the spy network he called the Geheimdienst (secret service). Operating nearly invisibly, the network conducted surveillance, engaged in sabotage, and provided protective service for visiting dignitaries.

When Koenig later came under suspicion, the NYPD's Thomas Tunney installed a wiretap at a switching station of the Metropolitan Telephone and Telegraph Company, 18 Cortlandt Street, only to discover the German

Disgruntled spy George Fuchs, who lived modestly in this apartment building at 630 West 139th Street, gave law enforcement its first lead in a World War I espionage case when he called his boss on a tapped phone line to complain about being cheated out of $2.57.

agent already assumed his phone was tapped. Koenig's protective measures included using a simple yet secure code that depended on word substitutions known only to the users. For instance, a stated meeting arranged for a particular restaurant was code meaning the contact would occur at a hotel several blocks away. With the substitutions changed regularly, Koenig's code was virtually unbreakable.

A break in the case came in December 1915 when an operative who felt cheated out of a single day's wage—$2.57—phoned Koenig. Furious, he called the spymaster a "bullheaded Westphalian" along with a string of expletives. The call was traced to a saloon in Lower Manhattan, which was a sufficient lead for the police to identify George Fuchs. Unlike other members of Koenig's network, Fuchs, a cousin of Koenig's then living at 630 West 139th Street, was not a disciplined Hamburg-America Line employee or agent. When questioned, the disgruntled relative gave up enough information for the NYPD to raid Koenig's office and garner a huge cache of evidence.

Among the spies rounded up was Richard Emil Leyendecker, an art and antiques dealer with an office at 345 Fifth Avenue, and Frederick Scheindl, a bank clerk in the commercial credit department of the National City Bank, living at 1165 Bryant Avenue, the Bronx. In his position at the bank, Scheindl was able to review and pilfer documents related to the arms and ammunition transactions of the Allied governments.

■ 34. THE WOULD-BE SABOTEUR

MAP 13 ▶ **Robert Fay residence:** 28 50th Street, Weehawken, New Jersey

Army lieutenant Robert Fay arrived in New York City in April 1915 at age 24. The German national, an expert electrician and chemist, was already a veteran of the trench warfare in France where he had witnessed the carnage caused by US artillery munitions supplied to European allies. Fay's mission was to sabotage munitions ships bound for Europe using a cleverly designed "rudder bomb."

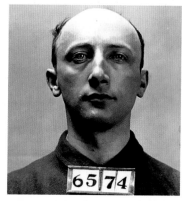
Robert Fay

For his mission, Fay was provided $4,000 and a fake Scottish passport in the name of H. A. Kearling and told to report to military attaché Franz von Papen's office at 60 Wall Street. Papen instructed him to describe the device to Capt. Franz von Rintelen, a German naval intelligence officer in New York City in charge of sabotage operations in New York Harbor. Fay's description was recorded in *The Secret War on the United States in 1915: A Tale of Sabotage, Labor Unrest, and Border Troubles* by Heribert von Feilitzsch:

Aspiring saboteur Robert Fay lived at this house at 28 50th Street in Weehawken, New Jersey. His plot to sabotage ships heading for Europe was thwarted by law enforcement. Fay lived at multiple locations in New Jersey, and addresses appearing in some published reports at the time of his arrest are likely incorrect.

Incriminating evidence collected in the Fay investigation included this saboteur's kit complete with explosives, tools, and disguises.

The contrivance reveals the mechanical ingenuity and practical efficiency of Fay's bomb. A rod attached to the rudder at every swing the rudder gave turned up by one notch the first of the beveled wheels within the bomb. After a certain number of revolutions of that wheel it in turn gave one revolution to the next and so on through the series. The last wheel was connected with the threaded cap around the upper end of the square bolt and made this cap slowly unscrew until at length the bolt dropped clear of it and yielded to the waiting pressure of the strong steel spring above. This pressure drove it downward and brought the sharp points at its lower end down on the caps of the two rifle cartridges fixed below it like the blow of a rifle's hammer. The detonation from the explosion of these cartridges would set off a small charge of impregnated chlorate of potash which in turn would fire the small charge of the more sluggish but stronger dynamite and that in turn would explode the still more sluggish but tremendously more powerful trinitrotoluol.

If all worked as planned, Fay believed his device was far better than a torpedo, which might miss the target. In theory, Fay's bomb would blow the stern off a ship and sink the vessel far off shore in deep water.

Fay, who lived at 28 50th Street in Weehawken, New Jersey, with his brother-in-law and coconspirator Walter L. Schultz (or Scholz), began work on the bomb from Schultz's nearby garage. Their explosive devices were tested in a wooded area in Grantwood, New Jersey. Aided by German engineer Dr. Herbert O. Kienzl, Fay purchased the needed explosives as well as 20 sticks of dynamite from a friendly local German contractor.

While the bombs were being assembled, the saboteurs reconnoitered New York Harbor from a 32-foot motor launch. They observed guards on the piers were so focused on examining what was loaded into the large transatlantic steamers that they paid no attention to the smaller boats scurrying around the harbor.

In June 1915, Rintelen demanded to see a demonstration of the bomb. To his dismay, after four attempts Fay's team could not get the device to perform properly. The potassium chlorate kept getting wet, the firing mechanism failed, and the dynamite did not cause the expected damage. Rintelen left for Europe in August, causing a sudden halt in Fay's operation. Fay did not know Papen was redirected to building a series of less complex "cigar bombs" that eventually sank or damaged dozens of ships en route to Europe.

Walter L. Schultz's Weehawken garage served as workshop and storage space for Fay.

Nevertheless, Fay and his small ring kept working on bombs, but the mistress of Fay's ammunition supplier, Countess de Beckendorf, tipped off the Secret Service about the plot in a fit of jealous pique. This came as no surprise to the Secret Service, which already had a double agent, Paul Seibe, inside the ring.

On October 25, 1915, Fay's Weehawken room was raided and found to contain dynamite, more than 80 pounds of TNT, eight completed bombs, maps, and disguises. Fay and Schultz were tracked to their garage workshop. Fay was arrested, convicted, and sentenced to eight years in prison.

As it turned out, Fay was a better escape artist than bomb maker. He broke out of the Atlanta federal prison, managed to reach Mexico and then Spain, but was recaptured after the war ended.

Disguises and false papers were found among Fay's spy equipment.

■ 35. PAYMASTER FOR SABOTEURS

MAP I ▶ G. **Amsinck and Company:** 6 Hanover Street (site redeveloped)

At the outbreak of World War I, Germany's popular military attaché in the United States, Capt. Franz von Papen, with a 25th-floor office at 60 Wall Street, was deeply involved with creating clandestine espionage and sabotage networks in the United States. Along with his naval attaché, Capt. Karl Boy-Ed, the two proved remarkably successful. The idea was to spy as well as disrupt the flow of munitions and raw materials to England and France.

Unexplained fires broke out in factories, such as the John A. Roebling facility in New Jersey, a steel company instrumental in the Brooklyn Bridge construction decades earlier. Explosions ripped through gunpowder and munitions plants in Delaware, New Jersey, and Pennsylvania. Ships sank at sea under suspicious circumstances, and at least one train was derailed. However, the most ambitious plot, sabotaging the Welland Canal to stall shipments of raw materials from Canada, failed.

Behind the scenes, financing the operations was the trading firm G. Amsinck and Company, 6 Hanover Street. Papen had purchased the firm to use its banking division as the covert paymaster for his intelligence activities and sabotage.

The operation ended in 1916 when the US government moved against Amsinck. Officials at the firm responded with a cover story: "The statement in the morning paper that Captain von Papen has made payments through G. Amsinck & Co. is wholly false. Because of his acquaintance with Adolf Pavenstedt, a member of the firm, the firm has from time to time cashed Captain von Papen's checks upon the Riggs Bank in Washington, he having no bank account in New York. . . . The checks cashed were for small amounts, never exceeding $1,000, and the aggregate amount was not large." When America entered World War I in 1917, the government closed the operation by selling Amsinck to the American International Corporation and purging the company of German nationals in executive positions.

By then, Papen had already returned to Germany to command a battalion on the western front, and after World War I, with an eye toward entering German politics, he

Karl Boy-Ed

attempted to clean up his wartime reputation in the United States as a ladies' man. "I made a sworn statement that the whole collection of affidavits and particularly one dated February 14, 1925, and made by someone named Mena Edwards née Reiss, known as the 'Eastman Girl,' were a complete invention from start to finish," Papen wrote in his memoirs. "I had never known a young woman of that name in the whole of my life."

Papen's plan to cleanse his past must have worked. In 1932, he became the chancellor of Germany and in 1933 and 1934 served under Adolf Hitler as vice chancellor. He is remembered for conspiring to dissolve the Weimar Republic and calling for a new election, which brought the Nazis to power. He was sentenced to 8 years by the Nuremberg war crimes court but released in 1949 on appeal. Although he was forbidden to publish in Germany, Papen's last years were spent in a futile attempt in books, articles, editorials, and speeches in other countries to clear his name and justify his role in bringing Hitler to power. He died in 1969, at the age of 89.

■ 36. ACE OF SPIES

MAP 7 ➤ **Sidney Reilly residence:** 260 Riverside Drive

Born Solomon or Sigmund Rosen-blum in Russia in 1874, Sidney Reilly has gained the reputation as one of the most colorful and mysterious spies of the 20th century. Reputed to be fluent in four or five languages and an avid collector of Napoleon memorabilia, Reilly likely spied for at least four nations, though some historians place the number even higher. Without specific attribution, Reilly is described as having "eleven passports and a wife to go with each one."

Before World War I, Reilly was involved in secret operations against Germany and credited with using lockpicks to break into an office in

Sidney Reilly

Essen, Germany, to steal important weapon designs for the British. Other details of his career remain murky. A healthy portion of his legendary exploits were likely self-created, and even historians who consider him a superspy agree the Reilly legend is inflated.

What can be confirmed is that from 1914 to 1916, Reilly operated out of a New York office on the 27th floor of the Equitable Building, 120 Broadway, as a spy, arms merchant, and con man engaged with the Russian Supply Committee, based in the Flatiron Building, 175 Fifth Avenue. His residences included 260 Riverside Drive; the Gotham Hotel (today the Peninsula New York), 700 Fifth Avenue; the St. Regis Hotel, 2 East 55th Street; and 38 West 59th (today Central Park South). Reilly's business involved selling and brokering arms to both the Germans and the Russians while rubbing elbows with New York's financial elites at the Bankers Club, which occupied the top three floors of the Equitable Building. By 1917, after the United States entered the war, Reilly's profitable munitions sales dried up, and he looked to rekindle his intelligence operations.

One of New York's grand old hotels, the Peninsula, previously named the Gotham, was home to Sidney Reilly during the early years of the 20th century.

In March 1918, Reilly began working with the British Secret Intelligence Service to launch an aggressive and ambitious anti-Bolshevik campaign in the wake of the Russian Revolution to rescue the Romanov family from imprisonment, restore Czar Nicholas II, and assassinate Vladimir Lenin. He even sold off his beloved collection of Napoleana to fund the effort. Considered to be his most daring plot, the operation was thwarted by unanticipated events on the eve of the coup. At the end of the war, the British recognized his service, and Reilly was

Among his numerous New York addresses over the years, Reilly also lived in this upscale apartment building at 260 Riverside Drive.

awarded the Military Cross in 1919 following a formal recommendation by Sir Mansfield Smith-Cumming, the head of British intelligence, "for distinguished services rendered in connection with military operations in the field." Details of the award and Reilly's real contributions remain controversial, even today.

Reilly met his fate in 1925 after he was lured back into Soviet Russia through Finland by an old nemesis, Felix "Iron Felix" Dzerzhinsky, the wily chief of the Soviet secret police, the Joint State Political Directorate (OGPU). Reilly was ostensibly to meet with the Trust, a notional anticommunist organization posing as the vanguard of a counterrevolution to overthrow the new Soviet government.

In reality, the Trust was an elaborate ruse engineered by Dzerzhinsky to consolidate and eliminate foreign opposition to the new Bolshevik government. After crossing the Finnish border into Russia, the "Ace of Spies" was captured and interrogated at the OGPU's Lubyanka Prison headquarters in Moscow. Realizing his position was hopeless, Reilly wrote out a lengthy confession to Dzerzhinsky and pleaded for his life but to no avail. He was executed in a forest near Moscow on November 5, 1925, and his corpse was photographed for documentation as it lay in Lubyanka. After Reilly's death, Soviet guards found his diary hidden in his cell. Photographic copies of it, along with his confession, are held in the Russian intelligence archive.

■ 37. DON'T SLEEP ON THE SUBWAY

MAP I ➤ **US Secret Service:** Alexander Hamilton US Custom House, 1 Bowling Green

Heinrich Albert, Germany's commercial attaché in Washington from 1914 to 1917, also operated from an office at 45 Broadway, the Hamburg-America Line Building. As a master of accounting manipulation, he hid Germany's financial support of intelligence activities through multiple bank accounts, funds transfers, and legitimate businesses sympathetic to his country's interests.

Heinrich Albert

By early 20th-century standards, Albert ran an efficient multi-million-dollar money-laundering scheme that allowed for the anonymous payment of agents and financed large-scale clandestine operations. Although America was still neutral in the war, the sinking of the *Lusitania* in May 1915 combined with NYPD reports of German spies and saboteurs prompted President Woodrow Wilson to order surveillance on German and Austrian diplomats.

Followed by a Secret Service agent on July 24, 1915, Albert left his Broadway office with the editor of a pro-German publication and headed

Germany's commercial attaché Heinrich Albert made his office in the no-longer-standing Hamburg-America Line Building on lower Broadway.

for the Sixth Avenue elevated train platform. While a cab ride would have cost under $2.00, Albert opted for the five-cent subway fare. Dozing on the ride back to his hotel, the Ritz-Carlton, then located on East 46th Street and Madison Avenue (since demolished), Albert exited the train at his stop without his brief-case. Immediately realizing his error, he returned to his seat and spotted the Secret Service agent leaving the station with his briefcase.

With the frantic Albert in pursuit, the agent made it to the street and hopped a streetcar. According to reports, the agent urged the con-ductor to pass stops. As recounted in *Dark Invasion* by Howard Blum, the agent told the streetcar conductor, "That guy's a nut." The conductor, believing an emotionally disturbed person was chasing them on foot, ordered the motorman to skip stops. Albert, unable to catch up but assuming his briefcase had been stolen by a common thief, placed an ad in the *New York Evening Telegraph*, offering a $20.00 reward for its return.

Meanwhile, at the Secret Service office in the Alexander Hamilton US Custom House, 1 Bowling Green, agents opened the briefcase to find a windfall of information about clandestine operations. Among the proposed operations was the purchase of American companies to corner the market on vital war materials and the instigation of strikes at plants producing armaments. It also contained lists of payments made to journalists and other public-opinion influencers. The operational scope and sums involved were staggering. One proposal alone to buy a company for $17 million repre-sented more than $500 million in current dollars.

The briefcase's contents were rushed to Washington but created some unanticipated problems. President Wilson and his Secretary of State, Robert Lansing, knew that as valuable as the information may be, legal action could not be taken against Albert or the German government without revealing the source of the intelligence. Its acquisition could be interpreted as theft, so rather than turning the matter over to the courts, Wilson's trusted adviser

Edward House took charge and arranged for publication of the briefcase's contents in the *New York World*. The articles created a sensation.

Remarkably, Albert faced little or no disciplinary action from his government for his carelessness. He remained in the United States until formal diplomatic ties with Germany were broken in 1917.

THE AMBASSADOR'S BATHING SUIT SCANDAL

The scandal surrounding Henrich Albert's lost briefcase extended beyond New York. Documents in the briefcase linked Midwestern industrialist turned Wall Street banker Archibald S. White to a German propaganda effort. A friend of then German ambassador to the United States, Count Bernstorff, White was implicated in a money-laundering scheme when the briefcase's documents revealed that he had supplied secret funds for the purchase of a pro-German newspaper called *Fair Play*.

White, who was forced to step down from the bank he founded in the wake of the scandal, also owned a luxury rustic retreat, the White Pine Camp, in the Adirondacks. Along with his then wife, Olive, the couple were reported to host memorable parties at the site. A photograph of Bernstorff at the White Pine Camp, flanked by two young women in bathing outfits, neither of whom was his wife, mysteriously emerged. The photo circulated first among diplomats—one fellow ambassador framed and displayed it on his mantelpiece—before it was leaked to the press in 1916. The photo seemed to confirm long-circulating whispered rumors about Bernstorff, who was reputed to have kept three mistresses in the Ritz-Carlton Hotel. Two British intelligence officers, Norman Thwaites and Guy Gaunt, were behind the acquisition and distribution of the photograph.

A photo of German diplomat Count Johann Heinrich von Bernstorff with two bathing beauties of the era caused a scandal when leaked to the press by British intelligence.

■ 38. MASTER SABOTEUR

MAP 3 ➤ **New York Yacht Club:** 37 West 44th Street

An imaginative World War I German saboteur, Capt. Franz Dagobert Johannes von Rintelen, arrived in New York City in April 1915. The former Deutsche Bank executive and German naval intelligence officer used a false Swiss passport with the alias Emile V. Gaché (also spelled Emile Gasche) to enter the United States. At his disposal was $500,000 ($11,000,000 in current value) to disrupt the flow of American munitions to the Allies. Checking into the Great Northern Hotel (now the modern Le Parker Meridien), 118 West 57th Street, Rintelen changed his alias to Frederick Hansen and opened an import-export front company on Cedar Street under the name E. V. Gibbons. However, it was necessary for him to use his true name at the New York Yacht Club at 37 West 44th Street, where his membership predated the war. Rintelen skirted the potential compromise by using the Deutscher Verein, 112 Central Park South, for his residential address.

Franz von Rintelen

World War I German spy Capt. Franz von Rintelen was a member and sometime resident of the New York Yacht Club. The club had only three German members at the start of the war: Kaiser Wilhelm II, his brother, Prinz Heinrich, and Rintelen.

The saboteur began working with a chemist, Dr. Walter Scheele, of 1133 Clinton Street, Hoboken, New Jersey, (today the site of the board of education parking lot), to devise timed explosive devices using an interned German ship in New York Harbor, the *Friedrich der Grosse*, as their bomb factory. Since the ship had a legal status under international law similar to embassies, the crew could work undisturbed, producing scores of the timed devices. Rintelen then recruited dockworkers to plant the bombs in ships' coal bunkers and munition holds. Numerous ships sunk in the Atlantic during that time can be attributed to Rintelen's efforts.

Next, with the clandestine seed money, he financed a front organization called Labor's National Peace Council, with offices at 55 Liberty Street, to organize strikes at munitions factories and promote American neutrality. He also moved forward with a plot to reinstall ousted Mexican dictator José Victoriano Huerta Márquez, conducting multiple meetings in the Ansonia Hotel, 2109 Broadway between West 73rd and 74th Streets. The plot entailed providing the former dictator with 10,000 rifles and a large amount of money in exchange for staging a coup in Mexico that would spur Mexico into declaring war on the United States.

Unfortunately for Rintelen, his cover unraveled after a few months. His communications were compromised when Room 40, the code-breaking section of the British Admiralty, decrypted a telegram to Rintelen from a colleague and alerted the Americans. The German intelligence officer and saboteur fled the United States but was arrested in England and jailed, then returned to the United States, where he received a four-year sentence.

Rintelen was also implicated in the 1916 munitions depot explosions at Black Tom Island—a thin peninsula that jutted out into New York Harbor from the New Jersey side. He denied direct involvement but in his 1933 book, *Dark Invader*, confessed to casing the facility during his time in New York. He died in England in 1949.

■ 39. THE BOMBER FROM HOBOKEN

MAP I 3 ➤ **New Jersey Agricultural Chemical Company:** 1133 Clinton Street, Hoboken, New Jersey (site redeveloped)

Dr. Walter T. Scheele, president of the New Jersey Agricultural Chemical Company, 1133 Clinton Street, Hoboken, New Jersey, created one of the most effective sabotage devices of World War I. A chemist by training and a former intelligence officer, Scheele designed the device as a tube not much larger than a cigar, approximately six inches long and an inch and a half in diameter. Its lead casing enclosed two chambers, each filled with a different acid. When the acid dissolved a copper divider between the chambers, the chemicals mixed, and the incendiary device exploded.

What made Scheele's bomb especially useful to saboteurs was that

This unexploded German incendiary device, suspected to have been planted by saboteurs at an American port, was discovered on a British supply ship when it docked in Liverpool.

the explosion could be timed by altering the thickness of the material dividing the two chambers. A thick divider might take weeks for the acid to do its work; a thinner one enabled an explosion in minutes or hours. A length of tin fastened along the side allowed a saboteur to mount the device in a fixed position, and lead's low melting point assured the explosion would destroy evidence of the device.

The operation lasted from January 1, 1915, to April 13, 1916, and may have destroyed as many as 36 ships at sea. When the plot was eventually uncovered, Scheele fled to Cuba but was captured there in March 1918. By accepting a plea bargain with an extraordinarily light sentence, he served only a single day in custody in exchange for his cooperation in the case. He then provided technical advice to the War and Navy Departments on techniques and tools for the safe loading of shells. Scheele died in 1922 in Hackensack, New Jersey.

■ 40. WOLF OF WALL STREET AND GERMAN AGENT

MAP I ➤ **Labor's National Peace Council offices:** 55 Liberty Street

Although best known for World War I sabotage operations, German naval intelligence officer Capt. Franz von Rintelen also ran effective covert action operations. In June 1915, he formed a front group called Labor's National Peace Council (LNPC), headquartered at 55 Liberty Street, which was designed to appear similar to the American Federation of Labor. However, the LNPC was not created to represent workers in collective bargaining. Instead, its mission was to provoke strikes at factories producing arms for the

David Lamar

Allies and encourage work stoppages by dockworkers who loaded the cargo. Generous strike benefits were paid to those willing to walk out.

In his postwar memoir *Dark Invader*, Rintelen recalled organizing a meeting at Carnegie Hall, Seventh Avenue and West 57th Street:

> The first thing I did was to hire a large hall and organize a meeting, at which well-known men thundered against the export of munitions. Messrs. Buchanan and Fowler, members of Congress; Mr. Hannis Taylor, the former American Ambassador in Madrid; Mr. Monnett, a former Attorney General; together with a number of University professors, theologians and labor leaders appeared and

raised their voices. I sat unobtrusively in a corner and watched my plans fructifying. None of the speakers had the faintest suspicion that he was in the "service" of a German officer sitting among the audience. They knew the men who had asked them to speak, but had no idea that the strings were being pulled by somebody else.

David Lamar, the most visible face of the LNPC, managed the organization's money. Called the "Wolf of Wall Street," Lamar came to the project with a history of questionable dealings. He once owned a townhouse at 618 Fifth Avenue, today the site of Rockefeller Center, and was said to have cheated the venerable J. P. Morgan out of a small fortune. Lamar's trademark was a diamond-tipped walking stick and a philosophy of what *The New York Times* dubbed "swagger and swank." In fact, Rintelen had unwittingly hired a local mob-connected con artist who was better at deception than being a labor organizer or spy. Nevertheless, the LNPC operation, despite Lamar, seemed to succeed temporarily as Rintelen spread money around and workers walked off their jobs in defense factories and on docks.

The scheme eventually fell apart. Lamar was indicted in December 1915. At his trial in late April 1916, he was given to courtroom outbursts and antics, at one point asserting a grand conspiracy against him. The histrionics were to no avail, and he was sentenced to a year in prison.

Rintelen was arrested on a Dutch ship as it passed through British waters in early July 1916. He subsequently spent 21 months in a British prison and was then deported to the United States, where he served an additional three years in the Atlanta federal prison.

Lamar, however, may have had the last laugh in deceiving Rintelen and pocketing most of the LNPC's funds for himself. It turned out that very little about Lamar was real, and even his southern accent was a fiction. A man more successful at conning people out of money than managing it, he died destitute in 1934 in a room at the Wellington Hotel, Seventh Avenue and West 55th Street. The "Wolf's" *New York Times* obituary was headlined "True Name a Mystery." Waiters, whom Lamar tipped generously during his prosperous years, paid for his funeral expenses.

Master-spy Franz von Rintelen teamed up with dubious financier David Lamar, known as the Wolf of Wall Street, to form the fraudulent Labor's National Peace Council, headquartered at 55 Liberty Street.

■ 41. SABOTAGE OR TERRORISM?

MAP 13 ▶ **Black Tom Island commemorative plaque:** Foot of Morris Pesin Drive in Liberty State Park, Jersey City, New Jersey

The highest viewing point from the Statue of Liberty is not her crown but rather her torch. It remains off-limits to visitors, however, as a result of an act of sabotage conducted by a foreign terrorist cell more than 100 years ago.

Kurt Jahnke

Ground zero for the attack was at nearby Black Tom Island in Jersey City. The first explosion at 2:08 a.m. on July 30, 1916, jolted millions of people from their sleep and caused property damage of $20 million dollars at the time—about $500 million today. The explosion of two million pounds of munitions, equivalent of a 5.5 magnitude earthquake, was felt as far away as Philadelphia and into Maryland. The true death toll will never be known as the housing barges and others in the vicinity of the blast disappeared in the inferno. The shock wave from the blast popped Lady Liberty's rivets, and flying debris damaged her arm holding the torch.

The investigations that followed the attack determined that German saboteurs were the culprits. The possibility of a careless accident was considered,

The devastation caused by the Black Tom Island explosion left the Lehigh Valley Railroad pier and surrounding area in ruins.

but other explosions across the country around the same time seemed more than coincidental. Although the United States was officially neutral in World War I at the time, Black Tom Island was a primary shipping point for arms and munitions sent to England. Through German eyes, the munitions from Black Tom Island's 24-hours-a-day operations were used to kill German soldiers, and America's neutrality was nothing more than a farce.

Investigations continued for more than two decades following the war as shipping companies were persistent in recovering compensation for their losses. By 1939, there were conclusive evidence and confessions to show that Germany sent spies and saboteurs to the United States in 1914 as part of the diplomatic staff of German ambassador Johann Heinrich von Bernstorff.

One German agent, Capt. Franz von Rintelen, set up a front company, the Austrian-subsidized Transatlantic Trust Company, at 57 William Street in Manhattan. The firm attempted, but failed, to buy the DuPont gunpowder factory and stop shipments to England. Rintelen was successful in developing small time-delayed incendiary devices, assembled in a bomb-making laboratory at 1133 Clinton Street, Hoboken, New Jersey, and recruiting Irish American dockworkers to sabotage the British war effort at a time when Ireland was actively seeking independence from Britain.

Rintelen fled the United States in August 1915 but left behind an operational network. Around midnight on July 30, 1916, two saboteurs, Rintelen operatives Kurt Jahnke and Lothar Witzke, planted the devices at the Black Tom target. By 1:00 a.m., fires were burning on the piers, and an hour later major explosions began. Jahnke and Witzke escaped Black Tom Island to continue their attacks elsewhere. A similar explosion in early 1917 at the Mare Island naval shipyard in Vallejo, California, was also attributed to the pair before both entered Mexico in April 1917.

Rintelen was eventually arrested and interned in the United Kingdom for 21 months, then extradited to the United States. He was tried in New York, found guilty on federal charges, and imprisoned in Atlanta for three years. He returned to Germany in 1920.

Today the land that was Black Tom Island, near the Liberty Science Center, is part of Liberty State Park. A small plaque in the flag plaza at the foot of Morris Pesin Drive commemorates the 1916 attack.

■ 42. THE HEROINE OF KINGSLAND

MAP 13 ► **Memorial at Vest Pocket Park former site of Canadian Car and Foundry Company:** 213 Clay Avenue, Lyndhurst, New Jersey

Following the explosions at Black Tom Island in July 1916, German saboteurs targeted the Canadian Car and Foundry Company (CCFC) at Kingsland, New Jersey, which produced artillery shells under contract for

Despite newly instituted security measures, saboteurs were successful in blowing up the munitions-producing Canadian Car and Foundry Company in Kingsland, New Jersey, in early 1917.

Russia. Aware of the vulnerability of Black Tom Island to saboteurs, the owners of CCFC constructed a six-foot fence around the plant and expanded the guard force to conduct 24-hour patrols. Each worker arriving at the plant was screened before being entering.

Frederick Hinsch, who headed the group tasked with sabotaging the facility, recruited countryman Curt Thummel. Having changed his name to Charles Thorne, Thummel became the company's assistant employment manager and influenced the hiring of several other operatives sent by Hinsch. One of the men, Theodore Wozniak, was known to the British Secret Intelligence Service as a German agent, though no action was taken when he was hired at Kingsland. The cost of overlooking the spy would be steep.

On January 11, 1917, the saboteurs attacked Building 30, where Wozniak worked cleaning out shell casings. On each of the 48 work benches in the building was a belt-driven lathe and a pan of gasoline used as a cleaning solvent. A blaze was ignited at Wozniak's work station, and the fire spread rapidly. Within minutes, flames engulfed the entire structure. The fires raged for four hours, detonating between a half-million and 1.25 million 3-inch explosive shells. With the exception of two concrete buildings, the entire plant was destroyed.

In the midst of the conflagration, Tessie McNamara, the company's switchboard operator, saved numerous lives of the more than a thousand men working at the time of the explosion. Despite personal danger, she remained at her post with six telephone lines leading to the buildings and the outside world. Her description of the event is inscribed on the Clay Avenue marker:

> My first thought was to save the lives of the 1700 men in the buildings. While making my calls, the first shell struck the building and passed about five feet from where I was sitting. About a dozen buildings were now on fire and I had completed all calls. I started to leave the building without a coat, but I couldn't walk. My courage left me and the arriving firemen picked me up, wrapped a big coat around and rushed for the gate.

The official investigation determined that the fires that began at Wozniak's workbench in Building 30 were no accident, but he had already slipped away to Mexico.

From the memorial to Tessie McNamara in a small park located at 213 Clay Avenue, Lyndhurst, New Jersey, the plant's location can still be seen. One of the smokestacks still stands. The marshy bog where the plant was situated is believed to be the site of the large crater caused by the 1916 explosions.

Germany made reparations for the damage caused by the explosion in 1979 but never officially accepted responsibility for the acts of sabotage.

■ 43. SPY AND PLAYWRIGHT

MAP | ➤ **World War I British consulate:** 44 Whitehall Street

Sir William George Eden Wiseman, 10th Baronet (of Canfield Hall, Essex), carried a biography as colorful as his name. A graduate of Cambridge, he was a boxer, playwright, and journalist before turning his attention to making money in banking, a profession interrupted by World War I. After surviving a combat gas attack in Flanders, he was recruited into the War Office Section of Britain's MI6, the country's foreign intelligence service, then called MIIc.

Wiseman and a traveling companion arrived in New York City in the fall of 1915 under the cover of merchants and gave their local business address as that of the accounting firm of Touche and Niven (a predecessor of Deloitte Touche Tohmatsu), 30 Broad Street. However, Wiseman was soon installed in the British consulate at 44 Whitehall Street in Lower Manhattan as a low-level functionary in the Purchasing Commission of the British Ministry of Munitions. He eventually took over British Empire intelligence operations from a Royal Navy captain, Sir Guy Gaunt, targeting German American organizations and anti-British groups advocating independence for India and Ireland.

Wiseman moved into the luxury Gotham Hotel (now the Peninsula New York) at 700 Fifth Avenue, which was also the residence of Col. Edward House, a trusted adviser to President Wilson. Together the pair acted as conduits of unofficial diplomacy between the British government and the president.

With World War I raging in Europe and America remaining neutral, Wiseman and his network attempted to discredit the Germans while urging America to enter the fray. After the war, Wiseman remained in New York City working for the investment house of Kuhn, Loeb and Company while dabbling in theater as a playwright and launching a play called *Her Lord and Master* in 1929. In 1939, he was called back to duty to help William Stephenson set up the British Security Coordination (BSC), modeled in large part on his original World War I intelligence operation.

■ 44. PROPAGANDA FOR THE KAISER

MAP | ➤ *New York Evening Mail* **offices:** 34 Park Row

The *New York Evening Mail*, which was located at 34 Park Row, dated to the 1830s and made front-page news itself in 1918 when its publisher,

Edward A. Rumely, was arrested. Three years earlier, the pro-German Rumely had purchased the paper and changed its editorial policy from anti- to pro-German. However, the funding source for Rumely's acquisition of the paper was suspect, and anti-German papers, including *The New York Times*, headlined that the *Evening Mail* was part of a massive German propaganda campaign.

The New York Evening Mail became the center of a German propaganda campaign in New York after its purchase by Edward A. Rumely.

Rumely was accused of financing the purchase from a $30 million German fund earmarked for influencing political opinions in America. Rumely denied the charges, claiming the funds came from an American living in Germany, but was convicted of violating the Trading with the Enemy Act in 1918. His sentence of a year and day in jail was shortened to one month, and in 1925, Rumely was pardoned by President Calvin Coolidge.

The *Evening Mail* ceased publication in 1924 following a merger with the *New York Telegram*. Rumely reemerged as a controversial public figure in the 1930s when he organized groups protesting against Roosevelt's New Deal and remained politically active until his death in 1964.

■ 45. JOURNALIST-SPY GEORGE VAUX BACON

MAP | ▶ **George Bacon cover office:** Central Powers War Films Exchange, 150 Nassau Street

George Vaux Bacon, a young New York reporter who covered celebrity news for magazines such as *Photoplay*, was recruited to spy in 1916 by German intelligence officers Albert O. Sander and Charles Wunnenberg. Operating under a commercial cover called the Central Powers War Films Exchange, 150 Nassau Street, the two maintained residences at Brooklyn's Clarendon Hotel, at the corner of Fulton and Washington Streets (today Cadman Plaza East).

Bacon must have seemed the ideal spy. Only in his twenties yet solidly established as a journalist, he was offered a salary of $125 a week in return for his espionage services. According to accounts at the time, Bacon used a secret writing compound impregnated into a pair of black wool socks. To reconstitute the ink, he soaked the top of a sock in distilled water to produce a light brown liquid that vanished when dry.

The system was secure because the ink was difficult to detect due to the small quantity of active ingredients required, and the message itself became readable only when multiple reagents were applied.

On his handlers' instructions, Bacon traveled to England, from where he reported on Allied antiaircraft defenses, fighting-ship technology, and the morale of the general population. He would later claim he had no intention of passing secrets that would harm Britain or America. "It was nothing but a crazy adventure designed to produce an exclusive story on espionage, if I had gotten

George Vaux Bacon

CHARMING SPY

An unsung American hero of the George Vaux Bacon spy saga is Roslyn "Ross" Whytock. A newspaperman by trade, Whytock was recruited by German agents Sander and Wunnenberg before their approach to Bacon. Apparently a more clever negotiator, Whytock was to receive $200 a week from the Germans for spying, compared to Bacon's $125. He reported the recruitment pitch to a British intelligence contact in New York and agreed to travel to Europe as a double agent. Unbeknown to the Germans, he provided information about Bacon until the latter's arrest.

Whytock, who worked for Joseph Pulitzer's *Evening World*, 53–63 Park Row, was a New York transplant from Missouri. He left that state after an affair with married department-store model Irma Jones forced him to resign his commission in the Missouri National Guard. Even worse, Mrs. Jones's husband had threatened to kill him. Whytock, a man of uncommon charm, calmed the offended husband, and in a few days the two became good friends.

Following his mission as a double agent, Whytock joined the US Army, which sent him to the War College in Washington. He emerged with the rank of major and then, as a port control officer, was assigned to the Military Intelligence Division, based in room 805 of 302 Broadway. Later he returned to the *Evening World*. Whytock died in 1964 in California.

away with it," Bacon wrote years later to code breaker Herbert O. Yardley. "However, I had to swear to keep what I knew to myself, so the story was never written."

When authorities arrested Bacon in Britain in mid-December 1916, they found incriminating evidence among his possessions, including secret-writing materials and the name and address of a known German intelligence contact in the Netherlands. Also discovered was a bottle of Argyrol, a commercial product used before the discovery of antibiotics to treat a variety of ailments, including gonorrhea. By coincidence, the medication had a chemical makeup similar to secret-writing ink.

Bacon confessed to spying, was put on trial in Britain, convicted, and sentenced to death. However, through the intervention of US authorities, he was returned to the United States to offer testimony against Sander and Wunnenberg, both of whom were subsequently sentenced to two years in prison and fined $2,500. Bacon received a year in prison, then, according to one report, relocated to Los Angeles and found work writing sales brochures. He died in 1972.

■ 46. WARTIME SLEUTHS FROM WALL STREET

MAP | ▶ **Office of Naval Intelligence, World War I branch office:** 14 Wall Street

In the fall of 1916, the chief of naval intelligence, Roger Welles, called on the newly organized Naval Reserve to fill the need for wartime spies. The first branch office of the Office of Naval Intelligence (ONI) opened in New York City a short time later. Comprised of a small undercover force of officers with temporary commissions, the unit was headed by Spencer Fayette Eddy, a Harvard graduate and career diplomat. Eddy, who moved in the elite circles of New York society, was known for his tennis game and prize-winning orchids.

Spencer Fayette Eddy

He also possessed a taste for adventure. A 1905 news story detailed his narrow escape in St. Petersburg, Russia, when caught between a crowd of protesters and a squadron of charging Cossacks. In James Bond style, the young Eddy made his escape by sleigh.

Relying on volunteers, Eddy set up the first ONI branch office at 14 Wall Street. Other branch offices in Chicago, San Francisco, Pittsburgh,

Philadelphia, Washington, Baltimore, and Boston soon followed and, in total, employed approximately 500 people by 1918.

Many of the new spies came from the same social set as Eddy. There were attorneys and Wall Street bankers along with Harvard and other Ivy League alumni. Among them was Ralph Pulitzer, son of Joseph Pulitzer, the newspaper magnate who owned the *New York World*, and por-

The Office of Naval Intelligence, 14 Wall Street, was an important hub of US intelligence activities during World War I.

trait artist DeWitt McClellan Lockman. Some were handpicked by Franklin Roosevelt, then Assistant Secretary of the Navy, from his social circle.

ONI agents secured waterfront facilities, searched ships, and worked with the management of large wartime industries to protect facilities against sabotage and espionage. The branch offices were largely seen as doing an admirable job against the threat of German sabotage, although some agents ventured into the unlawful surveillance of radical groups and individuals. For example, the pro-Soviet author and socialist John Reed, who lived at 147 West 4th Street, was surveilled while in New York.

Radical publications, unions, and other organizations also came under the scrutiny of ONI branch offices. In factories, troublemakers, slackers, and even those who did not participate in Liberty Loan or Red Cross drives could be singled out as being potentially disloyal and fall under suspicion. "ONI might be pursuing suspects a bit too enthusiastically," cautioned Rear Adm. Leigh V. Palmer, chief of the Bureau of Navigation, in an August 1918 report. Once World War I ended, ONI's branch-office intelligence program was discontinued.

■ 47. CRUSADER AND SPY

MAPS 2 AND 4 ➤ **Agnes Smedley residences:** 2 Bank Street, 156 Waverly Place, and 16th East 9th Street

Agnes Smedley—journalist, author, and activist—spied at various times for the Indian nationalist movement, the Soviet Union, and Chinese communists. After arriving in New York City in 1916 from California, newly divorced and with few employment prospects, Smedley immersed herself in the Greenwich

Agnes Smedley

Author, activist, and spy Agnes Smedley's apartment building at 2 Bank Street

Smedley's residence at 156 Waverly Place in Greenwich Village. Moving frequently made it more difficult for authorities to track her.

Village culture of causes, including the women's suffrage movement, Margaret Sanger's birth-control advocacy, and the push for Indian independence.

While working inside India's independence movement, Smedley gained her first experience in the clandestine world. She established herself as a communication conduit for a violent faction of the movement involved in arms smuggling. Financed by Germany during World War I, the group's activities soon came to the attention of British and US intelligence. Despite changing residences frequently—she lived at 2 Bank Street, 156 Waverly Place, and 16th East 9th Street—Smedley was arrested in 1918 by the US Naval Intelligence Bureau under the Espionage Act and imprisoned at City Prison (a.k.a. the Tombs), Manhattan's municipal jail at 125 White Street.

Smedley was eventually released when the government failed to provide her with a speedy trial. She then abandoned causes related to women's issues and committed herself to spying for the Communist International (COMINTERN). Initially she moved to Germany and then relocated to India before traveling to China.

In China she met Soviet master-spy Richard Sorge, with whom she became professionally and romantically linked, and assisted him in forming a spy network in Japan. She also began a romantic involvement with Ozaki Hotsumi, a correspondent for the newspaper *Asahi Shinbun* and Sorge's most important agent in Japan. During World War II, Smedley lobbied US general Joseph Stilwell to send arms to communist Chinese forces to be used against the Japanese.

By the late 1940s, Smedley's radical views and writings, as well as rumors of espionage, brought her name to the attention of the Federal Bureau of Investigation (FBI). She relocated to Britain, where she died in 1950.

Smedley's cover as a crusading journalist and author gained her a measure of renown and legitimacy. Her 1929 autobiographical novel *Daughter of Earth* offered a flattering self-portrait of a fearless and independent idealist.

For many, she seemed a woman ahead of her time. After her death, however, documents uncovered in Moscow confirmed her role as a wily and effective intelligence operative working for both the Soviet Union and China.

■ 48. AN ARTIST GOES UNDERCOVER

MAPS 4 AND 8 ➤ John Held Jr.
residences: 151 East 19th Street and 736 Riverside Drive

At the start of World War I, archaeologist Sylvanus G. Morley, then working for the ONI, recruited John Held Jr. as an assistant. The Utah-born Held, a cartoonist and illustrator living at 736 Riverside Drive and then 151 East 19th Street, signed on for an archaeological expedition along the coasts of Central and South America. In fact, the expedition was a cover to create maps and file reports on German submarine operations and potential amphibious landing sites. These maps and other materials were sent back to the United States using accommodation addresses.

Among the New York residences of popular Jazz Age illustrator and one-time spy John Held was an East 19th Street apartment.

Following the war, Held returned to New York and became one of the best-known illustrators of the Roaring Twenties. His work appeared in *Life* magazine, *Vanity Fair*, and the *New Yorker*. His artwork also adorned the cover of F. Scott Fitzgerald's *Tales of the Jazz Age* (1922), and he designed the landmark "Wise Men Fish Here" sign of the now-defunct Gotham Book Mart on West 47th Street.

When World War II began, Held enlisted in the US Army Signal Corps and was assigned to Camp Evans, Belmar, New Jersey, where radar technology was being developed and tested. Following the war, Held settled in Belmar at 3106 Hurley Pond Road. He died on March 2, 1958, and is buried in Woodlawn Cemetery, East 233rd Street and Webster Avenue, the Bronx.

■ 49. CITIZEN SPY CATCHERS

MAP 1 ➤ **American Protective League Headquarters:** 32 Nassau Street

Soon after the passage of the Selective Service Act in 1917, it became clear that federal and local authorities were unable to keep up with enforcement. With the nation at war, federal agencies, including the

The American Defense Society (ADS), a civilian organization headquartered at 303 Fifth Avenue with a mission similar to that of the American Protective League, called on citizens to hunt German spies and Bolsheviks and for America to enter World War I on the side of Great Britain.

Bureau of Investigation (BOI), sought help from a civilian organization, the American Protective League (APL). A national group of volunteers, the APL was given some enforcement authorities by Attorney General Thomas Gregory. The group's letterhead and other official documents noted that it was "Organized with the Approval and Operating under the Direction of the United States Department of Justice, Bureau of Investigation."

Founded in 1917 by businessman A. M. Briggs, the APL functioned as civilian counterintelligence corps. Members were issued a badge and identification card conveying a quasi-official status—"American Protective League—Secret Service"—but they received little training to hunt for wartime spies and German sympathizers. They also sought to counteract the activities of radicals, anarchists, antiwar activists, left-wing labor unions, and fringe political organizations. APL members illegally opened mail, made surreptitious office searches, and reported "word of mouth propaganda."

In 1915, the BOI had only 219 agents in offices around the United States and none authorized to carry weapons or make arrests. As a result, the resources of the APL's 250,000 members in 600 cities across the country were initially welcomed by federal authorities. The attorney general boasted of the manpower they provided: "I have today several hundred thousand private citizens . . . assisting the heavily overworked Federal authorities in keeping

A. M. Briggs

an eye on disloyal individuals and making reports of disloyal utterances." The APL established secret cells inside factories producing clothing and war matériel to identify disloyalty and sabotage. Suspects were identified, investigated, and reported to the BOI.

The APL's New York headquarters, 32 Nassau Street, was one of the largest and most active of the association's network. Problems arose as the result of poor communication with the overstretched BOI, and sometimes APL lost control of its far-flung field operations.

The American Protective League's slacker raids earned the ire of New Yorkers when civilian enforcers began entering offices, restaurants, and theaters demanding to see draft registration cards.

APL members grew impatient with the limited resources of the BOI and, at times, conducted operations independently.

On September 3, 1918, 2,000 APL members, accompanied by 35 BOI agents and NYPD officers, began rounding up suspected draft dodgers. Such so-called slacker raids had already taken place in Minneapolis, Cleveland, San Francisco, Philadelphia, and other cities without serious incident. However, the New York City slacker raid was a different matter. For three days, APL members positioned themselves outside office buildings such as the Equitable Building (120 Broadway), pool halls, public parks, and local diners and demanded young men show draft cards as proof they were registered. Similar demands were made of travelers at Grand Central Terminal. At the Lexington Theatre, 51st Street and Lexington Avenue, where Irving Berlin's patriotic revue *Yip Yip Yaphank* was playing, an announcement made from the orchestra pit ordered draft age men in the audience to stand up and present their draft cards.

As the raids progressed, men from throughout the city were hauled off to police precincts, the 69th Regiment Armory (68 Lexington Avenue), the 23rd Regiment Armory (1322 Bedford Avenue, Brooklyn), and other holding areas for processing. According to FBI records, 75,000 men were detained, many not even of draft age, including a 75-year-old gentleman on crutches. Public outrage followed, and a formal investigation was launched. No official number of draft dodgers apprehended was released, though an estimate in the *FBI Comprehensive Reference Guide* put the figure at one for every 200 men detained.

After the armistice with Germany ended the war, Attorney General Gregory officially credited the APL with the defeat of German spies and propaganda in America. But when A. Mitchell Palmer became attorney general on March 5, 1919, he stopped accepting intelligence provided by the APL, and within months the organization was disbanded.

■ 50. INTERNATIONAL WOMAN OF MYSTERY

MAP 5 ➤ **Maria de Victorica dead-drop site:** Pew 30, St. Patrick's Cathedral, Fifth Avenue and East 50th Street

Maria de Victorica

In the autumn of 1917, MI-8 established a laboratory and office in the US postal facility at 541 Washington Street to screen letters for secret writing. MI-8's mail-opening operation revealed letters written in invisible ink detailing chilling plots of sabotage. These included recruiting radical elements of the Irish American community to blowing up ships and importing explosives secreted in religious statues through unwitting priests. The office examined two thousand letters a week. In April 1918, censors identified a major German spy ring led by Herman Wessels, an employee of the Hamburg-America Line. The ring included Maria de Victorica (dubbed "the Blonde Mata Hari" by the New York press), the glamorous daughter of a Prussian general.

Born Baroness Maria von Kretschmann, de Victorica was the younger sister of Lily Braun, an early feminist, and an accomplished journalist who also wrote screenplays for silent films. She acquired multiple university degrees, spoke several languages, and was noteworthy as the only female newspaper editor in Germany.

Recruited for espionage around 1910 in Germany by Col. Walter Nicolai, head of Abteilung IIIB (military intelligence), de Victorica arrived in America in 1917. By then, she was an often-married, 38-year-old morphine addict with a once-promising literary career behind her. Under the cover of a journalist,

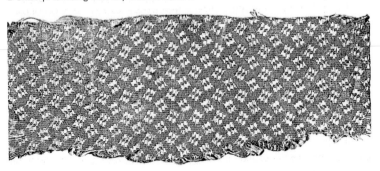

A section of Maria de Victorica's scarf contained chemicals she used for secret writing.

she communicated with her handlers, including Lt. Cdr. Karl von Rodiger of the German navy, through dead drops and accommodation addresses—addresses having no connection with an intelligence organization. One notable drop site was pew 30 in St. Patrick's Cathedral, Fifth Avenue and East 50th Street.

Capturing the mysterious spy proved difficult. De Victorica moved frequently from one hotel to another and always paid her bill in advance and in cash. Among her favorite hotels were the Knickerbocker Hotel, 6 Times Square, followed by the Waldorf Astoria Hotel, at the time located at Fifth Avenue and West 34th Street, and the Spencer Arms, 140 West 69th Street.

Carl von Rodiger

Fashionably dressed, she attracted little undue attention at the upscale hotels she seemed to favor. Nevertheless, before her ambitious sabotage operations could be carried out, de Victorica was arrested at the Hotel Nassau, today the Ocean Club apartments, 100 West Broadway at National Boulevard, in Long Beach (just off southwestern Long Island), where she had registered under the name Marie de Vussière.

Among the possessions police discovered following de Victorica's arrest were chemicals used for

The previous incarnation of the Waldorf Astoria Hotel, seen here, was a popular site for espionage operations and as a temporary residence for spies.

secret-writing inks that were impregnated in one of her scarves. These could be reconstituted by soaking the fabric in distilled water. More of the chemicals were found in a ballpoint pen, an exotic writing instrument at the time. To create the reagent to render the secret writing visible, iodine tablets were dissolved in vinegar.

Newspapers reported that de Victorica appeared in court in a sable coat and diamonds, as if dressed for the opera. The truth was much more grim. Far from the glamorous international woman of mystery depicted in the press,

De Victorica used St. Patrick's Cathedral for clandestine communication. Secret messages for her were concealed in a newspaper left in pew 30.

her medical condition required that doctors remove pustules and treat infections from her years of morphine addiction.

Despite the evidence against her and Wessels, the two were acquitted. De Victorica, who later cooperated with the US government, remained addicted to morphine and died in a private sanitarium at 41 East 78th Street in 1920. She was buried in Gate of Heaven Cemetery, 10 West Stevens Avenue, Hawthorne, New York.

■ 51. A REAL BOND GIRL

MAP II ➤ **Despina Storch grave:** Mount Olivet Cemetery, 65-40 Grand Avenue, Maspeth, Queens

Despina Davidovitch Storch

She was beautiful, mysterious, and a spy. Born in Turkey, Despina Davidovitch Storch married a suspected French spy when she was just seventeen but divorced him not long after. Whether she entered the intelligence world through her ex-husband or by some other way remains a mystery, but there is no doubt of her profession. Living under a string of aliases, including Madame Nezie, Madame Hesketh, and Madame Davidovitch, she crisscrossed Europe. Accompanied by Baron Henri de Beville, Storch sought out military and diplomatic contacts at parties and other social events.

The pair also attracted another couple, a German woman, Elizabeth Charlotte Nix, and Robert de Clairmont, who may or may not have been a French count. When the four landed in New York, they initially checked into the Biltmore Hotel at 335 Madison Avenue (now the Bank of America Plaza), then moved to the original Waldorf Astoria at Fifth Avenue and West 34th Street, where the Empire State Building now stands. The new arrivals were welcomed at fashionable society events, but authorities soon became suspicious of their activities. An investigation discovered unexplained large sums of money, bogus passports, coded correspondence, and a safe-deposit box with additional coded letters.

When Storch was identified as a spy by French authorities, the four were ordered out of the United States amid public speculation about firing squads in France. While held at Ellis Island awaiting deportation, the 23-year-old Storch became ill and died of pneumonia on March 30, 1918. Rumors accompanied her death. Some said she took her own life with a suicide pill, while others blamed cunning German assassins. She was buried in Mount Olivet Cemetery in Maspeth, Queens.

■ 52. THE HINDU–GERMAN CONSPIRACY

MAP 8 ➤ **Chandra Chakravarty residence:** 364 West 120th Street

The "Hindu-German Conspiracy" was a series of operational plans developed from 1914 to 1917 both abroad and in India by Indian nationalist groups to start a bloody revolution against British rule in India. The conspiracy gained support from the German Foreign Office and from Ottoman Turkey as a way to weaken the British Empire in the midst of World War I, and the Irish republican movement provided aid. The ambitious concept involved Japanese statesmen, Chinese mandarins, Russian Bolsheviks, and American leftists. Plans called for an uprising in Tibet, bombings in New York and California, and an armed expedition of anti-British US volunteers to India.

American and British intelligence services thwarted the conspiracy and captured 30 of the plotters. One of the leaders, Dr. Chandra Chakravarty, who lived at 364 West 120th Street, was arrested by NYPD inspector Thomas J. Tunney. Chakravarty was accused of receiving hundreds of thousands of dollars from Berlin for Indian revolutionary work in America and the bomb plot in New York City. A warehouse at 200

Thomas Tunney

West Houston Street was used as a storage and transit point for guns and other armaments.

American cryptanalyst William F. Friedman, the leading authority on ciphers and secret writing, broke the case when he established how the conspirators communicated using a dictionary code they considered to be unbreakable. Applying the new science of frequency analysis, he was able to decipher their messages without ever identifying the specific dictionary used.

The drama-filled trial of the Hindu-German Conspiracy case, held in San Francisco beginning in November 1917 and ending in April 1918, drew global interest. The German Foreign Office, the German embassy in Washington, and the German consulate in San Francisco were revealed as the nerve centers outside of India in the plot to subvert British rule there. The spectacle concluded when, on the last day of the trial, one of the defendants, Ram Singh, shot fellow defendant, Ram Chandra in court. Ram Singh was then shot and killed by US marshals.

Twenty-nine defendants, including Dr. Chakravarty, received fines and prison terms. Franz Bopp and E. H. von Schack from the consulate were given the maximum sentences of two years imprisonment and a $10,000 fine for violating neutrality laws.

■ 53. COMMERCIAL COVER EXPOSED

MAP | ➤ **German cover office:** 60 Wall Street (site redeveloped)

Wolf von Igel

In an odd incident leading up to America's entrance into World War I, on April 18, 1916, Secret Service agents raided the office of Wolf von Igel on the 25th floor of 60 Wall Street, today a modern office building. The space had been leased with private funds as an advertising agency, but agents discovered a large safe imprinted with the insignia of the German imperial government, leaving little doubt the company was a commercial cover for German espionage. Following a brief struggle with federal agents, Igel was subdued.

Documents recovered included detailed plans to sabotage the Welland Canal and fund radical Irish and Indian independence groups.

According to *The New York Times*, there was also correspondence regarding the purchase of a sizable amounts of explosives, one letter specifying 300 pounds of dynamite. "Those von Igel documents tell a story that would make your hair stand on end," a government official told the paper.

What happened next surprised both the investigators and the international community: Igel claimed diplomatic immunity. Not only was he protected as a registered diplomat, listed as an attaché with the German embassy, he argued, but the office itself—although rented with private funds under a bogus name—was a branch of the German embassy. His creative defense was nevertheless dismissed, and Ingel was arrested, then released on $25,000 bail. Not long afterward, he fled the country.

■ 54. THE PRESIDENT'S ANALYSTS

MAP 8 ➤ **American Geographical Society:** 3755 Broadway

The Inquiry, a presidential advisory group of more than 100 geographers, historians, legal scholars, economists, and philosophers, was established in September 1917 to prepare President Wilson for post–World War I peace negotiations. Overseen by Sidney Mezes, president of the College of the City of New York, and presidential adviser Edward House, the group has been described as "a temporary intelligence agency, a precursor in many ways to the CIA's own Directorate of Intelligence." The Inquiry first met in conference rooms of the New York Public Library, West 42nd Street and Fifth Avenue, then later moved to the American Geographical Society, 3755 Broadway (at West 156th Street).

During its brief existence, the Inquiry was comprised of 18 divisions, 11 dealing with issues regarding specific regions, including national boundaries. Among the areas of interest were the Austro-Hungarian Empire, the Ottoman Empire, the German colonies in Africa, and Alsace-Lorraine. In all, the Inquiry produced some three thousand reports. Two memos forwarded to the president by House served as the basis for Wilson's speech on January 8, 1918, "War Aims and Peace Terms," which outlined his Fourteen Points policy.

More than 20 members of the group were involved in the American Commission to Negotiate Peace and accompanied Wilson to the Paris Peace Conference in January 1919.

A temporary presidential advisory group, the Inquiry, formed in 1917 and met at the American Geographical Society building on upper Broadway. The function of the Inquiry bore a close resemblance to modern-day intelligence analysis.

■ 55. GREAT WAR SPYMASTER

MAP 10 ➤ **Nolan Park:** Governors Island

A veteran of combat in Cuba and the Philippines during the Spanish-American War and the Philippine Insurrection that followed, Maj. Gen. Dennis E. Nolan received two Silver Stars for gallantry in action. However, he is better known for organizing the US Army's first G-2 (military intelligence) unit, for the American Expeditionary Forces during World War I under Gen. John "Black Jack" Pershing.

Dennis Nolan

Nolan, the father of US military tactical intelligence, aggressively exploited new technologies such as aerial reconnaissance and radio intercepts. In one morale operation, his unit printed postcards featuring the text of an 1819 treaty obligating humane treatment of POWs. Millions were then dropped over enemy lines, and subsequent official reports credited the effort with prompting surrender of many German soldiers. Nolan also oversaw publication of the newspaper *Stars and Stripes*, which debuted under his command on February 8, 1918.

Nolan's work earned him the Distinguished Service Medal as well as France's Croix de Guerre, and Britain made him a Commander of the Order of the Bath. Other honors flowed from Italy, Belgium, and Panama. He served his final command on New York's Governors Island, where the Second Corps Area was headquartered. Nolan's last residence was the Blackstone Hotel, 57 East 57th Street, today the site of the Four Seasons Hotel.

In December 1988, President Ronald Reagan, President-elect George H. W. Bush, and Soviet leader Mikhail Gorbachev met in the Admiral's House on Governors Island overlooking the four-acre Nolan Park named in the war hero's honor.

■ 56. HIDDEN IN PLAIN SIGHT

MAP 1 ➤ **Suspected surveillance site:** 20 Broad Street (site redeveloped)

A top-secret program during World War I, the Naval Cable Censor, based in the Commercial Cable Building, 20 Broad Street (since demolished), monitored transatlantic telegraphic traffic. The activity employed 760 people, about half of them described as "yeomanettes" (enlisted women who worked alongside US Navy men during the war), and included representatives from Western Union, the Commercial Cable Company, and other communications firms. The Naval Cable Censor worked closely with the NYPD, the Secret Service, and British intelligence. Beginning operation in 1917, the censors sought to identify covert messages concealed in the cable traffic and other communications. Although similar efforts were conducted in other parts of the country, New York City had the largest facility.

A secret World War I intercept program, housed at the Commercial Cable Company at 20 Broad Street, employed more than 700 people searching international traffic for nefarious transmissions.

TAPPING BY INDUCTION

On March 16, 1918, John J. Carty, the American Telephone and Telegraph Company's chief engineer, on loan to the US Army Signal Corps, along with other engineers and a US Navy observer sailed from New York Harbor on the 150-foot Western Union cable steamer *Robert C. Clowry*. Four miles out, they lifted aboard a cable that ran from Manhattan to Nova Scotia and bolted to it an unusual device. Inside the device were five vacuum tubes connected to an external coil of wire that wrapped around the cable. When attached to the cable, the device picked up the transmission signals passing through the cable. Because the system relied on the principles of induction, there was no need to cut into the insulation or make a direct connection to the wires within the cable.

By comparing the signals recorded aboard the *Clowry* to those received at Western Union's Manhattan office, the team confirmed the system worked with 80 percent accuracy. Cables, once thought to be protected from covert tapping, were now vulnerable. And neither sender nor receiver could detect any interference from the eavesdropping operation.

In 1921, Carty was awarded the rank of brigadier general in the Officers Reserve Corps. Following the war, he returned as chief engineer to the company known today as AT&T, retiring in 1930 after 51 years with the firm.

■ 57. SOLDIER-SPY "WILD BILL" DONOVAN

MAP 5 ➤ **69th Regiment Armory:** 68 Lexington Avenue between East 25th and 26th Streets

The 69th Regiment Armory is the home to artifacts from the life of Maj. Gen. William Donovan, World War I Medal of Honor recipient and World War II head of the Office of Strategic Services.

New York City's Irish-heritage infantry regiment, the "Fighting 69th," was William "Wild Bill" Donovan's outfit during World War I. Wounded three times, he was awarded the Medal of Honor for bravery under fire at the River Ourcq during the second Battle of the Marne and became one of the most decorated soldiers of the war. When Donovan returned home to New York, he began a law practice and, with Theodore Roosevelt Jr., founded the American Legion.

Among Donovan's New York's residential addresses were 1 Beekman Place and 4 Sutton Place. He was a founding partner of the law firm Donovan, Leisure, Newton and

William Donovan

Among Donovan's New York homes was this prestigious 4 Sutton Place address.

Lombard, with an office at 2 Wall Street. At the start of World War II, President Franklin Roosevelt picked Donovan to lead the Office of Strategic Services (OSS), forerunner to the CIA. By the end of his distinguished military and government service, he had received the Distinguished Service Cross, the Distinguished Service Medal, and the National Security Medal in addition to the Medal of Honor.

■ 58. THE GENERAL ON EAST 83RD

MAP 6 ➤ **Marlborough Churchill residence:** 40 East 83rd Street

Brig. Gen. Marlborough Churchill, who lived at 40 East 83rd Street, was a distant relative of Britain's Prime Minister Winston Churchill. A Harvard graduate, he served on the general staff of the American Expeditionary Force in France during World War I. However, Churchill is better remembered for establishing, along with Ralph Van Deman, the Military Intelligence Division of the War Department. Churchill assumed the senior role after Van Deman's departure in 1918 and, by 1920, was working with code breaker Herbert O. Yardley to create the joint State

Brig. Gen. Marlborough Churchill

Department and War Department Cipher Bureau, better known as the American Black Chamber. Churchill, who died in 1947, was inducted into the Military Intelligence Hall of Fame in 1988.

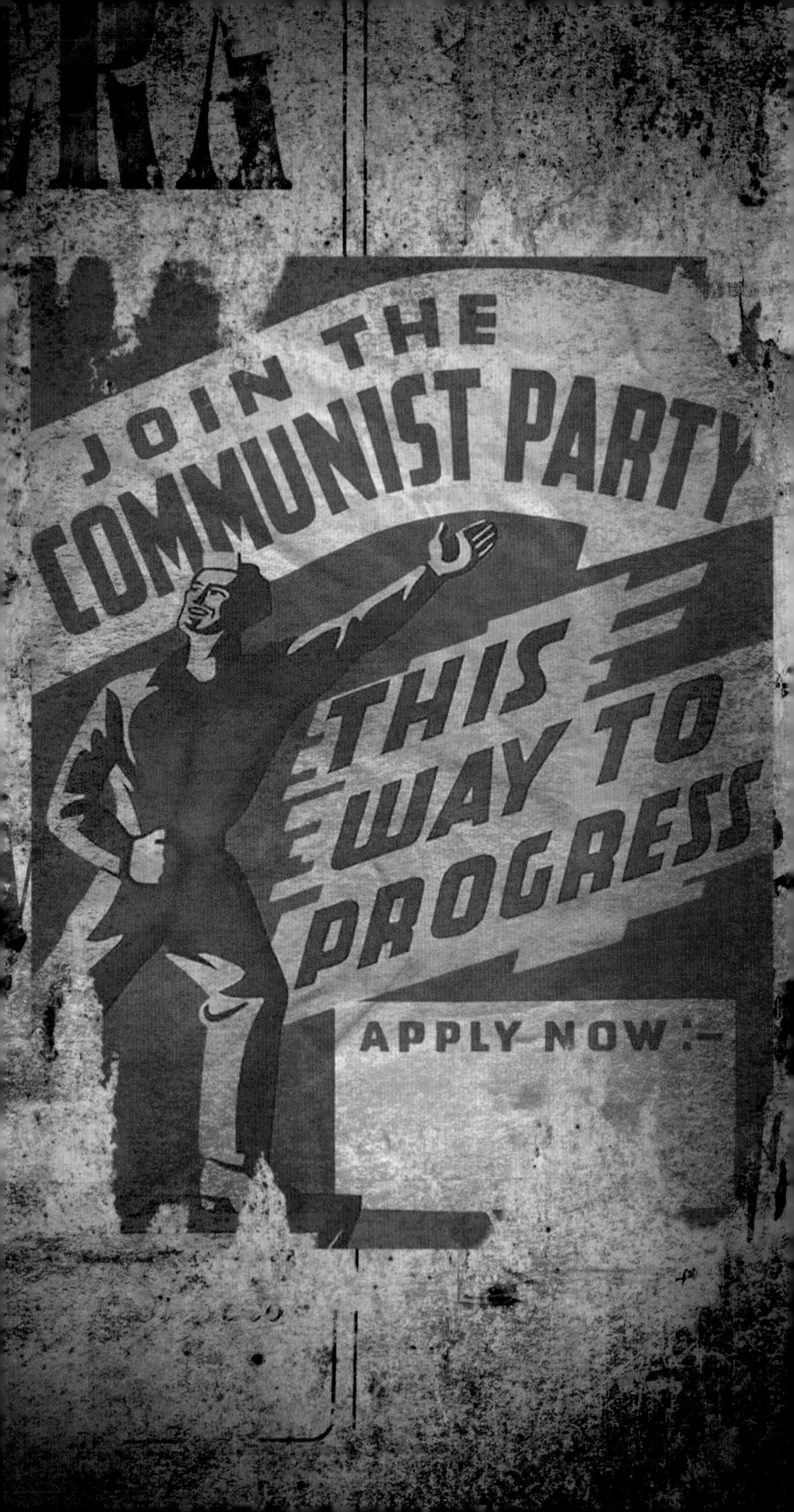
JOIN THE
COMMUNIST PARTY
THIS
WAY TO
PROGRESS
APPLY NOW :-

4

ANARCHISTS, REVOLUTIONARIES, AND SOVIET SPIES

(1919–1946)

Industrialization and World War I brought to the fore revolutionaries who agitated for the overthrow of the existing socioeconomic regimes in Europe and the United States. First, anarchists sought to disrupt civil society with radical publications and coordinated bombing attacks in major cities. This reached a fever pitch in 1919 and 1920, but the anarchists alienated the public rather than winning mass support. However, the successful Bolshevik Revolution of 1917 that overthrew the Russian czar shook the world. The Union of Soviet Socialist Republics (USSR) sought to spread revolution throughout the globe, in part through clandestine networks of party cells and intelligence officers. The Soviet Union sent skilled intelligence operatives to New York to provoke, incite, and exploit the unrest in America's largest and most influential city.

During the 1930s, the brutality and horrors of Joseph Stalin's government were minimized in the West, and USSR-style communism was packaged as an alternative to the economic crisis and hardships of both the Great Depression and totalitarian fascism. It became a golden age for ideological-agent recruitment of Soviet spies among Americans. In addition to compromising classified information, the Soviet operatives, often US citizens working in government jobs, stole American technology, ran clandestine networks, and conducted assassinations. Throughout the 1930s, the NKVD (the forerunner of the KGB, the main Soviet security agency from 1954 until 1991) laid the groundwork in New York for a permanent clandestine intelligence presence in America.

By contrast, US counterintelligence capabilities were under-manned, underfunded, and uncoordinated. Efforts of the FBI and the ONI failed to prevent the Soviets from penetrating virtually every fed-eral cabinet department as well as the White House and Congress. The years of an uneasy US-USSR wartime alliance (1941–1945) against Nazism did not halt Soviet espionage against the United States. On the contrary, the wartime alliance caused the United States to relax its guard further against Soviet espionage. This changed only as the wartime alliance soured and America realized that it needed to pro-tect the secrets of the emerging atomic age. A turning point came when US Army signals intelligence was able to break Soviet diplo-matic codes and then slowly decrypt messages about Soviet intelli-gence operations. The project, code-named VENONA, became one of America's most closely held secrets during World War II and the Cold War. When decrypted, the collection from 1942 to 1945 revealed a nationwide Soviet intelligence network intently focused on acquiring secrets, especially related to the atomic bomb.

■ 59. TROTSKY'S BRONX EXPERIENCE

MAP 9 ➤ **Leon Trotsky residence:** 1522 Vyse Avenue near East 172nd Street, Bronx

When Leon Trotsky, exiled from czarist Russia and on the run, arrived in New York in early Janu-ary 1917, even the hardcore Marxist could not contain his enthusiasm for the city. "Here I was in New York, city of prose and fantasy," he wrote in his 1930 autobiography, *My Life*. Then, catching himself, he tempered his language by adding, with obligatory revolutionary dour-ness, "of capitalist automatism, its

This Vyse Avenue address in the Bronx was the likely residence of Leon Trotsky during his brief stay in New York. Trotsky recalled in his memoirs the exact amount of his rent: $18 a month.

streets a triumph of cubism, its moral philosophy that of the dollar."

Trotsky's family was not as committed to the austerity of the communist cause. "That apartment, at eighteen dollars a month, was equipped with all sorts of conveniences that we Europeans were quite unused to: electric lights, gas cooking-range, bath, telephone, automatic service-elevator, and

Trotsky was employed during his few weeks in New York writing for the revolutionary paper *Novy Mir* (*New World*) on St. Mark's Place.

even a chute for the garbage," he conceded. "These things completely won the boys over to New York."

Exactly where Trotsky lived remains open to debate; he lived a life of secrecy and never publicized his address. The "workers' district" he described in his book is undoubtedly the Bronx, but a precise address is not mentioned. The best—though still disputed—location is 1522 Vyse Avenue near East 172nd Street, although another possibility is along Prospect Avenue south of East 186th Street.

More certain is where Trotsky worked. Despite a heavy lecture schedule, he wrote for the paper *Novy Mir* (*New World*) at 77 St. Mark's Place in the East Village. But his time in New York was short. Within a few weeks of Trotsky's arrival, Czar Nicholas II abdicated, so Trotsky promptly sailed for Russia. As years passed, an unverified legend emerged that the *Bronx Home News,* with somewhat outsized borough pride, published the headline "Bronx Man Leads Russian Revolution."

From Moscow, Trotsky rebuilt the Red Army, engineered a victory in the Russian Civil War, and became the second most powerful man in Russia after only Vladimir Lenin. Ultimately, however, he was outmaneuvered by Joseph Stalin and went into exile abroad again in 1929.

Ho Chi Minh (ca. 1921)

■ 60. THE MAKING OF A REVOLUTIONARY

MAP 8 ▸ **Crescent Theatre: 36–38 West 135th Street** (site redeveloped)

Vietnamese communist revolutionary leader Ho Chi Minh is recognized by most Americans as the chairman and first secretary of the Workers' Party of Vietnam during the Vietnam War. Ho's strategy to weaken American resolve by drawing out the conflict and minimizing direct confrontation with the conventional power of the US military proved successful. Less well known, however, is his life in the United States.

While in America in 1917 and 1918, Ho Chi Minh was known as Nguyen Ai Quoc. He had arrived as a cook's helper on a steamship and reportedly worked as a servant for a wealthy family in Brooklyn. He also had the opportunity to attend fiery lectures of pan-Africanist Marcus Garvey at the Universal Negro Improvement Association Hall at 36–38 West 135th Street, in the Crescent Theatre building. Garvey's words must have influenced him because in 1924 Quoc wrote a pamphlet, *Black Race*, in which he detailed the "horrors" of African American life in the "false democracy" of America. To date, little other information about Ho's stay in New York has been uncovered.

■ 61. HE SAW SOMETHING AND SAID SOMETHING

MAP 2 ➤ **James A. Farley Post Office Building:** Eighth Avenue and West 33rd Street

CHARLES KAPLAN, POST OFFICE CLERK WHO DISCOVERED THE BOMBS.

On April 27, 1919, 29-year-old postal clerk Charles Kaplan (sometimes reported as Caplan) was reading the newspaper on the subway after work, heading home to his apartment at 765 East 183rd Street, the Bronx. What caught his attention was an account of a bomb mailed to former US senator from Georgia Thomas Hardwick, cosponsor of the controversial Immigration Act of 1918. The explosion injured a maid who opened the package, blowing off both of her hands, and less seriously injuring Hardwick's wife, who was standing nearby. Wisely, Kaplan focused on the detailed description of the wrapping. He had seen similar packages at work.

Changing trains at 110th Street, Kaplan headed back to the main branch of the post office at 33rd Street and Eighth Avenue, where he alerted a supervisor. After a short search the pair found 16 packages wrapped similarly in brown paper with the same return address— "Gimbel Brothers / 32nd St. /

Anarchists sending mail bombs in 1919 failed to include sufficient postage on the packages. Some 16 packages were set aside at the James A. Farley Post Office Building on West 33rd Street, pictured here in 1910.

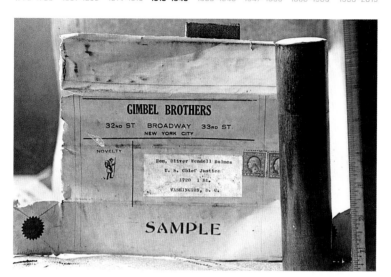

Mail bombs sent to prominent citizens around the country in 1919 were disguised as merchandise from the now defunct Gimbel Brothers department store.

Broadway / 33rd St. / New York City"—and each with a bright red stamp, "Novelties—A sample." All 16 packages had been undelivered for insufficient postage and contained explosive devices.

Information about the bombs was promptly passed to other post offices across the country, enabling discovery of similarly wrapped packages. In all, 36 mail bombs were intercepted, addressed to prominent citizens such as J. P. Morgan Jr., John D. Rockefeller, New York mayor John F. Hylan, and Supreme Court Justice Oliver Wendell Holmes Jr. Save for the alert and pro-active Kaplan, the packages could have arrived at their destinations on or around May 1—May Day.

A nationwide manhunt for the bombers resulted in the detention and questioning of several suspects, but no convictions were obtained.

■ 62. TERROR ON THE UPPER EAST SIDE

MAP 6 ➤ **Charles Nott residence:** 151 East 61st Street

New York did not escape the well-coordinated multicity attacks of anarchist bombings that occurred in the United States at approximately the same time on June 2, 1919. Late that evening, explosive devices detonated in Philadelphia,

One bombing target in 1919 was the residence (pictured here today) of municipal court judge Charles Cooper Nott Jr. The explosion killed a night watchman and a passerby.

Charles Cooper Nott Jr.

Law enforcement tracked the anarchist bombers involved in the 1919 and 1920 attacks to a Fifth Avenue print shop in Park Slope, Brooklyn.

Washington, Boston, and Cleveland. In Washington, the target was the home of US Attorney General Mitchell A. Palmer. In Manhattan, the target was municipal court judge Charles Cooper Nott Jr.'s residence. That bomb, placed in an outer vestibule of Nott's townhouse at 151 East 61st Street, killed a night watchman and a woman passerby as well as caused substantial damage to the building and shattered windows up and down the block. Clocks in the area stopped by the explosion put the blast time at 12:55 a.m. Questions linger as to why Nott, a

In February 1918, police discovered an unexploded bomb of this type at 119–125 West 25th Street.

relatively obscure city judge, was targeted. Possibly the bombers confused him with a Judge Knox, who earlier ruled on an anarchist deportation case.

■ 63. THWARTED BY SUICIDE

MAP | ➤ **Bureau of Investigation:** 15 Park Row (now the Park Row Building)

Frustrated law-enforcement officials never solved the 1919 bombing case, although distinctive pink flyers promoting the anarchist cause were found near the crime scenes. The paper was traced to a printing shop at 225 Fifth Avenue, Brooklyn, where two typesetters, Roberto Ellia and Andrea Salsedo, were taken into custody.

Under questioning, the pair agreed to cooperate. As a precaution against retribution by former terrorist compatriots, they were held in protective confinement in the offices of the Bureau of Investigation, 15 Park Row. In time, Salsedo began to show signs of distress under pressure, and on May 4, 1919, he jumped from a 14th-floor window. Authorities offered a false explanation for the suicide, but newspapers reported the true story, which allowed other bombing coconspirators time to escape. Ellia was transferred to Ellis Island, eventually raised bail money, and disappeared.

Federal law enforcement came close to solving the mystery of the anarchist bombings of 1919 and 1920. However, the trail turned cold when a suspect committed suicide while in custody by jumping from the 14th floor of this building at 15 Park Row.

■ 64. RADICAL ROUNDUP

MAP 4 ➤ **Union of Russian Workers:** 133 East 15th Street

In the wake of the coordinated bombings of 1919, the BOI created the General Intelligence Division to combat the threat posed by violent anarchists, communists, and militant unionists. The menace was real. The aftermath of World War I brought civil unrest to many major American cities, including riots and attempted assassinations.

Headed by the youthful J. Edgar Hoover under Attorney General A. Mitchell Palmer, the small division collected as much intelligence as possible on subversive groups. Palmer would have been particularly sensitive to the threats because he had been the target of a bombing that destroyed the front of his home in Washington, DC, a few months earlier.

A. Mitchell Palmer

Today it is a modern apartment building, but a century ago this East 15th Street address was the site of the Union of Russian Workers and a target for the Palmer Raids of 1919.

On November 7, 1919, the second anniversary of the Bolshevik take-over of Russia, law-enforcement officers raided the headquarters of the Union of Russian Workers, 133 East 15th Street, a well-known group that counted a radical faction among its membership. The headquarters of other subversive organizations were also raided in a coordinated action in several cities, including Chicago, Akron, Philadelphia, and Pittsburgh.

The raids were not gentle; suspects were beaten and thrown down stairs. A New York newspaper reported police were told to meet force with force and use nightsticks if members of the group put up a fight. "They used them freely. No chance was given to the 'Red Guard' to carry out the orders given them," reported the *Evening World*. "The effect of the police night sticks was shown on the appearance of the battered group which was headed for Ellis Island today." In all, 158 were arrested and ferried to Ellis Island to await hearings and eventual deportation.

The next month, on December 21, 249 radicals rounded up during the raids were put aboard the aging USAT *Buford*—nicknamed the *Soviet Ark*—which sailed from New York Harbor. Once at sea, the captain opened an envelope with his orders. He was directed to drop the prisoners off in Finland from where they were transported to the USSR. Political activists and authors Emma Goldman and Alexander Berkman, the would-be assassin of industrialist Henry Clay Frick, were among those aboard.

Another major raid occurred on January 2, 1920, followed by smaller raids over the next few weeks. In all, approximately 3,000 radicals were arrested across 30 states. However, public opinion began to swing from enthusiasm for law and order to outrage at the rough treatment afforded the suspects. Adverse political pressure on Palmer and the BOI mounted when details surfaced that suggested the raids were poorly planned, arrests were made without warrants, and some individuals were held for days without contact with their families.

For Palmer, whose name was once floated as a likely presidential candidate, the raids eroded his public image, and his once-promising political career never recovered.

■ 65. WALL STREET CARNAGE

MAP | ➤ **House of Morgan:** 23 Wall Street, corner of Wall and Broad Streets

A 1920 terrorist attack on Wall Street is largely forgotten a century later. The explosion that hit the heart of America's financial center at approximately noon on September 16, 1920, was the deadliest terrorist attack on American soil to that date. The death toll from the blast eventually rose to nearly 40 and left hundreds injured.

Scars from the shrapnel of the bomb that exploded on Wall Street on September 16, 1920, can still be seen on nearby buildings.

Investigators determined that a horse-drawn wagon pulled up in front of the former headquarters of J. P. Morgan and Company, 23 Wall Street, loaded with what is believed to be 100 pounds of dynamite and 500 pounds of scrap metal, including sash weights. A timer delaying the explosion allowed the driver to escape before the blast destroyed the wagon and propelled its load of deadly shrapnel through the air. Men who had witnessed the carnage of World War I described the aftermath of the explosion as like that of a battlefield.

Law enforcement focused attention on followers of the anarchist Luigi Galleani, called Galleanists, who were responsible for coordinated bombings

The 1920 Wall Street bombing killed 38 people and injured more than 100. Timed to cause maximum fatalities, the bomb exploded at around noon when lunch-hour crowds were on the street.

in several US cities a year before, though nothing was ever proven. However, in contrast to the bombings of 1919, the Galleanists did not claim credit for the Wall Street bombing, and there was no direct evidence linking them to the attack.

Today scars caused by the shrapnel are still visible on the old House of Morgan at 23 Wall Street, on Federal Hall at 26 Wall Street, and on other nearby buildings.

■ 66. FALSE EMBASSY, FAKE DIPLOMATS, REAL SPIES

MAP 3 ➤ **World's Tower Building:** 110 West 40th Street

US-Soviet relations following the 1917 Russian Revolution were contentious from the beginning. With the United States unwilling to establish formal diplomatic relations with the newly formed Bolshevik state, the Russian Soviet Government Bureau (RSGB) was established in 1919 on the third floor of the World's Tower Building, 110 West 40th Street. The new entity was neither an official embassy nor a consulate and purportedly served as a trade and information organization. Its true objective, however, was to foment a global communist revolution and recruit like-minded Americans to perform acts of political subversion.

Ludwig C. A. K. Martens

Because the RSGB's status was unofficial, its foreign employees did not operate with diplomatic immunity. Ludwig C. A. K. Martens, a Russian immigrant and engineer already living in the United States, headed the unorthodox organization. He had previously worked at the engineering firm Weinberg and Posner, 120 Broadway, but was best known as the editor of the radical newspaper *Novyi Mir* (*New World*), 77 St. Mark's Place, which briefly employed Leon Trotsky in 1917.

Although Martens's credentials as an official representative of the USSR were not accepted by the State Department, he remained undeterred. Martens hired staff and opened his door to American businesses. While the United States officially boycotted the Soviet Union, American companies were eager to do business and competed for heavy equipment and technology contracts reportedly worth millions.

Almost immediately Martens's organization was used as a cover for espionage activities. The director of the RSGB's Technical Department was Arthur Adams, a British citizen with degrees from the USSR's Kronstadt School of Science and Canada's University of Toronto. Adams was also a spy working for the Registration Directorate, the predecessor organization of the GRU (Soviet military intelligence service).

Although Martens claimed a fortune was available to American companies for foreign trade, in reality the new Soviet government was teetering on collapse following the revolution. With the RSGB chronically short of funds, rumors persisted that the Bolsheviks were even sell-

Beginning in 1919, the Russian Soviet Government Bureau occupied and ran intelligence operations from the third floor the World's Tower Building. Since the United States did not recognize the communist government at that time, the organization had no official diplomatic status.

ing off the Romanov jewels for quick cash, a claim that was somewhat substantiated by the arrest of a Swedish sailor, Neil Jacobsen, on July 23, 1920. According to press reports, Jacobsen was detained by US Customs officials with a package containing 131 diamonds and a note addressed to "Comrade Martens." Jacobsen, who had made previous trips to the United States, was also delivering packages to a Mrs. Keinanen at 113 West 80th Street. From there, the packages were picked up by a representative of Martens's office. Jacobsen told authorities later that he also delivered diamonds to an address on West 129th Street. Diamonds enabled substantial sums to be transferred in small, easily concealed packets.

Following the arrest of the Swedish sailor, reports that Martens's home at 572 Ocean Avenue, Brooklyn, had been searched created more headlines. Martens's continued presence in the United States was an irritant, and opponents of American "Reds" and the Bolsheviks feared the spread of subversive material in the city. Civic-minded groups, such as the Union League, lobbied for action against him.

New York's state government finally acted on June 12, 1919, when state police raided the 40th Street offices and seized virtually every scrap of paper. Local hearings were held, followed by more hearings in Washington in the Senate and at the Department of Labor. Martens and Adams, neither of whom held diplomatic status, were deported in January 1921. Adams's role as an intelligence officer went undetected, and he surfaced again two decades later to play a central role in penetrating the Manhattan Project.

■ 67. TALENT SPOTTING

MAP 4 ▶ **Union Square:** Broadway at East 14th Street

Union Square at East 14th Street and Broadway is a traditional New York venue for rallies, protests, and political debate by communists, socialists, and anarchists. In the decade before World War II, the Stalinist-led Communist Party of the United States of America (CPUSA) was headquartered a few blocks away at 35 East 12th Street. During the Great Depression, thousands assembled to hear Earl Browder, general secretary of the CPUSA, proclaim, "Communism is 20th Century Americanism." At the time, no one realized the native Kansan was a Soviet agent with the code name FATHER.

Both the CPUSA and the Socialist Party of America were vehicles for Soviet intelligence officers to spot ideologically motivated, often naive individuals who could be recruited as spies. For example, Flora Wovschin (code name ZORA) became a recruiter for Soviet intelligence, drawing Judith Coplon (code name SIMA), then a student at Barnard College, into espionage. Elizabeth Bentley (code name UMNITSA, meaning CLEVER GIRL), was recruited in much the same manner while in graduate school at Columbia University. So successful was the Soviet intelligence apparatus in the 1930s that by the time the United States entered World War II, the government was penetrated at multiple levels. These spies were the foot soldiers for what would later become the Soviets' most successful operation, the theft of the plans for the atomic bomb.

COMMUNIST HOME IN AMERICA

Founded in Chicago in 1919, the CPUSA moved its national headquarters to New York in 1927 and, over the years, occupied a variety of addresses, including 35 East 12th Street and 23 West 26th Street. The longtime headquarters on East 12th Street has been converted to multimillion-dollar loft apartments, and the organization now operates from 235 West 23rd Street. The CPUSA's historical records, including its founding documents, are housed at New York University's Tamiment Library.

■ 68. EDITOR BY DAY, SPY BY NIGHT

MAP 4 ▶ **Daily Worker:** 35 East 12th Street

First published by the Central Committee of the CPUSA in 1924, the newspaper *Daily Worker* had offices at 35 East 12th Street and reached an approximate peak circulation of 35,000. During the 1930s, Louis Budenz held a number of positions at the publication and was arrested more than 20 times prior to 1938 for his radical politics. With these quali-fications, he was eventually promo-

This 1897 building at 35 East 12th Street that today offers multi-million-dollar loft apartments was, in earlier years, headquarters for the radical newspaper *Daily Worker*, published by the CPUSA.

ted to editor and granted membership on the prestigious National Committee of the CPUSA. Less known was the active role Budenz played as a Soviet agent code-named BUBEN and TAMBOURINE.

In 1945, Budenz renounced communism and appeared as an expert wit-ness at government hearings as well as publishing a series of books on his life as a communist. Among his revelations to the FBI was his role in recruit-ing Ruby Weil, a member of the American Worker's Party, to facilitate a secret meeting in Paris in 1938 to introduce Trotskyite Sylvia Ageloff to Ramón Mercader (a.k.a. Jacques Mornard and Frank Jacson). Mercader would later assassinate Trotsky.

■ 69. A SPY BY ANY OTHER NAME

MAP II ▶ **J. Peters residence:** 83-46 118th Street, Queens

Alexander Stevens, whose birth name was Sándor Goldberger, adopted the pseudonym J. Peters to become one of the leading fig-ures in the Hungarian-language section of the CPUSA and the COMINTERN during the 1930s.

Peters immigrated to the United States in 1924 and by 1930 was in charge of building capabilities within the Communist Party to support Soviet foreign policies. He

J. Peters, a.k.a. Alexander Stevens (left), is sworn in by Rep. John McDowell for testimony before the House Committee on Un-American Activities in August 1948.

received additional training in Moscow in 1932 and adopted the name "J. Peters." When he returned, he was appointed to head the CPUSA's "secret apparatus."

In the pre–World War II years, while residing at 83-46 118th Street in the Kew Gardens section of Queens, Peters fabricated passports, recruited agents, and accumulated and reported secret information in support of Soviet intelligence. Peters was also the handler of Whittaker Chambers, who obtained valuable information from Alger Hiss, a spy inside the State Department.

During World War II, Peters worked on "special assignments" for the Central Committee of the CPUSA

Peters, a Soviet agent in the 1930s and 1940s, lived in this Kew Gardens apartment building.

and did "informational work" (clandestine activities) for the Soviet GRU.

Peters was betrayed to the FBI as a spy by Whittaker Chambers, who described him in testimony as "the head of the whole underground [of the] Communist Party United States." When Peters was summoned to appear before the House Un-American Activities Committee (HUAC), he refused to cooperate or answer sensitive questions. Rather than be deported, he fled to Hungary in May 1949. Peters was also identified as a Soviet agent in subsequent testimony by former communists Hede Massing and Nathaniel Weyl. Various deciphered Soviet cables later confirmed Peters's role in the Soviet espionage apparatus in the United States. Although Peters was a significant and successful spy, his death in Budapest in 1990 was barely noticed in the news.

■ 70. AMERICAN PROFESSOR IN THE GULAG

MAP 4 ▶ Isaiah Oggins residence: 308 East 18th Street

During the first two decades of the 20th century, New York City was a hotbed for radicalism. Among the early adherents to anarchism was Connecticut-born Isaiah (a.k.a. Cy) Oggins. Entering Columbia College in 1917, he graduated with a degree in history and joined the communist Workers Party of America in 1923. A year later he married a dedicated communist activist, Nerma Berman, and lived at 68 Perry Street before moving to 308 East 18th Street. Among their revolutionary friends was anarchist Emma Goldman, who resided at 36 Grove Street.

By 1926, Oggins and Berman were both members of the Soviet underground and among the first Americans recruited to spy abroad for the Soviet Union. They went to Berlin in 1928 under instructions to establish a safe house. In 1930, they left Berlin for Paris, posing as art dealers, then traveled onward to New York and San Francisco. Oggins went to China in 1935 to work with established Soviet espionage cells, enabled by training that prepared him to shift identity with ease and avoid leaving a trail to follow. He never returned to the United States.

Isaiah Oggins during his imprisonment in Soviet Gulag.

Berman briefly traveled abroad and then returned to New York City in 1939. In 1942, she lived at 322 West 15th Street and two years later moved to 8 Barrow Street. Meanwhile, Oggins was recalled to Moscow in 1939, arrested by the NKVD, and became a victim of Stalin's purges. Although few Americans operated longer as a Soviet agent, which should have earned trust, Oggins received a perfunctory trial and was sentenced to eight years in a gulag in January 1940.

Rather than being released at the conclusion of his sentence, Oggins was sentenced to death in 1947. Soviet authorities feared that he

Isaiah Oggins, an early true believer in the communist cause, became an effective spy for the Soviet Union but later was sent to a gulag and executed. This apartment on East 18th Street was one of his New York residences.

knew too much as a former spy and would reveal state secrets if allowed to return to the United States. He is believed to have been executed by an injection of curare poison on Stalin's orders at Moscow's notorious Laboratory Number One, a research facility of the Soviet security services.

Decades later, fellow prisoners only remembered Oggins as "the American professor." The little that is known of his espionage activities comes from a KGB release of a small, heavily redacted portion of his file. Otherwise, the case records remain classified in Kremlin archives even over seventy years after his death.

■ 71. SPY CENTRAL

MAP 3 ▶ **Taft Hotel (now The Michelangelo):** 152 West 51st Street

Opened in 1926 as the Manger Hotel and renamed for President William Howard Taft five years later, this centrally located Times Square hotel was often the hostelry of choice for visiting spies.

If you were a newly arrived Soviet spy in New York in the 1930s, chances are good you stayed at the Taft Hotel (now called The Michelangelo) at 152 West 51st Street. You might have enjoyed music from one of the big bands, such as Jimmy Dorsey or Glenn Miller, in the famed Taft Grill while waiting for your contact, who would likely welcome you with a parole such as, "Greetings from Fanny." Then, only if the required answer "Thank you. How is she?" was received, would the clandestine meeting begin.

Throughout the years, the Taft provided rooms for an assortment of spies, including notable Soviet operative Valentin Markin and Capt. Ulrich von der Osten from the Abwehr (German military intelligence). When the Soviet atomic spy Klaus Fuchs arrived in New York in 1943, he checked into the Taft Hotel before relocating to the Barbizon Plaza Hotel (now the Trump Parc) at 106 Central Park South.

Built in 1926 as the Manger, the hotel was renamed for President Taft in 1931. The largest hotel in the Times Square area at the time, the Taft was known for its direct walkway into the Taft Grill and the lavish Roxy Theatre on 50th Street, called "The Cathedral of the Motion Picture." Today the majority of its rooms have been converted into condos. The Roxy Theatre was demolished in 1960 to make way for an office building.

■ 72. BATHHOUSE DEATH OF A RUSSIAN SPY

MAP 3 ▶ **Luxor Baths:** 121 West 46th Street

Valentin Markin of the Soviet intelligence organization OGPU is credited with setting up the first *illegal* residency—a *rezidentura*—to run spy operations in the United States in 1933. As head of the residency, or *rezident*, Markin operated under a variety of code names, including ARTHUR, WALTER, OSKAR, HOWARD, and DAVIS. Markin's death is even more mysterious, however, than his secret intelligence work. In August 1934, he appeared at the now defunct Luxor Baths, 121 West 46th Street, a health spa that

Where the elite once met to sweat, the Luxor Baths are now a historical memory. During its heyday in the 1930s and 1940s, a mortally wounded Soviet spy stumbled into the bathhouse.

once hosted celebrities such as Jackie Gleason and Jack Dempsey, with a large gash on his forehead. Rushed to a nearby hospital, Markin gave a story that he had sustained injuries in a taxi accident, then died a few days later without revealing any other details.

Unsubstantiated stories about his death soon circulated. One asserted Markin was murdered on Stalin's orders for being a Trotskyite, while his wife back in the Soviet Union was told he had been killed by American gangsters. Another tale had him mugged leaving a midtown speakeasy. A fourth explanation implicated fellow Soviet intelligence officers seeking revenge for a memo he wrote criticizing colleagues.

Markin, who worked in a cosmetics company as cover, left behind an American business-partner and a girlfriend. There was also a bank safe deposit box containing sensitive documents, but the full story has never been revealed. Most significantly, the intelligence work begun by Markin's OGPU in New York City has continued in the United States for nearly a century.

■ 73. THE WILY PUPPETMASTER

MAP 6 ➤ **FBI observation post:** Pierre Hotel, 2 East 61st Street (opposite Russian consulate)

Gaik Ovakimian, sometimes known as "the Puppetmaster," became the NKVD *rezident* in the United States after arriving in 1933 under cover as an engineer for the Amtorg Trading Corporation, a Soviet entity based in New York that frequently provided cover for Soviet military intelligence officers. FBI agents called "the Bucket Squad" surveilled his activity at the Russian consulate, 7 East 61st Street, from an observation post across the

Gaik Ovakimian

Fifth Avenue's historic Pierre Hotel once hosted a secret FBI surveillance operation. From a room there, the FBI had line-of-sight to the East 61st Street entrance to a mansion that was home to Soviet diplomats.

street in the Pierre Hotel at 2 East 61st Street.

FBI special agent Robert Lamphere later said that "Ovakimian's recruits were scattered as far afield as Mexico and Canada. . . . Americans whom Ovakimian recruited or controlled described him as charming, serious, sympathetic, well read in English literature, knowledgeable in science, and a man who inspired loyalty in his agents. He must also have been agile and politically aware, for he survived the great purges of the late 1930s which decimated the upper ranks of the Russian espionage services."

Ovakimian facilitated the surveillance on members of the Socialist Workers Party (SWP) preceding the assassination of Leon Trotsky in August 1940. He was also involved in the recruitment of Earl Browder (later the head of the CPUSA) and Julius and Ethel Rosenberg. As the primary handler for Jacob Golos and Elizabeth Bentley, Ovakimian also received reporting from atomic spy Klaus Fuchs delivered by a courier, Harry Gold.

In 1939, while studying for his doctorate in chemistry at New York University, Ovakimian was appointed as the NKVD's chief of scientific intelligence in the United States. Following a meeting with Golos, he was arrested in May 1941 by the FBI. Since Ovakimian did not have diplomatic status, he was charged with being an unregistered agent of a foreign government and detained for several weeks until swapped for several Americans imprisoned in the Soviet Union.

■ 74. SOVIET MASTER-SPY AND CAPITALIST

MAP 3 ▶ **Itzhak Akhmerov hat shop:** 19 West 57th Street (since redeveloped)

Itzhak Akhmerov operated as a Soviet *illegal* (a foreign intelligence officer living undercover without diplomatic immunity) in New York as "Michael Adamec," with documentation to backstop the identity that was inserted covertly into Cook County, Illinois, birth records. Akhmerov arrived in the mid-1930s with the code name MER and used layers of cutouts between himself and his agents, who knew him only as Mr. Adamec. At some point, he left his Russian wife and married an American, Helen Lowery (code names NELLY and MADLEN), who was the niece of CPUSA head Earl Browder, himself a Soviet agent.

Itzhak Akhmerov

Following a recall to Moscow in 1939, the couple returned to New York in 1941. Living in Upper Manhattan at 115 Cabrini Boulevard, Akhmerov used a milliner shop, Henry Bookman Inc., at 19 West 57th Street, as cover. The Soviets invested $5,000 in the Bookman company, where Akhmerov's wife worked as the bookkeeper. Together the husband-wife team made the store a profitable venture.

Inspired by this commercial success and with a natural flair for high-end fashion, Akhmerov proposed a more ambitious venture, a furrier shop, to his Moscow bosses. "The business could look like this: A nice shop selling fur products on Madison Avenue or in the 50s between Fifth and Madison Avenues," he wrote Moscow. "What will be for sale will be silver foxes, Persian lamb, sealskin coats and jackets, and other fur products. Besides selling ready made items, custom orders will be accepted."

Moscow rejected his New York business proposal but later assigned Akhmerov and his dreams to Baltimore, where he did open his furrier shop. Although its commercial success is unknown, the shop became a safe house for clandestine meetings for NKVD agents such as Elizabeth Bentley and Michael Straight.

■ 75. RUSSIA'S THOMAS EDISON

MAP 3 ▶ Leon Theremin residence: 37 West 54th Street

Born into czarist Russia, Professor Leon Theremin was a musical prodigy who performed for Lenin before gaining fame as an inventor with a talent for physics. His genius was co-opted by the Soviet intelligence services, and for nearly ten years, beginning in the late 1920s, Theremin lived in a New York brownstone at 37 West 54th Street. There he established the Teletouch Corporation (later Teletouch Industries) and promoted a new musical instrument that bore his name, the theremin.

The revolutionary electronic device, which was played without being touched, created a sensation in a city eager for the new and the avant-garde. Performances of the theremin at Carnegie Hall sold out, while a home version of the device could be purchased at Macy's.

The Teletouch Corporation also patented a technology to activate advertising devices when shoppers entered their electronic field and developed the world's first passive burglar-alarm system to detect the presence of an intruder. Secretly, however, Theremin's clandestine mission was to collect information on American technology for Soviet military intelligence.

In early 1938, Theremin married the talented African American dancer Lavinia Williams. Born in Philadelphia, though raised in Brooklyn, Williams had studied on scholarship at the Art Students League before joining the American Negro Ballet Company. The biracial couple obtained a certificate of marriage at the Russian consulate, but this was never filed in New York.

Soviet musical genius, inventor, and spy Leon Theremin worked in this midtown townhouse for most of the 1930s. After he was recalled to Russia by Stalin at the beginning of World War II, his engineering talents were redirected to creating innovative audio eavesdropping devices for the KGB.

On September 15, 1938, Theremin was recalled to Moscow and escorted from his West 54th Street address in front of his wife by a contingent of Soviet officials. According to one account, he was promised Lavinia could join him, but the offer was withdrawn at the last minute. Another promise, that she could follow in a few weeks, proved equally hollow.

Coming at the height of Stalin's purges, Theremin's life in the West was sufficient reason for questioning the scientist's loyalty. First imprisoned, then consigned to a *sharashka* (an NKVD prison within a factory and laboratory), he turned out sophisticated covert-listening devices for the Soviet intelligence service. Among the most notable of these devices was an audio bug, the passive cavity resonator. That bug, concealed in a wooden replica of the Great Seal of the United States, was presented to the US ambassador in Moscow as a token of friendship on July 4, 1945, by a contingent of the Young Pioneers, a Soviet youth group.

The device operated undetected as the Great Seal hung on the wall behind the ambassador's desk until 1952. After the bug was discovered, frustrated CIA engineers unsuccessfully attempted to duplicate the technical functionality of the sophisticated device that they called "the thing" (as in "How does 'the thing' work?"). For his secret efforts, Theremin never gained public recognition, but he was released from the sharashka in 1947 and privately awarded the prestigious Stalin Prize First Class.

Theremin's passive cavity resonator made a dramatic and unanticipated public appearance in New York in May 1960 when US ambassador Henry Cabot Lodge Jr. displayed it during a meeting of the United Nations (UN) Security Council. The revelation of Soviet spying defused the calculated Soviet diplomatic histrionics that followed the downing of Gary Powers's U-2 spy plane over Russia. Theremin remained unrecognized in the West and, back in the USSR, continued his technical work for Soviet intelligence.

Lavinia, who had since remarried and divorced during a career as a dancer and teacher, learned in 1974 Theremin was alive. Correspondence began, and remarriage was proposed as Theremin's Russian wife had recently died. In the end, nothing came of the plans for a reunion. Williams died in 1989 and Theremin in 1993.

> ### SPY TONES
>
> Leon Theremin's musical genius left the legacy eerie sound heard in the *Green Hornet* radio program, numerous horror and sci-fi motion pictures, and the Beach Boys' hit song "Good Vibrations."
> The Russian engineer-musician-prisoner-spy's electronic instrument inspired a new generation of musical instruments (including the Moog synthesizer), and his technology enabled a new class of covert surveillance devices.

■ 76. EINSTEIN MEETS THE GRU

MAP 2 ▶ **Sergei Konenkov and Margarita Konenkova residence and studio:** 37 West 8th Street

During the 1930s, a Soviet intelligence officer succeeded in seducing Albert Einstein by playing to his vanity and loneliness. In 1935, Einstein sat for noted Russian sculptor Sergei Konenkov at the artist's fifth-floor

An Albert Einstein sculpture by Sergei Konenkov resides in the Institute for Advanced Study in Princeton, New Jersey. Einstein was unaware the artist's wife, Margarita, was a Soviet spy.

studio at 37 West 8th Street. There he became acquainted with the artist's wife, Margarita Konenkova.

It is uncertain exactly when an affair began, but the Einstein-Konenkova relationship intensified following the death of Einstein's wife, Elsa, in late 1936. What Einstein did not know was that his love interest was a Soviet military intelligence officer code-named LUKAS. At her urging, he met for an hour in August 1945 with a man he believed was the Soviet vice consul. In reality, Einstein was introduced to Pavel Mikhailov (code name MOLIÈRE), who headed Soviet GRU operations in the United States.

The long-rumored affair was confirmed when a collection of nine love letters Einstein sent to Margarita Konenkova came up for auction following the Cold War. Written in 1945 and 1946, the letters reveal a flirty and lovelorn side of the physicist. "Just recently I washed my head by myself, but not with the greatest success; I am not as careful as you are," he wrote, "but everything here reminds me of you: 'Almar's [his pet name for her] shawl, the dictionaries, the wonderful pipe that we thought was gone, and really all the many little things in my hermit's cell; and also the lonely nest."

Konenkova, who was trained as a lawyer and reportedly spoke five languages, was assigned to target and influence American scientists. But she may not have been successful with Einstein. In at least one of the physicist's love missives, he was critical of the Soviet Union's traditional ostentatious display of military might during the annual May Day parade. He also turned down invitations to visit the USSR.

The sculpture of Einstein by Sergei Konenkov is displayed at the Institute for Advanced Study at Princeton University.

■ 77. CODE NAME: REDHEAD

MAP 5 ➤ **Mail-drop address:** 121 Madison Avenue (at East 30th Street)

Hede Massing (also known as Hede Tune, Hede Eisler, and Hede Gumperz) was a Viennese actress with red hair and a flashy appearance who spied for the Soviets in Europe and New York. In the late 1920s, legendary OGPU *illegal* Ignace Reiss trained Massing in countersurveillance, teaching her to never go directly from her apartment to a meeting, to travel circuitously, and to create opportunities to detect anyone who might be following. Massing learned to select meeting sites in public spaces with a rear exit and to avoid becoming flustered or rushed if followed. As a result, Massing chose sites such as the New York Public Library Main Branch (42nd Street and Fifth Avenue) and the lobby of the Radio City Music Hall (1260 Sixth Avenue) for clandestine agent meetings.

Soviet spy Hede Massing used 121 Madison Avenue as an accommodation address to receive mail delivered to her under the name Mrs. Brucker

When Massing (code name RED-HEAD) first arrived in the United States, she used a mail-drop address: c/o Mrs. Brucker, 121 Madison Avenue. She showed a special talent for recruiting for the NKVD, based on training received from Reiss. Massing could identify the vulnerabilities of young American idealists by tapping into their anger at perceived social injustices, then leverage that moral outrage as an inducement to work for Soviet intelligence. Later in an interview she said sex was also sometimes part of her pitch.

The famed art deco lobby of Radio City Music Hall was among Massing's favorite operational sites. The anonymity offered by crowds, along with multiple entrances and exits, made it a well-considered choice for clandestine meetings.

Massing claimed credit for recruiting State Department officer Lawrence Duggan in 1935, who would become another of the Soviet Union's spies. During her time as a Soviet agent, she also became acquainted with such notable spies as Vassili Zarubin, Boris Bazarov, Elizabeth Zarubina, Joszef Peter, Earl Browder, Richard Sorge, Noel Field, and Alger Hiss.

Massing's disillusionment with communism followed news that the NKVD had murdered her mentor, Reiss, in Switzerland in 1937. At the time of the Great Purges, dozens of loyal NKVD officers were recalled to Moscow to defend themselves against baseless allegations of being either Trotskyites, German spies, or both. Massing and her husband, Paul, went to Moscow in 1938 to resign from the NKVD and, against the prevailing political winds, were successful. Remarkably, both were allowed to return to the United States. They purchased the Courtney Farm in Haycock Township in Bucks County, Pennsylvania, and operated it as a bed-and-breakfast. During World War II, she worked as a carpenter at the Todd Shipyard at Weehawken Cove, Hoboken, New Jersey, and later in the personnel department at the shipyard's headquarters at 15 Whitehall Street in New York.

In 1947, the Massings were questioned by the FBI about their contacts with Soviet spies. She agreed to become a confidential informant and served in that role for two decades. She corroborated Whittaker Chambers's story that Alger Hiss was once a member of the communist underground and became one of the FBI's most important witnesses against Hiss. Afterward, in the late 1940s and early 1950s, Hede resided at 17 West 82nd Street and died at her Washington Square home in 1981.

■ 78. THE REAL DRAMA WASN'T ON THE SCREEN

MAP 10 ➤ **RKO Prospect Theatre:** 327 9th Street, Brooklyn (today condos and Steve's 9th Street Market)

Whittaker Chambers (code name CARL), whose 1948 testimony accused State Department officer Alger Hiss (code names ALES, JURIST, and LEONARD) of being a Soviet spy, asserted that he personally arranged a meeting between Hiss and GRU handler Col. Boris Bykov (also spelled "Bukov"; code names PETER and JEROME) in the spring of 1937. The three met on the mezzanine of the RKO Prospect Theatre, 327 9th Street,

Whittaker Chambers

The documents, known as the Pumpkin Papers, that made headlines and implicated Alger Hiss as a Soviet spy, were not papers at all. Whittaker Chambers secreted five canisters of 35mm film in a pumpkin on his Maryland farm.

Brooklyn where Steve's 9th Street Market and condos now occupy the original building.

Following brief introductions, the three left the theater and drove back to Manhattan to eat at the Port Arthur Restaurant, 7–9 Mott Street, notable as the first restaurant in Chinatown to be issued a liquor license. Today the space is occupied by the Chinatown Community Center.

At the time of the meeting in Brooklyn, New York's movie palaces were popular entertainment venues and favored sites for clandestine meetings. Theaters such as the landmark Radio City Music Hall (1260 Sixth Avenue) and the Roxy Theatre (once on West 50th Street) could seat up to six thousand patrons. Even smaller outer-borough theaters, such as the RKO Prospect, offered features making them attractive for spies. These were easy-to-find locations, generally near public transportation, and the buildings had multiple entrances and exits. Going to the movies was an everyday, nonalerting activity, and once patrons were inside, the darkness of the theater made their identification difficult.

■ 79. MARXIST, ECONOMIST, SOVIET SPY

MAP II ▶ **Victor Perlo residence:** 72-15 37th Avenue, Queens (sometimes listed as Long Island)

Soon after graduating from Columbia College in 1933, New York–born Victor Perlo joined an informal discussion group that included members of the CPUSA. The group was organized by Harold Ware and secretly coordinated by Joszef Peter, the head of the communist underground in Washington, DC. Far from promoting a free exchange of ideas, the group's purpose was to influence US government policies and nurture its young members to attain prominent government positions in the years ahead. The group's membership included many individuals who either were, or would later face accusations of being Soviet agents. Included among them were Alger Hiss, Nathaniel Weyl, Laurence Duggan, Harry Dexter White, Abraham George Silverman, John Abt, Nathan Witt, Marion

An active communist and NKVD agent, Victor Perlo lived in Jackson Heights, Queens, at 72-15 37th Avenue.

Bachrach, Julian Wadleigh, Lee Pressman, and Henry Hill Collins.

Assigned the code name RAIDER by the NKVD, Perlo secured a position in the Department of Commerce and the following year was promoted to senior economic analyst in the Bureau of Foreign and Domestic Commerce. He later worked in the Office of Price Administration and, at the end of World War II, headed the aviation section of the Bureau of Programs and Statistics at the War Production Board.

In 1938, Perlo extended the scope of his espionage by organizing a new group of spies working in government agencies and departments, who provided information to Earl Browder, the general secretary of the CPUSA. Following the death of Soviet spy Jacob Golos in 1943, the ring was controlled briefly by American NKVD agent Elizabeth Bentley.

During his time in the federal government, Perlo was an active contributor to the CPUSA's publications, using a variety of pseudonyms. He also secretly passed information to assist writer and one-time NKVD agent I. F. Stone in his exposés. After Bentley betrayed Perlo to the FBI in late 1945, he was placed under physical and technical surveillance at his residence, 72-15 37th Avenue in Queens. In August 1948, Whittaker Chambers accused Perlo and his group in testimony before the HUAC.

Perlo, however, continued to deny allegations that he spied for the Soviet Union, only admitting that he was a Roosevelt "New Dealer." He then invoked the Fifth Amendment when asked about his membership in the CPUSA and other matters. In the public's eye, "taking the Fifth" was tantamount to an admission of guilt.

In his later life Perlo admitted he was a veteran communist and chairman of the CPUSA's economic commission, but he was never prosecuted. He moved to Westchester County, New York, and resided at 30 Park Trail, Croton-on-Hudson, until his death in 1999.

Perlo's spy network and his activity as a Soviet agent became public in 1995 with the release of VENONA communication #687. This once-encrypted message from the Soviet's New York station to Moscow dated May 13, 1944, confirmed Perlo's role in Soviet espionage.

■ 80. THE VANISHING BELIEVER

MAP 3 ➤ **American Women's Association:** 353 West 57th Street

American communist Juliet Stuart Poyntz vanished before she could write a book critical of Stalinist Russia.

On June 3, 1937, Juliet Stuart Poyntz left her room at what was then the American Women's Association Clubhouse (formerly the Henry Hudson Hotel and now the Hudson Hotel) at 353 West 57th Street and vanished, never to be seen again. A police investigation into her disappearance turned up no clues. All her belongings, clothing, and hand luggage were found untouched in the room. Even a page of writing was left uncompleted on the desk.

Poyntz, who taught at Columbia University and Barnard College, was a founding member of the CPUSA and once considered among the top ten communist leaders in the United States. She began as a progressive activist, then drifted increasingly to the left but is reputed to have publicly withdrawn from the party in 1934 to work underground as an agent for the GRU. However, a trip to Stalin's Russia in 1936 apparently reversed her views. Returning to New York disillusioned, she spoke openly of plans to write a book exposing the Stalin purges.

Along with news of her disappearance were unsubstantiated rumors about the circumstances surrounding the incident and the identities of those involved with her apparent murder. Multiple accounts assert Poyntz was abducted and murdered by an NKVD assassination squad to prevent her defection. One theory in *Stalin's Agent: The Life and Death of Alexander Orlov* by Boris Volodarsky holds that she was killed and her body sealed in a wall of a Greenwich Village home.

Another disillusioned CPUSA member, Benjamin Gitlow, described the abduction, murder, and burial of the body on the grounds of an estate outside the city, in his book *The Whole of Their Lives: Communism in America*. "The body was covered with lime and dirt. On top were placed dead leaves and branches which the three killers trampled down with their feet," Gitlow wrote. A third account describes the disaffected spy as taken aboard a ship docked in the harbor, murdered, and her body thrown overboard while at sea.

However she died, Poyntz's mysterious disappearance was used as a warning to other party members should they ever consider defecting. In October 1944, the courts officially declared Poyntz dead and turned her estate over to her sister. The case remains unsolved.

■ 81. SPY ON THE RUN

MAP 3 ➤ **Alexander Orlov residence:** Wellington Hotel, 871 Seventh Avenue

Gen. Alexander Orlov (code name SCHWED, meaning SWEDE) played a leading role in multiple Soviet intelligence operations during the 1930s, first in England, then Spain. During the Spanish Civil War, he persuaded the Spanish government to move its gold reserves, the fourth largest in the world—approximately 500 tons—to Moscow, allegedly for safekeeping. Soviet assassin Ramón Mercader, who murdered Leon Trotsky in 1940, was Orlov's student in a training camp for guerrilla fighters in Spain several years earlier. George Mink, a feared American enforcer and assassin, was similarly schooled under Orlov.

Alexander Orlov

Despite his successes, Orlov received a notice to return to Moscow from Spain in July 1938 during the height of Stalin's purges. He had good reason to believe his loyalty would likely be repaid with a show trial and a bullet. Orlov fled to Canada with a horde of cash from the *rezidentura's* safe; estimates of the theft ranged between $22,000 and $60,000. He left behind two letters, one to the NKVD's vicious chief, Nikolai Yezhov (known as the Poison Dwarf), and another to Stalin. Both contained the same message: Orlov would reveal everything he knew

When Alexander Orlov defected with his wife and daughter, his first stop was the Wellington Hotel, where he registered under the name Leon Koornick. The wily master-spy evaded detection by both the KGB and FBI for years.

about Soviet intelligence if he was pursued. Only his safety and that of his family, and the stolen cash, could buy his silence.

From Canada, Orlov slipped across the US border with his wife, Maria, and terminally ill child, Vera. The family arrived in New York and settled into the Wellington Hotel, 871 Seventh Avenue, under the name Leon Koornick, an identity borrowed from a cousin living in Astoria, Queens.

Orlov then became invisible. He cut off ties to his old life, except for a single letter written anonymously to Leon Trotsky, warning of an imminent assassination plot. In the letter, he offered a detailed description of the assassin, but he did not know his name. Trotsky, assuming the letter was the work of NKVD agent provocateurs, ignored the warning.

Eventually the Orlov family moved from New York to Philadelphia, then to Boston and westward to Los Angeles. There Vera died from a heart weakened by rheumatic fever, after which Orlov and his wife settled in a Cleveland suburb under the alias Berg. For a decade, they led a spartan lifestyle, reportedly subsisting on breakfast cereals while eluding Soviet and FBI attention.

Then, a month after Stalin's death, Orlov surfaced by publishing in the April 6, 1953, issue of *Life* magazine an exposé, *The Ghastly Secrets of Stalin's Power*. In a series of articles, Orlov methodically outlined Stalin's corrupt and bloody regime. A year later, his first book, *The Secret History of Stalin's Crimes*, appeared. Orlov's sudden appearance surprised American spy catchers as much as the Soviets.

The Orlovs returned to New York for a brief time, living at 711 West End Avenue before moving to Michigan where he obtained a teaching position. He was contacted officially by KGB officer Oleg Kalugin in the 1970s, who told Orlov that his former colleagues appreciated his continuing discretion since the book's publication. Orlov died in the United States in 1973 without ever revealing that he also had handled several Soviet spies in the United Kingdom before World War II. Had Orlov revealed that information when he arrived in Canada or the United States, it would have severely crippled Soviet intelligence operations.

MEMORIES OF NEW YORK

Alexander Orlov's 1938 flight from Stalin was not the Soviet spy's first time in New York. In 1932, he visited the city using the alias Leon L. Nikolaev, claiming to be on a trade mission to buy American cars for the USSR. Upon arrival in New York with his family in 1938, Orlov was eager to show his daughter, Vera, sights he remembered from his previous trip. They stayed at the Wellington Hotel, a few blocks from Central Park, and made an excursion to Coney Island. At a shooting gallery, Orlov, a skilled marksman, won a small plaster-of-Paris kitten. Vera named the kitten Schatzi and carried the prized possession with her through all the family's numerous moves.

■ 82. LIPSTICK AND LIES

MAP 4 ► **Commercial cover:** Phantom Red Cosmetics, 67 Fifth Avenue (site redeveloped)

Soviet intelligence operatives in the United States made use of legitimate businesses as cover for their spying. Often with the cooperation of a company owner, Soviet officers established themselves as businessmen and developed a work history with a known firm.

Willie Brandes (also known as Mikhail Borovoy), an *illegal* who operated in England, Canada, and the United States in the 1930s, adopted the cover of a sales representative for Boston's Charak Furniture Company, a manufacturer of colonial furniture. As was later revealed, Soviet intelligence gave the owner of the company, Walter Charak, funds from which Brandes received a monthly $300 salary. At another point, Brandes became a sales representative for the interestingly named Phantom Red Cosmetics Company, headquartered at 67 Fifth Avenue (today the site of the New School).

Brandes, like several other Soviet intelligence officers in the United States, was eventually caught up in Stalin's purges and sent to a gulag when he returned to Russia in 1938.

■ 83. CODE NAME CROOK

MAP II ► **Samuel Dickstein burial site:** Union Field Cemetery, 82-11 Cypress Avenue, Queens

Samuel Dickstein, who represented New York's 12th District in Congress, was on the NKVD payroll from 1937 to 1940, working under the code name CROOK. A congressman at the center of American political power must have seemed like a prize asset. Dickstein, who promised to deliver material to his NKVD handler on fascists, German agents, and White Russians, received $1,250 a month for his services.

How much useful intelligence the congressman actually provided to the Soviets is uncertain. Responding to requirements to collect information on the Soviet defector Walter Krivitsky, for example, Dickstein delivered a short memo that read suspiciously close to the defector's public statements in the media, and he sponsored legislation that failed to have Krivitsky deported. Dickstein also advocated for more funding for J. Edgar Hoover's FBI, which was gearing up to fight fascist spies, and he helped form an antifascist House Special Committee on Un-American Activities in 1934 and later, in 1938, the House Un-American Activities Committee (HUAC). Ironically, both the FBI and HUAC would eventually focus on communist subversion.

Samuel Dickstein

After twenty-two years in office, Dickstein resigned from Congress in 1945, then became a judge on the New York State Supreme Court. His spying attracted no suspicion and was not made public until discovered in Moscow archives in the early 1990s. Dickstein died in 1954 and is buried in the Union Field Cemetery, 82-11 Cypress Avenue, Queens.

TINY TRIBUTE

Today Samuel Dickstein remains an obscure figure, although a short Lower Manhattan street named Samuel Dickstein Plaza (between Grand and Henry Streets) commemorates the public servant who kept secret his time as a Soviet spy.

■ 84. RUNNING FROM STALIN

MAP ⊝ ➤ **Walter Krivitsky apartment:** 36 West Gun Hill Road, Bronx

The first high-ranking Soviet intelligence officer to defect to the West was Walter Krivitsky (code name ENEMY). An *illegal* officer of the NKVD and GRU, he walked into a French ministry in Paris with his wife and young child in 1937 rather than return to the Soviet Union and Stalin's purges. He reemerged in 1939 living in an apartment at 36 West Gun Hill Road in the Bronx. In his book *In Stalin's Secret Service* and interviews in major

Walter Krivitsky

publications, Krivitsky offered a vivid personal account of the murderous regime. For the general public, the previously unreported brutality of the Soviet government was appalling. Krivitsky's information further enabled Western intelligence agencies to identify scores of Soviet agents around the world.

After defecting to the West to avoid Stalin's purges, Walter Krivitsky and his family lived in this modest apartment house in the Bronx.

On a February evening in 1941, Krivitsky checked into room 532 at the Bellevue Hotel (today the Kimpton George Hotel) in Washington, DC, under the name Walter Poref. The next day a maid found him dead, with a single gunshot wound to the head. Although his death was officially ruled a suicide, suspicions that Stalin had ordered the murder of the defector were widely believed. Decades later, the circumstances surrounding the defector's death remain inconclusive.

■ 85. SOVIET ASSASSIN IN GOTHAM

MAP 4 ► **George Mink mail drop:** 26 East 10th Street, apt. 5-F

Among the notorious NKVD enforcers of the 1930s, few were more feared than George Mink, who gained a bloody reputation as assassin, harbor pirate, and spy for the COMINTERN. Born in Russia in 1899, Mink came to the United States in 1913 to live with relatives in Philadelphia and later served in the US Navy for three years. In 1921, Mink joined the Seamen's International Union and the International Workers of the World but, judging both groups as insufficiently radical, switched his allegiance to the CPUSA and the COMINTERN. By 1928, after a trip to Moscow, he began working in the Foreign Section of the OGPU (predecessor of the NKVD).

Mink bounced between jobs in the 1930s. He was a taxi driver in Philadelphia and made frequent trips along the East Coast to strong-arm longshoremen into union membership while serving as the chairman of the Marine Workers Industrial Union. He first became known to law enforcement in 1935 when arrested

George Mink

in Copenhagen on accusations that he had raped a hotel maid. A search of his hotel room by Danish police revealed codes, false passports, and $3,000 in cash—more than enough evidence to conclude that Mink and his two traveling companions were spies. As a result, he received a four-year sentence but was released and deported to Moscow in 1936.

Mink next went to Spain, where he earned a fearsome reputation as an executioner under Alexander Orlov. Murders of multiple individuals throughout Europe seen as disloyal to the communist cause were attributed to Mink. Authorities believe he also directed or participated in several high-profile assassinations, including that of defector Ignace Reiss in Switzerland and anti-Stalinist Italian professor Camillo Berneri in Barcelona.

After returning to the United States, Mink is believed to have murdered Juliet Poyntz in New York City but her body was never found. During this same time period, Walter Krivitsky, who defected to the West in 1937 and lived in New York, reported having been accosted by three men, one of whom he recognized as Mink. Krivitsky escaped into a subway.

Throughout most of his life, Mink operated internationally and virtually invisibly. He used multiple passports under various names; some were clever forgeries in which his photograph replaced the original, while others were genuine passports issued under a false name. When arrested in Copenhagen, Mink was carrying four passports—one in his true name and the others in the names of Al Gotlieb, Abraham Wexler, and Harry Herman Kaplan. The true-name passport was issued to Mink in care of the union lawyer William "Bill" Standard, 26 East 10th Street, apartment 5-F. Another passport listed Mink's address as 235 East 13th Street, which he may have used as an accommodation address or mail drop.

Suspected assassin George Mink used 235 East 13th Street as an accommodation address to receive a US passport.

Mink was reportedly part of the NKVD plot to assassinate Leon Trotsky. In 1938, Trotsky, then living near Mexico City, publicly announced that Mink was in Mexico to assassinate him. Two years later, just before the failed NKVD attack on Trotsky's compound on May 23, 1940, Mink was reportedly captured by Trotsky's bodyguards. George Hansen, Trotsky's chief secretary, later told the FBI that in 1940 Mink's captors threw him into a volcano's crater southeast of Mexico City. This account of his death is consistent with one that appeared in the February 1941 Soviet publication *Novoye*

Russkoye Slovo (*New Russian World*), which reported, "According to the latest confirmed information Mink was liquidated in December [1940]." Whatever Mink's fate, it was the last credible report of his whereabouts and remains the best explanation for his sudden disappearance.

Not far from Union Square, the epicenter for New York's early 20th-century political radicals, the Socialists Workers Party once occupied offices above the deli on this site. The rival CPUSA headquarters was located within walking distance of each other.

■ 86. REVOLUTION IN NEW YORK

MAP 4 ► **Socialist Workers Party headquarters:** 116 University Place (now redeveloped)

The SWP, loyal to Leon Trotsky, moved its headquarters to 116 University Place from a site at the Labor Book Store at 28 East 12th Street in 1939. Led by James P. Cannon (code name DAK), party members were devout followers of the exiled Trotsky (code name OLD MAN) and his Fourth International. Trotsky had been forced into exile from the Soviet Union in 1929. Mortal enemies of the Stalinists, the group had been nonetheless thoroughly infiltrated by Stalin's agents, including Cannon's secretary, Sylvia Caldwell (also known as Sylvia Callen; code names SATYR and RITA). Trotsky depended on the SWP for living costs, funds to upgrade security at his residence in Coyoacán, Mexico, and salaries for American bodyguards. Caldwell reported all correspondence between the exiled Trotsky and Cannon, which provided the NKVD intelligence to refine their plans to assassinate Trotsky.

■ 87. THE NAIVE ASSASSIN

MAP 6 ► **Robert Sheldon Harte residence:** 1148 Fifth Avenue

The SWP provided the small contingent of American bodyguards to protect Trotsky at his compound in Coyoacán, just outside Mexico City. One of the guards, Robert Sheldon Harte, who had lived at 1148 Fifth Avenue, was the son of wealthy businessman Jesse S. Harte. Trotsky was unaware

Raised by a wealthy family in this Fifth Avenue apartment building, Robert Sheldon Harte entered radical politics at an early age. He became one of Leon Trotsky's bodyguards.

that Harte (code names AMUR and CUPID) had been recruited by legendary Soviet intelligence officer Iosif Grigulevich (code name PADRE) as an agent for Stalin.

Harte, the lone guard on duty in Coyoacán on the night of May 23, 1940, allowed a group of two dozen attackers dressed as Mexican policemen to enter the compound and storm Trotsky's living quarters. The assassins were led by famed Mexican muralist David Alfaro Siqueiros (code name KON) and fellow painter

On the gatehouse of Trotsky's compound in Coyoacán, Mexico, is a commemorative plaque for Harte. Harte allowed would-be assassins into the compound who failed to kill Trotsky but subsequently murdered Harte. Trotsky refused to believe Harte's complicity and paid for the plaque.

Luis Arenal Bastar (code name RAFAIL). Grigulevich remained at the entrance gate guarding Harte, who prepared Trotsky's two vehicles to serve as getaway cars. The attackers fired hundreds of rounds into Trotsky's bedroom and living quarters, but miraculously Trotsky survived the attack unscathed.

Efforts by the SWP to raise funds to strengthen the defenses of the compound after the attack were woefully inadequate, and Trotsky's trustful nature—he refused to permit his guards to search guests—prevailed over recommendations for enhanced physical security. Trotsky's misguided sense of civility contributed to his death less than three months later.

■ 88. TROTSKY'S ATTACKERS IN HIDING

MAP 10 ➤ **Safe house for murderers:** 881 Washington Avenue, Brooklyn

Following the failed assassination attempt on Trotsky in Mexico on May 23, 1940, Robert Sheldon Harte, the lone guard on duty, appeared to leave willingly with the attackers in Trotsky's two vehicles. His father rushed to Mexico from New York to search for his son. A month later, Harte's decaying remains were discovered buried beneath the kitchen of a remote safe house used by the attackers. Trotsky refused to believe Harte had betrayed him and commissioned a commemorative plaque to be erected near the

Luis Arenal

Following a botched attempt on Leon Trotsky's life, would-be assassin Luis Arenal returned to this New York apartment building at 881 Washington Avenue, which served as a safe house for him and his wife, Rose.

guard post in his honor. A search of the family's 1148 Fifth Avenue residence, however, revealed a different story, evidenced by a large painting of Joseph Stalin on a wall of Harte's room.

Later accounts revealed that Leopolo (or Leopoldo) Arenal (code name ALEXANDER) and his brother, Luis (code name RAFAIL), both hardened veterans of the Mexican Brigade of the Spanish Civil War, killed and buried Harte when they feared he would go to the authorities and confess his role. It was reported that Iosif Grigulevich, who had recruited the naive Harte, led him to believe the attack was intended only to destroy Trotsky's archive, not kill him.

Luis fled Mexico after Harte's body was discovered and resided secretly with his wife, Rose Arenal, at 881 Washington Avenue, Brooklyn. Rose later admitted to the FBI that her address was used as a mail drop for the brothers. The messages were picked up by Elizabeth Bentley, an American spy for the Soviets.

■ 89. THE ASSASSIN'S HONEY TRAP

MAP 10 ➤ **Sylvia Ageloff residence:** 50 Livingston Street, Brooklyn

Following the failure to assassinate Leon Trotsky by an armed assault, an elaborate NKVD backup plan was activated. In the works for more than two years, the second operation to eliminate Trotsky used seduction as the tool to infiltrate the exiled revolutionary's compound and kill him.

In 1938, the NKVD asked a prominent CPUSA member, Louis Budenz (code names BUBEN and TAMBOURINE), who resided at 328 East 15th Street, apartment 22, to identify a female supporter of Trotsky who might be vulnerable to manipulation

Mark Zborowski

by a charming lover, known as a Romeo agent. Budenz recommended Sylvia Ageloff as the target. She was a social worker, Trotsky supporter, and Columbia University graduate living alone at 50 Livingston Street in Brooklyn. The petite Ageloff was of average appearance with sharp features, wore large round glasses, and was without a boyfriend or love interest. Equally important, her sister, Ruth, had served as a secretary to Trotsky in Mexico a year earlier and was close to Trotsky and his wife, Natalia.

The plan called for the assassin, Ramón Mercader, in alias as Jacques Mornard, to meet and woo Ageloff, who, in turn, would use her sister's friendship with Trotsky to introduce Mornard into the exiled leader's trusted inner circle. The operational challenge was to find a way for the assassin and Ageloff to meet without appearing contrived.

Budenz proposed to have another local party member, Ruby Weil, who knew the plan, appear to break with the pro-Stalinist CPUSA and espouse pro-Trotsky views. Weil would then befriend Ageloff and invite her to travel with her to France for the founding conference of the Fourth International (Trotsky's version of communism), where Ageloff could be introduced to Mornard and seduced by him.

The plan proceeded without a hitch as the key planner of the Paris conference, Mark Zborowski, was secretly an NKVD agent (code name TULIP) and arranged for Ageloff to be seated next to Mercader. Posing as Mornard, the debonair son of a wealthy Belgian diplomat, he wined and dined Weil and Ageloff for ten days. On the tenth night, Weil withdrew and Mercader/Mornard seduced Sylvia.

Harvard-educated Soviet spy Mark Zborowski's greatest achievement was penetrating the Trotskyites' inner circle in Paris. In later years he lived here on West 108th Street.

Thereafter the couple traveled throughout Europe for several months before Ageloff returned to New York. Mercader/Mornard, traveling under a false passport in the name of Frank Jacson, followed her to New York in the fall of 1939. Soon afterward, he left for Mexico City, supposedly to establish a business there. Ageloff joined him in 1940 and renewed her friendship with Trotsky but never introduced the two. On May

This short-handled ice ax was the weapon used to kill Leon Trotsky in 1940. The ax is displayed at the International Spy Museum in Washington, DC.

28, four days after the failed assault on Trotsky's compound, Mercader/Mornard/Jacson went to New York City and, following a meeting in the Hotel Pierrepont, 55 Pierrepont Street, Brooklyn, was designated as the primary assassin.

Prior to May 28, 1940, Mercader had never met Trotsky or been inside the compound. To the guards and the Trotsky family, he was known by his passport alias, Frank Jacson. They considered him to be Ageloff's common-law husband who dropped her off at the compound for visits but was apolitical and never ventured inside.

Over the next three months, however, Mercader befriended Trotsky's American bodyguards, loaned them his car for six weeks, and was welcomed into the armed compound on 10 occasions. He became the only visitor ever allowed to meet alone with the exiled revolutionary. Alone with Trotsky on the 10th visit in August, he struck the deadly blow with an ice axe. Trotsky did not die instantly and let out a terrible scream. Guards in the next room quickly overwhelmed the assassin.

Ageloff was arrested as a suspect following the attack. The police could not believe that she had no knowledge of the crime, but a lengthy investigation proved her innocence, and she returned to New York City. Mercader never admitted to his true name during questioning. Despite the overwhelming proof against him, the assassin-spy never broke cover and maintained throughout his imprisonment that he was Jacques Mornard. He served a full 20-year prison sentence before his release and resettlement to the USSR in 1960. Honored as a Hero of the Soviet Union upon his return to Moscow, he was awarded in 1965 an engraved gold watch by the Central Committee inscribed with a previously undisclosed code name, AGENT LOPEZ.

■ 90. PLOTTING TROTSKY'S DEATH

MAP 10 ▶ **Hotel Pierrepont:** 55 Pierrepont Street, between Henry and Hicks Streets, Brooklyn (building remains on rehabilitated site of St. Charles Jubilee Senior Center of Brooklyn)

For $15.00 a week in 1940, Soviet agent Ramón Mercader, a Spaniard, stayed in the unassuming Hotel Pierrepont at 55 Pierrepont Street in Brooklyn Heights to plan the final attack to kill Leon Trotsky. Code-named RAYMOND, later GNOME, Mercader operated under the aliases

Mercader entered Mexico using a forged passport under an alias, Frank Jacson.

Jacques Mornard and Frank Jacson. Following the failed first attack on Leon Trotsky in Mexico on May 23, 1940, Mercader traveled to New York City to meet with his mother, Eustacia María Caridad del Río Hernández (code names KLAVA and MOTHER), who served as the NKVD operational controller for the backup plan to eliminate Trotsky. In the Brooklyn hotel room, supported and guided by the chief NKVD intelligence officer in the United States, Gaik Ovakimian (code name GENNADI), the mother and son finalized the plan that killed Trotsky two months later.

Built in 1928, the Hotel Pierrepont was a stone's throw from downtown Brooklyn and the temporary headquarters for Trotsky assassin Ramón Mercader.

■ 91. ATTEMPTING TO FREE TROTSKY'S KILLER

MAP 6 ➤ **Jacob Epstein residence:** 958 Madison Avenue

The assassination of Leon Trotsky on August 20, 1940, marked the successful conclusion of an elaborate NKVD intelligence operation known as UTKA (meaning DUCK), which took place on different continents, spanned several years, and involved multiple subplots. With the assassin Ramón Mercader (a.k.a. Frank Jacson and Jacques Mornard) serving a 20-year prison sentence in Mexico, the NKVD planned an operation, code-named GNOME, to free him.

During 1942 and 1943, a number of letters that passed between Mexico City and New York City were intercepted by the US Office of Censorship. Laboratory examination of the letters determined they contained ciphered messages in invisible ink related to efforts of Soviet agents in the

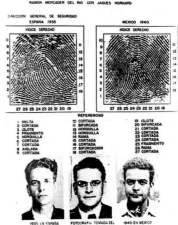

Leon Trotsky's assassin, Ramón Mercader, was identified through fingerprint arrest records predating the Spanish Civil War.

Jacob Epstein, one of the plotters to break Mercader out of a Mexican jail, lived at 958 Madison Avenue.

United States and Mexico to free Frank Jacson from imprisonment. Further investigation disclosed that an elaborate system of mail drops on both sides of the border was used for this correspondence. Subsequently, each of these mail drops was investigated to determine the scope of the conspiracy.

A few of the agents participating in the plot knew of the operation to break Frank Jacson out of prison, but not all were aware of the purpose of the plot. Individuals and addresses subsequently identified by US congressional investigators included:

- Jacob Epstein (HARRY): 958 Madison Avenue

- Lydia Altschuler (LYDIA): 97 Perry Street

- Barnett Sheppard: 47-14 261st Street, Great Neck, Long Island

- Fanny McPeek: 846 Prospect Place, Brooklyn

- Mrs. Pauline Baskind: 1045 Anderson Avenue, Bronx

- Mrs. Frances Silverman: 134 St. Johns Avenue, Yonkers

- Ethel Vogel: 137 West 82nd Street

- Anna Vogel Colloms: Park Trail, Mount Airy Road, Croton-on-Hudson

Participants in operation GNOME to free Ramón Mercader from prison included multiple New York plotters. Among them was Fanny McPeek, who lived at 846 Prospect Place, Brooklyn.

Ultimately GNOME was a failure. The NKVD's Mexico City mission lacked the resources and skills to pull off such a daring caper, despite the personal interest of NKVD chief Lavrentiy Beria. In 1945, following the conclusion of World War II, the plan was abandoned.

■ 92. THE FIRST "ATOMIC SPY"

MAP 5 ➤ **Arthur Adams residence:** Peter Cooper Hotel [now the Tuscany St. Giles Hotel], 120 East 39th Street

The life of Arthur Adams, an early Soviet spy in the United States, remains shrouded in mystery. Adams, a Soviet *illegal* working for military intelligence, moved in and out of America and traveled between New York and the West Coast with little problem. Older and seemingly frail, he suffered the effects of severe rheumatism that often increased or decreased according to operational necessity. His health problems were said to be genuine and the result of severe beatings by the Okhrana, the czar's secret police. However, despite his frail appearance and infirmities, Adams played a significant role in penetrating security of the top-secret Manhattan Project, America's atomic bomb program.

Adams's first unconfirmed entrance into the United States was on July 4, 1910; he entered again on October 9, 1915. Juliet Poyntz—who later served as a Soviet spy and was murdered during Stalin's reign—acted as a character witness to support his travel to America. According to one source, during the

Arthur Adams

Members of Arthur Adams's spy ring included Eric Bernay of Keynote Records, 522 Fifth Avenue.

1915 visit he lived at 151 West 14th Street before moving to Detroit in 1917, where he was employed by the Ford Motor Company.

Adams appeared again in September 1925 as part of a Soviet trade delegation, then in September 1928 in an official capacity representing the Moscow Automotive Society, seeking information on the American auto industry. In December 1932, he was a member of a commission shopping for aircraft from the Curtiss-Wright Corporation and was, apparently, attached to the Amtorg Trading Corporation.

Then, on May 17, 1938, using a false Canadian passport, Adams returned to the United States on a long-term mission for the GRU. He filled out forms declaring his intention to become an American citizen, gave his place of birth as Canada, and set up a cover company called Technological Laboratories Inc. The company briefly occupied room 839 at 1775 Broadway, though it seems to have been a largely a paper entity. A Macy's charge account he opened in February 1940 listed his address as the Hotel Commander, 240 West 73rd Street. By the time he closed the account in early 1945, he was living at the Peter Cooper Hotel (today the Tuscany), 120 East 39th Street.

Adams operated with a support network of dedicated communists. Chief among them was Samuel J. Novick, who lived at 91 Central Park West and owned the profitable Wholesale Radio Service Company, 100 Sixth Avenue, and the Electronics Corporation of America, then located at 45 West 18th Street. During the war years, the latter company became even more profitable from government contracts. Another member of the spy ring was Eric Bernay, owner of Keynote Records, 522 Fifth Avenue, a record company specializing in jazz and folk music. A third person providing cover was Samuel J. Wegman, who reportedly owned engineering and machine-design offices in New York and California. Adams gave Wegman $1,875 in cash, which was to be paid back to him as a $75-a-week salary, showing employment in the California office, and with checks sent to the Peter Cooper Hotel in New York.

Novick and Bernay both gave Adams employment as a cover for spying. A fourth member of the group was Victoria Stone, who owned a high-end jewelry store, 510 Madison Avenue. Likely Adams's lover as well as his assistant, she lived at 39 West 55th Street, apartment 9-E.

Adams's targets, the Manhattan Project and American radar technology, were two of the most closely guarded technologies of the war years. Eventually his contacts extended from New York to Chicago and California, constituting a network of agents in universities, the military, and the top-secret facility at Oak Ridge, Tennessee.

Tipped off to Adams's involvement in espionage, the FBI searched his Peter Cooper Hotel apartment and found sensitive material on fission technology and equipment for creating microdots. Since an arrest and trial would reveal the existence of the Manhattan Project, Adams and his network were surveilled but not arrested. When he became aware of the surveillance in 1945, Adams sought to flee but was prevented from boarding a ship in Portland, Oregon. Returning to New York, he became a virtual recluse in his hotel. Then, in 1946, he left the hotel, evaded surveillance, and vanished.

Adams resurfaced in Moscow a few years later as a political columnist for the Soviet news agency TASS. He died in 1969 and was interred in a columbarium in Moscow's Novodevichy Cemetery. He was awarded the title Hero of the Russian Federation by Russian president Boris Yeltsin in 1999.

■ 93. FROM FASCIST TO COMMUNIST TO FBI SOURCE

MAP 2 ➤ **Elizabeth Bentley apartment:** 58 Barrow Street

Elizabeth Bentley graduated from Vassar College in 1930, then entered graduate school at Columbia University. During a fellowship in Italy she flirted with fascism but, after returning to the United States, swung to the far left and communism. She soon came to the attention of Yakov Reizen, a Soviet intelligence officer in New York operating under the identity of Jacob Golos (code name SOUND). Bentley first caught Golos's interest when she volunteered to spy on her Italian fascist friends. Later she would become his protégée and lover. Golos, then one of the Soviet Union's senior intelligence officers in the United States, was subsequently involved in plans to assassinate Leon Trotsky. In 1938, he gave Bentley the code name UMNITSA (meaning CLEVER GIRL) and initially put her to work in supporting roles as his courier and something of a Girl Friday.

Jacob Golos

Elizabeth Bentley

In 1940, Golos's company, World Tourists Inc., at 60 Fifth Avenue and later 175 Fifth Avenue, was exposed as an unregistered foreign agent.

Golos, a naturalized American, avoided arrest, but his World Tourist cover was blown. However, with his spy network still intact, Golos set up another front company, United States Service and Shipping, at 212 Fifth Avenue, with laundered funds. He installed Bentley as vice president. The new company was quietly connected with Intourist, 545 Fifth Avenue, the official travel bureau of the Soviet Union. Intourist itself was closely aligned with the NKVD and provided cover for operations and sometimes assisted in entrapping foreign visitors to the USSR.

Elizabeth Bentley lived in this Barrow Street home in the West Village during the later years of her spying for the Soviets.

Over time Bentley became one of the NKVD's most trusted agents, serving as a courier for passing stolen secrets from other spies to Golos and meeting other agents in Washington and in New York. When spies Gregory and Helen Silvermaster made trips to New York from Washington to deliver materials to Bentley, they stayed at the Hotel Victoria (today site of an office building), 145 51st Street, or the Times Square Hotel, 255 West 43rd Street. Duncan Lee (code names KOCH and PAT), another spy who lived in Washington, met with Bentley at one of the Longchamps chain restaurants on Fifth Avenue at East 12th Street and once at a Longchamps on 57th Street. On other occasions Bentley received money from a Soviet agent at meeting sites on Fourth Avenue and 10th Street and at 23rd Street and Eighth Avenue, near a Bickford Cafeteria.

Based in Washington, DC, Soviet spies Gregory and Helen Silvermaster sometimes stayed at the Hotel Times Square, 255 West 43rd Street, when delivering information to Bentley.

Bentley was living at 58 Barrow Street, next to the former speakeasy Chumley's, when Golos died of a heart attack in her apartment in 1943. Becoming distraught and paranoid, she moved into the Hotel St. George at 100 Henry Street in Brooklyn. Living in fear of both the FBI and her Soviet handlers, she began drinking heavily and acting erratically. Bentley had good reason to be afraid. Her new Soviet handler wanted her killed, but Moscow refused. By August 1945, she had enough and walked into the New York FBI field office to tell her story. Bentley made a full statement in November, and then spent years testifying and lecturing about the dangers of Soviet espionage. She died from cancer in 1963.

■ 94. BLUE BLOOD AMONG THE REDS

MAP 6 ➤ **John Hazard Reynolds residence:** 825 Fifth Avenue

John Hazard Reynolds, a coconspirator with Soviet spies Elizabeth Bentley and Jacob Golos, must have seemed the perfect front man for a commercial cover operation to Soviet intelligence in the fall of 1940. The son of a New York State Supreme Court judge and a member of old-money Manhattan society, Reynolds was a war veteran who had increased his inherited wealth working in Wall Street finance. He then married into the even larger fortune of the Fleischmann Yeast family, lived at 825 Fifth Avenue on the Upper East Side, and joined the prestigious Racquet and Tennis Club, 370 Park Avenue.

John Hazard Reynolds created a stylish front company for Soviet intelligence when he furnished the offices of the US Service and Shipping Corporation, 212 Fifth Avenue, with family antiques and portraits.

Despite his capitalist heritage, Reynolds was no stranger to the communist cause. Before becoming involved with Golos and Bentley, he donated money to left-wing magazines such as *Soviet Russia Today* and *New Masses*. When the Soviets needed a reputable American to run a commercial cover called US Service and Shipping Corporation, Reynolds was willing. He accepted $15,000 cash to start the company, added another $5,000 of his own money, then laundered the funds through his numerous bank accounts.

Bentley found office space for the new company on the 19th floor of 212 Fifth Avenue. Golos, a known Soviet intelligence officer, planned to stay in the background. Almost immediately, however, Reynolds clashed with his Soviet handlers by rejecting their hand-picked staff. Bentley, in her autobiography,

Out of Bondage, recalled Golos describing their partner as "the sort of person who likes to sit behind a desk and look important." After hanging an oversized oil painting of one of his ancestors in the office, Reynolds bragged to Golos, "That's my great-grandfather hanging there." Golos answered, "My great-grandfather was hanged too, but under slightly different circumstances."

Reynolds escaped prosecution but died in 1951 of a heart ailment at age 54.

From a nondescript building amid the bright lights of Times Square, the film distributor Artkino brought Soviet films such as *Ballad of Siberia* (1947) and *Cossacks of the Kuban* (1949) to American audiences. Artkino's president, Nicola Napoli, was also an agent for Soviet intelligence.

■ 95. FILMS AND SPIES

MAP 3 ➤ **Artkino Pictures:** 723 Seventh Avenue

For more than four decades beginning in the 1930s, Nicola Napoli, president of Artkino Pictures Inc., 723 Seventh Avenue, was the primary distributor of Soviet films in the United States. Less well known was his role in passing information from the CPUSA to Soviet intelligence during World War II.

Napoli became involved in supporting Soviet intelligence after he came to the attention of Jacob Golos, a founding member of the CPUSA. Shortly before his death in 1943, Golos told his protégée and lover Elizabeth Bentley that he was turning Napoli over to another Russian contact to continue the covert relationship. Napoli was later identified when the VENONA project decrypted an NKVD communication dated December 1944 sent from New York to Moscow.

Napoli was contacted by would-be spies Theodore Hall and Saville Sax after the two were rebuffed by Earl Browder of the CPUSA. Napoli recognized the potential value of Hall, a physicist and youthful member of the Manhattan Project team, as a spy. Hall, given the code name MLAD (meaning YOUTH), was handled by Sergi Kournakoff (code names CALVERYMAN and BEK), who operated under the cover of being a journalist at the *Daily Worker*. Sax became a courier for Hall's information.

■ 96. FRIENDS HELPING FRIENDS

MAP I ➤ **International Development Company:** 19 Rector Street

Lauchlin Currie, an economist and senior official in the administration of President Franklin Roosevelt from 1939 to 1945, spied for the USSR.

Although the evidence was inconclusive at the time, Currie was suspected as a Soviet agent as early as 1939. He adamantly denied the accusation, but in 1945 Soviet-agent-turned-FBI-informant Elizabeth Bentley identified Currie as part of a large espionage ring run by Nathan and Helen Silvermaster in Washington, DC. The Silvermasters used an agent in the US military, William Ullmann, as both a source of information and secret photographer. Ullmann copied documents in the Silvermasters' basement photo laboratory, then passed the undeveloped film to Bentley, the spy ring's courier.

Lauchlin Currie

Before Ullmann became a major in the US Army Air Corps, he was an assistant to Harry Dexter White, another spy for the USSR. When applying for a security clearance early in World War II, Ullmann listed Currie, then at the International Development Corporation, 19 Rector Street, as a character reference.

Currie died in 1993, and any remaining uncertainty about his spying was resolved a few years later. Transcripts of Soviet intelligence cables intercepted during the 1940s were released in 1995, revealing Currie's guilt and NKVD code names of PAGE, CECIL, and VIM.

■ 97. UNSUITED FOR ESPIONAGE

MAP 6 ➤ **Ernest Hemingway apartment:** 1 East 62nd Street

Ernest Hemingway became involved with espionage multiple times throughout his life. Even the NKVD claimed to have recruited the American writer. An impassioned article Hemingway wrote for the left-wing magazine *New Masses* on the government failures in responding to a 1935 hurricane, followed by an antifascist speech he gave while sharing a stage with the CPUSA's Earl Browder, likely caught the NKVD's attention.

The first contact may have been made during the Spanish Civil War in Madrid, where he met legendary Soviet spymaster Alexander Orlov and the two bonded over vodka, caviar, and a mutual love of hunting. Orlov gave the writer safe passage to NKVD guerrilla-training camps of the kind described in *For Whom the Bell Tolls*.

According to Soviet files made public following the Cold War, Hemingway was recruited by Jacob Golos in 1941 in New York and assigned the code

Author Ernest Hemingway volunteered to spy for the United States during World War II.

name ARGO. "I am sure that he will cooperate with us and will do everything he can," Golos reported to Moscow.

In 1942, Hemingway was living on his Cuban estate, Finca Vigía, and volunteered to spy for Washington. A 2012 *Studies in Intelligence* article published by the CIA's Center for the Study of Intelligence described the FBI's response. "Hemingway is the last man, in my estimation, to be used in any such capacity," J. Edgar Hoover wrote. "His judgment is not of the best." Nor did Hemingway have much love for the FBI, which he called "Franco's Bastard Irish" and "the American Gestapo."

Nevertheless, the popular writer found a receptive ear in Ambassador Spruille Braden of the American embassy in Havana. Soon Hemingway was running a small network of informants to hunt fascists. Colorfully nicknamed the Crook Factory, the effort produced little useful intelligence. Unsatisfied, Hemingway sought to get into military action by petitioning the ONI to outfit his boat, the 38-foot *Pilar*, with machine guns, bazookas, hand grenades, and other gear to hunt German subma-rines under the guise of fishing.

In addition to arming his boat, Hemingway envisioned recruiting jai alai players to throw grenades into hatches of submarines once they surfaced. It was a madcap scheme, though US officials reluctantly relented and sent the author off to patrol the seas from the second half of 1942 through most of 1943. By 1944, Hemingway was in France as a war correspondent, where he joined

Although he was reputed to have disliked New York, Hemingway rented an apartment just off Fifth Avenue at 1 East 62nd Street in the late 1950s.

a group of Resistance fighters based outside Paris. He eventually entered the city and, according to self-created legend, "liberated the Ritz."

For its part, the NKVD expressed continued frustration with keeping in touch with its famous author, who seemed to drop them after multiple meetings. An internal NKVD dispatch noted, "Our meetings with 'Argo' in London and Havana were conducted with the aim of studying him and determining his potential for our work. Through the period of his connection with us, 'Argo' did not give us any polit. Information [*sic*], though he repeatedly expressed his desire and willingness to help us. 'Argo' has not been studied thoroughly and is unverified."

In 1959, Hemingway rented an apartment at 1 East 62nd Street, although he disliked New York and typically stayed in hotels, such as the Sherry-Netherland, 781 Fifth Avenue, when visiting or passing through to other destinations. According to some accounts, the apartment may have been rented at the insistence of his fourth wife, Mary Welsh. A persistent New York urban legend asserts Hemingway wrote *The Snows of Kilimanjaro* in the 900-square-foot apartment; in fact, the short story was written twenty-three years earlier. By the late 1950s, Hemingway's health was declining, and in July 1961 he committed suicide at his home in Ketchum, Idaho.

■ 98. MURDER MYSTERY OF A WHITE RUSSIAN

MAP 8 ➤ **Michael Borislavsky murder site:** St. Nicholas Terrace side of the Convent of the Sacred Heart, West 133rd Street and Convent Avenue

On February 24, 1941, Michael Borislavsky left his apartment at 510 West 135th Street for an early evening walk. A former colonel in the Russian Imperial Army, the 60-year-old soldier and engineer had fled his native country shortly following the 1917 revolution. Now a naturalized US citizen, Borislavsky was in contact with the War Department. Press reports stated the Russian engineer was designing an unidentified form of large-scale armament.

In 1941, Russian émigré and US weapons designer Michael Borislavsky was killed near his apartment on West 135th Street by a single gunshot through the eye. Police attributed the murder to a street mugging, a conclusion many questioned.

Borislavsky's body was discovered later that evening, according to *The New York Times*, on the sidewalk on St. Nicholas Terrace, at the rear of the Convent of the Sacred Heart (Convent Avenue at West 133rd Street, now owned by the City College of New York). An examination determined the Russian émigré had been shot, the fatal bullet shattering a lens of his glasses and penetrating an eye.

Within 24 hours, the NYPD announced Borislavsky had been murdered by street thugs. The thieves, police theorized, were attracted by his Kodiak-bear-skin coat and walking stick. According to the police theory, the mugger or muggers panicked after shooting him and fled without stealing any of the victim's possessions, which included a watch and a small amount of money. The shot that killed him, which would seem more the work of an expert marksman than muggers, was dismissed as beginner's luck.

According to friends, Borislavsky was the type of person to put up a fight if accosted. The murder briefly caught the media's attention. Just two weeks earlier, another Soviet defector, Walter Krivitsky, had been found dead in a Washington hotel room. Although that incident was officially ruled a suicide, doubts remained about the true cause of both deaths. No arrests were ever made in either case.

■ 99. WHEN TREASON TURNED A PROFIT

MAP 3 ► **Tempus Import Company:** 119 West 57th Street

Joseph Katz, an aircraft engineer and American citizen, was recruited into the NKVD's Foreign Intelligence Directorate in 1937. For more than a decade, he supervised dozens of agents while managing profitable cover companies that supported Soviet espionage in the United States.

In 1939, Katz, with NKVD money, launched his first business, Meriden Dental Laboratories and Supplies, in Meriden, Connecticut. Five years later he founded the Tempus Import Company at 119 West 57th Street to import leather goods, such as gloves, handbags, and wallets, from South America. He also owned several parking lots, one on West 130th Street.

Katz's wide-ranging contacts included Earl Browder and Bernard Schuster of the CPUSA. He oversaw the clandestine work of Elizabeth Bentley and Harry Gold. He surveilled Walter Krivitsky during the high-profile defector's time in New York City and Trotskyites in the Socialist Workers Party. Katz once installed a listening device in the home of the SWP leader, James Cannon, to monitor conversations with Leon Trotsky and others.

Katz came to the attention of the FBI in November of 1945 when Elizabeth Bentley described a man she met with in 1944 and 1945 but knew only as Jack. Her recollections were vague; she remembered Jack as colorless and nondescript. But when the FBI tentatively identified Katz by name in 1947,

Bentley confirmed that he was Jack from a photo.

Bentley may not have fully understood the potential danger Jack posed. When the NKVD's New York station contemplated assassinating the increasingly erratic Bentley in 1945, Katz was chosen as the best person to arrange the murder. Among the methods considered were poisoning her food or cosmetics, using slow-acting poisons over a longer term, or simply having an assassin stab her at home at night. Katz balked at the latter idea because Bentley was tall, healthy, and strong. The outcome of such an attack would be uncertain, he reasoned.

In the end, Moscow Center vetoed the assassination plans, a decision the NKVD may have later regretted. As feared, Bentley switched sides and contacted the FBI in August 1945, making a full confession on November 7 that revealed the names of more than 150 Soviet agents, including 37 federal employees.

During his time in the United States, Katz used many code names, such as STUKACH (meaning WHISTLER), DUGLAS (meaning DOUGLAS), and INKS (meaning X), which appeared in 26 partially decrypted VENONA cables. It was later revealed that both Katz and Bentley received the Order of the Red Star in absentia during a secret ceremony in Moscow in 1944. By the time the FBI gathered sufficient evidence to arrest Katz, the NKGB, successor to the NKVD, had relocated its spy to France to protect him and his knowledge of Soviet intelligence operations.

Katz fled to Israel in 1951. He died there in 2004, leaving an estate in excess of $3 million.

■ 100. SLEEPING WITH MANY ENEMIES

MAP 7 ➤ **The Majestic:** 115 Central Park West

Martha Dodd, the daughter of American ambassador William E. Dodd, arrived in Germany in 1933 and soon began an affair with Gen. Ernst Udet, a decorated officer of the German air force. Another of her lovers, Ernst Hanfstaengl, an American aide to Adolf Hitler, tried unsuccessfully to promote an unlikely romantic liaison between Dodd and his boss. When no romantic chemistry materialized between the diplomat's daughter and the Fürher, she began a

Martha Dodd and Alfred Stern

Known as an "art deco masterpiece," the Majestic features Central Park views and fit the status and lifestyle of a young, well-off couple like Martha Dodd and Alfred Stern in the 1930s.

passionate affair with Boris Vinogradov, an NKVD officer operating under the cover of a press attaché in the Soviet embassy.

Moscow Center encouraged Vinogradov to pursue the romantic relationship and gave Dodd the code name LIZA. The affair paid off. Dodd informed the Soviets of secret embassy business and provided details of her father's official reports to the State Department. The couple eventually separated when Dodd returned to America. Vinogradov, recalled to Moscow, was caught up in Stalin's purges and executed.

Back in New York, Dodd married a wealthy stockbroker, Alfred Stern, took up residence in a penthouse of the Majestic, an art deco masterpiece at 115 Central Park West, threw lavish parties, and dabbled in liberal politics. However, the NKVD did not forget about their potentially valuable agent and put her to work. On one hand they assessed her as "gifted and clever" but also realized she "needed constant control over her behavior." According to NKVD cables quoted in *Haunted Wood* by Allen Weinstein and Alexander Vassiliev, Moscow Center viewed her with open disdain as "a typical representative of American bohemia, a sexually decayed woman ready to sleep with any handsome man."

Eventually, Dodd brought her husband into the ring and the couple took an active role by providing support functions for the Soviet espionage apparatus, acting as spotters of potential recruits, and maintaining a substantial bank account for laundering money through front companies, including a music business with a record label.

When called to testify before the Senate Sub-Committee on Un-American Activities in 1956, Dodd and her husband fled the United States, eventually turning up in Mexico, Prague, Cuba, and Moscow. Martha Dodd died in Prague in 1990.

■ 101. PRODUCER-DIRECTOR, DOUBLE AGENT

MAP 7 ➤ **Boris Morros residence:** 50 Riverside Drive

A musical prodigy in czarist Russia, Boris Morros claimed that as a child he played the cello in a performance for the Romanovs. After the 1917 revolution, he immigrated to the United States and became musical director for live performances of the Paramount Theatre chain and then for films such as *Stagecoach* (1939) and the *Bulldog Drummond* series.

Even as Morros worked on popular movies through the 1930s, Soviet intelligence used threats against his family in St. Petersburg to coerce him into hiring Soviet agents as talent scouts for Paramount. The talent-scout cover enabled the spies to travel freely as representatives of a recognized company in a glamorous industry. Morros and his Soviet secret police contact met on the first Tuesday of each month for a time at 58 West 58th Street and later at the Simón Bolívar monument at the Sixth Avenue entrance to Central Park.

Then, in the early 1940s, Morros was instructed to work with two Americans, Alfred Stern and Martha Dodd. The well-to-do married couple would be his partners in a record company venture, American Recording Artists, located in 30 Rockefeller Plaza. Stern supplied the money while Morros offered industry credibility for the commercial cover. That the couple knew virtually nothing about the music business was insignificant as far as Soviet officials were concerned, but not to Morros.

Trouble soon arose. A song Morros wanted to purchase, "Chattanooga Choo Choo," was vetoed by Stern because of its "vulgar title." Stern's reject went on to become the first song to receive a Gold Record for RCA Victor. According to Morros, a move into the potentially lucrative record-production business was stalled by Stern with the ill-advised

Double agent Boris Morros lived a comfortable, music-mogul lifestyle in his Riverside Drive residence.

Morros met his Russian contact at the Simón Bolívar statue at the Sixth Avenue entrance to Central Park.

purchase of antiquated and largely useless equipment. They also passed on the opportunity to purchase the company that created Muzak.

The company's only hit was "Nobody's Home on the Range" (1944) by Joe Reichman and His Orchestra. The novelty song featured such memorable lines as "Gramma doesn't ride her geldin' / She's out at Lockheed weldin'" and "Everyone's in the battle / punching time clocks 'stead of cattle."

Meanwhile, Martha Dodd presented problems of a different kind with her unrestrained habit of seducing men who caught her eye, including her NKVD handlers. Authors Herbert Romerstein and Eric Breindel recount in their 2000 *The Venona Secrets: Exposing Soviet Espionage and America's Traitors* that Bennett Cerf, then head of Random House, quipped about Dodd's book *Through Embassy Eyes* (1938) "that if each man she had been to bed with had bought a copy, the book would be a great success."

In a life demanding constant travel between California and New York, Morros's preferred New York address was the Sherry-Netherland, 781 Fifth Avenue, but by 1947 he had enough of both the NKVD and the Sterns. He contacted the FBI, became a double agent, and reported on Soviet intelligence operations during the next decade. In January 1957, the FBI moved on the spy ring and arrested brothers Jack Soble and Dr. Robert Soblen (their last names were spelled differently), along with Soble's wife, Myra. Stern and Dodd had fled the United States in 1956.

Morros described the operation in his memoir *My Ten Years as a Counterspy* (1959), which became a film, *Man on a String* (1960), starring Ernest Borgnine and Kerwin Mathews. Morros was living at 50 Riverside Drive at the time of his death in 1963.

■ 102. DENOUNCED AND PROMOTED

MAP 7 ➤ **Vasily Zarubin residence:** 2788 Broadway, apt. 4-A

Vasily Mikhailovich Zarubin, the senior NKVD officer stationed in the United States from 1941 to 1944, operated under the aliases of Vasily Zublin and Edward Joseph Herber. His multiple code names included MAKSIM, LUCHENKO, PETER, and COOPER. This was Zarubin's second tour in the United States. He replaced another intelligence officer, Gaik Ovakimian, who was arrested by the FBI in June 1941, then swapped for several Americans the following month.

Vasily Zarubin

Zarubin was sent to America at a time when the German army was advancing on Moscow and the Soviet Union's prospect of stopping the invasion seemed unlikely. Stalin, fearing President Roosevelt might pursue a separate peace agreement with Germany, demanded the most current intelligence on US policy.

Zarubin was described by those who knew him as capable of either charm or menace, as circumstances demanded. Zarubin's wife, Elizabeth (code name HELEN), also an experienced intelligence officer, joined him in the United States. The couple resided at 2788 Broadway, apartment 4-A, in the 1930s, then moved to the Soviet School, also known as the Russian Aid Society, 349 West 86th Street.

To many of the NKVD officers in the New York *rezidentura*, Zarubin was unpopular and criticized for relying only on his wife along with a few hand-picked NKVD officers he brought with him. The VENONA intercepts revealed he was once denounced in a cable to Moscow for "crudeness, general lack of manners, use of street language and obscenities, carelessness in his work, and repugnant secretiveness."

For some of his time in New York, Soviet spy chief Vasily Zarubin lived with his wife at the Soviet School on West 86th Street.

Zarubin came to the attention of the FBI when he traveled to California to meet with Steven Nelson, a member of the CPUSA. Nelson headed a small counterintelligence group for the party working to root out spies and informants that had infiltrated the California branch. Zarubin's first trip to locate Nelson was unsuccessful, and his misfortune continued during a second trip when his meeting in Nelson's home was captured by the FBI's hidden microphones. The subsequent investigation discovered that Zarubin "organizes secret radio stations, prepares counterfeit documents, obtains industrial and military information for transmittal to the Soviet Union."

Zarubin and Elizabeth were again denounced and accused of contact with the FBI in a 1944 letter sent from the *rezidentura* directly to Stalin. All those involved were recalled to Moscow. After an investigation, the accusations were found to be groundless, and the accuser was sent to a labor camp. In the end, Zarubin's career prospered, and he became the deputy chief of foreign intelligence in Moscow.

■ 103. FATHER OF THE ATOMIC BOMB: A SPY?

MAP 7 ➤ **J. Robert Oppenheimer childhood home:** 155 Riverside Drive

Native New Yorker and physicist J. Robert Oppenheimer directed research and design for the atomic bomb at the Los Alamos Laboratory

Physicist J. Robert Oppenheimer, who led the Manhattan Project, grew up in a luxury apartment on Riverside Drive. Oppenheimer's security clearance was revoked following the war when his leftist politics and associations with known CPUSA members were revealed.

during World War II. His childhood home was the entire 11th floor of a Riverside Drive apartment building. His mother was a painter and his father a successful businessman in the fabric industry. Their brilliant son graduated from Harvard in 1925, then studied for his doctorate at the Cavendish Laboratory in Cambridge, England, and in Göttingen, Germany, receiving it in 1927. His arrival in Europe coincided with the development of the revolutionary theory of quantum mechanics.

When the Manhattan Project was created in 1942, Oppenheimer was a recognized advanced theoretical physicist already involved in exploring the possibility of an atomic bomb. Despite his past secret membership in the Communist Party, he was appointed director of the Los Alamos Laboratory and led the team that developed the bomb.

In 1944, Oppenheimer was named in a secret message to NKVD chief Lavrentiy Beria describing Soviet efforts to obtain information about the design of the atomic bomb and specifically uranium-related problems. The letter noted that Professor Oppenheimer was an unlisted member of the apparat of Earl Browder, the head of the CPUSA. Oppenheimer, it recounted, "provided cooperation in access to research for several of our tested sources." Because of the sensitivity of the project, the NKVD sought to protect Oppenheimer by severing his contacts with the CPUSA.

A deliberate spy or not, Oppenheimer, from the Soviet perspective, provided valuable technical intelligence and access for other "sources of information." However, he was not the only family member aiding the Soviet Union. His younger brother, Frank, a nuclear physicist and scientist on the Manhattan Project, was also a source for Soviet intelligence. The younger Oppenheimer was a member of the CPUSA and is mentioned in the VENONA intercepts with the code names RAY and CARL.

Robert Oppenheimer, who clashed with others in government regarding development of the hydrogen bomb and nuclear weapons policy, had his security clearance revoked in 1954 and was called to testify before the HUAC. Later his professional reputation was recognized when he received the Atomic Energy Commission's 1963 Enrico Fermi Award based on scientific achievement.

■ 104. THE ATOMIC SPIES

MAP 4 ➤ **Julius and Ethel Rosenberg residence:** 10 Monroe Street, apt. GE-11

The most widely recognized of the USSR's "atomic spies" were Julius Rosenberg (code names LIBERAL and ANTENNA) and his wife, Ethel, both dedicated communists who lived at 10 Monroe Street, apartment GE-11, in the Knickerbocker Village housing development on the Lower East Side. Julius Rosenberg was recruited by Soviet intelligence officer Jacob Golos in 1942, and in turn Julius recruited Ethel in 1944. The couple served as couriers, cutouts, and recruiters.

The case of Julius and Ethel Rosenberg made sensational headlines at the time of the spies' arrest and eventual execution.

While the Rosenbergs conducted much of their espionage from their apartment, Julius used two additional apartments, at 65 Morton Street and 131 East 7th Street, for photographing and copying documents. Known as the "atomic spies" when they were arrested in 1950, the couple was convicted of espionage in 1951 and executed in June 1953 at the Sing Sing Correctional Facility in Ossining, New York.

The arrest of the Rosenbergs and their coconspirators prompted outcries of anti-Semitism against the US legal system, and conspiracy theories thrived. Controversy surrounding the case continued for four decades until the declassification of the VENONA materials in 1995 provided conclusive evidence implicating the Rosenbergs.

The Rosenbergs lived in Knickerbocker Village, a housing development located between the Manhattan Bridge and the Brooklyn Bridge in Lower Manhattan.

A SPY'S DECADES-LATE CONFESSION

The guilt or innocence of Soviet spy Morton Sobell (code name SENYA) was debated for decades. During World War II, the Stuyvesant High School and City College graduate worked at the Reeves Instrument Corporation, 215 East 91st Street, a contractor for ballistic-missile defense systems. Following the war, he came under suspicion as part of the Rosenberg spy ring and fled to Mexico. Sobell was eventually returned to the United States, tried, and convicted and served 18 years in prison. During a 2008 *New York Times* interview, he finally confessed that he had spied for the USSR. Ten years later, at the age of 101, Sobell told the *Wall Street Journal*, "I bet on the wrong horse." He died in December 2018 in Manhattan.

■ 105. ALL IN THE FAMILY

MAP 4 ➤ **David Greenglass residence:** 265 Rivington Street

David Greenglass, a US Army sergeant, was a key operative in the "atomic spy ring" that stole secrets from the Manhattan Project for the Soviet Union. Born in 1922 on Manhattan's Lower East Side, Greenglass married Ruth Printz in 1942. The couple shared left-leaning beliefs and were members of the Young Communist League, which had an office at 799 Broadway. Greenglass joined the army in 1943 and a year later was assigned to the Los Alamos Laboratory as a machinist for the Manhattan Project. To obtain his security clearance, he omitted mention of his prior membership in the Young Communist League.

David Greenglass

Greenglass's sister, Ethel, was married to Julius Rosenberg, a longtime NKVD agent who, when he learned that his brother-in-law was working on the Manhattan Project, recommended the Greenglass couple be recruited as spies. Ruth (code name OSA) was to maintain their Albuquerque, New Mexico, residence at 209 High Street NE (today the Spy House B&B) as a safe house for photographing documents. David, an eager recruit code-named KALIBR, wrote to Ruth: "My darling, I most certainly will be glad to be part of the community project [espionage] that Julius and his friends [the Russians] have in mind." David passed his secrets to a courier from Philadelphia, Harry Gold, or directly to a Soviet official in New York City.

In 1946, Greenglass was honorably discharged and opened a small machine shop, G&R Engineering, at 300 East 2nd Street in partnership with Julius Rosenberg. It seemed the ring had not been detected, but when Soviet agent Klaus Fuchs was arrested in 1950, he revealed the name of his New York City courier, Harry Gold. The Soviets informed Julius of Fuchs's arrest and gave Greenglass and Ruth $5,000 to escape to Mexico. Instead, they went to the Catskill Mountains in New York and sought legal advice.

Ruth Greenglass

The FBI investigation of Gold led to the arrest of David Greenglass in June 1950. When questioned, Greenglass identified his brother-in-law Julius Rosenberg as a spy while denying that his sister, Ethel, was involved. Later Greenglass testified that she typed his notes for the Soviets.

At trial, Greenglass recounted giving details of the atom bomb implosion process to the Soviets and revealed that Julius passed designs

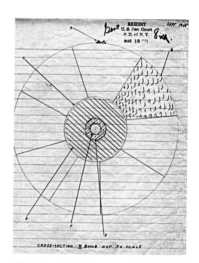

This drawing by David Greenglass provided the USSR a rudimentary illustration of the implosion process vital to the atomic bomb.

for the classified artillery proximity fuze to his Soviet handlers. He also admitted to stealing a few ounces of uranium-238 from Los Alamos years earlier but said he had thrown it into the East River in 1950 to rid his residence, 265 Rivington Street, of evidence.

David Greenglass was sentenced to a 15-year prison sentence and released in 1960. For many years prior to his death in 2014, he lived with his wife, Ruth and their children, at 130-73 228th Street in Laurelton, Queens, under assumed names. Ruth died in 2008.

■ 106. SECRETS SERVED AT THE AUTOMAT

MAP 3 ➤ **Horn & Hardart Automat:** 1391 Broadway (now a drugstore)

Although called the "atomic spies," Julius and Ethel Rosenberg, along with their coconspirators, delivered other secrets to Soviet intelligence as well. In all, an estimated 20,000 pages of nonatomic material was given to their handlers, including technical details on an advanced radar system and America's first jet fighter.

Passage of one of the most highly classified secrets happened on Christmas Eve 1944. That night, Julius Rosenberg (LIBERAL) met with his Soviet handler, Aleksandr Feklisov (KALISTRAT), at the Horn & Hardart Automat, 1391 Broadway at West 38th Street. The ubiquitous budget eatery chain was then considered a New York staple. Large, anonymous, open around the clock, and often with multiple entrances, the Automat was an attractive meeting place for spies.

The two men exchanged packages in what would have looked like ordinary Christmas gift giving to anyone watching. Feklisov gave his spy three boxes. One contained an Omega stainless steel watch for Rosenberg, in the second package was a handbag for his wife, Ethel, and the third held a teddy bear for Michael, the couple's only son at the time.

The single package that Rosenberg proffered in return was significantly heavier than the watch, handbag, or teddy bear, and far more valuable. Inside was a proximity fuze, one of America's most closely guarded weapon secrets of the war. Stolen by Rosenberg from the US Army Signal Corps Engineering Laboratories at Fort Monmouth, New Jersey, the 15-pound device represented a major technological breakthrough in armaments. When mounted on an antiaircraft shell, it employed a rudimentary onboard radar system to detonate as it passed near an aircraft. By eliminating the need for a direct hit, the proximity fuze rendered antiaircraft batteries far more deadly.

Sixteen years later, on May 1, 1960, an advanced Soviet version of the proximity fuze received by Feklisov at the automat was part of the system used to shoot down CIA pilot Francis Gary Powers's U-2 aircraft as it made an overflight of the USSR.

■ 107. TEENAGE PRODIGY AND ATOMIC SPY

MAP 8 ➤ **Theodore Hall family home:** 725 West 172nd Street

American physicist Theodore Hall was a science prodigy and Soviet spy. As a teenage scientist and the youngest member of the Manhattan Project technical team, he provided the Soviet Union with details of the Fat Man bomb and plutonium-purification processes.

Hall was born in 1925 in Far Rockaway, Queens, though the family moved to 725 West 172nd Street in Washington Heights, where he spent his youth. He attended Public School 173, 306 Fort Washington Avenue, then briefly Columbia University before graduating from Harvard University at age 18. He then began working on the Manhattan Project in January 1944.

In October 1944, Hall attempted to make an initial contact with Earl Browder at the CPUSA headquarters in New York City but was unable to get past his secretary. Undeterred, Hall and his Harvard roommate, Saville Sax, went to the Amtorg offices several days later at 238 West 28th Street and expressed Hall's willingness to pass Manhattan Project secrets to the Soviet Union.

Their initial meeting was with Sergei Kurnakow (code name BEK), a mid-level NKGB officer working under journalistic cover. Sax became Hall's courier and later met Kurnakow at the Soviet consulate at 7 East 61st Street to deliver an initial report identifying scientists at Los Alamos and the basic science behind the bomb. The NKGB station chief, Anatoly Yatskov, who lived at 3 West 108th Street, received the report, and Hall was assigned the code name MLAD (meaning YOUTH). Sax was assigned the code name STAR.

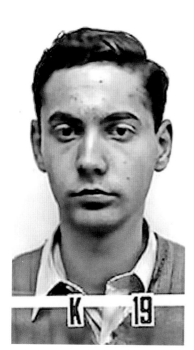

Theodore Hall

Theodore Hall, a physics prodigy, lived on West 172nd Street in Washington Heights as a young child. While still in his teens, he began working on the Manhattan Project and became an important spy.

Sax and Hall were initially so apprehensive about FBI surveillance that the only place they deemed safe to talk was in a rented rowboat in the middle of the Central Park lake. Sax communicated with Hall in New Mexico via mail. To evade the postal censors, the clever young spies employed a private book code they developed using Walt Whitman's *Leaves of Grass*.

Anatoly Yatskov, depicted on a Soviet stamp

The Soviet *rezident* in New York, Anatoly Yatskov, who operated under diplomatic cover, controlled some of the USSR's most valuable Cold War spies, including the Rosenbergs, Harry Gold, and Theodore Hall. Yatskov lived in this unassuming apartment house on West 108th Street.

Sax traveled to Los Alamos to receive information until the spring of 1945, when Lona Cohen replaced him. Though the Soviets had other agents, such as Klaus Fuchs, at Los Alamos supplying secrets, Hall was the only person to provide details of the atomic bomb's design. In 1946, Hall attended the University of Chicago, where he received his master's and doctoral degrees, and continued to provide information to the Soviet Union about a follow-on generation of nuclear weapons.

Hall was never prosecuted for his espionage. The VENONA decrypts provided some information about MLAD, but his only contact with the FBI was in 1951. Eventually Hall confessed his actions during a televised 1999 interview for a Cold War documentary: "I decided to give atomic secrets to the Russians because it seemed to me that it was important that there should be no monopoly, which could turn one nation into a menace and turn it loose on the world as . . . Nazi Germany [had] developed. There seemed to be only one answer to what one should do. The right thing to do was to act to break the American monopoly."

Hall died in 1999 in Cambridge, England, at the age 74.

■ 108. THE ALL-AMERICAN SOVIET SPY

MAP 4 ➤ **GRU station at the Raven Electric Company:** 889 Broadway

Among the spies most damaging to America's national security in the 20th century was George Koval. His name is not widely recognized, although the secrets he stole directly advanced the development and testing of the Soviet atomic weapon.

Koval was born in 1913 in Sioux City, Iowa, to parents who had emigrated from Russia three years earlier. In 1932, during the Great Depression, the family returned to the USSR, where Koval showed himself to be a bright student, graduated from the Mendeleev Institute of Chemical Technology in Moscow, and was recruited by Soviet military intelligence. They could not have asked for a better spy candidate. Koval spoke unaccented American English and understood American culture. "He played baseball and played it well," a former friend remembered.

Soviet spy George Koval worked at Raven Electric, a defense subcontractor that also served as a cover for the GRU operations, located at 889 Broadway.

Leaving his wife in the USSR, Koval (code name DELMAR) returned to the United States around 1940 and lived at 3470 Cannon Place in the Bronx while attending classes at Columbia University. His primary job, however, as deputy *rezident* of the secret GRU station, was performed under the cover of employment at the Raven Electric Company, 889 Broadway. A defense contractor in the Flatiron District that supplied equipment to General Electric, Raven provided Koval with a deferment that protected him from the military draft until February 1943.

By the time he was eventually drafted, Koval had moved to 3451 Giles Place, the Bronx. His initial testing indicated an exceptionally high IQ, which gained him a posting at the Army Specialized Training Program based in the former Hebrew Orphan Asylum of New York, Amsterdam Avenue between West 136th and 138th Streets.

Older than most of the other students, Koval sailed through the program, no doubt assisted by his previous training in the USSR. He was subsequently assigned to the top-secret Manhattan Project and worked at several locations, including Oak Ridge, Tennessee; Dayton, Ohio; and Philadelphia. Koval passed classified information to a yet-to-be-identified courier known only by the code name CLYDE.

Following the war, Koval enrolled in the City College of New York Engineering School, West 137th Street

APPLICATION DENIED!

George Koval lived long enough to see the breakup of the Soviet Union. Before his death in 2006, Koval is reported to have applied for Social Security benefits through the US embassy in Moscow. The application was denied.

and Convent Avenue (today the Grove School of Engineering), and received a bachelor's degree in electrical engineering. He came under scrutiny in 1948 after US counterintelligence agents discovered a story about the Koval family in the Soviet publication *Rossiiskaia Gazeta*, which described a happy immigrant family from America. Koval then fled the country, traveled to Poland as a tourist, and eventually reemerged in Moscow.

Koval's role in stealing atomic secrets came to light slowly. In 2002, a book appeared in Russia titled *The GRU and the Atomic Bomb*, by Vladimir Lota, which referenced the spy only by code name. Then, in 2007, Vladimir Putin posthumously recognized Koval, a private in the Soviet army, with Hero of the Russian Federation honors and revealed the identity of DELMAR.

■ 109. THE PHYSICS OF ESPIONAGE

MAP 7 ➤ **Klaus Fuchs residence:** 128 West 77th Street

British physicist and Soviet spy Klaus Fuchs held top-security clearances when working on the Manhattan Project.

German-born physicist and naturalized UK citizen Klaus Fuchs (code names REST, CHARLES, and BRAS) spied for the Soviets first in England, then in the United States, and then again in England. He lived for a time at the Hotel Taft (now the Michelangelo), 152 West 51st Street, then at the Barbizon-Plaza Hotel (now the Trump Parc), 106 Central Park South. In New York City, Fuchs worked on gaseous-diffusion theory as a consultant to the Kellex Corporation, headquartered in the Woolworth Building, 233 Broadway, and later out of the British Mission of Supply at 37 Wall Street. By February 1944, he had moved into a furnished brownstone at 128 West 77th Street.

In the previous years, Fuchs passed information about America's top-secret nuclear program in Oak Ridge, Tennessee, to the Soviets and, when reassigned to the facility in Los Alamos, New Mexico, continued spying. Not until 1949, after he returned to Britain to work on that country's nuclear program, did Fuchs come under suspicion by US and British counterintelligence. During interrogation by William James Skardon of MI5, Britain's internal security service, in 1950, Fuchs confessed to espionage.

Since the Soviet Union was considered an ally during World War II, Fuchs could not be convicted of high treason, a capital offense, but was found guilty of a lesser charge and sentenced to 14 years in prison. He was released in 1959, immigrated to East Germany, and became director of that country's Institute of Nuclear Physics, a post he held until retiring in 1979. Fuchs died in 1988.

■ 110. THE INDISPENSABLE MIDDLEMAN

MAP I I ➤ **Harry Gold meeting site:** Newsstand (no longer exists) beneath the 90th Street Station at Elmhurst Avenue, Queens

Dr. Klaus Fuchs was arrested in England on charges of espionage in 1950. He confessed that while in New York City during World War II, he passed US atomic secrets to the Soviet Union on four occasions through a courier the FBI later identified as Harry Gold.

When questioned by the FBI, Gold revealed his code name was GOOSE and that he had been recruited by the NKVD in 1934. From 1944 to 1946, he served as a courier, passing atomic secrets from Fuchs and other agents to his handler, JOHN. The FBI subsequently identified JOHN as Anatoli A. Yakovlev, the former Soviet vice-consul based in New York City. Information from Gold also led the FBI to arrest David Greenglass and Julius and Ethel Rosenberg.

During questioning, Gold detailed the tradecraft training he received. The NKVD taught that meetings with agents were preceded by recognition signals: an object such as a piece of paper, paroles (a code phrase in the form of a greeting and often a physical attribution such as wearing gloves), and use of pseudonyms. Two different signals, one verbal and one visual, were required before each meeting could begin.

Harry Gold

Gold was to be available for meetings in New York City on the same day and time each month. One such scheduled meeting was at 10:00 a.m. on the first Sunday of each month at a newsstand beneath the elevated subway platform at 90th Street and Elmhurst Avenue. For a visual recognition signal, Gold was to be smoking a pipe with a curved stem, while his contact was to be smoking a cigar. If business was to be transacted, one man would ask, "Can you direct me to the Horace Harding Hospital?" Gold would reply, "Yes, I am going that way. Come along with me." Only if both paroles were correct would the meeting continue.

A newsstand once located under the elevated-train platform in Elmhurst, Queens, was a regular meeting site for Harry Gold and his Soviet handler.

Another meeting in 1945 between Gold and Yakovlev, regarding a trip to New Mexico to meet Greenglass, took place at the Volks Bar on Third Avenue and East 42nd Street. They also met in the Ferris Wheel Bar in the basement of the Henry Hudson Hotel at 353 West 57th Street (today the Hudson Hotel), 358 West 58th Street.

Gold pleaded guilty to espionage and was sentenced to a 30-year prison sentence in 1951. He was released on parole in 1965 and died seven years later in Philadelphia.

■ 111. SMALL MAGAZINE, BIG PROBLEMS

MAP 5 ➤ *Amerasia* **offices:** 225 Fifth Avenue, 11th floor

Amerasia, a left-leaning journal covering American-Asian foreign affairs, had a small circulation of 2,000 subscribers in the 1940s. The magazine's cofounders were Philip Jaffe, who had made his fortune from Wallace Brown Inc., a company that enlisted housewives and Boy Scouts to sell greeting cards door-to-door, and Frederick Vanderbilt Field, great-great-grandson of railroad titan Cornelius Vanderbilt.

The journal, primarily a vanity operation of the two wealthy men, espoused Marxist doctrine and would probably have gone unnoticed had it not published verbatim sections of a top-secret 1945 OSS report on British policy in Thailand. In response, the OSS assigned Frank Bielaski, its director of investigations, to the case. On March 11, 1945, Bielaski and four other agents surreptitiously entered *Amerasia's* offices on the 11th floor of 225 Fifth Avenue. A methodical search uncovered more than 300 classified documents from

A small-circulation journal, *Amerasia*, based at 225 Fifth Avenue, set off a firestorm when it published verbatim sections of a top-secret OSS report.

the OSS, the ONI, G-2, the State Department, and British intelligence as well as photographic document-copying equipment.

The FBI entered the case, and the editors were put under surveillance. On June 6, 1945, with President Truman's approval, six individuals were arrested. As the case moved forward, however, procedural and prosecutorial problems arose. The initial entry into the journal's office had been made without a warrant, as were the subsequent wiretaps by the FBI. When prosecutors could not definitively link *Amerasia* or its editors to the USSR, four of those arrested were not charged. The remaining two were charged with possessing stolen documents and paid relatively small fines. Not long afterward, the journal closed.

Nevertheless, the case stubbornly lingered for over a decade and was cited as example of the government's tolerance of communist sympathizers, if not outright spies. In 1950, Sen. Joseph McCarthy pointed to the *Amerasia* case as evidence the country was flooded with Soviet agents.

5

FASCISM, COMMUNISM, AND WORLD WAR II

(1933–1945)

When German fascism enveloped Europe and Japanese imperialism rose in Asia, New York again became a clandestine battlefield for England and Germany and now Japan. From Midtown's luxury hotels and restaurants to tree-lined streets of the outer boroughs, foreign spies gathered intelligence, recruited agents, and sought to influence American opinion. Nazi Germany sponsored pro-German societies to support Hitler's government and promote American isolationist sentiments. Britain, through its New York–based BSC, sought support from the Franklin D. Roosevelt administration for financial aid and war materials. Japan recruited spies for its war effort. Each country saw intelligence operations in New York as pivotal to its individual strategic interests.

In the spring of 1941, President Roosevelt authorized the first civilian US national intelligence structure, the Office of the Coordinator of Information (COI), under William Donovan. The COI, authorized to collect and analyze information from across the government, became the forerunner of the Office of Strategic Services (OSS). After 1941, in a war against German fascism and Japanese imperialism, the OSS and other US intelligence organizations, such as the FBI and the ONI, drew on the talent and patriotism of thousands of New

Yorkers, including its artists, socialites, immigrants, academics, Wall Street titans, longshoremen, and writers. Even crime bosses and felons who possessed specialized skills needed for the war effort were recruited.

After the war, the OSS was disbanded, and most of its officers and staff returned to their civilian professions, while a few continued working in government intelligence positions that would form the backbone of the CIA. For some, the new United Nations headquarters, built on the edge of the East River, rose as a shared international vision for lasting peace. For others, UN missions in New York provided foreign governments a new avenue of cover for spies that made the city an even more significant and enduring center of international espionage.

■ 112. WRITER, POET, SOLDIER, SPY

MAP 4 ➤ **Edwin Emerson residence:** 215 East 15th Street

Edwin Emerson acted as Hitler's representative and the emissary for the National Socialist German Workers' Party in America in the 1930s. His grand mission was to unite the disparate Nazi supporters in New York City and throughout the country.

Emerson was born in Germany of American parents, graduated from Harvard, and spent his early years as a soldier of fortune, writer, war correspondent, journalist, editor, secret agent, historian, poet, playwright, scholar, and lecturer. In 1918, he was accused by the president of Guatemala of being a German spy and in 1922 and 1923 was expelled from Austria and Switzerland, respectively, for engaging in subversive activity.

In 1933, he became the principal Nazi propagandist in America and the editor of the German-language paper *Amerikas Deutsche Post*, the

Edwin Emerson

Col. Edwin Emerson, who acted as Hitler's emissary and a propagandist for the National Socialist German Workers' Party, lived at several New York addresses, including here at 215 East 15th Street.

first pro–National Socialist publication in the United States. A year later he had a personal meeting with Hitler.

Emerson lived at 215 East 15th Street and operated from an office at 17 Battery Place, room 1923. Propaganda from Germany was sent to Emerson through the postal system or smuggled into the United States by courier. Emerson's couriers included Guenther Orgell of 606 West 115th Street and Frank Mutschinski of 116 Garland Court, Brooklyn.

■ 113. SEX, SPIES, AND SECRETS

MAP 12 ➤ **William Lonkowski and Senta de Wanger residence:** 83 Lincoln Boulevard, Hempstead, Long Island

William Lonkowski, an agent of Germany's Abwehr military intelligence service, used a small ring of spies to steal some of America's most secret aircraft designs in the early 1930s. An engineer and aircraft designer, Lonkowski worked at the Ireland Aircraft Corporation on Long Island in 1927. His code name, SEX, was a play on one of his many aliases, William Sexton.

SEX recruited agents from among German American workers at the aircraft plant. As the agents were transferred to other plants in the normal course of business, the range of secrets accessible to Lonkowski only increased. By 1934, his network could provide answers to almost any of the military questions asked of them by the Abwehr. Eventually Lonkowski became a reporter for the popular German aviation magazine *Luftreise*, which provided an ideal cover for his espionage on visits to US aircraft plants.

In 1935, Lonkowski and his wife moved into a Long Island residence at 83 Lincoln Boulevard in Hempstead, owned by Senta de Wanger. Lonkowski installed a private telephone line, a luxury at the time, and built a secret darkroom for microfilming documents.

Lonkowski used the fast German luxury liners crossing the Atlantic to transport his stolen military secrets. On each ship the Abwehr stationed couriers—*forschers*—working under the cover of steward or engineer. A prearranged set of signals ensured that the secrets were passed to the correct individual. On the other side of the Atlantic, other Abwehr couriers, called *Umleitungsstelle*, took possession of the material and rushed it to Hamburg or Berlin.

Lonkowskis' landlady, de Wanger, also operated a large liquor store at 330 Clinton Street in Hempstead and previously owned an interior decorating firm at 7 Park Avenue in Manhattan. After the Lonkowskis moved in, de Wanger privately questioned how the new German boarder could maintain his lavish lifestyle on a reporter's salary. The truth was revealed when Mrs. Lonkowski got drunk and spilled the family secret that her husband was selling US military secrets to Germany.

Indignant at the thought, de Wanger told them both to leave the house. William Lonkowski retaliated by threatening to have de Wanger's parents in Stuttgart, Germany, arrested and put into a concentration camp unless she cooperated. Afraid and bewildered, de Wanger reluctantly became a part-time courier for the spy network, shuttling packages of information to couriers on the German liners *Europa* and *Deutschland* when they docked at New York City.

In September 1935, evidence surfaced of Lonkowski's spy operations when a guard stopped and queried him about a violin case he was carrying as he boarded the *Europa* at Pier 86 in Manhattan. The guard, a violin enthusiast, had been simply curious about the instrument, but inside the case he discovered strips of microfilm and aircraft drawings. After an unproductive round of questioning by authorities, Lonkowski was released and told to return the next morning to answer more questions.

Predictably Lonkowski pulled his money from the bank that day, borrowed a car, and fled to Canada, where he boarded a German freighter for the return trip to the homeland. US investigators inexplicably failed to pursue the matter and missed an opportunity to break up the spy ring he left behind.

■ 114. THE CANARY FLEW THE COOP

MAP 6 ➤ Ignatz Griebl residence and office: 56 East 87th Street

Dr. Ignatz Theodor Griebl was a German American gynecologist and spymaster based in Yorkville, a largely German community on Manhattan's Upper East Side. Griebl had obtained American citizenship after arriving in 1928 and became a first lieutenant in the US Army Medical Corps Reserve. Griebl's medical practice flourished among wealthy German American women visiting his distinctive office in a beaux arts building at 56 East 87th Street. The office doubled as his residence and featured a large portrait of Field Marshal Paul von Hindenburg.

In early 1934, Griebl wrote a letter to German propaganda minister Joseph Goebbels volunteering to spy. The letter was passed to the Gestapo and eventually the Abwehr. The volunteer was accepted and assigned agent number A.2339 and the code name ILBERG. He became head of a German spy network in New York responsible for recruiting other German agents, collecting their information, and passing it to Abwehr couriers.

Griebl's activities eventually came to the attention of the FBI following the arrest of German spy Gunter Gustav Rumrich (code name CROWN) in 1938. Rumrich, improbably posing as US Secretary of State Cordell Hull, was apprehended after attempting to acquire blank American passports by phone from a Grand Central Terminal phone booth. When questioned, Rumrich almost immediately implicated Griebl.

The subsequent investigation included an early use of a polygraph. Griebl and six other suspects were questioned using the device and, to the FBI's surprise, the doctor "sang like a canary." He betrayed other agents, including Otto Voss and Werner Gudenberg, and described the German government's support of his spy ring. The FBI examiner later stated that Griebl "made us relax all vigilance, all watchfulness over him," and the spy was released from custody. However, Griebl's cooperative appearance proved deceiving. Five days later, the FBI's canary flew the coop to Germany aboard the SS *Bremen*.

German spy Dr. Ignatz Griebl maintained a residence and medical practice at 56 E. 87th Street. He fled the country after his arrest and questioning.

Nevertheless, Griebl's confession provided the FBI with valuable intelligence. His questioners learned of deep German penetration of US military installations, defense plants, and high-level government agencies. Two Gestapo leaders in the United States, Karl Herrmann and Fritz Rossberg, were exposed along with a spy ring responsible for stealing blueprints and specifications for US warships, aircraft, and weapon systems. Two factory employees, Werner George Gudenberg and Otto Herman Voss, were apprehended as German spies. The FBI also arrested the purported Gestapo chief Herrmann at his mistress's apartment at 75 West 89th Street as well as New York storm trooper leader Wilhelm Boning and John Baptiste Unkel, an officer of the pro-Nazi German American Bund.

■ 115. SPIES, LIES, LOVERS, AND BUGS

MAP 7 ➤ **Kate Moog residence:** 276 Riverside Drive

Katherine Moog Busch, a.k.a. Kate Moog, a six-foot-tall blonde, stood in sharp contrast to her lover, the short, pudgy Dr. Ignatz Griebl. Descended from a wealthy German family, she had arrived in New York as a young girl and lived well. The educated Moog owned a nursing home and was accepted into the upper level of the German American social scene. Though a nurse by day, her evenings were attended to by servants at a 14-room luxury apartment at 276 Riverside Drive.

On a crossing to Germany in 1937, Moog and Griebl were lavishly wined and dined by Capt. Erich Pfeiffer, a German naval intelligence officer. "I was there to dance and have a good time," Moog would later testify in the 1938 spy trial against the agents in the Griebl network.

For its part, German intelligence had bigger plans for her. According to interviews with the FBI and her testimony in court, she was offered the

The German spy Kate Moog lived in fashionable luxury at 276 Riverside Drive.

opportunity to create a salon in Washington, DC, that would attract politicians and power brokers and promote the virtues of National Socialism. Covert funds from the Abwehr were to be used to establish a Washington venue that could become a brothel controlled by German intelligence. At the time the offer was made, Berlin's infamous brothel Salon Kitty was open for business with bugged rooms and recording devices feeding pillow-talk secrets to the Nazi SS's intelligence service, the *Sicherheitsdienst des Reichsführers-SS* (*SD*).

Moog reemerged in the press when she joined a libel lawsuit

THE FBI GOES TO HOLLYWOOD

The case of Nazi spies Kate Moog and Ignatz Griebl was not without bureaucratic intrigue. The lead FBI special agent on the case, Leon G. Turrou, contracted to write a series of articles on the Nazi spy hunt for the *New York Post*. With the stories about to begin appearing in the paper on June 23, 1938, Turrou tendered his resignation, citing concerns for his family and health issues as reasons for his departure. However, when the first article appeared, Turrou's resignation was declined, and he was "terminated with prejudice."

It then became clear that more than the newspaper articles prompted Turrou's resignation. He had also signed an agreement with Warner Brothers for a movie based on the case. The film deal, reportedly worth $25,000, culminated with the release in 1939 *Confessions of a Nazi Spy*, starring Edward G. Robinson in the fictionalized role of Turrou. It was the first openly anti-Nazi film produced by a major studio.

Following the war, 20th Century Fox released an FBI spy film, *The House on 92nd Street* (1945). This film, based on the apprehension of the Duquesne Spy Ring, the largest single roll-up of spies in the FBI's history, was made with the full cooperation of the bureau and featured J. Edgar Hoover and other FBI agents in small roles.

brought by Fritz Kuhn and his German American Bund to halt distribution of the 1939 Warner Brothers film *Confessions of a Nazi Spy*. The character of Erika Wolff (played by Lya Lys) was said to be based on Moog, who sought $75,000, a modest sum compared to Kuhn's $5 million. Both claims were unsuccessful.

■ 116. THE NAZIS OF YORKVILLE

MAP 6 ▸ **German American Bund headquarters:** 178 East 85th Street at Third Avenue

Twenty thousand people packed Madison Square in February 1939 for a pro-German rally marking the pinnacle of pro-German influence in the United States before World War II. The event's sponsor, the German American Bund, or German American Federation, was an American Nazi organization active from 1933 to 1941. With a stated mission to unite "similar people," membership in the Bund was restricted to those of "Aryan" descent. The leader, or *Bundesführer*, was Fritz Julius Kuhn, a German army veteran of World War I who lived at 33-42 73rd Street in Jackson Heights, Queens.

The Bund's headquarters on East 85 Street

Nazi supporters march on East 86th Street prior to America's entrance into World War II. The Yorkville neighborhood was the home to the German American Bund and a center of German espionage.

The Bund used the traditional language and symbols of American patriotism to try to make fascism palatable to fellow citizens.

The German American Bund's primary objective was to promote a favorable view of Nazi Germany. The Abwehr was careful to maintain distance from the Bund for fear that, if discovered, it would inflame the public's anti-German sentiment. Individual Bund members were not so constrained, however, and were often recruited as spies for the Abwehr.

Following Germany's 1939 invasion of Poland and a series of arrests, including that of Kuhn for tax evasion and embezzlement, public sentiment turned against Germany, and Bund membership plummeted. The protection under the First Amendment that allowed the Bund to operate ended when war was declared on Germany in 1941 and it became illegal to swear an oath of loyalty to a national enemy.

■ 117. THE SPY WHO COULD NOT ESCAPE

MAP 6 ➤ **Gerhard Kunze residence:** 211 East 87th Street (site redeveloped)

American-born Gerhard Kunze, sometimes referred to as the American Joseph Goebbels, rose to prominence in 1939 as the last leader of the German American Bund. When registering for the Selective Service in 1936, he listed his home address as 211 East 87th Street. Kunze was instrumental in building the Bund's American youth movement, which was modeled on the Hitler Youth. Boys and girls of so-called Aryan descent were encouraged to attend Bund-sponsored summer camps, where they were indoctrinated into Nazi culture, received paramilitary training, and attended lectures on the importance of breeding with others "who look and think like you."

Kunze replaced Fritz Kuhn as head of the Bund in 1939 after Kuhn was charged with tax evasion and embezzlement. By then the tide of American

Gerhard Kunze

opinion was turning against Hitler, and news of the Molotov-Ribbentrop Pact in August 1939 further hastened the decline in Bund membership. By the time of the attack on Pearl Harbor in December 1941, the Bund was finished.

In the face of increasing US anti-Nazi sentiment, Kunze fled to Mexico in November 1941. He was eventually apprehended aboard a small motor launch in Mexico by local police and FBI agents on June 30, 1942. He was indicted on espionage charges on June 10, along with four other spy ring members. Subsequently Kunze was found guilty and received a 20-year sentence for conspiring to send US military information to the Axis powers. Thomas J. Dodd, who successfully prosecuted Kunze, later gained fame for his role in the Nuremberg Trials.

■ 118. NAZI TRAINING CAMP

MAP 12 ► **Long Island Nazi camp:** Intersection of Mill Road and German Boulevard, Yaphank, Long Island (private side road)

Nazi symbols and ideology permeated the grounds of Camp Siegfried.

In the years prior to World War II, a Nazi indoctrination camp operated on a 40-acre campground in the German Gardens section of Yaphank, Long Island. The Camp Siegfried site, owned by the German American Settlement League, was operated with the support of the German American Bund and its leader, Fritz Kuhn. At the height of its popularity in 1938, as many as 40,000 supporters participated in German Day festivities at the camp. To accommodate the crowds, the Long Island Railroad operated a daily 8:00 a.m. train from Pennsylvania Station known as the "Camp Siegfried Special."

Male pro-Nazi sympathizers at the camp wore the Bund uniforms of black breeches, boots, gray shirts, and black ties, and on weekends the camp's beer hall resonated with the sound of the German national anthem, with its lyrics *Deutschland über Alles* (Germany above all). Flagpoles at the camp's entrance gate flew both the American and Nazi flags, as the Bund promoted George Washington as the "first fascist." The assertion that fascism and Americanism were compatible echoed the claim made by communists earlier in the decade. Swastikas were proudly displayed on homes and buildings along the streets and even in the arrangements of flowers and meticulously trimmed topiary.

Bund training resembled the paramilitary training provided to the Hitler Youth in Germany. Uniformed teens marched to the "Horst Wessel Song"

Street names at Camp Siegfried reflected admiration for Nazi leaders.

[the joint national anthem of Nazi Germany from 1933 to 1945) along streets named for Nazi leaders, such as Adolf Hitler Strasse, Joseph Goebbels Strasse, and Hermann Göring Strasse.

The Bund believed that future leaders in America would likely have German blood, and the camp was preparing a generation of young people to assume their rightful roles. It is not coincidental that of the eight Abwehr saboteurs who landed in 1942 in nearby Montauk as part of OPERATION PASTORIUS, four were past attendees of Camp Siegfried.

The camp was never entirely welcome on Long Island but was protected by the First Amendment. One of the most vocal critics of Camp Siegfried, US congressman Samuel Dickstein, headed a committee investigating the Bund. No one knew that Dickstein was secretly a Soviet spy (code name CROOK) operating under the NKVD.

The US government seized the land during World War II, but the German American Settlement League managed to wrest back control of the property following the war. Today the organization still owns the land and leases the

American and Third Reich flags hung side by side at the Camp Siegfried swimming pool, giving the illusion of an alliance between the two nations.

houses back to the occupants in a community closed to outsiders and accessible only by a private road. While many of the homes and buildings remain almost as they were in the late 1930s, the swastikas are gone, and the street names have been changed. Adolf Hitler Strasse is Park Boulevard, Hermann Göring Strasse is Oak Street, and Joseph Goebbels Strasse has become Northside Avenue.

■ 119. MORE THAN A PORTRAIT STUDIO

MAP 9 ➤ **Wilhelm Grote studio:** 946 East 181st Street, Bronx [site redeveloped]

Carl Alfred Reuper

The Little Casino bar and restaurant on East 85th Street, now a French bistro, was once a notorious Nazi spy nest.

One of the most successful German agents in America prior to World War II was Carl Alfred Reuper, a 37-year-old skilled mechanic employed at Air Associates in Bendix, New Jersey. Reuper, who worked on classified government contracts, came to the United States from Germany in 1929 and became a naturalized citizen in 1936. He attended an Abwehr spy school in Hamburg while on a trip to Germany in 1939 and, upon return to the United States in late December of that year, began recruiting a small network of spies. Reuper's new agents, all members of the German American Bund, worked at defense plants along the East Coast. Each agent was meticulously selected by Reuper and assigned to collect code books, documents, and blueprints related to America's national defense.

In managing his spy ring, Reuper developed an operational pattern. After returning from work to his home at 9062 Palisade Avenue, Hudson Heights, North Bergen, New Jersey [now redeveloped into apartments], he changed clothes, took a bus to New York's Pennsylvania Station, and met unobserved with his subagents in the crowded bustle of the arriving and departing passengers.

His prize recruit, US Army private Peter Franz Donay, was posted on Governors Island and gave Reuper a top-secret field manual that Wilhelm Grote, a commercial photographer based at 946 East 181st Street in the Bronx, photographed, reducing each page to less than a 2mm microdot. The microdots were hidden inside a used book, which was wrapped in a plain brown cover and passed to a German sympathizer, Paul Alfred Scholz, the proprietor of a Yorkville bookshop on East 85th Street.

Scholz concealed the book beneath the counter for two days before a man called for it. After exchanging passwords, the unidentified man was observed by the FBI as he carried the package to the SS *Manhattan*, an ocean liner about to depart from New York harbor. A later investigation revealed that the individual was an Abwehr courier posing as the ship's librarian.

Frederick Joubert Duquesne

German spy Frederick Duquesne lived at this stately Upper West Side townhouse with his accomplice and lover, Evelyn Clayton Lewis, a well-to-do writer and artist.

■ 120. INMATE OF A HOSPITAL FOR THE CRIMINALLY INSANE

MAP 7 ➤ Frederick Joubert Duquesne residence: 24 West 76th Street

Frederick Joubert Duquesne, head of a major World War II German spy ring, lived under the alias Dunn at 24 West 76th Street and worked at Air Terminal Associates, 120 Wall Street. Duquesne, a South African adventurer and mercenary, harbored a pathological hatred of the British after the Second Boer War. Alleged to have been involved in sabotage operations that destroyed British ships during World War I, he was held in police custody at Bellevue Hospital in New York in 1919. At the time, Duquesne described himself as a "British prisoner of war, confidential emissary of King Leopold II in the Belgian Congo, big game hunting instructor to Theodore Roosevelt, reporter, author, publicity man, inventor and inmate of a hospital for the criminally insane."

Duquesne was also apparently a convincing performer. During his stay at Bellevue, he faked paralysis for two years before escaping by climbing over the hospital wall dressed as a woman, then managed to remain at large for the next two decades before his misadventures in an FBI-controlled double-agent operation at the beginning of World War II.

Arrested in 1941 and later convicted of spying, Duquesne served 12 years in prison, then returned to New York. In the last report of his whereabouts, the frail, sickly and destitute former spy was living on public assistance at 526 East 83rd Street. In 1954, he made his final known public appearance, a lecture

at the now defunct Adventurers Club titled "My Life—In and Out of Prison." A fall in 1956 sent Duquesne to a charity hospital ward on Welfare Island, now Roosevelt Island, where he died of a stroke at age 78. His body, unclaimed, was buried on Hart Island, New York's potter's field.

Reputed by some to be the birthplace of the martini, the Knickerbocker Hotel was built by John Jacob Astor IV in 1906. The FBI staged one of its most successful counterintelligence operations during World War II at the site.

■ 121. FBI'S DOUBLE-AGENT: WILLIAM SEBOLD

MAP 12 ➤ **Secret radio transmitter:** 28 Bankside Drive North, Centerport, Long Island

In the late 1930s, William Sebold held a steady job as a mechanic at a California company, Consolidated Aircraft. The native German, born Wilhelm Georg Debrowski, fought in World War I as a machine gunner before jumping ship in Galveston, Texas, changing his name, marrying, and becoming a naturalized US citizen. On a visit to Germany in the summer of 1939, Sebold's life took an unexpected turn when he was approached by German intelligence to spy on America. After agreeing to cooperate, Sebold

This modest cottage in Centerport, Long Island, housed William Sebold's transmission station.

A concealed FBI surveillance camera photographed Frederick Duquesne in Sebold's office at the Knickerbocker Hotel on June 25, 1941.

Axel Wheeler-Hill

went to the American consulate in Hamburg to report the attempted recruitment. Recognizing a counterintelligence opportunity, US officials instructed Sebold to play along with the Germans.

German intelligence trained Sebold in clandestine tradecraft and sent him back to the United States with an alias, Harry Sawyer, under the cover of being an engineering consultant. When met at a New York dock by the FBI on February 8, 1940, Sebold reaffirmed his loyalty to the United States and became one of America's most valuable double agents.

Sebold's mission was to be the communications officer for the Duquesne spy network, managing transmissions of their stolen secrets to Germany and receiving and delivering return messages to the spies.

Sebold initially resided at 223 East 82nd Street and established a front company, Diesel Research, in the Knickerbocker Hotel at 152 West 42nd Street, rooms 627 and 628. (The hotel's address was later changed to 6 Times Square.) Unbeknown to Duquesne and his spy network, the FBI wired the rooms with microphones and motion picture cameras to capture everything that was said or done in subsequent meetings. The FBI also constructed and controlled a secret radio-transmitting station on Long Island that Sebold used to send information and disinformation to the Abwehr.

The transmitter site at 28 Bankside Drive North, Centerport, Long Island, was selected for its privacy and the

Josef Klein

atmospheric conditions necessary for long-range radio signals. Sebold then moved to Hempstead, Long Island, to be closer to the site.

Over the next eighteen months, the Abwehr station in Hamburg received hundreds of shortwave radio transmissions from the Long Island site they believed were originating from their agent in America using the call sign CQDXVW-Z. The FBI-controlled radio station eventually transmitted some 300 messages to Germany and received more than 200 replies.

Through Sebold, the FBI identified dozens of German agents in the United States, Mexico, and South America. When the US government moved against the Duquesne spy ring in 1941, 33 German spies were arrested and convicted in a trial that concluded less than a week after the attack on Pearl Harbor.

With his mission complete, Sebold received a new identity from the US government in an early version of the Witness Relocation Program and was resettled to an undisclosed location. He died in 1970 following years of emotional distress from his role in the operation and is buried in Queen of Heaven Cemetery, Lafayette, California.

A little-known part of the case was the existence of another, lower-power radio transmitter operating at 562 Caudwell Avenue in the Bronx. One of the Duquesne spies, Felix Jahnke, arrived in the United States in 1924 and became a citizen in 1930. He had previously attended a military school in Germany and served in the German army as a radio operator.

Jahnke and fellow agent Axel Wheeler-Hill secured the services of a third spy, Josef Klein, a radio technician, to build a wireless shortwave radio set for Jahnke's Caudwell Avenue apartment. The radio transmitted information Jahnke collected while visiting New York docks to observe vessels bound for England. Unfortunately for Jahnke, his messages were intercepted by the FBI, and the three spies were arrested.

At their trials, Jahnke, Wheeler-Hill, and Klein all pleaded not guilty but were convicted on December 13, 1941. Jahnke was sentenced to 20 months in prison and a $1,000 fine. Wheeler-Hill was sentenced to 15 years in prison for espionage and two concurrent years for violating the Registration Act. Klein received five years imprisonment for espionage with two one-year sentences to run concurrently under the Registration Act.

■ 122. THE HOUSE ON 92ND STREET WAS REALLY ON 93RD

MAP 6 ➤ **FBI secret residence:** 53 East 93rd Street

The real "House on 92nd Street" was at the 53 East 93rd Street site indicated. While the house no longer exists, a nearly exact duplicate still stands nearby at 55 East 93rd.

The 1945 award-winning movie *The House on 92nd Street* was based on a 1941 FBI double-agent operation against the German-directed Duquesne spy ring. The address of the actual house used in the operation at 53 East 93rd Street was changed by the movie's director because he thought 92nd Street was a better-sounding title. The original house no longer stands, but its sister building at 55 East 93rd Street (the Alamo Apartments) is almost a visual duplicate and is often confused with the original building.

The movie won the Academy Award in the Original Motion Picture Story category. Its sense of realism draws from the cooperation of the FBI, which provided surveillance footage of the real Nazi spies. FBI special agents played themselves in nonacting roles, and J. Edgar Hoover appeared in an introduction to the film.

■ 123. NAZI HONEY TRAP

MAP 6 ➤ **Lilly Stein residence:** 780 Madison Avenue

Lilly Stein

One notable agent rolled up in the Duquesne spy ring arrests was Lilly Stein. The Viennese fashion model arrived in New York in October 1939 and, although Jewish, must have seemed an attractive recruit when she joined the Abwehr. Fluent in English, she was socially adept and reportedly had an affair with US State Department official Ogden H. Hammond Jr.

Stein, like William Sebold, was trained for intelligence operations in Germany by Hugo Sebold (no relation to William). In New York, she first lived

Lilly Stein's residences at 780 Madison Avenue and another at the Hotel Windsor (today the Windsor Park) were sites for German intelligence honey traps.

at the Hotel Windsor, 100 West 58th Street (today the Windsor Park), then moved through a series of addresses, including 780 Madison Avenue, 127 East 54th Street, apartment 2-A, and 232 East 79th Street, apartment 2-B. Stein's apartments were used as accommodation addresses for operational communication.

Stein was one of four people to whom Sebold was instructed to deliver instructions on microdots when he arrived in the United States. She, in turn, passed Sebold information for transmittal to Germany. Stein also acted as a honey trap, cruising Manhattan bars and social events to meet men with access to secrets. Frequently in need of money, she eventually turned to prostitution to support herself. By the time of her arrest, Stein was begging her handlers for small amounts to pay her phone bill.

Stein pleaded guilty for her part in the compromised spy ring and received a sentence of 10 years and two concurrent years' imprisonment for violations of espionage and registration statutes, respectively. She served 12 years before being released and moving to France near Strasbourg.

■ 124. WHEN THE NAZIS TARGETED AMERICA'S LARGEST COMPANIES

MAP 5 ▶ **Texaco headquarters:** Chrysler Building, 405 Lexington Avenue

Torkild "Cap" Rieber was an American success story. Born in Norway, he went to sea as a teen, then immigrated to the United States and rose from ship's captain to head the Texas Corporation (Texaco), one of the world's largest oil companies. Although Rieber traded merchant seamanship for membership in the New York Yacht Club, he retained an expletive-laced, plain-spoken style. His reputation was one of a tough businessman given to berating bankers and subordinates alike. Living in an apartment on the 35th floor of the Hampshire House, 150 Central Park

German intelligence once infiltrated Texaco's headquarters in the landmark Chrysler Building, seen here in a 1930s photograph

West, he was a much feared and admired captain of industry.

Rieber sided with Francisco Franco during the Spanish Civil War, and the company was fined for providing oil to the rebels. In 1940, Rieber met Hermann Göring in Germany and was asked to deliver a proposal to President Roosevelt. In the brief meeting, FDR warned the businessman, "Cap, if I were you, I'd keep out of this thing."

Rieber chose not to follow the president's advice and eventually met Nikolas "Niko" Bensmann. Born in Germany, Bensmann attended Columbia University, then spent years working in the oil and auto industries in the United States. Bensmann understood the oil industry, possessed an unapologetic appetite for fine food and wine, and unlike doctrinaire Nazis occasionally ridiculed Hitler. He seemed just the type of man Rieber needed for his increasingly complicated dealings with Germany. Bensmann was hired as the company's attorney in Bremen.

Rieber did not know that his efficient German lawyer was also an Abwehr officer. Bensmann, in turn, placed his own representative in Texaco's Chrysler Building headquarters, 405 Lexington Avenue, and devised a code for secret communication based on patent numbers inserted into seemingly routine business correspondence.

The operation ended quickly for both Rieber and Bensmann. A report smuggled out of Texaco headquarters included an estimate of potential US aircraft production and fuel requirements. The number, an impressive 50,000 aircraft, was of such significance to Abwehr chief Wilhelm Canaris that he personally handed it to Hitler. "You must be out of your mind to take such crap seriously," Hitler is reported to have said. "Fifty-thousand rubber tranquilizers [pacifiers] maybe, for the poor little babies of America. But 50,000 planes? Don't be ridiculous!" Discredited despite providing accurate intelligence, Bensmann's spy ring ceased to be of value to the Third Reich.

Rieber's Texaco career eventually ended due to his German associations. In New York, British intelligence traced a German propagandist, Gerhard Westrick, to Texaco's offices in the Chrysler Building, which he listed as his local address on a driver's license. Leaked to the press, the ensuing scandal touched both Rieber and Texaco. A lavish banquet held at the Waldorf Astoria after the fall of France, paid for by Rieber, featured Westrick as guest of honor and further linked the Nazi regime to the American company. After a public outcry, Rieber resigned from Texaco the same week Westrick sailed back to Germany in August 1940.

Rieber continued in business for several years, most notably turning around the Barber Asphalt Corporation, owned by the wealthy Guggenheim family, although his reputation as a Nazi sympathizer remained. He died in 1968 in his apartment at 812 Fifth Avenue, an address that later become the home of Nelson and Happy Rockefeller.

■ 125. GERHARD WESTRICK'S FAILED INFLUENCE OPERATION

MAP 9 ➤ **Gerhard Westrick residence:** 188 Mamaroneck Road, Scarsdale

Gerhard Alois Westrick, accredited as a German diplomat, arrived in the United States in the spring of 1940 with a mission to solidify Germany's relationship among American business leaders. Assistance came from Torkild "Cap" Rieber of Texaco. Westrick rented a house at 188 Mamaroneck Road, Scarsdale, New York, and worked from an office in Texaco's Chrysler Building headquarters, 405 Lexington Avenue. As it was later revealed, Texaco also paid for Westrick's car, a Buick purchased for $1,570.

Westrick's operational timing seemed ideal. Hitler's army was on the march across Europe. On June 26, 1940, the day after France fell, Westrick was the guest of honor at a dinner at the Waldorf Astoria, 301 Park Avenue, attended by executives from some of America's largest companies. The event furthered Westrick's goals to recruit businessmen to pressure President Roosevelt to discontinue shipments of arms to England, promote an American stance of isolationism, and secure a loan to Germany from the United States.

For British intelligence officers operating in New York, Westrick's successes were alarming. British surveillance placed on the diplomat's Scarsdale home revealed visits from businessmen who seemed to believe Westrick's propaganda of Germany's inevitable victory and promises of commercial rewards from a Europe under the control of the Axis powers.

Finding a cooperative outlet in the *New York Herald Tribune*, the BSC planted a story that revealed Westrick's mission along with his Scarsdale address. The article prompted an angry crowd to gather outside the house. Westrick retaliated by blasting "God Bless America" and the "Star-Spangled Banner" at the protesters on his phonograph. Hostile letters and threats followed, then increased as the story was picked up by news outlets around the country. Business leaders, fearful of being labeled fifth columnists, deserted the German diplomat, and the FBI was forced to post a 24-hour guard on the Scarsdale property.

The end came when another *New York Herald Tribune* story revealed Westrick wore a prosthetic leg, a fact he had not disclosed on his driver's license application. The license was then revoked, followed by an eviction notice from his Scarsdale landlord. Finally, a request, prompted by the FBI, came from the State Department that Germany remove him from the country. By August 20, 1940, less than six months after arriving, Westrick was on a Japanese ocean liner back to Germany.

■ 126. SCHOOL FOR CODE BREAKERS

MAP 10 ➤ **Boys High School:** 832 Marcy Avenue, Brooklyn

In 1930, William Friedman, the senior civilian in the Army's Signal Intelligence Service (SIS), hired an additional three civilians, all former mathematics teachers, to work as cryptanalysts. The small team of SIS cryptanalysts compiled ciphers for military use and attempted to break foreign codes.

Two of the code breakers, Abraham Sinkov and Solomon Kullback, were graduates of Boys High School, 832 Marcy Avenue, Brooklyn. Both attended the City College of New York, then continued in postgraduate studies at different universities before reuniting as part of the US code-breaking efforts.

Dr. Sinkov and the team had early success with Japanese diplomatic machine ciphers and were sent to the Panama Canal Zone in 1936 to open the first SIS intercept site outside the continental United States. In 1941, on a secret trip to Bletchley Park known as the Sinkov Mission, the Americans were briefed by the British on the challenges of breaking the codes created by the Germans' ENIGMA cipher machine.

Dr. Sinkov, with the rank of colonel, headed the Central Bureau Brisbane (CBB) in Australia during World War II, which provided cryptological support for Gen. Douglas MacArthur. The CBB's signals intelligence success against Japanese communications was instrumental to some of MacArthur's critical victories in New Guinea and the Philippines.

Brooklyn's Boys High School's notable graduates include code breakers Abraham Sinkov and Solomon Kullback along with author Isaac Asimov and sports announcer Howard Cosell.

When the Armed Forces Security Agency (AFSA), the first US centralized cryptological organization, was formed in 1949, Dr. Sinkov became chief of the communications security program. He remained in this position as the AFSA made the transition into the NSA. Dr. Sinkov, one of the nation's master cryptanalysts, retired from the NSA in 1972 and died in 1998.

■ 127. THE CODE-BREAKING ARCHITECT

MAP 6 ➤ **Hunter College:** East 68th Street and Lexington Avenue

The esteemed architect Rosario Candela designed many of New York's most desirable luxury apartment buildings, including 740 Park Avenue, which has been called "the world's richest apartment building." At the height of his success and creative output in the 1920s, he designed more than two dozen buildings. Today a Candela cooperative apartment in Manhattan can command $20 million or more.

Candela became interested in cryptology in the 1930s after reading Herbert O. Yardley's *The American Black Chamber*, a popular book at the time. Yardley's revelations generated controversy as well as a government rebuke for his descriptions of code breaking and the secretive world of intelligence. The subject matter fascinated Candela, even though he found Yardley insufferable. "He carried on and on about the 'cryptographic mind,' and how there are only a half dozen in the world or something like that—just to make himself seem holy, I guess," Candela later told a reporter from the *New Yorker*.

Hunter College was the first civilian institution to have a course in cryptography. It was taught by famed architect and amateur cryptographer Rosario Candela.

Still, intrigued by the subject, Candela sought books on it from Europe while teaching himself code breaking. In 1938, he published *The Military Cipher of Commandant Bazeries*, explaining how he broke a difficult World War I French cryptogram. Praised in Europe, the book also gained notice in the United States, and Candela was invited by the US Army Signal Corps to take a cryptology course by mail. He then received an offer from Hunter College, East 68th Street and Lexington Avenue, to teach a night course. Candela did so while still maintaining an architectural practice, then located at 19 East 53rd Street.

Hunter, founded as a training college for teachers, was at the time the nation's largest college for women. Many of its students commuted to classes from Brooklyn, the Bronx, and Queens by subway. When asked by *The New York Times* whether women could make good cryptographers, Candela replied, "Capable women make just as good cryptographers as men. . . . Actually some of the most highly successful cryptographers have been women."

This would be proved true during World War II. At Arlington Hall, the code-breaking facility outside of Washington, DC, women made up a significant portion of the decryption workforce, with some, such as Elizebeth Friedman and Agnes Meyer Driscoll, rising to the highest levels of the craft.

Candela served a brief stint in the COI, predecessor to the OSS, at its Foreign Broadcast Quarterly Corporation, a short-lived intelligence component that intercepted foreign radio broadcasts. Following the war, he became president of the New York Cipher Society, hosting the group's meetings at his architectural offices at 654 Madison Avenue. The renowned architect continued to practice until his death in 1953. Among the last buildings he designed is the William T. Sherman School, Public School 87, located at 160 West 78th Street.

In the lead-up to World War II, the FBI established a cover organization, Importers and Exporters Service Company, at 30 Rockefeller Center to collect foreign intelligence.

■ 128. SMALL BUSINESS, LARGE MISSION

MAP 3 ➤ Importers and Exporters Service Company: 30 Rockefeller Plaza, room 4332

Prior to 1940, intelligence operations of the US government were primarily run as independent activities by separate departments, such as the Department of State and the individual armed services. Officially accredited attachés and diplomats collected the bulk of America's foreign intelligence. Then in June of 1940, the FBI created a Special Intelligence Service with responsibility for conducting "foreign intelligence work in the Western Hemisphere." Of special interest was information about Nazi espionage, counterespionage, subversion, and sabotage planned or conducted in South America, Central America, and the Caribbean.

The SIS opened an undercover office as the Importers and Exporters Service Company at 30 Rockefeller Plaza, room 4332. With Europe already at war and many neutral countries doing business in the United States, New York City was a hotbed of spying. It was also convenient that the BSC was located in the same building along with Soviet, German, Italian, and Japanese tenants.

The Importers and Exporters Service Company may have never imported or exported anything, but it operated for the duration of the war handling the necessary logistics and cover positions to deploy SIS agents throughout the hemisphere.

In 1941, the COI, headed by William Donovan, became America's first centralized intelligence service and was succeeded a year later by the OSS. The FBI retained responsibility for the Western Hemisphere while the OSS ran spies, conducted sabotage operations, and supported the war effort in the rest of the world. In 1947, the collection of foreign intelligence was consolidated and assigned as a primary responsibility to the newly formed CIA.

■ 129. A "BROKEN-DOWN BOARDING HOUSE" FOR SPIES

MAP 5 ▶ **St. Regis Hotel:** 2 East 55th Street

American and British spy-masters met at the luxury St. Regis Hotel to plot strategies for World War II intelligence operations. Afterward, Ian Fleming used the hotel as a setting in the James Bond novel *Live and Let Die*, calling it "the best hotel in New York."

The luxury St. Regis Hotel, 2 East 55th Street, catered to intelligence officers during World War II. The "spy friendly" hotel frequently hosted Gen. William "Wild Bill" Donovan, who, as head of the COI, was assembling America's first centralized intelligence service. Donovan and William Stephenson, the spymaster who set up the BSC in New York prior to World War II, first met at the St. Regis.

Another British intelligence officer, Ian Fleming, liked the hotel so much he incorporated it into his James Bond novel *Live and Let Die*. As Fleming weaves the story, Bond meets his CIA contact, Felix Leiter, at the St. Regis. One can imagine the two spies plotting operations in the hotel's iconic King Cole bar with its Maxfield Parrish mural.

Built by John Jacob Astor IV in 1904, the beaux arts St. Regis was then owned by his son, Vincent Astor, who once referred to the hotel as his "broken-down boarding house."

■ 130. PLAYWRIGHT SPY

MAP 5 ➤ **Coordinator of Information, New York branch:** 270 Madison Avenue

Pulitzer Prize–winning dramatist Robert E. Sherwood, who lived at 25 Sutton Place, was among William Donovan's first hires in 1941 for the Coordinator of Intelligence office.

Among William Donovan's first hires in the summer of 1941 for the newly authorized organization COI was Robert E. Sherwood. The Pulitzer Prize–winning dramatist was also friends with President Roosevelt, often pitching in as one of the president's speechwriters. Sherwood, then living at 25 Sutton Place, ran what has been called Donovan's "propaganda" component.

Sherwood viewed his unit, the Foreign Information Service (FIS), based at 270 Madison Avenue, as a "positive" influence and means of "truth spreading." The influential America First Committee, partly financed by Germany, with aviation hero Charles Lindbergh as its most visible spokesman, promoted isolationism. Sherwood's organization countered the America First claims by exposing the threat of fascism.

COVERING THE WATERFRONT

A little-known component of the OSS was the Ship Observer Unit (SOU). Established in December 1942, the unit was headquartered at 42 Broadway. SOU representatives worked through the maritime unions to interview crew members of ships from neutral countries. Seaman who may have distrusted military officials or FBI agents opened up to SOU representatives in less formal interviews at waterfront bars, seamen's restaurants, and union halls. Radio operators and ship stewards provided valuable information on port fortifications, enemy vessels under repair, and cargo movements in Axis or occupied ports. In some cases, the seamen provided photos of foreign facilities or accepted cameras from the SOU to photograph ports they were scheduled to visit.

Sherwood's small group was put to the test on December 7, 1941, with Japan's attack on Pearl Harbor. As Sherwood pointed out to Donovan, most Americans did not even know where Pearl Harbor was located. Sherwood and his team sent a bulletin to newspaper editors across the country, explaining where Pearl Harbor was located and that the American fleet was the target. Among the notable broadcasting efforts by COI was Voice of America, launched in February 1942. Its name is credited to Sherwood.

A few weeks after establishing the FIS, Donovan expanded his organization's New York presence by forming the Oral Intelligence (OI) Unit. Members of the OI interviewed foreign travelers and refugees, first from the Madison Avenue address, then moving to 21 East 40th Street. The small staff, made up of newspaper reporters, skilled interrogators, and a pollster, was the first effort by Donovan's organization to provide raw intelligence reporting. Many of the new arrivals interviewed came from France, Germany, and Poland. Interviews were typically scheduled with cooperation by the ONI and through access to shipping manifests. The interviews were voluntary and, reportedly, the reports were shared with the BSC office in New York. This activity represented one of the first points of cooperation between the COI and the BSC.

■ 131. THE APOSTLE SPY

MAP 6 ➤ **Ridgway Brewster Knight residence:** 45 East 82nd Street

Nearly two years prior to America's entrance into World War II, President Roosevelt assigned a dozen vice-consuls to diplomatic posts in the North African French colonies of Tunisia, Algeria, and Morocco. Initially called the Murphy Mission because the vice-consuls reported to Robert D. Murphy, counselor of embassy in Vichy, the group eventually became known as the Twelve Apostles. Their diplomatic status enabled them to acquire information and provide reporting that would support the future Allied military action of OPERATION TORCH, the invasion of North Africa.

German intelligence in the region dismissed the significance of the group. One memo sent to Berlin sneeringly called them

> a perfect picture of the mixture of races and characteristics in that wild conglomeration called the United States of America. We can only congratulate ourselves on the selection of this group of enemy agents who will give us no trouble. In view of the fact that they are naturally lacking in method, organization, and discipline, the danger presented by their arrival in North Africa may be considered as nil. It would merely be a waste of paper to describe their personal idiosyncrasies and characteristics.

For their part, the Twelve Apostles identified sites for observation posts, captured code books, and recruited agents from within the Vichy government.

Ridgway Knight

Eventually they conducted sabotage operations and worked with local groups opposed to Germany.

Among the twelve was Ridgway Brewster Knight. Born in France to American artist parents, he was educated in France, followed by a degree from the Harvard Business School. After working at Cartier Jewelers, 653 Fifth Avenue, Knight partnered with Frederick S. Wildman to buy out the long-established Bellows and Company, where he pioneered the importation of French wines before selling the business in the lead-up to the war.

Knight, then living at 45 East 82nd Street, prepared for military service by taking flying lessons but was turned down by the US Army Air Forces. Nevertheless, he was recruited for the Murphy Mission by the State Department and left behind a wife and three young children when he departed to North Africa.

Following OPERATION TORCH in 1942, Knight joined the US Army in time for the invasion of Italy and eventually became assistant to Ambassador David K. E. Bruce in Paris. After the war, Knight rejoined the US State Department for a distinguished career that included multiple foreign ambassadorial postings. He died in 2001 at his home in northern France.

■ 132. UNINTENDED CONSEQUENCES

MAP 3 ▶ **Madison Square Garden:** Eighth Avenue between West 49th and 50th Streets (since relocated)

Among the covert operations conducted by British intelligence prior to America's entrance into World War II was an attempt to disrupt an America First Committee rally in New York. British intelligence discovered America First was partially funded and directed by Germany to promote a hard line on isolationism and keep America out of the war. One of the organization's most popular and high-profile spokesman, aviation hero Charles Lindbergh, was scheduled to give a rousing speech on October 30, 1941, at Madison Square Garden, then located on Eighth Avenue between West 49th and 50th Streets.

To counter the rally, the BSC printed and distributed duplicate tickets. The plan envisioned those with bogus tickets creating a disruption over seating with legitimate ticket holders. The operation might have worked if more legitimate ticket holders had attended the rally. However, the event was far from sold out, even with an appearance by Lindbergh. Ushers noticed, but ignored, the duplicated tickets and escorted prospective troublemakers to available vacant seats. In the end, the operation fizzled as holders of forged tickets only increased the attendance at the event.

■ 133. SPY HEADQUARTERS AT ROCK CENTER

MAP 3 ▶ **British Security Coordination**: 630 Fifth Avenue, International Building of Rockefeller Center

Beginning before World War II, room 3603 in the International Building of Rockefeller Center at 630 Fifth Avenue housed the BSC, which operated under nominal cover as the British Passport Control Office. The New York office of the OSS was later located conveniently nearby in room 3663. From this prestigious midtown address, guarded at its Fifth Avenue entrance by a 45-foot-high art deco statue of Atlas supporting a globe, both the American and the British spymasters, William Donovan and William Stephenson, coordinated intelligence operations throughout the war.

British Security Coordination established its US headquarters at the landmark Rockefeller Center on Fifth Avenue prior to America's entry into World War II.

■ 134. BIG BILL AND LITTLE BILL

MAP 3 ▶ **Dorset Hotel**: 30 West 54th Street (demolished in 2000)

William Stephenson, who served as the senior British representative for the BSC for the Western Hemisphere during World War II, is widely known by the code name INTREPID. In fact, INTREPID was the telegraphic address for BSC headquarters at Rockefeller Center, 630 Fifth Avenue, not Stephenson's code name.

Whatever his code name, many consider him to be the inspiration for the fictional character James Bond, of whom Ian Fleming once wrote, "James

The no-longer-standing Dorset Hotel was one of the homes of BSC chief William Stephenson. A Museum of Modern Art expansion now occupies the site.

Bond is a highly-romanticized version of a true spy. The real thing is . . . William Stephenson."

Stephenson established BSC offices in New York City with a main office in Rockefeller Center, but he also conducted business in the now demolished Dorset Hotel at 30 West 54th Street and the Hampshire House at 150 Central Park South. Known as "the quiet Canadian," Stephenson worked closely with President Roosevelt's administration in the years before America entered World War II. Then his primary mission was moving American public opinion away from an isolationist position and encouraging the United States to intervene in the war against Germany. Stephenson also gathered intelligence on Axis spy networks operating in Central and South America and fed updates on Vichy French activities to London.

Stephenson played a major role in the establishment in 1941 of America's first centralized intelligence service, the COI, and a year later the OSS. OSS chief Maj. Gen. William J. "Wild Bill" Donovan later said, "Bill Stephenson taught us all we ever knew about foreign intelligence." The pair worked so closely together colleagues took to calling Donovan "Big Bill" and Stephenson "Little Bill."

Rather than adopt the structure of the British foreign intelligence service, MI6, which only gathered secret intelligence, Stephenson urged the United States to model itself after the lesser-known British Special Operations Executive (SOE). Accordingly, the OSS was created to collect secret intelligence, perform research and analysis, and conduct special operations and counterintelligence.

The UK government knighted Stephenson in 1946 for his wartime exploits, and from America he received what was then the nation's highest civilian award, the Medal for Merit.

James Joseph "Gene" Tunney

■ 135. BRITISH SPIES AND LIES IN NEW YORK CITY

MAP 3 ▶ Vichy French consulate: 610 Fifth Avenue

Before the United States entered World War II, the BSC intelligence apparatus engaged the Axis powers in secret spy operations in New York. In one instance, a BSC agent seduced a woman known only as "Madame Cadet," who worked as the secretary to the financial attaché in the Vichy French consulate at 610 Fifth Avenue. The affair paid off when the BSC agent began receiving copies of correspondence that confirmed the existence of Nazi sympathizers in Quebec City. When the woman transferred to Washington, she was handed off to another BSC operative to whom she provided a host of blank passports and official stamps that supported other espionage operations.

THE QUIET CANADIAN AND THE CHAMP

When William Stephenson, head of the BSC, wanted an informal and discreet introduction to FBI chief J. Edgar Hoover in 1940, he turned to an old friend and native New Yorker, Gene Tunney. Stephenson first met the future world heavyweight boxing champion during World War I when they both fought in an interservice boxing competition. Tunney, son of a longshoreman, was born at 416 West 52nd Street, joined the US Marine Corps in 1917, won the light heavyweight championship of the American Expeditionary Force in 1918, and afterward lived at 111 Bank Street.

Tunney recalled that Stephenson once "wrote a confidential letter from London. I arranged to get the letter into the hands of Mr. Hoover because Sir William did not want to make an official approach.... He wanted to do so quietly and with no fanfare." Following the Hoover-Stephenson meeting in Washington on April 16, 1940, Tunney wrote, "Naturally, I had to stay out of whatever business was between them, but it was my understanding that the thing went off extremely well." Stephenson's account of the meeting, as recounted by Jennet Conant in *The Irregulars: Roald Dahl and the British Spy Ring in Wartime Washington*, was far less positive.

The BSC also launched an explosive propaganda campaign to expose Kurt Heinrich Rieth, a German operative who had entered the United States through Brownsville, Texas, on a tourist visa in 1941. From a wealthy German family (his father represented Standard Oil in Hamburg), Rieth was a skilled diplomat who operated in the shadows of international trade. After setting himself up in a $600-a-night luxury suite at the Waldorf Astoria, 301 Park Avenue, he began exploiting business contacts with Standard Oil of New Jersey and other companies. Based on its intelligence about Rieth's activities, the BSC leaked details of his operations to the press. Within days the BSC-friendly *New York Herald-Tribune* blared a headline: "Nazi Agent Here on Secret Mission Seeks Oil Holdings." Standard Oil denied ever hearing of Mr. Rieth, who locked himself in his hotel suite and refused to answer questions other than to say he was in New York on personal business. Five days after the headlines first appeared, he was deported.

The Vichy French government operated from this Rockefeller Center building during the early days of World War II.

■ 136. BRITAIN'S WARTIME PROPAGANDA MACHINE

MAP 5 ➤ **Overseas News Agency:** 101 Park Avenue (site redeveloped)

Among the tricks up the tailored sleeves of World War II spymaster William Stephenson and the BSC was a covert propaganda program called the Overseas News Agency (ONA). Originally a division of the small Jewish Telegraph Agency, the British spies invested in the venture, expanded it, and eventually took control of its content.

With offices at 101 Park Avenue, the news organization rapidly increased the number of papers in which its stories appeared. Among the 45 publications that printed ONA stories were *The New York Times*, the *New York Post*, the *Washington Times*, the *San Francisco Chronicle*, and the *Kansas City Star*. Whether the publishers were aware British intelligence was behind the articles remains a mystery.

In addition to providing occasional cover for SOE operatives posing as reporters, many of the ONA's stories were written by the BSC to confuse and mislead enemies. For example, in an attempt to lower morale among U-boat crews, the ONA circulated a November 1941 dispatch that the British had discovered a "super explosive" for depth charges. Following the war, the ONA struggled unsuccessfully as a legitimate news organization before finally closing.

READING THE HEAVENS

Charlatan astrologer Louis de Wohl, dispatched to the United States by British intelligence in 1941, toured the nation predicting, based on his reading of the positions of the stars, victory for America in military ventures and Hitler's impending death. The ONA broadcast Wohl's predictions and reported similar starry assertions from other astrologers to add credibility to Wohl's claims. "At the time, there was a perception of American people, in the minds of the British Security Services, that they were more gullible than us Brits," author William Boyd said in a 2008 interview.

■ 137. PLAYWRIGHT SPY

MAP 3 ➤ **Noel Coward meeting site:** Hampshire House, 150 Central Park South

Noel Coward, the famed play-wright, was among Britain's most unlikely World War II spies. Coward was active in prewar propaganda operations in Paris. A fact-finding tour of Eastern Europe and Scandinavia followed, with visits to Leningrad, Moscow, Warsaw, and Helsinki. "Celebrity was wonderful cover," Coward said, "My disguise would be my own reputation as a bit of an idiot . . . a merry playboy."

Noel Coward

Coward was recruited by William Stephenson into the BSC, who initially met with him in London, then again at Stephenson's suite in the Hampshire House, 150 Central Park South. Coward is said to have attended training at a secret BSC facility known as Camp X on the northwestern shore of Lake Ontario. How much actual spying Coward did during the war remains in dispute.

The Nazis almost certainly knew of his espionage activities, earning him a place on the *Sonderfahndungsliste G.B.* (Special Search List Great Britain), which included nearly 3,000 names of British citizens to be rounded up following an invasion. After the war, Coward sent a telegram to another member of the elite list, author Rebecca West, which read: "My dear—the people we should have been seen dead with." By then Coward had resumed his old globe-trotting, high-society life with few regrets, later saying, "Could have made a career in espionage, except my life's been full enough of intrigue as it is."

■ 138. DEATH OF A JAYWALKING SPY

MAP 3 ➤ **Compromise of the Ludwig spy ring:** Taft Hotel (now The Michelangelo) 152 West 51st Street

Rain was falling the evening of March 18, 1941, when a well-dressed middle-aged man wearing horn-rimmed spectacles and carrying a brown briefcase stepped into traffic near the corner of West 45th Street and Seventh Avenue. Struck by a cab, he was propelled into the path of another car. An

Kurt Frederick Ludwig

ambulance rushed the victim to St. Vincent's Hospital at 203 West 12th Street in Greenwich Village (closed in 2010), where he died the following day without recovering consciousness. The man was identified as Don Julio Lopez Lido, a Spanish citizen with a home address in Shanghai and guest of the Taft Hotel (today The Michelangelo) at 152 West 51st Street. The Spanish consulate claimed the body and paid for the funeral.

The incident seemed like just another big-city tragedy, except for some troublesome details. First, Lopez Lido's unidentified companion at the scene of the accident suspiciously grabbed the mortally injured man's briefcase and fled, vanishing into the gathering Times Square crowd. Then, a notebook found on Lopez Lido, written in German, contained names and assignments of US soldiers. Finally, his clothing bore no identifying labels. More suspicions mounted after a search of his hotel room discovered a *Fortune* magazine article detailing the history of aviation, a story in *Harper's* magazine about "ferry pilots" flying bombers to Britain, and the book *Winged Warfare* by Maj. Gen. Henry H. Arnold and Col. Ira C. Eaker.

Even more clues emerged after British censors in a Bermuda mail-opening operation intercepted a letter from New York found to contain secret writing informing Lopez Lido's handlers that an American car had mysteriously run over and killed "PHIL." The BSC notified the FBI that PHIL was actually Capt. Ulrich von der Osten of the Abwehr, who had entered the United States one month earlier via Japan.

Piecing together the clues, the FBI identified the victim's companion as an American citizen, Kurt Frederick Ludwig, who had moved to Germany at an early age, then returned to the United States, and was living in a boarding-house on Fresh Pond Road in the Ridgewood section of Queens. He was also an agent for German intelligence.

By keeping Ludwig under surveillance, the FBI eventually identified other

Dr. Paul Borchardt, analyst.

Evelyn C. Lewis, accomplice.

René Mezenen, Nazi steward.

Lucy Boehmler, Ludwig aide.

Agents of the Ludwig spy ring

members of the spy ring, including 18-year-old Lucy Boehmler of 62-02 60th Street, Maspeth, Queens. The teenager, working as Ludwig's $25-a-week secretary, composed meticulous records about US Army airfields, camps, and factories engaged in manufacturing wartime matériel by writing with a toothpick dipped in an ink that, when dry, was invisible to the naked eye. The final piece of the puzzle fell into place when Ludwig, who was in jail at the time, tried unsuccessfully to bribe a police officer to send a telegram warning of potential arrest to Paul Borchardt, the last free member of the ring.

In all, eight other members of the spy ring, including a Long Island housewife and active military personnel, were arrested in the summer of 1941. Found guilty of spying, Ludwig received a 20-year prison sentence. When paroled in 1954, he returned to New York to work, surprisingly, as a security guard at the Morgan Library and Museum, 225 Madison Avenue, before eventually moving to Germany in 1960. Boehmler, who testified for the prosecution, was sentenced to five years. Borchardt, sentenced to 20 years, was released in 1952 and died the next year.

The Whitehall Building, named for Peter Stuyvesant's home, "White Hall," housed Nazi Germany's consulate until America entered World War II in 1941.

■ 139. SPIES WITH HARBOR VIEWS

MAP I ➤ **German consulate:** Whitehall Building, 17 Battery Place

Before America's entrance into World War II, the German Consulate and International Commercial Agency on the 19th floor of the Whitehall Building, 17 Battery Place, operated an espionage hub run by Nazi Party member Ernst Hopf. The consulate, with spectacular harbor views, was bombed in 1940 but sustained only minimal damage. The attackers were never identified.

A short time later, the building's furnace operator, Walter Morrissey, was ordered to burn official looking papers. Instead, he smuggled the documents out of the building to the FBI. Those documents would later provide vital evidence in the Ludwig spy ring case. The consulate was closed in late 1941 when America entered the war.

■ 140. TWO LADIES AND THE SPY

MAP 6 ➤ **Duško Popov penthouse:** 530 Park Avenue

Dušan "Duško" Popov passport photo

Nothing was low profile about World War II double agent Duško Popov. He lived in a luxury Park Avenue Building and dated beautiful women, including French film star Simone Simon.

Dušan "Duško" Popov, a Yugoslavian businessman, was first recruited by the Abwehr before volunteering to become a double agent for British intelligence. Given the code name TRICYCLE for his proclivity for entertaining two women at once, Popov became a valuable source of information on German tradecraft, including use of microdots for covert communication. As a double agent, he was also useful for relaying disinformation to Berlin.

In addition to his fondness for beautiful women, Popov possessed an appetite for expensive living. Arriving in New York in 1941 on a secret mission for German military intelligence, he checked into a suite at the Waldorf Astoria, 301 Park Avenue, before moving to a penthouse in a new luxury building just up the street at 530 Park Avenue. Never fully trusted by J. Edgar Hoover's FBI because of his flamboyant lifestyle, Popov asserted in his memoir *Spy/Counterspy*, "If I bend over to smell a bowl of flowers, I scratch my nose on a microphone."

Neither Popov nor Hoover relented in their mutual disdain. While Popov vacationed in Miami with British fashion model Terry Richardson, two FBI agents, wearing suits and ties, approached the couple on the beach. To Popov's surprise, the double agent was threatened with arrest under the 1910 Mann Act, a law that proscribed travel across state lines with a woman "with the intent and purpose to induce, entice, or compel [her] to become a prostitute or to give herself up to debauchery, or to engage in any other immoral practice."

Popov left the United States soon afterward but continued working for Allied intelligence and played a key role in OPERATION FORTITUDE, the 1944 deception campaign preceding the Normandy landings in France.

In Popov the US government missed an intelligence opportunity by failing to recognize the significance of one microdot that contained tasking requirements for an agent in the United States. The requirements were detailed questions, apparently requested by Germany's ally Japan, about US defenses at Pearl Harbor. Decades later Popov claimed he informed the FBI on August 12, 1941, of an impending attack. The FBI said the information was forwarded to the Navy Department.

■ 141. NEW YORK'S LANDLORD, AMERICA'S SPY

MAP 2 ➤ **Astor family office:** 23 West 26th Street

Vincent Astor, a boyhood friend and distant cousin of Franklin Roosevelt, inherited an estimated $200 million when his father, John Jacob Astor IV, died in the *Titanic* disaster in 1912. Vincent Astor became known as "New York's landlord" and, from the family office at 23 West 26th Street, oversaw a business empire of New York real estate and substantial interests in premier companies such as Chase National Bank and the Western Union Telegraph Company.

The Astor family offices on West 26th Street, in a once-fashionable neighborhood portrayed in Edith Wharton's novels, became headquarters for the Communist Party USA after Vincent Astor's death.

Astor was no stranger to espionage. During World War I, he loaned his 265-foot luxury yacht, the *Norma*, to the US Navy, which outfitted it with small arms and commissioned it as the USS *Norma*. Astor then served on his own vessel as a junior officer as it escorted troop and cargo ships across the Atlantic Ocean and hunted German submarines. During the 1930s, Astor was a founding member of the Room, 34 East 62nd Street, an unofficial organization of businessmen who shared closely held international information among themselves and government officials.

Vincent Astor

Then in 1938, he used another yacht, the 263-foot *Nourmahal*, for a scouting expedition of Japanese defenses in the Marshall Islands under cover of an oceanic expedition. Astor also persuaded other wealthy boat owners to follow his example. The result was that at least 89 yachts of members of the New York Yacht Club, including J. P. Morgan's 304-foot *Corsair III*, saw wartime service.

In April 1941, President Roosevelt offered Astor, who held the rank of commander in the Navy Reserve, an intelligence position as "Area Controller for the New York Area." Astor accepted in a personal letter that characterized the responsibilities as coordination of intelligence and investigational activities in the New York area undertaken by representatives of the Departments of State, Navy, War and Justice. In this intelligence role, Astor operated from an office at 50 Church Street, today the site of the Millennium Hilton Hotel, working with the other intelligence organizations to settle bureaucratic turf disputes. He also served as a liaison to British intelligence and, in that role, became a back channel for relaying to the president sensitive information collected by the British. From his position on the boards of Western Union and Chase National Bank, Astor enjoyed access to otherwise difficult to obtain foreign intelligence information. Finally, he also allowed the Astor estate in Bermuda, Ferry Reach, to be used by British intelligence for a mail-opening operation.

The millionaire-spy resigned his role as area controller for New York in August 1944 and died in 1959 at his home at 120 East End Avenue.

J. P Morgan's 1898 yacht was commissioned into the US Navy on May 15, 1917, as the USS *Corsair*. It would again serve the United States during World War II as the USS *Oceanographer*.

■ 142. UNDERCOVER RECRUITING

MAP 5 ➤ **Clayton Knight studio:** 291 Fifth Avenue (site redeveloped)

At the beginning of World War II in Europe, Clayton Knight was an artist living in Greenwich Village working from a studio at 291 Fifth Avenue. His days as a World War I pilot were long behind him when he was unexpectedly contacted by Canadian flying ace Billy Bishop. The British Commonwealth was woefully unprepared for an air war, Bishop explained, and in desperate need of pilots.

The two enlisted E. Homer Smith, heir to a Canadian oil fortune, to launch the Clayton Knight Committee. From a luxury suite at the Waldorf Astoria, 301 Park Avenue, they recruited American pilots for training in Canada and onward deployment to Europe. The committee opened branches in Atlanta, Los Angeles, Chicago, and other major cities. Discreet posters and word-of-mouth attracted applicants, and for 18 months the committee supplied a steady stream of pilots to Canada.

The Clayton Knight Committee faced continuing legal problems because of America's official neutrality and laws that prohibited Americans from fighting in the armed services of foreign nations. Officially the committee recruited for a private enterprise called Dominion Aeronautical Association (DAA), not the Canadian military. Nevertheless, the FBI and the State Department launched investigations, citing DAA's close ties to the Royal Canadian Air Force. Knight staunchly maintained his committee was simply interviewing, providing physicals, conducting flight tests, and then recommending applicants to a private Canadian company.

Once America entered World War II, Knight turned his artistic attention to painting recruiting posters for the US Army Air Forces and patriotic illustrations of air combat for magazines. At the end of the war, Knight was awarded the Order of the British Empire, though likely not for his paintings.

■ 143. HITLER'S FAILED SABOTEURS

MAP 2 ➤ **OPERATION PASTORIUS safe house:** Governor Clinton Hotel (now the Stewart Hotel), 371 Seventh Avenue at West 31st Street

By mid-1942, American factories were working at full capacity building the warships, planes, and tanks needed to defeat the Axis powers. To disrupt military production, Hitler and his generals planned to bring the war to American soil by sending Abwehr agents to sabotage American manufacturing. Designated OPERATION PASTORIUS, the plan was named for the leader of the first German settlement in America, near Philadelphia.

Just after midnight on June 13, 1942, four men infiltrated the country on a Long Island beach near Amagansett from the submarine *U-202*. They dragged ashore explosives, primers, and incendiary devices along with more than

$175,000 in cash to support two years of sabotage. Four days later, in the second phase of the operation, *U-584* delivered a similarly equipped group to Ponte Vedra Beach near Jacksonville, Florida.

The New York saboteurs, all in their thirties, were led by George John Dasch and included Ernest Peter Burger, Heinrich Harm Heinck, and Richard Quirin. All members of the New York and Florida teams were German nationals who had spent significant time in the United States prior to the war.

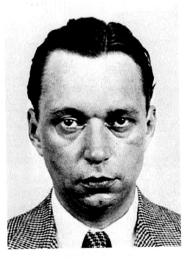

Ernest Peter Burger

George John Dasch

Almost immediately the New York team ran into trouble. A Coast Guardsman on watch, armed with a flare gun, encountered the four would-be saboteurs as they were burying their equipment and changing from military uniforms into civilian clothing. Clumsily shoving more than $200 in cash into the surprised sentry's hands, they escaped up the beach, but he promptly reported the encounter to his superiors. Knowing they had been compromised, the four caught the Long Island Railroad to Manhattan and broke up into two groups. Dasch and Burger checked into the Governor Clinton Hotel (now the Stewart Hotel) at 371 Seventh Avenue, while Heinck and Quirin rented rooms at the Hotel Martinique (now the Radisson Martinique), 49 West 32nd Street. The following night they rejoined for dinner and hit the town, going to clubs along Swing Street (West 52nd Street) and freely spending the Abwehr's cash.

The next day Dasch lost his nerve and called the New York FBI office. The agent who answered the phone hung up on him, thinking it a prank call. Undeterred, Dasch took a train to Washington, checked into the Mayflower Hotel, and surrendered to the FBI, revealing details of the plan along with descriptions of his fellow saboteurs.

Dasch's three companions were picked up in New York City on June 20. Two members of the Florida team were arrested on June 23, also in New York. The other two members of the Florida team were rounded up in Chicago on June 27.

From beginning to end, OPERATION PASTORIUS lasted less than two weeks. The eight were tried before a military commission, found guilty, and sentenced to death. Attorney General Francis Biddle and FBI director J. Edgar Hoover appealed successfully to President Roosevelt to commute the sentences of Dasch and Burger in recognition of their cooperation. Dasch's sentence was reduced to 30 years in prison, and Burger got life. The remaining six were executed at the District of Columbia jail on August 8, 1942, after the United States Supreme Court ruled against them in *Ex Parte Quirin*.

Three years after the war ended, President Harry S. Truman granted executive clemency to Dasch and Burger on condition of deportation. Both were eventually freed in the American Zone of Germany. Burger died in 1975 and Dasch in 1992.

German saboteurs Heinrich Harm Heinck and Richard Quirin stayed at the Hotel Martinique during the failed OPERATION PASTORIUS.

The Stewart Hotel, once called the Governor Clinton and now the Affinia Manhattan, was built in 1929 near Pennsylvania Station and briefly hosted two would-be German saboteurs, George John Dasch and Ernest Peter Burger, during OPERATION PASTORIUS.

■ 144. ESPIONAGE ON RIVERSIDE DRIVE

MAP 8 ➤ **Simon Koedel residence:** 660 Riverside Drive

Simon Emil Koedel, a naturalized American citizen who served in the US military prior to World War I, remained loyal to Germany through two wars. As a volunteer spy during World War I, he sent meticulous reports to German intelligence on shipping activity in New York Harbor. Following the war,

With money received from German paymasters for his espionage, Simon Koedel lived comfortably at 660 Riverside Drive.

he was given a small stipend should the need arise to reactivate him.

During World War II, Koedel became Agent A2011, a high-value spy. In addition to providing detailed reconnaissance reports of the lightly guarded harbor, he posed as a wealthy armaments merchant and joined a trade group, the American Ordnance Association (AOA). Although his day job was projectionist at the Lyric Theatre, 213 West 42nd Street, Koedel received confidential reports from the association and other information from the War Department's official mailing list. Following a well-earned raise from the Abwehr, he moved into a luxury building at 660 Riverside Drive with his wife, while his daughter, Marie Hedwig Koedel, lived at 542 West 112th Street.

Koedel wrote letters on AOA stationery, which prompted responses containing secret information and invitations to tour armament facilities. In one instance, while visiting the Edgewood Arsenal in Bel Air, Maryland, he was able to detach labels from containers and mail them to his handlers. As an active member of the AOA, he regularly attended meetings and corresponded with the association's president. In one instance, Koedel chided the AOA for lack of security at defense plants. US senator Robert Rice Reynolds from North Carolina, a member of the Military Affairs Committee, unwittingly eased the way for Koedel into secure facilities.

Not all of the information Koedel sent back to Germany was classified. He made good use of open sources and regularly scanned the papers for significant tidbits. For example, in October 7, 1939, a *New York Times* story announced, "Roosevelt Protected in Talks to Envoys by Radio 'Scrambling' to Foil Spies Abroad." Beginning with only the few facts included in the story, German technicians began building a descrambling device, which became operational by March 1942.

Aware that mail to Europe was passing through censors, Koedel devised a simple yet clever countermeasure. He steamed-open official manila envelopes from the AOA, added his intelligence reports, then forwarded them to an accommodation address in Milan, Italy. He calculated correctly that the censors would not tamper with envelopes stamped "Official Business" from the AOA. Koedel even recruited his reluctant daughter, Marie, instructing her to cruise waterfront bars to pick up information from merchant seamen and US Navy sailors about their ships, cargoes, and schedules.

Koedel's activities eventually came to the FBI's attention. With the war going against Germany, he ranted in an angry letter to a Maj. Gen. Morris B.

Payne of the Connecticut National Guard, "The average American is a double-crosser, a chronic draft-dodger, and crooked at heart." Payne turned the letter over to the FBI. Then, when Koedel ordered Marie to break her engagement to her fiancée, she told the young man of the spying, and he, in turn, contacted the FBI.

Koedel was apprehended in October 1944. He was convicted of espionage and sentenced to 15 years in prison. After the war, he was released and deported to Germany.

■ 145. PLANNING OPERATION UNDERWORLD

MAP ı ➤ **Mob boss headquarters:** Meyer's Hotel, 119 South Street

Charles "Lucky" Luciano

In 1942, the outcome of World War II was undetermined and the waters off New York and New Jersey teemed with U-boat wolf packs. At night, the flames of exploding oil tankers were visible from the shoreline. Commercial fishing fleets were suspected as sources of fuel and supplies for enemy submarines off shore.

Many longshoremen were of Italian heritage, and some were suspected sympathizers of Benito Mussolini and his fascists. The ONI, realizing the security threat, also understood that the Italian American Mafia controlled the docks. These circumstances prompted a bold move, code-named OPERATION UNDERWORLD, to recruit infamous crime bosses to help maintain security.

Heading the operation for naval intelligence was Cmdr. Charles R. Haffenden, who worked closely with legendary New York district attorney Frank Hogan. In March 1942, they contacted Joe "Socks" Lanza, a mob boss who governed the Fulton Fish Market and docks along the East River from his headquarters in Meyer's Hotel at 119 South Street, above a longshoremen's bar called the Paris Café.

The initial meeting with Lanza was held at West 135th Street and Riverside Park on a bench, after which Haffenden, sensitive to the fact mobsters were wary of meeting in public or in a federal office building, established a "field office" for subsequent meetings in a room in the Hotel Astor, 1515 Broadway (today 1 Astor Plaza).

From the Fulton Fish Market, then known as a venue for organized crime, underworld figures were recruited during World War II to preclude fuel or provisions from being supplied to German submarines patrolling the Atlantic.

Joseph "Socks" Lanza, a known racketeer who allegedly controlled the New York waterfront, was approached by federal authorities in the Meyer's Hotel for assistance in keeping the docks safe from sabotage during World War II.

Sensitive to potential political concerns about meeting with alleged mobsters in federal buildings, World War II's OPERATION UNDERWORLD chief, Cdr. Charles R. Haffenden, set up his headquarters in the Hotel Astor at 1515 Broadway.

Lanza suggested an approach be made to organized crime kingpin Charles "Lucky" Luciano, who was in prison at the time. Working through lawyers and another reputed gangster, Meyer Lansky, the government offered Luciano clemency in exchange for cooperation. Luciano agreed to rally the underworld, though he insisted on secrecy, telling ONI, "When I get out—nobody knows how this war will turn out—whatever I do, I want it kept quiet, private, so that when I get back to Italy I'm not a marked man."

Luciano was then transferred to Great Meadow Prison, where he was allowed to meet mob contacts, posing as regular visitors, in a conference room adjacent to the warden's office. Over the next two years, he made available to the ONI his full list of contacts and associates willing to cooperate in the program.

Lanza, for his part, would safeguard the piers from sabotage and keep the fishing fleet free of rogue elements who might be tempted to sell fuel to surfacing German U-boats. Reporting about suspicious activities on the waterfront, acting as lookouts for sabotage and espionage, and obtaining and altering union books and union cards to enable naval intelligence agents to work in hotels, restaurants, bars, trucking, factories, and on the docks were all part of the support provided. Numerous Italians of Sicilian birth or background and their relatives were also enlisted to provide intelligence about Sicily's terrain, harbors, and other geographical features in anticipation of the Allied invasion.

The US Navy calculated that the value of the information provided by Lanza, Luciano, and their contacts was invaluable to the war effort. In return for his help, Luciano's prison sentence was commuted, and he was deported to Italy on January 3, 1946. The mobster was driven under guard to Pier 7 of the sprawling Bush Terminals (now Industry City) in Brooklyn, given a rousing bon voyage party, and put aboard the *Laura Keane* for Italy.

Under the deportation agreement, Luciano was banned from reentering the United States and died in Italy in 1962. His body was returned for burial at St. John's Cathedral Cemetery in Queens.

■ 146. SECRET SITES OF THE SECRET BOMB

MAP I ▶ **First headquarters of the Manhattan Project:** Arthur Levitt State Office Building, 270 Broadway

Uranium ore for the Manhattan Project was stored in the Baker and Williams warehouses on West 20th Street prior to its distribution to government facilities for processing.

From 1942 to 1945, America's program to create the world's first nuclear weapon was among the nation's most closely guarded secrets. Security surrounding the Manhattan Project was so tight that President Roosevelt never told Vice President Truman of its existence.

The enriched uranium needed for the bomb was produced at a laboratory in Oak Ridge, Tennessee, while components of the weapon were assembled at Los Alamos, New Mexico. However, the project also operated in a network of secret offices, laboratories, and warehouses throughout the country, including many in New York City, where the initial effort began:

■ Manhattan Project Headquarters, 270 Broadway: In June 1942, the 18th floor of the (now) Arthur Levitt State Office Building was the first office for the Manhattan Engineer District, or "Manhattan Project." Though the headquarters was relocated in the summer of 1943 to Oak Ridge, the "Manhattan Project" name stuck.

■ Pupin Hall and Schermerhorn Hall, 2912–2952 Broadway, Columbia University: Important particle research was carried out on Columbia's campus by physicists Isidor I. Rabi and Enrico Fermi to investigate atomic particles. A cyclotron—an "atom smasher"—was installed in the basement of Pupin Hall to induce collisions of atoms at speeds of up to 25,000 miles per second.

The Kellex Corporation, headquartered in the landmark Woolworth Building, was the contractor responsible for building the Manhattan Project's gaseous diffusion plant.

An early cyclotron was installed in the basement of Columbia University's Pupin Hall as part of the Manhattan Project's research efforts.

Physicist Enrico Fermi assembled the first experimental nuclear pile in Schermerhorn Hall on the campus of Columbia University

■ Nash Garage, 3280 Broadway: The site, originally a Nash automobile dealership, was acquired by Columbia University to create the barrier material used in the gaseous diffusion process necessary to enrich uranium.

■ Union Carbide and Carbon Corporation Building, 30 East 42nd Street: The former site of Union Carbide's headquarters has been replaced by a new office building. However, from the 18th floor of the original building on the southwestern corner of 42nd Street and Madison Avenue, Union Carbide and its subsidiary, the Union Mines Development Corporation, managed the acquisition of raw uranium ore. The US Army's Murray Hill Area Engineers Office was conveniently located on the same floor.

■ Baker and Williams warehouses, 529 West 20th Street: The enormous warehouses stored tons of uranium ore, much of it from Canada, secretly off-loaded from ships at the nearby docks. It was then shipped to government facilities and laboratories for processing.

■ Kellex Corporation, Woolworth Building, 233 Broadway: The Kellex Corporation was contacted by the Manhattan Project to build the gaseous diffusion plant, or K-25, for Columbia University in the Nash Building. Soviet spy Klaus Fuchs worked at the Kellex Corporation from December 1943 until his transfer to Oak Ridge in August 1944.

The statue of Shinran Shonin, 13th-century founder of Jodo Shinshu Buddhism, standing outside the New York Buddhist Church on Riverside Drive survived the atomic bombing of Hiroshima, Japan.

■ Madison Square Engineers office, 1 East 29th Street (also listed at 261 Fifth Avenue): A 300-person team worked from this office to procure the materials needed for the atomic weapon, including uranium, graphite, and beryllium.

■ Office of Edgar Sengier, Cunard Building, 25 Broadway: Sengier was a Belgian businessman and director of the Union Minière du Haut Katanga, a mining company in the Belgian Congo. Through him, the Manhattan Project gained access to vital uranium sources.

■ 147. BROADCASTING LIVE FROM LONG ISLAND

MAP 12 ➤ **Secret transmitter site:** 408 North Side Road, Wading River, Long Island

From January 1942 until June 1945, the FBI conducted a secret radio operation at Benson House, 408 North Side Road, Wading River, Long Island, that communicated with the Abwehr in Hamburg. While German intelligence believed it was receiving reporting from an agent inside the United States, it had actually fallen for an elaborate FBI deception. Cooperating with the US military, the FBI sent hundreds of messages to Germany designed to confuse and mislead the Nazi leadership.

The agent that the Abwehr believed it was in contact with was Jorge Mosquera, an Argentine businessman who had spent the previous 20 years living in Germany. When Mosquera sold his German business to return to Buenos Aires, Nazi authorities stopped the transfer of funds unless he agreed to become a spy for them in the United States. He accepted the dubious deal, only because there was no other choice.

Mosquera was provided with microdots containing a list of information needed by the German military and sent on his way. His first stop en route to the United States was Montevideo, Uruguay, where he contacted the American legation, told the entire story, and volunteered to act as a double agent.

When Mosquera arrived in the United States in late 1941, the FBI read the microdots, which validated his authenticity. Preparations were then made to carry out the Abwehr's plan by establishing a secret radio station in the New York City area and communicating using the code name ND98. The site needed to be remote but also possess the necessary atmospheric conditions for transatlantic high-frequency transmissions. A lonely three-story house on a high bluff on Long Island overlooking the sound and a mile from the small fishing village of Wading River met all operational and technical requirements.

By early January 1942, the FBI had installed sophisticated high-frequency radio equipment in the house, concealed the aerials, and acquired a generator to diminish otherwise suspicious high-electricity

Benson House in Wading River, New York, was the site of a sophisticated radio-deception operation launched by the FBI. German intelligence believed it was communicating with a high-value agent operating in the United States.

usage. The bureau then moved sickly-looking special agent Donworth Johnson, along with his wife and two-year-old daughter, into the house. Donworth's cover story, which was needed at a time when able-bodied men were in the military, was that he had communicable tuberculosis and needed seclusion. The cover explained his reclusive lifestyle and kept curious neighbors at a distance. The most visible member of the family was Clifford, a 70-pound German shepherd, whose fierce growl would frighten uninvited visitors. The Johnsons manned the radio 24 hours a day under such secrecy that the family was not allowed to leave the site, even to go into the nearby town.

The first radio contact with Hamburg occurred in late February 1942. The Abwehr believed the brilliant and motivated Mosquera was successfully recruiting subagents in important positions in the government, military, and industry. There was WASCH, a senior civilian in the War Department; NEVI, a secretary working for an admiral; REP, an employee of Republic Aviation based in Farmingdale, New York; and OFFICER, a worker in the Brooklyn Navy Yard. Together they provided a stream of harmless truths to establish credibility, along with misleading lies in response to a barrage of Abwehr requests for military intelligence.

Among the most important transmissions sent by Germany was an April 1942 instruction for Mosquera's network to gather all possible information on atomic research. This message reinforced President Roosevelt's decision to build an atomic bomb. A series of messages in early 1944 was part of an operation designed to deceive the German military about the timing and location of the Allied invasion of Europe. Other messages to Hamburg were relayed to Tokyo and served to confuse the Japanese about US advances in the Pacific.

By June 1945, the Abwehr radio station in Hamburg was in Allied hands, and the war in Europe over. The FBI removed almost every trace of the secret operation, and today, nearly unchanged from its appearance in World War II, the house is an office for the Camp DeWolfe Conference Center of the Episcopal Diocese of Long Island.

■ 148. LITTLE SHOP OF ESPIONAGE

MAP 6 ➤ **Velvalee Dickinson doll shop:** 718 Madison Avenue

As Velvalee Dickinson's doll shop at 718 Madison Avenue began to fail in 1941, she and her husband turned to spying for the Japanese. Coded messages were embedded in letters that outwardly appeared to document doll sales.

Velvalee Dickinson arrived in New York during the Great Depression after her husband's San Francisco produce-brokerage business failed in 1937. During their years in California, the couple had developed an affinity for their many Japanese customers and became friendly with officials in Japan's San Francisco consulate. In New York, Dickinson first took a job in the doll department at Bloomingdale's, then opened her own doll shop at 680 Madison Avenue, moved up the street to 714 Madison, and eventually settled at 718 Madison in 1941. By the time Japan attacked Pearl Harbor in December 1941, the doll shop was failing, yet, inexplicably, the couple continued to have plenty of money for trips back to the West Coast.

Then in 1943, some American residents unexpectedly began receiving strange "return to sender" mail addressed to Inez Lopez de Malinali in Buenos Aires, Argentina. The letters mysteriously bore US return addresses of people with no knowledge of the correspondence. The contents, detailing unfamiliar doll sales, aroused suspicion, so a few were turned over to the FBI. From analysis of the letters, the FBI identified de Malinali as a Japanese intelligence contact in Buenos Aires and traced the letters back to Velvalee Dickinson.

Something was hidden in the letters, but what? Breaking the "doll code" fell to Elizebeth Friedman, a veteran cryptanalyst who previously broke Prohibition-era bootlegger codes for the US Coast Guard. Working with the seemingly benign descriptions of dolls, Friedman discovered each doll mentioned in the letters was a code for a specific type of American warship. Dickinson's intelligence was gleaned from multiple trips to the West Coast, where she observed shipyards and struck up conversations with employees.

With this discovery, authorities apprehended a kicking and screaming Dickinson in January 1944 at a bank where a large amount of money was discovered in her safe deposit box. Indicted for espionage, she blamed her husband, who had died in March 1943, for leading her astray and eventually accepted a plea bargain that reduced the charges to violating censorship laws. Dickinson was sentenced to 10 years in prison, was paroled in 1951, and died in 1980.

■ 149. JOLLY GOOD CENSORSHIP

MAP 3 ➤ **Mail-opening operation:** Park Central Hotel, 870 Seventh Avenue

The basement of the Park Central Hotel on Seventh Avenue was reportedly the site of an OSS mail-opening operation during World War II.

During World War II, the OSS was an apt student of ungentlemanly warfare learned from the British security service MI5. An example of lessons learned involved breaking into diplomatic containers and pouches, whose security was protected by international law but in practice was vulnerable to MI5's ingenious safecrackers and flaps-and-seals experts. OSS spy-techs reportedly established a special lab for opening mail and diplomatic pouches in the boiler room of the midtown Park Central Hotel, 870 Seventh Avenue.

Among the British ploys they learned was requesting couriers to place their diplomatic bags in locked safes at international arrival points. The couriers were unaware that the backs of the safes were hinged and easily opened for technicians to access the bags. Aided by the Postal Censorship Department, the OSS also developed methods for breaking, reconstituting, and repairing wax seals on the bags without leaving a trace.

When in New York City, Dietrich called 993 Park Avenue home. A naturalized US citizen, the star of *The Blue Angel* and *Shanghai Express* worked tirelessly against the Nazis during the war years.

■ 150. THE SINGING SPY

MAP 6 ➤ **Marlene Dietrich apartment:** 993 Park Avenue (at East 84th Street)

Movie star Marlene Dietrich resided at 993 Park Avenue after becoming an American citizen in 1939. A tireless opponent of Nazism, the star of *The Blue Angel* (1930) and *Shanghai Express* (1932) sold war bonds, entertained US troops, and worked for the OSS Morale

Operations Branch. Dietrich, along with other entertainers such as Bing Crosby and Dinah Shore, recorded songs in German aimed at lowering enemy morale and countering German propaganda. Dietrich's version of "Lili Marlene" for the Allied broadcaster *Soldatensender* (Soldiers Radio) proved particularly powerful as a propaganda tool, inciting German soldiers to write protest letters after listening to the station was banned by Nazi authorities. When Dietrich received the Presidential Medal of Freedom for her wartime support to the OSS in 1945, she described the recognition as "the proudest accomplishment of her life." She died in 1992 at age 90.

Marlene Dietrich's broadcasts during World War II were so popular that she later released an album of "greatest hits" recorded for the OSS.

■ 151. MAJOR LEAGUE SPY

MAP 8 ▶ **Moe Berg birthplace:** East 121st Street (exact address unknown — approximately at East 121st Street and Lexington Avenue)

Morris "Moe" Berg

Born in a cold-water tenement on East 121st Street in 1902, Morris "Moe" Berg studied at Princeton, then Columbia Law, and, briefly, the Sorbonne. After signing a professional baseball contract in 1923 at age 21, Berg played primarily as a catcher for a series of minor and major league teams, including the Brooklyn Robins (later called the Dodgers), the Toledo Mud Hens, the Chicago White Sox, the Cleveland Indians, and the Washington Senators. Berg, who spoke at least eight languages and read half a dozen newspapers a day, was so different from the other players that Casey Stengel described him as "the strangest man ever to play baseball." Berg's performance at the plate did not match his enthusiasm for the game: He compiled a .243 lifetime average, modest for players at the time.

Just when Berg began spying is uncertain. Possibly it was in 1934 while playing an exhibition series in Japan. Feigning illness to sit out a game, he donned traditional Japanese clothing and filmed the Tokyo skyline from a hospital room with a Bell and Howell 16mm camera, ostensibly for Movietone News. Once World War II began, Berg joined the OSS and worked behind enemy lines, first in Yugoslavia, then in German-occupied Norway.

However, perhaps Berg's most famous OSS assignment was PROJECT AZUSA. The mission was to assess the state of the German nuclear weapon program by attending a lecture in Switzerland in late 1944 by German physicist Werner Heisenberg. If Berg, code name REMUS, judged the program close to producing a nuclear device, he was to shoot Heisenberg on the spot. The gun stayed in his pocket.

After the war, Berg undertook one final clandestine mission for US intelligence. From 1952 to 1954, the CIA had him assigned to gather information about Soviet atomic science. Eventually the former ballplayer and spy drifted into public obscurity while maintaining a lifelong love for America's pastime. Nicholas Davidoff's biography, *The Catcher Was a Spy*, recounts Berg's last words on May 29, 1972: "How did the Mets do today?" They beat the Cardinals 7 to 6.

■ 152. NOT TOO TALL TO SPY

MAP 5 ➤ **Julia Child apartment:** 400 East 59th Street

Julia McWilliams began her career as a copywriter in New York and lived in an apartment close enough to the East River to hear the waves against the pilings. She served in the OSS before becoming the world-renowned television chef Julia Child.

Before becoming a world-famous celebrity chef, Julia Child was Julia McWilliams, an OSS officer from Pasadena, California. After graduating from Smith College in 1934, Child moved to her first New York apartment, at 400 East 59th Street, and began her professional career as an advertising copywriter for the now defunct W. J. Sloane home-furnishings store at 575 Fifth Avenue.

When the war began, she sought to enlist. Rejected by the services because of her height of over six feet, McWilliams joined the OSS as a typist. She advanced to researcher for OSS director William Donovan and was then posted to Ceylon (now Sri Lanka) and China. Her subsequent culinary fame, combined with her intelligence work, made McWilliams/Child a legendary OSS officer.

■ 153. OSS "TRUTH" DRUG

MAP 5 ➤ **Drug-testing site:** Belmont Plaza Hotel (today the Maxwell Hotel), 541 Lexington Avenue

Hopes were high in 1943 among OSS scientists that tetrahydrocannabinol acetate, a derivative of the cannabis plant, could elicit truth from an unsuspecting subject. To test the potential of this alleged truth serum, an OSS officer and former NYPD detective George Hunter White invited August "Little Augie" Del Gaizo, a Lower East Side gangster whom he knew from his previous years in law enforcement, to meet in a midtown room at the Belmont Plaza Hotel, 541 Lexington Avenue. The drug was

OSS operatives, along with NYPD detective, tested a cannabis-derived "truth drug" on an unsuspecting gangster at the Belmont Plaza during World War II.

administered to the unwitting Del Gaizo in a cigarette and appeared to have positive results when the gangster began describing some of his illegal activities, which included importing narcotics into the United States. However, subsequent testing demonstrated the drug was unreliable and ineffective.

■ 154. COLD-FOOTED SABOTEUR

MAP 5 ➤ **Operational safe house:** 39 Beekman Place

A German U-boat quietly put two Abwehr spies ashore in Maine during November 1944. Erich Gimpel, a German national with a background in radio work, and William Colepaugh, a Massachusetts Institute of Technology dropout who had defected to Germany, worked their way undetected from the shoreline through Boston to New York and checked into the Kenmore Hotel at 145 East 23rd Street. Their mission was to collect intelligence and transmit it back to Germany by ciphered radio messages.

The pair spent the next few weeks subletting an apartment at 39 Beekman Place, bought and modified a shortwave radio, and lived well on $60,000 cash and a stash of diamonds courtesy of German intelligence. They shopped for new clothes at stores near Rockefeller Center, watched National Velvet at Radio City Music Hall, and frequented classic nightspots such as the Copacabana at 10 East 60th Street, El Morocco at 154 East 54th Street, and the Stork Club at 3 East 53rd Street. Once the money was spent, Colepaugh decided he was not cut out for spying and confessed the nature of the mission to a friend from Queens, who assisted in his surrender. Colepaugh then told the story to the FBI, and Gimpel was arrested while buying a newspaper at the Seventh Avenue and 42nd Street subway station newsstand.

The Kenmore Hotel, a hangout for writers such as Nathanael West, S. J. Perleman, and Dashiell Hammett, rented rooms to two German spies, Erich Gimpel and William Colepaugh, during their failed World War II sabotage operation.

Their mission, code-named MAGPIE, had lasted a little more than a month. Tried on Governors Island before a military court, both were found guilty of conspiracy to commit espionage and sentenced to death. Fortunately for the pair, the war ended two months after their conviction, and President Truman reduced their sentences to life. Gimpel served 10 years in Alcatraz, then returned to Germany. Colepaugh was paroled in 1960, got married, and settled in Pennsylvania.

■ 155. NIGHTLIFE FOR SPIES

MAP 3 ➤ **21 Club:** 21 West 52nd Street

Originally called Jack and Charlie's Place, the townhouse at 21 West 52nd Street was a speakeasy before it became the internationally recognized 21 Club. The upscale eatery and bar was already legendary during World War II, attracting notable intelligence patrons, including William Donovan of the OSS, BSC chief William Stephenson, and suspected German spies.

First operating as a speakeasy during Prohibition, the 21 Club survived the Depression to become a favorite with British and American intelligence operatives during World War II. Ian Fleming and the fictional James Bond were both devotees of the restaurant's wine cellar and menu.

Ernest Cuneo, a behind-the-scenes World War II operator who worked with both British and US intelligence services, later lived on East 62nd Street.

Ian Fleming, who frequented New York as a British intelligence officer, liked the 21 Club so much he later incorporated it into one of his James Bond novels. In *Diamonds Are Forever*, Bond dines at 21 with the beautiful diamond-smuggling "Bond girl" Tiffany Case. Fleming, who often included his personal tastes in the Bond books, detailed a 21 menu in the narrative. Actor David Niven, another of 21's notable frequent customers, was a member of the GHQ Liaison Regiment, known as the Phantom Signals Unit, which reported on enemy positions from the front lines following the D-Day invasion.

One of Fleming's American contacts was Ernest Cuneo, a fellow 21 Club enthusiast. Cuneo worked as liaison between British intelligence, the OSS, and President Roosevelt. Following the war, he married one of the British intelligence secretaries stationed in New York and moved into a former Rockefeller-owned townhouse at 9 East 62nd Street. Cuneo maintained his friendship with Fleming, and the pair often conducted "nightlife research" expeditions in New York, Las Vegas, and Chicago. Fleming's *Thunderball* is dedicated "To Ernest Cuneo, Muse."

■ 156. TOUGH SPOUSE OF AMERICA'S SPYMASTER

MAP 6 ➤ Clover and Allen Dulles home: 239 East 61st Street

A townhouse at 239 East 61st Street was home to Allen Dulles, the future director of Central Intelligence, when he worked as a lawyer in the powerhouse Wall Street firm Sullivan and Cromwell. During World War II, while Dulles was posted in Bern, Switzerland, with the OSS—code name AGENT 110—his wife, Clover, continued to live in the Upper East Side townhouse and commute by subway to her job in Brooklyn as a defense plant supervisor. *Gentleman Spy: The Life of Allen Dulles* by Peter Grose recounts that after Clover took a firm stand against what she viewed as racial discrimination in the plant, one Brooklyn factory worker told her, "You're probably the toughest son-of-a-bitch in the place!"

The Upper East Side residence acquired a footnote in intelligence history while Dulles was posted in Bern. His secretary, Mary Bancroft, claimed that she could guess the combination of his secure briefcase. Incredulous, he challenged her to open it. And she did, correctly guessing the lock was set for 23961, his home address.

Following the war and a short stint on Wall Street, Dulles became the longest-serving Director of Central Intelligence, holding the position from 1953 to 1961. He later served as a member of the Warren Commission

Allen Dulles lived in a modest townhouse during his time in New York. His wife, Clover, worked in a Brooklyn defense plant and played hostess to spies passing through town while Dulles was on an OSS assignment in Europe.

investigating President John F. Kennedy's assassination. Dulles was recognized in 1997 as one of the CIA's 50th Anniversary Trailblazers for "creating the architecture of the modern CIA."

■ 157. CENTRAL PARK'S WILD WILDLIFE

MAP 7 ➤ **Central Park:** Fifth Avenue, Eighth Avenue, 59th Street, and 110th Street

William Donovan, director of the OSS, was known to encourage innovation by saying, "Go ahead and try it." Inevitably, ideas ranged from the practical and pragmatic to the madcap. PROJECT FANTASIA fell into the latter category. When someone in OSS recognized that the fox was an important figure in Japanese folklore and culture, it was also noted that a glowing fox was seen in that culture as a bad omen. To exploit this belief and inspire pessimism about the outcome of World War II among Japan's population, PROJECT FANTASIA was proposed as a psychological operation.

The operation envisioned releasing glowing foxes into selected Japanese locations, and in late 1944 the concept was field-tested. Reportedly, 30 foxes, painted with a radiant compound supplied by the United States Radium Corporation, were released at night in Central Park. The sight of the cavorting glow-in-the-dark animals set off a small panic among park goers, described by the *New York Herald Tribune* as "screaming jeemies."

Judged a success, FANTASIA was given operational approval, but the war came to an end before it could be implemented.

■ 158. NAZI PROPAGANDIST FROM BROOKLYN

MAP 10 ➤ **Lord Haw Haw childhood residence:** 1377 Herkimer Street, Brooklyn

British troops captured Brooklyn-born German propagandist William Joyce (a.k.a. Lord Haw Haw) in 1945 and executed him the following year.

During World War II, William Joyce acquired notoriety for his pro-Nazi propaganda radio broadcasts from Germany aimed at the British public. Joyce's sonorous, upper-class English accent often mocked British war efforts. On the air from 1939 to 1945, his broadcasts opened with the phrase "Germany calling," repeated twice in a condescending and calm tone.

Although Joyce was not identified by name, the *Daily Express* columnist Jonah Barrington, a.k.a. Cyril Carr

Dalmaine, imagined him to be a well-educated, imperious upper-crust type, perhaps an Oxford or Cambridge graduate, who wore a monocle and was given to Britishisms such as "cheerio" and exclamations that sounded like "haw haw." The name stuck.

In fact, Joyce was an American citizen by birth, born April 26, 1906, at 1377 Herkimer Street, Brooklyn, to Irish immigrant parents. The family later returned to Ireland where Joyce became a racist, profascist political activist in the 1930s before immigrating to Germany. At the end of the war, Joyce was captured by the British, tried, and hanged on January 3, 1946.

Joyce was born at 1377 Herkimer Street in Brooklyn.

■ 159. FORGIVEN PROPAGANDIST

MAP 6 ➤ **P. G. Wodehouse residence:** 1000 Park Avenue

Sir Pelham Grenville Wodehouse, better known as P. G. Wodehouse, the prolific author of the beloved Jeeves novels, is viewed as quintessentially British but remained in gentlemanly American exile for much of his later life. Arrested during the German occupation of France at the start of World War II, he was shuttled by his captors among internment camps. A series of recorded radio broadcasts Wodehouse made while held in Germany led to questions as to just which side he was on.

Whether the broadcasts were explicitly pro-German is questionable, but they were taken that way by the British. With the press and public turned against him in post–World War II England, Wodehouse moved to New York in the late 1940s to live comfortably at 1000 Park Avenue.

P. G. Wodehouse

British writer P. G. Wodehouse made a series of odd propaganda broadcasts following his capture by German troops in France. Shunned in his home country following the war, he lived in a penthouse at 1000 Park Avenue.

He later worked that address into his book *Service with a Smile* as the home of American millionaire Jimmy Schoonmaker. Eventually Wodehouse and his wife, Ethel, traded life in the Park Avenue penthouse for a house at 21 Basket Neck Lane, Remsenburg, on the South Shore of Long Island. He became a US citizen and never returned to Europe but was later knighted by the British government.

■ 160. SAM SPADE OF THE OSS

MAP 4 ▸ **Frank Bielaski office:** Hotel Van Rensselaer, 17 East 11th Street (now apartments)

Frank Bielaski

Frank Bielaski, who directed investigations for the OSS, was not a well-known counterintelligence figure. The one-time Wall Street broker, who maintained an office in a small suite at the Hotel Van Rensselaer, 17 East 11th Street, came from a family of government officials. His brother, Bruce Bielaski, headed the Bureau of Investigation, predecessor organization of the FBI, from 1912 to 1919. His sister, the formidable Ruth Shipley, was in charge of the State Department's passport division.

Some believed Bielaski's assignment was an effort by OSS chief William Donovan to placate Shipley who, at times, blocked issuance of passports to overseas OSS operatives. Shipley would not be placated and eventually President Roosevelt intervened.

Regardless of how he landed in the position, Bielaski displayed a natural aptitude for the work. In one case, he situated a female agent in a New

At one time known as the Hotel Van Rensselaer, this East 11th Street building was headquarters for OSS spy catcher Frank Bielaski.

York brownstone in the East Sixties to successfully infiltrate an Eastern European spy ring. When President Truman disbanded the OSS, Bielaski opened the Research and Security Corporation at 521 Fifth Avenue, and former OSS director William Donovan hired him to investigate his one-time OSS protégé Soviet spy Duncan Lee. Bielaski, who lived at 41 Park Avenue, died in 1961.

■ 161. FROM SPY TO HOLLYWOOD

MAP 7 ▶ **Robert Ryan apartment:** The Dakota, 1 West 72nd Street

A graduate of Dartmouth College, actor Robert Ryan appeared in nearly 100 films, including *The Set-Up* (1949) and *The Wild Bunch* (1969), almost always playing tough-guy roles of a gangster, gunslinger, or a boxer. The legendary star was indeed a tough Marine who reportedly worked with the OSS during World War II to assist partisan fighters in Yugoslavia. After the war, Ryan launched his movie career and became a champion of civil rights and liberal political causes. When he died in 1973, Ryan's apartment in the Dakota, 1 West 72nd Street, was sold to John Lennon and Yoko Ono.

The Dakota, built by Singer Sewing Machine heir Edward S. Clark, acquired its name because some New York residents thought its location was as remote as the Dakota Territory. Actor Robert Ryan, a World War II Marine and a star of *The Wild Bunch*, lived here.

■ 162. FROM INTELLIGENCE OFFICER TO FASHION ICON

MAP 6 ▶ **John Weitz residence:** 710 Park Avenue

To the fashion world, the name John Weitz defined elegance. The celebrity designer, who often served as model for his own clothing line, cut a glamorous swath through Manhattan society. Weitz lived on the Upper East Side at 710 Park Avenue and frequently appeared on society page photos dressed in a tuxedo or in fashion magazines unveiling a new line of clothing. In a parallel career as historian and author, Weitz wrote multiple books on World War II, including *Hitler's Banker* and *Hitler's Diplomat*, along with novels such as *Friends in High Places* and *The Value of Nothing*. However, he remained scrupulously circumspect about his experiences as an intelligence officer during the war.

As an immigrant to the United States from Germany with his family at the start of World War II, Weitz spoke fluent German and French. After a brief stint with Voice of America, he was recruited into the OSS and sent back into France, where he made contact with a German officer planning the failed July 20, 1944, plot to assassinate Hitler. Weitz offered few details about his other OSS assignments, even to his family. One exception was his

Fashion designer and OSS operative John Weitz became known as the epitome of elegance, often serving as model in advertisements for his clothing line. However, he remained stubbornly quiet about his harrowing OSS missions.

mention of posing as a German to infiltrate the Dachau concentration camp complex, where German prisoners were held after liberation, to determine whether an uprising was planned. He discerned that the report of a possible incident was only a matter of an officer giving pep talks to the men. Weitz said he also searched for scientists thought to have been interned at Dachau but found none.

Weitz also reportedly infiltrated a Munich-based Werwolf cell at the end of the war as part of OPERATION NURSERY to break the organization's Munich branch. Comprised of fanatical Nazis, the Werwolf organization operated as a stay-behind guerrilla force to create mayhem in occupied Germany. Formed in 1944, the organization boasted the motto "Hate Is Our Prayer, Revenge Our Resolve." The well-outfitted and armed recruits came primarily from the SS and Hitler Youth. Weitz was said to have simulated burns on himself similar to those an SS officer would

Weitz's prestigious 710 Park Avenue address befitted the celebrity designer and former OSS officer.

have gotten in trying to remove the unit's identifying tattoo with a lit cigarette. The operation was deemed a success, as 16 members of the cell were arrested in Munich in April 1946.

This episode is recounted in *The Last Hero: Wild Bill Donovan* by historian Anthony Cave Brown, who casts Weitz under the name Johanne Werner. In crediting the interview, Brown writes, "At Werner's request, the facts about his origins have been rearranged to make his identification impossible."

BLASS HAD CLASS

Born in 1922 in Fort Wayne, Indiana, William "Bill" Blass lost both his parents early in life and moved to New York City at age 17 to study fashion. He joined the army in 1942 and was assigned its tactical deception unit, the 23rd Headquarters Special Troops. The mission of the 1,100-man unit, known as the Ghost Army, was to deceive and confound the enemy by providing misleading intelligence. Blass subsequently joined the 603rd Camouflage Engineers, the visual deception unit, where inflatable tanks, artillery batteries, and aircraft as well as bogus airfields and bivouacs were deployed to deceive enemy aerial reconnaissance. Often operating close to the front lines, Blass saw combat in North Africa, Sicily, the Normandy breakout, and the Battle of the Bulge.

Before he became a legendary fashion designer, Bill Blass served in the secret Ghost Army, a US tactical deception unit during World War II.

Following the war, Blass returned to New York to launch a fashion career that became an estimated $700-million-a-year giant. Living at 444 East 57th Street, he received numerous professional honors, including the Fashion Institute of

Blass's former apartment building, just off Sutton Place, was once also home to film icon Marilyn Monroe while she was married to playwright Arthur Miller.

Technology's Lifetime Achievement Award. Blass's generosity made possible the renovation of the landmark Public Catalog Room of the Main Branch of the New York Public Library, 42nd Street and Fifth Avenue, which now bears his name. The spy, designer, philanthropist, and longtime trustee and benefactor of the New York Public Library died in 2002.

■ 163. NOBEL LAUREATE, DIPLOMAT, SPY

MAP II ▶ **Ralph Bunche residence:** 115-24 Grosvenor Road, Queens

Although best known as a Nobel laureate diplomat and civil rights advocate, Ralph Bunche began his illustrious career in 1941 as an analyst in William Donovan's newly formed COI, the predecessor to the OSS. Born in poverty and orphaned at age 13, Bunche nonetheless excelled in school. Working manual labor jobs to supplement a scholarship at the University of California at Los Angeles, he eventually went on to Harvard and a course of study that led to a doctorate in government and international relations. When World War II began, Bunche was teaching at Howard University and serving on President Roosevelt's Federal Council of Negro Affairs (known informally as the "Black Cabinet"), advising the president on minority affairs during the Great Depression.

Following the war, Bunche transferred to the State Department and became its first African American desk officer. A self-described "incurable optimist," he became an adviser to the US delegation at the 1945 United Nations "Charter Conference" and played a critical role in the adoption of the landmark Universal Declaration of Human Rights.

Bunche later served as the UN undersecretary-general, a role that would see him awarded the Nobel Peace Prize in 1949 for his work in negotiating an armistice between Israel and neighboring nations. A small park directly across from the United Nations on First Avenue and 42nd Street pays tribute to the diplomat.

Bunche's last residence in New York was 115-24 Grosvenor Road, Kew Gardens, Queens. Built in 1927, the Tudor-style home is a National Historic Landmark. Bunche, who died in 1971, is buried in Woodlawn Cemetery in the Bronx.

Ralph Bunche began his career as part of William Donovan's Coordinator of Information organization, then later served as the UN's undersecretary-general. A small park on First Avenue and 42nd Street honors the Nobel laureate.

6

SPIES, NOT GUNS, IN THE EARLY COLD WAR

(1947–1959)

The early history of the Cold War included an armed conflict in Korea and smaller proxy wars around the globe, but within the United States espionage also played a central role in defining the era. New York was the frontline for many Moscow-directed intelligence operations as the country woke to the threat of Soviet espionage beginning in the 1940s. Some of the USSR's and America's greatest espionage triumphs and failures took place in the city. While New York was the hub of *illegal* Rudolph Abel's spy network and the UN provided official cover for KGB operatives, several of America's most significant Soviet recruitments also occurred in the city.

New York proved a dynamic battlefield for the clandestine operations with the city's ethnic diversity, subways, parks, office buildings, theaters, restaurants, and hotels. All were used by spies from every region of the world. Many of the city's cherished landmarks were the sites of clandestine meetings and dead drops. From the heavily trafficked Manhattan tourist attractions to quiet outer-borough enclaves, spies identified, evaluated, and chose sites for their clandestine work. Even long-closed eateries, such as Bickford's cafeterias, Longchamps, and the Horn & Hardart Automat chain, are part of New York's espionage history.

Working primarily from their respective consulates and UN missions, foreign intelligence officers used every neighborhood of every borough for recruitments, dead drops, brush passes, and clandestine meetings. These rarely noticed Cold War warriors blended into city life, working unseen in the shadows. Only when exposed, or when they were arrested, did their operations become front-page news.

■ 164. HIDING IN PLAIN SIGHT

MAP I ➤ **Central Intelligence Group field office:** 39 Broadway

The post–World War II organizational forerunner of the CIA, the Central Intelligence Group, opened a branch office here at 39 Broadway.

Sensational allegations about illegal CIA activities within the United States made front-page headlines in *The New York Times* during Christmas week of 1974. That the CIA maintained offices and conducted operations within the borders of America surprised the public and even some politicians.

Expressions of shock that American intelligence-gathering organizations were working discreetly with US companies and other institutions seemed either disingenuous or reflected historical ignorance. New York City had been a hub for intelligence collection by US government agencies, led by the Office of Naval Intelligence, since before World War I.

During World War I, in addition to the ONI's activities, a parallel and sometimes overlapping collection program was run by the War Department's Military Intelligence Division under the command of Brig. Gen. Marlborough Churchill. After the war, Churchill sought to continue collecting information from domestic sources by maintaining the program in New York from 1920 to 1923. This activity exploited information voluntarily obtained from the city's international businessmen and foreign travelers and was the forerunner of post–World War II collection programs subsequently conducted by the Central Intelligence Group (CIG) and then the CIA.

In July 1946, the CIG established a branch for domestic collection of foreign intelligence information and located its first field office in New York. The office at 39 Broadway was activated in January 1947, with former ONI officer James Ramsay Hunt Jr. serving as chief. New York and offices in other American cities established by the CIG during 1947 became part of the new CIA's

Office of Operations in October, after the founding of the agency. The domestic offices had the common purpose of capturing the intelligence acquired and volunteered by private citizens during the course of their professional or personal travel abroad.

As the nation's leading business and financial center, New York became the flagship of the CIA's domestic foreign intelligence-collection program. During a rare interview in the early 1970s with reporter Edward Hershey, senior officers from the New York office of the Domestic Contact Service traced the New York history of the activity. While the work was overt, and the office had a listed phone number, the physical address was not made public to provide protection against protestors, cranks, and worse. Officers carried official government credentials identifying themselves as representatives of the CIA but had no domestic law-enforcement or investigative authority. Those powers were reserved for the FBI.

■ 165. THE MODEL SPY

MAP 5 ➤ **Gompers Research Library:** 406 East 58th Street

Prior to her work in intelligence, Louise Page-Morris appeared in a Lucky Strike cigarettes advertisement during her early modeling career.

Born into an upper-class Boston family in 1904 and descended from the presidential Adams family by marriage, Louise Page-Morris demonstrated an adventurous streak early in life. Following a short-lived marriage to John Boucher Morris, she became a model with the famous John Robert Powers Agency in New York City. As a "Powers Girl," she appeared in advertisements for Lucky Strike cigarettes and the Remington Typewriter Company. Her string of off-camera adventures included an affair with a White Russian émigré that prompted her to take Russian language classes at Columbia University.

After World War II began, Page-Morris was recruited by the OSS and posted to London as the deputy chief of the fledgling intelligence service's Research and Analysis Division. She later recalled that the focus of her assignments was to convince reluctant British counterparts to share intelligence with their American cousins. As told by author Ted Morgan in his 1999 biography of Jay Lovestone, *A Covert Life: Jay Lovestone, Communist, Anti-Communist and Spymaster*, Page-Morris subsequently worked with labor organizer Lovestone to infiltrate communist front organizations before and after the formation of the CIA.

During her association with Lovestone, Page-Morris was employed by the Free Trade Union Committee, an arm of the American Federation of Labor. Lovestone's activity received covert funding as it attempted to curtail or eliminate communist influence in international unions. Lovestone's effectiveness was such that he enjoyed access to powerful government officials in the United States and abroad.

With a generous salary and expense account, Page-Morris—called "Pagie" by her colleagues—managed the Gompers Research Library, 406 East 58th

Street. She and Lovestone became lovers but lived separately, in a relationship that endured, often stormily, for more than two decades. From her home at 125 East 57th Street, she traveled the world while keeping up an active New York social life that sometimes landed her in society and gossip columns. She would later live at 25 West 54th Street. Page-Morris died in 2002 at the age of 98.

Page-Morris's West 54th Street apartment building was among the addresses of the colorful and fearless socialite turned fashion model turned spy.

■ 166. INTERNATIONAL BANKER-SPY

MAP 7 ➤ **Harry Dexter White residence:** 334 West 86th Street

The 1944 Bretton Woods Conference, convened to determine the global financial architecture for postwar economic development, created the World Bank and the International Monetary Fund (IMF). The meeting's chief architect, Harry Dexter White, was a top adviser to Secretary of the Treasury Henry Morgenthau Jr. and to President Franklin Roosevelt. He was also a Soviet spy.

On November 7, 1945, defector Elizabeth Bentley made a startling

Harry Dexter White, a senior US Treasury Department official, was among the Soviet Union's most valuable agents but died without being prosecuted. His New York residence was a Rosario Candela–designed building at 334 West 86th Street.

confession to the FBI and identified White among a number of other Soviet agents. The next day, FBI director J. Edgar Hoover sent a handwritten note to the White House listing the names provided by Bentley. White's was the second name on the list. A month later, on December 4, 1945, the FBI provided a more detailed report about Soviet espionage in the United States, citing additional sources who asserted White was supporting Soviet espionage.

White expected to become the head of the World Bank or the IMF. However, the new, but yet unconfirmed, accusations of espionage led President Truman to nominate him to a lesser IMF position. White was put under surveillance, and on February 4, 1946, a 28-page FBI report for the White House focused exclusively on the allegations against him. Two days later, the Senate approved White's nomination to the IMF without having been briefed on the investigation into his alleged espionage activity.

In June 1947, Attorney General Tom Clark ordered a federal grand jury investigation of the espionage allegations made by Bentley. When he learned of the investigation, White abruptly resigned from the IMF, vacating his office the same day. He was again accused of spying by former Soviet operatives Whittaker Chambers and Bentley during a hearing of the House Un-American Activities Committee chaired by Richard Nixon in July 1948. White, living at 334 West 86th Street, steadfastly denied all charges against him when testifying before the HUAC on August 13, 1948, then died three days later of a heart attack.

Eventually it was revealed that White had been recruited to spy in the 1930s by NKVD agent Jacob Golos, Bentley's handler and lover. White's initial code name, KASSIR, was later changed to JURIST, then LAWYER, and eventually RICHARD. White's first work for the Soviets was with the Ware Group, a small network of aspiring officials being positioned to penetrate the US government at senior levels. As the chief monetary expert for the Treasury Department, White provided his primary contact, Whittaker Chambers, sensitive documents to be photographed and passed to the NKVD. An NKVD communication to Moscow in early 1942 labeled White as "one of the [NKVD's] most valuable agents."

■ 167. SPY WITH ONE OVERSHOE

MAP 3 ▶ **Death scene:** Institute of International Education, 2 West 45th Street

There were no witnesses on December 20, 1948, when Laurence Duggan plummeted 16 floors from his 2 West 45th Street office window at the Institute of International Education. Duggan's body was discovered in the snow around 7:00 p.m. Bystanders observed that he was wearing only a single overshoe, and the NYPD concluded the dead man either fell accidentally from the window while pulling on his second overshoe or intentionally jumped.

The death of suspected spy Laurence Duggan remains a mystery. Did he jump from the 16th floor window on West 45th Street, or was he pushed by Soviet handlers wishing to protect their secrets?

Nevertheless, the incident may have been linked to the FBI's questioning Duggan about possible contacts with Soviet spies ten days earlier. In the decades that followed, a belief emerged that Duggan's death, if a suicide, might have been the result of an overzealous investigation of an innocent public servant hounded by unfounded accusations.

After five decades, when the decrypted VENONA intercepts were made public, the truth about his espionage was finally revealed. From 1937 to 1944, Duggan, then head of the Latin American desk at the State Department, was known to colleagues as a left-leaning idealist and supporter of President Roosevelt's New Deal. Duggan's good friend Noel Field (NKVD code name ERNST), a State Department informational officer on the European desk, had recommended Duggan's recruitment to the Soviets in 1934. (Field defected to the Eastern Bloc in 1948 and was presumed to be a spy.)

A year after Field's recommendation, actress and NKVD agent Hede Massing (code name REDHEAD) pitched Duggan about becoming a spy. Duggan rejected the first proposal, but the offer was made again by a young Soviet *illegal*, Norman Mikhailovich Borodin (code name GRANIT). Duggan declined again but after several months agreed to cooperate and was assigned the NKVD code name 19TH.

Duggan was, at best, always a conflicted and reluctant agent. News of the bloody purges in Moscow in 1937 was weighed against his long-standing hatred for the Nazis. A message to Moscow from his NKVD handler, Iskhak Akhmerov (code name MAYOR), gave a frank portrayal of him: "You know that he is neither a compatriot nor a paid probationer. He is a deeply honorable and progressive American. He used to assist and is assisting us out of his understanding that we are the advance guard of the progressive humanity. He has not taken a single kopeck from us. Our personal friendship has played a significant role in our relationship."

Duggan's spying continued sporadically for years. Nine cables sent in 1943 and 1944 that were deciphered in the VENONA project referenced him using the names FRANK, SHERWOOD, and PRINCE. He provided valuable information to Moscow on the US plans to invade Italy and a possible invasion of

Norway. Other important information Duggan passed to the Soviets outlined the US postwar Middle Eastern oil policy.

In late 1944, Duggan resigned from the State Department and accepted an assignment as the deputy of the assistant secretary-general for the United Nations Relief and Rehabilitation Administration. By 1947, he was the president of the Institute of International Education, where he worked on cultural diplomacy until his death.

Whether the reluctant spy's fatal fall was precipitated by his conscience or something more sinister remains a mystery.

■ 168. DECADES OF DENIALS

MAP 4 ➤ **Alger Hiss residence:** 22 East 8th Street

Alger Hiss

Behind the Grand Hyatt's covering of reflective glass lies the espionage history of the landmark Commodore Hotel. In room 1400, with Congressman Richard Nixon present, Whittaker Chambers accused Alger Hiss of being a Soviet spy.

Alger Hiss possessed the perfect résumé for success at the highest levels of the federal government. With degrees from Johns Hopkins University and Harvard Law School, he was a protégé of professor and future Supreme Court Justice Felix Frankfurter and later clerked for Supreme Court Associate Justice Oliver Wendell Holmes Jr. For a brief time, Hiss practiced law in New York and Boston before joining the Agricultural Adjustment Administration in 1933. He then held positions of legal assistant for the Senate Munitions Committee and special assistant to the solicitor general before moving into the State Department.

The brilliant lawyer and rising star, however, was also a Soviet spy. An early penchant for leftist politics in college had evolved into full-blown espionage. Hiss photographed classified documents from work and passed them to couriers for delivery to Soviet officials. By the late 1930s, some of Hiss's accomplices, such as Whittaker Chambers, had become

This Park Slope neighborhood supermarket, 329 9th Street, Brooklyn, was once the site of the RKO Prospect Theatre where Alger Hiss and Chambers met with their Soviet handler.

disillusioned with Stalin and broke contact with Soviet intelligence. Chambers retained incriminating documents about Hiss and other spies as an insurance policy against reprisals by the Soviets and their American sympathizers.

Hiss's spying became known to the FBI in March 1945 when Chambers revealed his involvement in the Soviet infiltration of the US government. Questioned by State Department security officers, Hiss alleged that he had left the CPUSA in 1937 and was never a Soviet agent.

More allegations emerged following World War II when Soviet defector Igor Gouzenko offered additional information regarding major spy rings in America. By then Hiss had not only accompanied FDR to the historic Yalta Conference but was also named acting secretary-general of the United Nations founding conference in San Francisco.

The still unsubstantiated, but persistent, rumors of spying forced Hiss to resign from government. With the assistance of influential friends, including future Secretary of State John Foster Dulles, he became head of the Carnegie Endowment for International Peace and moved to a third-floor, two-bedroom walk-up at 22 East 8th Street in Greenwich Village.

As part of the ongoing investigations into possible Soviet infiltration of the US government, the HUAC convened a special session in August 1948 in room 1400 of the Commodore Hotel (today the Grand Hyatt New York), 109 East 42nd Street. There Hiss was accused by Chambers of spying for the Soviets. The accusation forced Hiss out of his position at the Carnegie Endowment, but he fought back, vehemently denying involvement in Soviet espionage, and sued Chambers for libel.

In response, Chambers produced documents in Hiss's handwriting and five rolls of film, hidden for 10 years at the Brooklyn apartment of Nathan Levine at 960 Sterling Place. This evidence later became known as the Pumpkin Papers when it was revealed that after the first HUAC hearing, the film canisters were moved and concealed inside a pumpkin on Chambers's Maryland farm. The dramatic HUAC hearings rocketed a young California congressman, Richard Nixon, to overnight fame.

Hiss was charged with perjury and tried in 1949 (the statute of limitations for espionage having expired). The first proceedings ended in a hung jury, though a second trial found him guilty on two counts. Sentenced to five years in 1950, Hiss served 44 months in prison and returned to New York City after his release in 1954. Disbarred as an attorney, he became a salesman for the S. Novick and Son stationery company, located in the Puck Building, 225 Lafayette Street.

Hiss outlived most of his accusers, including Chambers, who died in 1961, asserting his innocence until his death in 1996. Over the years, Hiss appeared to be winning public sympathy in a war of attrition. The perceived excesses of the HUAC investigations and his steadfast refusal to admit guilt persuaded his friends and political supporters that he was wrongly accused all along.

In 1995, the question was definitively settled with the declassification of the VENONA decryptions. Some of these previously secret Soviet communications identified Hiss as a Soviet agent. The US government had possessed this proof of guilt for decades but was unwilling to produce the evidence to protect the secret World War II code-breaking operation.

> **BAMBI CONNECTION**
>
> Before Whittaker Chambers gained fame in the Alger Hiss spy case, he was best known for his translation of the classic *Bambi: A Life in the Woods*. Originally published in German by Austrian author Felix Salten, an English-language edition from Simon and Schuster in 1928 captured the hearts of Americans and was later turned into the 1942 Walter Disney animated film.

■ 169. SEDUCING THE SPY WHO SEDUCED AMERICA

MAP 7 ➤ **Valentin Gubitchev residence:** 64 West 108th Street, apt. 3-A

Valentin Gubitchev

For a brief time in 1949 and 1950, the American public couldn't get enough of Judith Coplon. Her multiple, dramatic trials for espionage were the 1950s versions of a reality television show. Smart and ambitious, the petite young woman from Brooklyn had won a citizenship award at James Madison High School, 3787 Bedford Avenue, graduated cum laude from Barnard College, and went to work for the Department of Justice.

Through a college friend and Soviet talent spotter, Flora Don Wovschin (code name ZORA), Coplon was identified as a potential

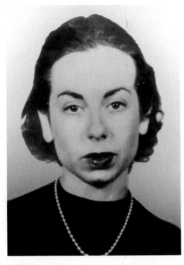
Judith Coplon

asset and recruited by Valentin Gubitchev (sometimes spelled Gubichev), who arrived in the United States around 1946. Code-named CARP, Gubitchev was an engineer/ architect working for the United Nations Secretariat's Department of Conferences and General Services, 1270 Sixth Avenue.

Gubitchev's recruitment of Coplon seemed uncomplicated. The married Russian intelligence officer took the young single woman for romantic walks to Rockefeller Center during the Christmas season, rowing in Central Park in the summer, and cozy dinners in Greenwich Village bistros, before eventually seducing her. "She [Coplon] gives the impression of a very serious, modest, thoughtful young woman. . . . There is no question about the sincerity of her desire to work for us," read a report on her to Moscow. Coplon (code name SIMA) was identified as a spy in 1948.

Coplon and Gubitchev were eventually arrested in 1949 on Third Avenue between 15th and 16th Streets, tried, and convicted. The first American to be tried and convicted of spying for the Soviet Union following World War II, Coplon was much later positively identified in the highly secretive VENONA decryptions, but classification of that program precluded use of the information by the prosecution. Instead, secret documents found in her handbag, which the press dubbed "Pandora's Purse," were presented. Gubitchev was declared persona non grata by the US government and left the country.

Coplon's first conviction was overturned, but she was retried, convicted a second time, and the verdict was again invalidated on procedural grounds. She eventually married one of her lawyers, Albert Socolov, and later operated two now-closed Manhattan restaurants, the Beach House in Tribeca and Alameda on the Upper West Side. Coplon died in 2011 at age 89.

■ 170. SPIES EVERYWHERE

MAP 5 ▶ **United Nations headquarters:** Manhattan's East Side between East 42nd and 48th Streets

The 17-acre compound of the United Nations, completed in 1952 on Manhattan's East Side between East 42nd and 48th Streets, along with scores of diplomatically accredited foreign missions scattered throughout the city, are centers of espionage. Even before completion of the first UN building on the banks of the East River, Soviet spies, working under diplomatic cover as representatives to the UN, were spying against the United States. For example, Valentin Gubitchev handled Judith Coplon from a temporary UN office at 1270 Sixth Avenue. By 1950, Soviet operatives were being posted to the USSR's mission to the UN in the Percy R. Pyne House at 680 Park Avenue and East 68th Street, now home of the Council of the Americas.

The Percy R. Pyne House, home to the Soviet mission to the UN from the late 1940s through the early 1960s, was designed by the notable firm of McKim, Mead and White.

The presence of the UN enhanced New York's historic reputation as a center of espionage as diplomats from virtually every nation took up residence in the city. Amid its vibrant, ethnically diverse populations, a foreign accent arouses no suspicion. With hundreds of hotels, thousands of restaurants, scores of public parks, more than 600 miles of subway, and round-the-clock activity, the city presents nearly unlimited options for surveillance detection routes, dead drops, signal sites, brief encounters, and clandestine meetings. Should an operation go bad, the UN also offered an international forum to levy accusations and air grievances.

PRACTICING FOR NEW YORK

During the Cold War, Soviet Bloc countries packed as many intelligence officers as possible into their UN missions under a variety of diplomatic and trade covers. New York became a highly desired posting for KGB and GRU officers who were allocated funds to live and entertain well.

Knowing social protocol was important for Soviets unaccustomed to the United States. Trainees were instructed, "It is the practice in all restaurants to tip the waitress 10 percent of the amount shown on the check. . . . It is not enough to ask, 'Give me a glass of beer.' It is also necessary to name the brand of beer, for example, 'Schlitz, Rheingold.'"

▪ 171. GRU COMMERCIAL COVER OPERATIONS

MAP 3 ➤ **Amtorg Trading Corporation:** 49 West 37th Street

Robert Philip Hanssen

Robert Hanssen lived in this Scarsdale residence when he began spying for the Soviets in 1979.

The American Trading Organization, founded by Armand Hammer with help from Vladimir Lenin, became an often-used cover for Soviet intelligence officers.

If you wanted to find a Soviet military intelligence officer in New York during the Cold War, the Amtorg Trading Corporation, conveniently listed in the telephone book, was a likely location. Set up by American businessman Armand Hammer in 1924 to represent Soviet trade in the United States, Amtorg was packed with intelligence officers from the GRU, who operated under the veneer of a commercial cover. Over the years, Amtorg's multiple New York locations included 165 Broadway, 261 Fifth Avenue, 238 West 28th Street, 49 West 37th Street, and 210 Madison Avenue.

FBI special agent and later spy Robert Hanssen first made contact with the GRU in 1979 by visiting Amtorg's New York office. At the time, Hanssen and his family were living at 150 Webster Road in Scarsdale, an affluent suburb in Westchester County. When his spying activities were discovered by his wife, Bonnie, who was never involved in them, Hanssen confessed to her and a priest. Hanssen vowed to end unauthorized contact with the Soviets, and temporarily kept his word. However, in 1985, after being transferred to Washington, DC, he resumed spying, this time for the KGB.

■ 172. LAW AND ORDER (AND DIPLOMACY)

MAP 6 ▶ **Pratt Mansion:** 7–9 East 61st Street (no longer standing)

The FBI set up a permanent observation post in the luxurious Pierre Hotel to surveil the Soviet consulate in the former Pratt Mansion, located directly across East 61st Street.

The Pratt Mansion, which once housed the Soviet consulate and *rezidentura*, has been replaced by a private garden for a Fifth Avenue apartment house.

From 1933 to 1948, Soviet diplomats occupied the John T. Pratt Mansion, which stood at 7–9 East 61st Street. The structure was built by John Teele Pratt, a wealthy Wall Street lawyer, on the adjoining lots of two existing townhouses. Although designed for a successful capitalist, the mansion became the center of Soviet espionage in the city after the newly recognized USSR chose it for a New York consulate. The top three floors of the structure were reportedly the site of the NKVD and GRU *rezidenturas*, from which North American espionage operations were directed. Secret reports from some of the most damaging early Cold War spies passed through the consulate, including those from the Rosenberg atomic spy ring. Secure cable traffic between the NKVD and Moscow used the code name ZAVOD (FACTORY) for the facility.

The FBI reportedly maintained a permanent observation post overlooking the consulate in the upscale Pierre Hotel, 2 East 61st Street. Called the Bucket Squad, the FBI team was said to have used 35mm newsreel cameras to film the comings and goings of the Soviet diplomats, intelligence officers, and spies.

On August 12, 1948, Oksana Stepanova Kasenkina, a 52-year-old schoolteacher from Moscow assigned to teach the diplomats' children, jumped from a third-floor window of the consulate in an effort to defect. In an earlier bid for asylum, she had been caught and forcibly returned to the consulate against her will. A full-fledged diplomatic flap over her attempted defection was in progress at the time of her desperate leap from the window.

Kasenkina's fall was broken by telephone wires, and she lay injured and unable to move in the courtyard as a crowd gathered on the street. Two New York City cops, Sgt. Lester Abrahamson and Patrolman Frank Candelas, rushed the compound, going over a 7-foot-high fence, subdued the Soviet security officers, and put the woman in an ambulance to Roosevelt Hospital, later St. Luke's Roosevelt Hospital Center (now Mount Sinai West). Soviet diplomats in pursuit were met at the hospital by a blue wall of NYPD uniforms, which kept them at bay. Kasenkina was given asylum, and the consulate ordered closed shortly thereafter.

The mansion was torn down in the 1970s to accommodate a private garden for the adjoining apartment house at 800 Fifth Avenue.

KGB *illegal* Yevgeni Brik acquired his distinctive Brooklyn accent when he lived at 1119 Foster Avenue in Brooklyn as a child. It added legitimacy to his meticulously curated cover.

■ 173. SOVIET SPY WITH BROOKLYN ACCENT

MAP 10 ➤ **Yevgeni Brik childhood residence:** 1119 Foster Avenue, Brooklyn

Yevgeni Brik, a KGB deep-cover *illegal*, spoke in a distinctive Brooklyn accent acquired as a child living at 1119 Foster Avenue, Brooklyn. His family had moved from Novorossiysk, Russia, to New York in the 1930s while his father was employed by Amtorg, the Russian-American trading company.

Brik entered Canada in 1951 and for the next two years sought to establish an identity as David Soboloff, a Montreal photographer. With his wife back in the USSR, however, Brik fell madly in love with Larissa Cunningham, the wife of a Canadian army corporal. After Cunningham left her husband to prove her love for Brik, the Soviet spy felt compelled to confess his own secret to her.

Cunningham then pressured Brik to turn himself in to the authorities for protection. The couple traveled to Ottawa where Brik met with the Royal Canadian Mounted Police Security Service (RCMP) and told his story. The RCMP seized the opportunity to turn Brik, gave him the code name GIDEON, and assigned him to work against the KGB in a project code-named KEYSTONE.

Brik was recalled to Moscow in 1955 for briefings and to reunite with his Soviet wife. While he understood that he could be returning to a counterintelligence trap, Brik was confident in his ability to deflect any suspicion. What he did not know was that Soviet authorities had already confirmed his betrayal. A member of the RCMP, Cpl. James Morrison, who once drove Brik from Ottawa to Montreal, sold Brik's name to the Soviet embassy for $3,500 to pay debts.

When the unlucky Brik arrived in Moscow, he was arrested, interrogated, and convicted of treason. Then he disappeared and was assumed executed.

To the RCMP, GIDEON was a regrettable casualty of the Cold War who passed into obscurity.

Morrison confessed his misdeeds to his superiors in 1957 but was only demoted and then dismissed from the service a year later. The failure to prosecute him was decried by some as a government cover-up. The case remained quiet for nearly three decades until Morrison, in heavy disguise, unexpectedly appeared in a Canadian documentary and confessed that he had given agent identity information to the Soviet Union.

Canadian authorities were incensed, impounded a tape of the show, and filed charges against Morrison. At trial in 1986, he surprised prosecutors by pleading guilty to violating Canada's Official Secrets Act and passing secrets to the Soviets from 1955 to 1958. In doing so, he revealed classified information about the Distant Early Warning line radar network and technical surveillance of the Soviet embassy in Ottawa. Morrison, however, denied that he had betrayed his country, insisting he had only "sold one man down the drain." He was sentenced to 18 months in prison, after release settled in Victoria, British Columbia, and died in 2001. That "one man," GIDEON, was also forgotten until 1992 when he unexpectedly appeared at the British embassy in Lithuania with a coded message asking for Canada's help. The Canadian Secret Intelligence Service, a new organization formed in the 1980s which superseded the RCMP Security Service for counterintelligence, confirmed the validity of the man as Brik. An exfiltration operation was mounted that brought Brik back into Canada where he was extensively debriefed and resided until his death in Ottawa in 2011.

■ 174. ARTIST, MUSICIAN, MASTER SPY

MAP 10 ➤ **Rudolph Abel studio:** 252 Fulton Street, Brooklyn (site redeveloped)

Rudolph Ivanovich Abel (code name MARK) was the chief Russian *illegal* in the United States after the collapse of the wartime Soviet networks and represented one of the FBI's biggest counterintelligence success at the time of his arrest in 1957. Raised in the United Kingdom, Abel, whose given name was Vilyam Genrikhovich Fisher, operated under multiple aliases, including Andrew Kyotis, Emil

СОВЕТСКИЙ РАЗВЕДЧИК

Р. И. АБЕЛЬ
1903—1971
5 к ПОЧТА СССР 1990

Spy Rudolph Abel was honored by being depicted on a Soviet postage stamp after his exchange for U-2 pilot Francis Gary Powers.

Abel's apartment, illustrated here with some tools of his tradecraft, stood on the site of what is now Brooklyn's Cadman Plaza.

Soviet master-spy Abel was apprehended by the FBI in room 839 of the Latham Hotel in 1957.

Goldfus, and Mark Collins. He spoke nearly flawless Polish, German, and English to match his varied identities. Abel entered the United States in 1948 with instructions to rebuild the effective wartime Soviet spy network (code name VOLUNTEER) that had smuggled atomic secrets to the USSR. In 1950, Abel, using the alias Emil Goldfus, rented his first apartment at 216 West 99th Street.

The Soviet *illegal's* English, spoken with a slight British accent and a touch of Brooklynese, enabled him to blend into a Brooklyn neighborhood near what is now Cadman Plaza. A talented painter, excellent photographer, accomplished linguist, and amateur musician, Abel was also a master at tradecraft. He constructed many of his own concealment devices, which included pieces of jewelry, hollowed-out pencils, and various artist's tools. Other artists in the now demolished Ovington Building at 252 Fulton Street, Brooklyn, where he maintained a studio, saw only a mild-mannered older man always willing to lend a hand. "I wish I had a couple like him in Moscow," CIA head Allen Dulles later commented.

Abel conducted operations throughout the city's boroughs, including Fort Tryon Park in Upper Manhattan, where he located dead-drop sites under lampposts; the Symphony Theatre at Broadway and West 95th Street; Prospect Park, Brooklyn; the cement wall between East 165th and 167th Streets on Jerome Avenue, the Bronx; Central Park's Bridle Path adjacent to Tavern on the Green; and under mailboxes between West 74th and 79th Streets along Central Park West.

The master-spy's downfall was due to his undisciplined, hard-drinking assistant, Reino Häyhänen (also known as Nicolai Maki; code name VIC), who defected to the West in Paris in 1957. Having once visited the site of

Soviet *illegal* Abel, using the alias Emil Goldfus, rented his first apartment in New York at 216 West 99th Street.

Abel used classic concealments for his spy gear, such as hollowed-out wooden blocks and pencils that he likely fashioned himself.

ARTISTIC SPY

One element that set Rudolph Abel apart from other post–World War II Soviet spies was the subculture that enhanced his cover. The talented artist ingratiated himself into New York City's bohemian, sometimes called beatnik, community during the 1950s. Abel befriended younger artists sharing studios in the Ovington Building. In one instance, a fellow artist, Burt Silverman, painted a portrait of the *illegal* with his Hallicrafters S-38D shortwave radio used for receiving coded instructions clearly visible, though upended, in the background.

Abel also haunted the jazz clubs of Greenwich Village, such as the original Five Spot Café at 5 Cooper Square, frequented by musicians such as John Coltrane, Charlie Parker, Charles Mingus, and Thelonious Monk; writers Jack Kerouac and Allen Ginsberg; and painters Willem de Kooning, Jackson Pollock, and Mark Rothko. After Abel's arrest, many of his artist friends expressed disbelief. "If he was a Red spy, what the hell was he doing hanging out with a bunch of loudmouth Brooklyn lefties?" Jules Feiffer, the famed cartoonist and playwright, wrote. "Weren't we the very people a real spy would avoid, lest he get snared in a cross-investigation?"

Abel's studio, Häyhänen tipped off the FBI to the location as well as Abel's penchant for white hatbands. Agents then staked out the *illegal's* Brooklyn studio and apartment before spotting Abel and trailing him to room 839 at the Latham Hotel, 4 East 28th Street, where he was arrested on June 21, 1957.

The arrest solved the mystery of a hollow nickel containing microfilm with ciphered information that a drunk Häyhänen mistakenly had spent earlier. The nickel eventually turned up in the hands of a young Brooklyn newspaper boy, James Bozart, in 1953 after he collected payments from customers at 3403 Foster Avenue. When Bozart accidentally dropped the nickel, it split apart and revealed the cavity and microfilm. Häyhänen's defection provided the FBI the key to decrypting the message.

Abel was tried, convicted, and sentenced to 30 years in prison in the fall of 1957. Five years later, the *illegal* was swapped for downed American U-2 pilot Francis Gary Powers and honored as a hero upon his return to Moscow. Despite his status at the time as a Soviet "spy hero," his KGB colleagues in Moscow never forgot that Abel's tradecraft error in taking Häyhänen to the site of his studio in Brooklyn violated the compartmentation of the network and led directly to his detection and arrest.

FBI photos of the lamppost in Fort Tryon Park that Abel used as a dead drop. The enlargement shows the drop site under the base of a lamppost.

NEVER-USED DEAD-DROP SITE

In 1952, the Soviet Ministry of State Security (MGB), a forerunner of the KGB from 1946 to 1953, designated a new drop site for *illegal* Rudolf Abel at the base of a lamppost in Fort Tryon Park. According to Department of Justice documents, Abel received precise location instructions:

> To locate this lamp post you take the Eighth Avenue subway to the 190th Street station and then take the elevator to the top of the Park. When you leave the elevator you turn left, take the steps down and at the bottom of the steps make another left turn and follow the path that is located there. You continue following the path past the first set of steps on the right and go to on to the second set of steps on the right. At the bottom of these steps is a lamp post, the base of which is about three or four inches above the ground.

A second site was designated, but never used:

> In order to approach this bank or drop one would enter Central Park by means of the entrance at 95th or 96th Streets and then follow the foot path that borders around the Northern end of the reservoir. If you continue along this path you will reach a small bridge over a bridle path. Upon arrival at the bridge you go off the path and walk down and into the end of the bridge closest to the reservoir. Situated approximately between the second and third stones is a hole [for] the drop.

■ 175. THE SPY WHO LOST HIS NICKEL

MAP 10 ➤ **Reino Häyhänen residence:** 3403 Foster Avenue, East Flatbush, Brooklyn

Reino Häyhänen (code name VIC) was a KGB lieutenant colonel posted to the United States as an *illegal* officer to support Rudolf Abel, the senior *illegal* in the United States and head of the VOLUNTEER spy network. Häyhänen entered the country in 1949 from Finland under the false identity of Eugene Nicolai Mäki, a purported American-born laborer. One signal site used by Abel and Häyhänen was Brand's Bar, 58th Street and Fourth Avenue, Brooklyn, where different arrangements of thumbtacks on the wall offered a means of communication.

THE ABANDONED DEAD-DROP SITE

This drop was not used because the MGB decided its location was inconvenient for use by "official people." The MGB understood that individuals with an official status, such as diplomats or under Amtorg cover, were often under FBI surveillance, and there was no plausible reason for them to visit and service the site. The MGB's concern was that surveillance of the official person might lead to the exposure of the agent.

KGB lieutenant colonel Reino Häyhänen operated in the United States under the false identity of Eugene Nicolai Mäki. He defected to the United States in 1957.

The railing along 151 Central Park West was a signal site for Soviet spy Häyhänen. A simple chalk mark could indicate whether a dead drop had been loaded or if a clandestine meeting was needed.

This misplaced hollow nickel played a major role in the detection of Soviet *illegal* Rudolf Abel.

Häyhänen lived in this apartment complex at 3403 Foster Avenue, Brooklyn. Here he inadvertently passed the famous hollow nickel to a newspaper boy.

Häyhänen lived at various addresses in the New York area, including 806 Bergen Street in Newark in 1955 and 1956. However, the *illegal's* assignment in the United States did not go well. He drank excessively, was late for meetings, and was sloppy in his tradecraft. His most egregious error may have been losing a special hollow nickel sent to him by the KGB containing a message on microfilm.

Häyhänen's story took a curious twist in 1953, when a newsboy for the local newspaper, the Brooklyn Eagle, was collecting delivery payments from a sixth-floor apartment at 3403 Foster Avenue in East Flatbush, Brooklyn. As he departed the apartment, the coins fell to the floor. One split open and revealed a small piece of microfilm filled with seemingly random numbers. What appeared to be a solid coin was actually two pieces with the middle hollowed out as a concealment device for microfilm. Detectives from NYPD's 67th Precinct could make nothing of the incident and turned the hollow coin and microfilm over to the FBI. The FBI realized these bore the marks of a Soviet spy operation, but efforts to decipher the numbers on the microfilm proved unsuccessful. Häyhänen's defection and his description of Abel led to the spy's arrest. Häyhänen, recalled to Moscow in 1957, realized he had accomplished little during his time in America. He also understood that he would be called into account for his drunkenness and operational failures and likely would never be allowed out of the USSR again, or worse. Rather than continuing to Moscow, as he passed through Paris he went to the US embassy and said, "I'm an officer in the Soviet intelligence service. For the past five years [sic], I have been operating in the United States. Now I need your help."

Häyhänen agreed to help the FBI decipher the message found in the coin four years earlier, was granted political asylum, and returned to the United States. The information he provided led the FBI to his two primary KGB contacts in New York City, Mikhail Nikolaevich Svirin (a former UN employee) and Vilyam Genrikhovich Fisher (Rudolph Abel).

Häyhänen was relocated under a new identity with his wife, Hannah, to Keene, New Hampshire. The couple was later moved to a two-acre property near East Prospect Road in the small town of Delroy in York County, Pennsylvania, where they lived under the names John Eugene and Anita Linden. Despite attempts to give up drinking, Häyhänen died of what was likely cirrhosis of the liver in August 1961 and buried as John Linden.

■ 176. A GOOD TIME WAS HAD BY SOME

MAP 5 ▶ **Clandestine meeting site:** Sutton-East Hotel (now AKA Sutton Place), 330 East 56th Street

The traitorous Harold "Kim" Philby received the traditional honor for Soviet spies of appearing on a postage stamp.

Valeri Mikhailovich Makayev was a 32-year-old intelligence officer when he arrived in New York from Poland in 1950. Working for the MGB, he entered the United States on a falsely obtained American passport bearing the name Ivan Kovalik. This bogus identity was "borrowed" from the real Kovalik who, as a child, accompanied his parents when the family immigrated to Poland from Chicago. A clerk working in the US embassy in Warsaw was blackmailed, then paid $750, for renewing Kovalik's expired passport and passing it to the MGB.

The Soviet intelligence service invested heavily in training Makayev, including more than a year in Poland establishing his legend. Now, in New York, he was given $25,000 to establish a new *illegal rezidentura* to support spies Harold "Kim" Philby and Guy Burgess, two members of the yet-to-be-exposed Cambridge spy ring. Philby was in Washington, acting as liaison between British and American intelligence

While undetected as a spy, British diplomat Guy Burgess delivered messages from the embassy in Washington to the United Kingdom's UN ambassador, Gladwyn Jebb. During these trips, Burgess met clandestinely with Soviet intelligence officer Valeri Makayev at the Sutton-East Hotel on East 56th Street.

Burgess, a member of the Cambridge spy ring, regularly visited the Everard gay bathhouse on West 28th Street. The site has been redeveloped as the Wholesale Center.

organizations, while Burgess was a diplomat in the British embassy there.

During his first months in the United States, Makayev worked in a cover job as a furrier and clandestinely passed Philby a camera to copy documents. He also activated two communication channels back to Moscow. The first was through a series of mail cutouts in New York and London, and the second used a Finnish seaman-courier who made regular stopovers in New York.

Remarkably, several operations involving some of the Soviet Union's most valuable spies in the United States depended on Makayev. The young, inexperienced intelligence officer was in New York for the first time, and things went badly. The initial $25,000 was spent quickly, likely not all of it for intelligence operations. Makayev reportedly gave up his furrier cover job for a position teaching music composition at a New York college. Finally, without advising Moscow Center, he began a romantic relationship with a Polish ballet dancer (code name ALICE) who operated a studio in Manhattan.

During the same time, Guy Burgess was making frequent official trips to New York City to meet with the United Kingdom's UN ambassador, Gladwyn Jebb. This travel provided the cover for Burgess to deliver messages from Philby to Makayev, whom he met at the Sutton-East Hotel at 330 East 56th Street. Burgess also took advantage of his New York sojourns to visit the Everard Turkish Baths, a gay bathhouse located at 28 West 28th Street.

As US codebreakers deciphered the VENONA ciphers and authorities began closing in on the Cambridge spy ring, Donald Maclean, a member of the ring in the British Foreign Office, and Burgess defected. Philby was understandably alarmed and fearful for his own security. At a time when Philby needed the reassurance and calm advice of his handler the most, the Soviet New York station sent a supportive letter to him along with $2,000, which were left in a dead drop for Makayev. For reasons never explained, Makayev failed to clear the drop, and Philby never received the letter, money, or instructions.

Whether Makayev's behavior was the result of intoxication from his first taste of the Western campus life of a New York college or complications with his girlfriend is not known. Regardless, Philby, one of the Soviet Union's most important spies, had been assigned an inept handler.

Makayev was recalled to Moscow and then, unexplainably, sent back to the United States to work under the older and more experienced *illegal* Rudolf Abel. Makayev showed little improvement and lost a hollow Swiss coin he was given for concealing microfilm. Recalled again in 1951, Makayev was dismissed from the service for "lack of discipline" and "crude manners."

The UK government issued "wanted" posters for two of its diplomats, Guy Burgess and Donald MacLean, who were Soviet spies.

■ 177. AN AMERICAN IN THE CAMBRIDGE SPY RING

MAP 6 ▶ **Michael Whitney Straight childhood home:** 22 East 67th Street

Born into a privileged family, Michael Whitney Straight spent his early childhood in a townhouse on 22 East 67th Street before moving to England with his mother, Dorothy Whitney, and his stepfather, Leonard Elmhurst. He attended a private progressive school run by the Elmhurst family, then Cambridge University where, in the 1930s, he was recruited by Anthony Blunt as an agent for the Soviets and given the code name NIGEL.

Returning to the United States in 1937, Straight continued his espionage, sometimes meeting his Soviet handler, Iskhak Akhmerov (alias Michael Green), at the now defunct restaurant chain Longchamps. Straight ceased spying at the start of America's involvement in World War II, joined the Army Air Corps, and piloted B-17s during the conflict. Following

From a luxurious townhouse on Manhattan's Upper East Side, Michael Whitney Straight moved to England at a young age and was recruited as a Soviet agent. The prominent New Yorker only confessed to his espionage decades later.

the war, Straight worked without drawing a salary at the State Department and edited his family's magazine, the *New Republic*.

Although he no longer spied for the Soviet Union, Straight remained silent about other members of the Cambridge spy ring he knew to be active. Eventually the prospect of a routine FBI background check in 1963 required for an appointment to the National Endowment for the Arts prompted him to confess his communist connections and identify members of the Cambridge spy ring, including Kim Philby, who had defected to the USSR in January 1963, Guy Burgess, who had defected 12 years earlier, and Anthony Blunt, still living in London at the time. Straight died in 2004 at the age of 87.

■ 178. POETRY, POISON, AND PLOTTING

MAP 8 ➤ **Christina Krotkova residence:** 561 West 141st Street, apt. 78

During World War II, Christina Krotkova, a linguist and NKVD agent, operated under the code name of OLA (after 1945 as ZHANNA). Employed by the Office of War Information (OWI) at 250 West 57th Street, she lived at 561 West 141st Street, apartment 78.

The OWI's work included producing pro-American news and stories for dissemination in the United States and abroad. Krotkova worked as an editorial assistant for *Amerika*, an OWI Russian-language magazine that featured trans-

The Office of War Information on West 57th Street was the one-time employer of Christina Krotkova, a Russian émigré poet who also moonlighted for Soviet intelligence.

lations of stories and photographs from other magazines intended for distribution in the USSR. Whether the magazine, which offered a glimpse into life beyond the Iron Curtain, ever found widespread readership in the USSR is unclear. However, Krotkova's 1951 book of poems *Belym po Chernomu* (*White on Black*) enhanced both her literary standing and cover.

The FBI first suspected Krotkova of reading the mail of Countess Alexandra Tolstoy in 1940 and 1941 while employed at Reed Farm in Valley Cottage, New York, a rural retreat favored by Russian émigrés and defectors. Later, through an intermediary, Krotkova landed a job as typist and translator for the noted Soviet defector Victor A. Kravchenko, gaining direct access to the anti-Stalinist author and his unpublished writings. She was also believed to be the author of a threatening letter to Kravchenko warning that his life was at risk if he traveled again to Europe.

In 1957, when Krotkova dined with former KGB assassin Nikolai Khokhlov at an Italian restaurant in Frankfurt, she may have slipped him a potentially lethal dose of radioactive thallium. Khokhlov had defected to the United States in 1954 after receiving orders to murder Georgi S. Okolovich, the exiled leader of a Russian anticommunist organization. Khokhlov survived the poisoning, but suspicion of Krotkova's role in the assassination attempt lingered.

In later years Krotkova worked as a confidential informant for the FBI and multilingual interpreter at the United Nations. She retired in 1964 and died in 1965 on a trip to Moscow, where she is buried in the city's Khimkinsky Cemetery.

■ 179. HOUNDED BY SOVIET INTELLIGENCE

MAP 6 ➤ **Victor A. Kravchenko residence:** 14 East 69th Street

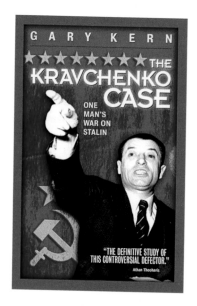

Victor A. Kravchenko, a Soviet official assigned to the Soviet Purchasing Commission in Washington, DC, defected to the United States on April 4, 1944. The Soviets claimed Kravchenko was a captain in the Red Army, although his passport clearly listed him as a civilian "Representative of the Soviet Government." When the United States recognized the official civilian title on the passport and refused his extradition back to the USSR, tensions between the wartime allies were raised. For Kravchenko, the difference meant either a likely death sentence in Moscow or asylum in the United States.

That diplomatic rift deepened when Kravchenko publicly revealed atrocities and daily fears Soviet citizens experienced during Stalinist rule. Despite living under the assumed name Peter Martin, Kravchenko's whereabouts in the United States became known to the NKVD almost immediately following his defection. Kravchenko was hounded and harassed by Soviet sympathizers who labeled him a mere clerk, a traitor, and a coward. He later claimed Soviet intelligence services attempted to kill him four times. In one bizarre 1956 incident, newspapers reported Kravchenko shot and seriously wounded a young

Victor A. Kravchenko's apartment at 14 East 69th Street was kept under surveillance by the Soviets following his defection. A smear campaign initiated by the USSR to discredit him and his claims of barbarism behind the Iron Curtain proved ineffective.

Puerto Rican man who had forced his way into his apartment, an incident subsequently described as a drunken scuffle that got out of control.

Kravchenko's best-selling 1946 book *I Chose Freedom* detailed the brutality of the Soviet system. For the first time, many American readers learned the realities of gulags, mass starvation, and other horrors. Although condemned by Soviet front organizations in Europe and America, the book gained a wide readership as the Soviet Union and the West entered the Cold War.

After being slandered by a French communist magazine, *Les Lettres Françaises*, Kravchenko sued the publication, and in 1949 the matter went to trial in Paris. The magazine, supported by Soviet authorities, produced witnesses who portrayed the defector as incompetent, feeble-minded, and of little importance. The wife Kravchenko left behind in the Soviet Union was paraded out to testify he was impotent. The trial found in favor of the defector but conveyed only a small symbolic monetary award. If Soviet authorities had hoped to silence Kravchenko, they were wrong. In 1950, he detailed the trial in his book *I Chose Justice*.

Sixteen years later, on February 25, 1966, Kravchenko died of a single gunshot wound to the head in his apartment at 14 East 69th Street. A note was found near his body along with a .38-caliber gun licensed to him. Friends commented that Kravchenko was despondent over America's role in Vietnam and personal financial setbacks, and police ruled the death a suicide. Others questioned the official finding. Kravchenko's ashes were scattered, in accordance with his wishes, on the Dniepr River near Zaporizhia, Ukraine.

■ 180. JEWELER, CRYPTOLOGIST, SPY

MAP 10 ▶ **Weisband jewelry stores:** 8016 Third Avenue, Brooklyn, and 8320 Fifth Avenue, Brooklyn

William Weisband is one of the least known but most damaging of the early Cold War spies. He claimed to be born in 1908 in Alexandria, Egypt, but his parents were probably living in Odessa, Russia, at the time of his birth. After the family immigrated to the United States, Weisband

William Weisband

William Weisband, who was recruited to spy by the Soviets in the 1930s and penetrated the Armed Forces Signal Security Agency in the 1940s, lived in this apartment building in Bay Ridge, Brooklyn, during his youth.

worked at his family's small chain of Brooklyn jewelry stores, first at 8016 Third Avenue and later at 8320 Fifth Avenue. He was also employed at times as a bookkeeper at the Stork Club, 3 East 53rd Street, and the Waldorf Astoria Hotel, 301 Park Avenue, but the jewelry business provided a cover for his espionage activities.

On a summer trip to Russia to study communism in the mid-1930s, Weisband was recruited by the NKVD and then served as a courier and sometime agent handler for several years. Drafted into the US Army in 1942 and promoted to the rank of first lieutenant in the Signal Corps, he continued spying. The VENONA decryptions later revealed that his letters to the Soviets were likely serviced at a mail drop by Lona Petka Cohen (code name LESLIE), who was then living at 178 East 71st Street.

After the war, Weisband went dormant until he was reactivated by the Soviets in 1948 while working as a civilian at the Armed Forces Signal Security Agency's Arlington Hall complex in Arlington, Virginia. Weisband's gregarious personality, combined with knowledge of the jewelry business, provided him with a credible pretext to roam the secret facility selling a selection of gems and inexpensive fashion accessories. His real purpose, however, was to elicit secrets from secretaries and other personnel about a startling new project, code-named VENONA, to decrypt wartime Soviet communications between Moscow and the United States.

Independently, Weisband and Kim Philby both reported on the VENONA intercepts and provided progress reports on the US code-breaking successes. As a result, the Soviets abruptly changed their communications ciphers in 1948, slamming shut one of America's few windows into Soviet espionage activities.

Weisband's family operated a small chain of neighborhood jewelry stores, one of which was located at 8016 Third Avenue, Brooklyn.

One intercepted message reported, "We received from 'Zhora' [Weisband] [highly valuable documents] . . . on the efforts of Americans to decipher Soviet ciphers. . . . Our state security agencies implemented a set of defensive measures, which resulted in a significant decrease in the effectiveness of the efforts of the [US] decryption service."

When confronted by the FBI about his alleged spying, Weisband staunchly refused to cooperate. Because the government possessed limited evidence against him, Weisband served only one year in jail for contempt when he failed to appear before a grand jury. Steadfastly maintaining his innocence, he dropped from public sight to become a door-to-door insurance salesman in Washington, DC. In May 1967, the World War II veteran who had compromised some of America's most closely guarded communications secrets suffered a fatal heart attack. His gravestone at the Presbyterian Cemetery in Alexandria, Virginia, identifies the spy by his military officer rank and the organization he betrayed.

■ 181. SPIES TO THE END

MAP 6 ▸ **Morris and Lona Cohen residence:** 178 East 71st Street (site redeveloped)

US-born Morris and Lona Cohen were committed communists who served as couriers in the Soviet penetration of America's atomic weapon development program. Morris used the alias names of Morris Pickett and Israel Altman. He was known by the code names VOLUNTEER and LUIS, while his wife was LESLIE.

A native New Yorker, Morris exhibited an affinity for Russian culture, having worked at the Soviet pavilion at the 1939 New York World's Fair. The couple played a supporting role in the Julius and Ethel Rosenberg operation and also crossed paths with the Soviet spymaster Rudolph Abel. When Abel was arrested, the Cohens' passports were found in his bank safe deposit box.

From 1948 to 1950, the pair lived at 178 East 71st Street, apartment 3B, while Morris Cohen worked at a public school once located at Lexington Avenue and East 96th Street. Fearing discovery after the arrest of scientist

Soviet postage stamps sometimes recognized spies during the Cold War. Morris Cohen received such a tribute.

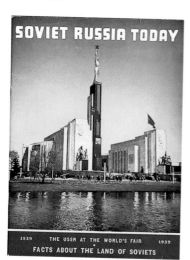

Among the meeting places—called *yavkas*—for Morris Cohen to contact his Soviet handlers in New York was the Soviet pavilion of the 1939 World's Fair in Flushing Meadows–Corona Park, Queens.

and Soviet spy Klaus Fuchs in Britain in 1950, the couple left New York, telling friends they were heading to Hollywood for screenwriting jobs. Instead, they fled to Moscow via Mexico, where Lona received additional training in ciphers and as a radio operator. Next they moved to England in 1954 on New Zealand passports as Helen and Peter Kroger and ran an antiquarian bookstore in London's East Ruislip area.

The Cohens' secret work in England supported London *illegal* Konon Trofimovich Molody, a Soviet intelligence officer with the alias Gordon Lonsdale (code name BEN). Molody directed a cell of Soviet spies, known in the United Kingdom as the Portland spy ring, under cover of his vending and jukebox business. The Cohen residence in East Ruislip became a covert communications center from which Molody's information was converted to microdots and concealed inside books shipped abroad. Molody was finally captured by MI5 in an operation code-named WHISPER, using information from a Polish defector Michael Goleniewski. A search of the Cohen residence revealed a secret radio transmitter under the house, accessed through a trap door beneath a refrigerator in the kitchen.

The Cohens and Molody were convicted of spying in 1961. Lona was sentenced to 20 years of prison time while her husband was given 25 years. After serving eight years, they were exchanged in a spy swap and relocated to Moscow. Once there, the pair taught espionage and trained Soviet intelligence agents for assignments in the West. Lona died in 1992 and Morris in 1995.

■ 182. "TALK TO ME, HARRY WINSTON!"
—FROM "DIAMONDS ARE A GIRL'S BEST FRIEND"

MAP 3 ➤ **Harry Winston Inc.:** 718 Fifth Avenue

Prominent jeweler Harry Winston was reportedly once investigated for assisting Soviet intelligence in converting diamonds into cash to fund intelligence operations.

Diamonds, a girl's best friend as Marilyn Monroe sang in the movie version of Anita Loos's novel *Gentlemen Prefer Blondes*, can also be a very good friend to spies. Espionage historian Nigel West has written that the "jeweller to the stars," Harry Winston, 718 Fifth Avenue, was once under investigation by the FBI for laundering diamonds to fund Soviet espionage. If true, it follows a pattern of past Soviet intelligence use of jewels for a source of hard currency. In the 1920s, a sophisticated Soviet smuggling operation in Europe turned an enormous horde of Romanov jewels into cash, some of which was used for espionage.

Nothing came of the FBI's investigation of Winston, but he again drew the attention of law enforcement when it was discovered that the family governess, Lona Petka (code name LESLIE and a.k.a Lona Cohen and Helen Kroger), was an NKVD operative. According to West, Petka made contact with her handler, Rudolph Abel, while taking the Winston children, Ronald and Bruce, on outings in Central Park. There, as Abel painted at an easel, she received instructions while pretending to admire his artwork.

A nephew of Harry Winston, Richard Alan Winston, likely assisted Abel. Richard, an aspiring artist, was introduced to Abel by Petka. Abel then convinced the young man to open a safe deposit box at Manufacturers Trust, 1511 Third Avenue, where the Soviet spy stashed $15,000 in cash along with the documents used to establish a false identity.

Harry Winston's name also surfaced during the investigation of Soviet spy William Weisband, who was employed at the Armed Forces Security Agency. Using a part-time sideline of selling jewelry as a reason to gain access to restricted areas of the Arlington Hall code-breaking facility near Washington, Weisband displayed a few pricey Harry Winston pieces to potential customers. He claimed the upscale merchandise had been inherited from his brother, Mark. Two decades later, Czech spy Hana Koecher worked for Winston grading diamonds.

Whether or not Anita Loos was correct about gentlemen preferring blondes, history seems to agree with Ian Fleming, who made the sparkling rocks an enduring part of espionage in *Diamonds Are Forever*.

■ 183. BROTHERS IN ESPIONAGE

MAP I ▶ **Morris and Jack Childs brush-pass site:** 11 Broadway, 9th floor

Russian-born brothers Morris and Jack Childs were active in the Communist Party in the 1920s before drifting away to pursue careers and get on with their lives. However, in the early 1950s, the two brothers returned to the communist fold, rose through party ranks, and resumed spying after receiving operational training in Moscow and neutral countries.

Morris Childs

In the 1960s, with the CPUSA budget running a deficit, Morris Childs (code name MARAT) received more than a million dollars a year from the Soviets to keep the organization going. A courier would execute a brush pass with Childs, delivering the cash, always at 3:05 p.m. at various downtown locations, including the 10th floor of 10 Pine Street (code name DINO), the ninth floor of 11 Broadway (code name FRED), the seventh floor of 120 Wall Street (code name POST), and the second floor of 81 New Street (code name ROLAND).

Soviet operational security for these brief encounters was nearly perfect. Each building was chosen for its multiple entrances and exits, and the two brothers were superb agents—disciplined, calm, and reliable. To their Soviet handlers, they seemed to be true believers in the cause, with the ideal cover of being prosperous American businessmen.

Russian-born brothers Morris and Jack Childs seemed eager to serve the communist cause. In reality, they were double agents reporting to the FBI. Their clandestine meetings occurred at multiple Manhattan office locations, including 11 Broadway.

In 1975, they received the Order of the Red Banner, with Morris traveling to Moscow to accept the tribute during a banquet in his honor presided over by Leonid Brezhnev, general secretary of the Central Committee of the Communist Party of the USSR.

Throughout the years, the handlers of Morris and Jack Childs did not realize the brothers were skimming as much as 5 percent of the money. Even more damaging, they had been working as double agents for the FBI under an operation code-named SOLO since rejoining the CPUSA in the early 1950s. Not until the 1980s were Soviet suspicions aroused and the operation closed down by the FBI. For their service, President Ronald Reagan awarded the brothers (Jack posthumously) the Presidential Medal of Freedom.

■ 184. AMERICA'S STRANGEST SPY AGENCY

MAP 3 ▶ **The Pond:** Steinway Hall, 109–113 West 57th Street (site redeveloped as 111 West 57th Street)

John V. Grombach

John V. Grombach is a nearly forgotten name in US intelligence history. Born in 1901 in New Orleans to a French consul, he was given the sobriquet "Frenchy," which would last throughout his life. According to legend, he displayed a combative personality early on while working as a teenaged bouncer in a New Orleans brothel. At age 18, Grombach renounced his French citizenship and entered West Point. Although a standout athlete, excessive demerits prevented his graduation. He then enlisted in the US Army, was assigned to the military police, and was eventually posted to the Panama Canal Zone.

Grombach left the military in the late 1920s, became a successful radio producer, and operated a side business as a boxing promoter. In 1941, he was called back into the army, given the rank of captain, and assigned to William Donovan's Coordinator of Information organization. The pugnacious Grombach clashed with Donovan almost from the start.

Within the Department of War another intelligence function, designated the Special Service Branch, better known as "the Pond," was created under Grombach's command. In the words of one of its Pentagon architects, the

Pond would be "a perpetual, a far-seeing, a far-distant, continuing secret intelligence service." Grombach, with a natural proclivity for secrecy, led the Pond for 13 years. He claimed the organization attempted to negotiate the surrender of Germany with Hermann Göring and tried to recruit Mafia kingpin Charles "Lucky" Luciano to assassinate Benito Mussolini.

One of the Pond's agents was a French serial killer, Dr. Marcel Petiot, whose recruitment Grombach attempted to justify in his 1980 book *The Great Liquidator*. Grombach asserted that Petiot provided reports on the Katyn Forest massacre of an estimated 22,000 Polish military personnel and civilians by the NKVD, the German missile site at Peenemünde, the opening of American diplomatic pouches by the British, and the names of German agents operating inside the United States. The veracity of Grombach's claims about Petiot remain in doubt, and French authorities gave no credit to them. When Petiot was captured in France at the end of the war, he was given a speedy trial and executed in 1946.

Following the war, the Pond maintained a New York office in Steinway Hall, then located at 109–113 West 57th Street, under the cover name Universal Service Corporation. However, Grombach's funding from the State Department and the CIA began a slow decline. By 1955, senior CIA officers concluded that the Pond's intelligence value was minimal, and the organization was shuttered. Grombach died in 1982 and is buried in New Orleans.

HISTORICAL FIND

Much of the Pond's history was forgotten or unknown until the discovery of several safes containing Grombach's papers in 2001 on an estate near Culpeper, Virginia, owned by the American Security Council Foundation. The documents were turned over to the government and are now in the National Archives. Grombach, for his part, remains a controversial and colorful character in the history of US intelligence operations.

■ 185. FRANK WISNER'S MIGHTY WURLITZER

MAP I ▶ Information Department of Cable and Radio Censorship: 90 Church Street

Frank Gardiner Wisner began his career in 1934 right out of law school at the esteemed white-shoe law firm of Carter, Ledyard, Milburn, at 2 Wall Street. The firm, where Franklin D. Roosevelt was once as an associate, was three floors below William Donovan's firm of Donovan, Leisure, Newton, and Lumbard.

Wisner joined the Naval Reserve in 1940, went on active duty in July 1941, and became assistant head of the Information Department of Cable and Radio Censorship, 90 Church Street. By 1943, the young lawyer had joined the OSS

Frank Wisner began his intelligence career in 1940 as a Naval Reserve lieutenant liaison officer and assistant head of the Information Department of Cable and Radio Censorship, 90 Church Street. Later he headed the CIA's worldwide operations.

and eventually served in Africa, Turkey, Romania, and France. Following the war, he briefly returned to his old law firm and lived at 1050 Park Avenue. In 1947, he accepted a position in the State Department as the deputy assistant secretary of state for occupied countries and in 1948 was reassigned to the newly formed CIA's Office of Policy Coordination (OPC).

Wisner became alarmed by the aggressive expansion of the Soviet Union after World War II and advocated for the CIA to respond to the USSR's hostile actions with covert actions similar to those used by the OSS in World War II. He dismissed the traditional functions of intelligence gathering and analysis as akin to "a bunch of old washerwomen, exchanging gossip while they rinse through the dirty linen." This attitude may have provided the OPC with a dashing panache, but Wisner and his staff were not universally admired. FBI director J. Edgar Hoover dubbed them "Wisner's gang of weirdos." In 1952, the CIA merged the OPC with the Office of Special Operations to form the Plans Directorate, with responsibilities for all clandestine-collection and covert-action operations.

Under Wisner, who served as the CIA's deputy director of plans from 1951 to 1958, the agency's covert actions included efforts to counter Soviet propaganda through covert funding of international student organizations, foreign labor unions, friendly journalists, and publications to create pro-American voices. He called these operations "the mighty Wurlitzer," after the well-known large theater organ, implying that he could play a tune heard around the world.

The Plans Directorate's campaigns involved a diverse and often surprising collection of personalities. In the late 1950s, the not-yet-famous Gloria Steinem was part of an organization that disrupted communist rallies abroad. "In my experience the agency was completely different from its image: it was liberal, nonviolent and honorable," she later told the *Washington Post* in 1967 after her participation was revealed.

Wisner left the agency in 1961 and died of a self-inflicted gunshot wound in 1965. He is buried in Arlington National Cemetery.

■ 186. HIDING THE MONEY

MAP 4 ▶ **J. M. Kaplan Fund:** 55 Fifth Avenue

Hiding the true sponsor's hand is a fundamental requirement for all intelligence organizations when conducting covert influence operations. During

During the Cold War's early years, the CIA used private foundations, such as the J. M. Kaplan Fund, located at 55 Fifth Avenue, to covertly fund educational and cultural causes in combating the spread of communism.

the early years of the Cold War, the CIA sought to counter Soviet expansion and subversion of European democracies by secretly working through US-based educational and cultural foundations with the shared objective of securing political freedom and maintaining democratic institutions throughout Western Europe.

The goal was to combat the growing influence of Soviet front groups, such as the World Peace Council and its affiliate organizations. Although masquerading under the guise of anodyne names and noble causes, the true Soviet goals were the subversion of democratic movements and promotion of the USSR's foreign policies.

Both public and private foundations accepted CIA funds for their own programs or forwarded the funds to other organizations without disclosing the true source of the money. Many of the foundations cooperating with the CIA were based in New York City, and their relationship with the agency was revealed in news reports beginning in the late 1960s and during congressional investigations in 1975 and 1976.

According to press reports, a partial list of New York–based foundations through which secret CIA funds passed in the 1950s includes:

- David, Josephine and Winfield Baird Foundation, 67 Broad Street
- Leveland R. Dodge Foundation, 300 Park Avenue
- J. M. Kaplan Fund, 55 Fifth Avenue
- Lucius N. Littauer Foundation, 345 East 46th Street
- Aaron E. Norman Fund, 40 Wall Street
- Benjamin Rosenthal Foundation, 350 Fifth Avenue

Some other domestic- and overseas-based organizations reported to have benefited from CIA monies funneled through these foundations were:

- African American Institute, New York
- Congress for Cultural Freedom, Paris
- Institute of International Labor Research, New York

- International Development Foundation, New York

- Radio Free Europe, New York

- United States Youth Council, New York

Once the European democracies survived and the USSR offensive seemed contained, the critical role played by the CIA became obscured by a torrent of questions about the legality and propriety of such covert relationships. As a result, the programs were curtailed, many organizations refused to accept funds originating from the CIA, and new laws and presidential executive orders defined and restricted the CIA's relationships with American citizens and organizations.

■ 187. BEST COVERT ACTION

MAP 2 ▶ **National Committee for Free Europe Inc. headquarters:** Empire State Building, 350 Fifth Avenue, room 301

Covertly funded by the CIA, Radio Free Europe was based at 2 Park Avenue.

A modest public announcement on June 1, 1949, launched the National Committee for Free Europe Inc. (NCFE). Comprised of lawyers, politicians, and businessmen, the new organization, headquartered in the Empire State Building, 350 Fifth Avenue, room 301, was to assist refugees escaping from behind the Iron Curtain. Joseph C. Grew, former undersecretary of state and ambassador to Japan, headed the NCFE, while notables such as Gen. Dwight D. Eisenhower, future director of Central Intelligence (DCI) Allen Dulles, *Time* magazine's Henry Luce, and movie producer Darryl Zanuck were also associated with the effort. The announcement, which attracted little press coverage, stated the committee would be funded by private donations from philanthropists.

In fact, the NCFE was established as a covert action operation by the young agency's OPC. The organization received covert funding from the CIA and, in turn, funded Radio Free Europe, based at 2 Park Avenue. The broadcast service went on the air on July 4, 1950, to become one of the few sources of accurate news about world affairs available to those confined behind the Iron Curtain.

Radio Free Europe was an unqualified success in countering the Soviet attempt to isolate Eastern Europe's population from news and information about the West. For two decades its broadcasts were among the CIA's most successful covert action operations, but in 1971 US senator Clifford P. Case exposed the agency's funding. As a result, the CIA relationship was ended, but Radio Free Europe's influence was so significant that Congress continued to fund the broadcasts through annual appropriations to the Board of International Broadcasting.

By the time it became known as a CIA operation, Radio Free Europe was the longest-lasting and arguably among the most successful covert actions ever mounted by the United States.

■ 188. WINNING THE COLD WAR THROUGH ART

MAP 3 ➤ **Museum of Modern Art:** 11 West 53rd Street

The Cold War represented a cultural as well as political challenge from Soviet communism. In Europe, America was often viewed as a nation uninterested in, even hostile to, art. This view was reinforced by Soviet propaganda that extolled the supposed virtues of communism over capitalism.

In fact, during the 1940s, American artists such as the so-called Irascible 18 were challenging the established art world and its institutions, including New York's Metropolitan Museum of Art. Originating in the West Village and incubated in locations such as the now defunct Cedar Tavern, 82 University Place, their art, abstract expressionism, was bold, exuberant, and distinctly American.

In 1950, Thomas Braden, an OSS veteran, an associate of Nelson Rockefeller, and a former executive secretary of the Museum of Modern Art (MoMA),

The Museum of Modern Art played an integral role in CIA-backed cultural operations.

was hired as a special assistant for Allen Dulles at the CIA and within two years was heading the agency's International Organizations Division (IOD). Among the IOD's responsibilities were covert political and psychological operations.

Braden, who is better remembered for his book and television show *Eight Is Enough* and the political commentary show *Crossfire*, managed covert funding of international events to promote American cultural values. Performances by American jazz musicians, opera recitals, tours by the Boston Symphony Orchestra, and the animated film of George Orwell's *Animal Farm* were all underwritten through private foundations, such as the Congress for Cultural Freedom.

In communist nations, the work of free artists was a revelation. A *Washington Post* article in 2008 reflected on the time by quoting a Polish admirer of Dave Brubeck after the jazz legend toured Poland during the Cold War: "Mr. Brubeck, you come to Poland, you did not bring jazz. You brought the Empire State Building, you brought the Grand Canyon, you brought America."

Fine art and MoMA would also have a role. Founded in 1929 by Abigail Aldrich Rockefeller, MoMA was originally housed in an exhibit space in the Hecksher Building, 730 Fifth Avenue, prior to moving to its current 11 West 53rd Street location. Her son, Nelson, frequently referred to it as "Mummy's museum" and was himself an early enthusiast of abstract expressionism, calling it "free enterprise painting."

In addition to Braden's employment by MoMA, several members of the museum's postwar board also had connections to the intelligence community. Together they recognized that MoMA offered both a prestigious name and an attractive vehicle for showcasing the talents of American artists such as Jackson Pollock, Willem de Kooning, and Robert Motherwell to the world. A 1952 exhibition that toured Europe, Masterpieces of the Twentieth Century, featured 200 paintings curated by James Johnson Sweeney, the former director of MoMA and the Solomon R. Guggenheim Museum. Other

LIFE AFTER THE CIA

William F. Buckley, Yale class of 1950, a leading voice of conservatism for decades, and founder of the *National Review*, served in the CIA for two years and, while posted to Latin America, edited a book by former Peruvian communist Eudocio Ravines, *The Road from Yenan*. After leaving the agency, his home was at a Rosario Candela–designed building, 778 Park Avenue, from which he oversaw the *National Review*, ran for mayor of New York City, and hosted the long-running television show *Firing Line*. Buckley's continued fascination with espionage was apparent in his 11 spy novels featuring the globetrotting Blackford Oakes. Among the titles are *Who's on First* (1980), *Marco Polo, if You Can* (1982), and *See You Later, Alligator* (1985).

exhibitions followed, including Modern Art in the United States (1955) and The New American Painting (1958–1959).

The shows were designed to present America in the vanguard of the art world. It is unlikely the artists realized the CIA was funding exhibits of their work, though several spoke openly against communism and Soviet government restrictions, comparing them to those Nazi Germany had placed on the creative community.

Some of the exhibits were controversial and drew criticism from a few US politicians. Congressman George A. Dondero, who called modern art "depraved" and "destructive," saw it as part of a communist conspiracy. Looking for meaning in one painting, Dondero claimed he detected a map of American military installations obscured in the work.

The CIA dismissed the naysayers. "Regarding Abstract Expressionism, I'd love to be able to say that the CIA invented it just to see what happens in New York and downtown SoHo tomorrow!" former CIA officer Donald Jameson told historian Frances Stoner Saunders. "But I think that what we did really was to recognize the difference. It was recognized that Abstract Expressionism was the kind of art that made Socialist Realism look even more stylized and more rigid and confined than it was. And that relationship was exploited in some of the exhibitions."

■ 189. OPERATION MIDNIGHT CLIMAX

MAP 2 ➤ **Secret drug-testing apartment:** 81 Bedford Street

During the early years of the Cold War, as part of the MKULTRA program, the CIA researched the effect of a variety of drugs on human behavior. Experiments code-named MIDNIGHT CLIMAX were conducted on both witting and unwitting subjects in New York and San Francisco. Potential "truth drugs" such as LSD were administered in a West Village apartment at 81 Bedford Street to unsuspecting individuals, including Russian sailors and paid prostitutes. The subjects were secretly observed and photographed after consuming alcoholic beverages laced with various drugs.

On November 27, 1953, the Statler Hotel (now the Hotel Pennsylvania), 401 Seventh Avenue, which gained fame with Glenn Miller's 1940 big band hit song "Pennsylvania 6-5000,"

This Bedford Street apartment in the West Village was used for drug tests on unwitting subjects in the 1950s as part of the CIA's MKULTRA program.

US government scientist Dr. Frank Olson jumped to his death from the 10th-floor window of the Hotel Pennsylvania on November 27, 1953. A week earlier, Olson had participated in an LSD experiment that was part of the MKULTRA program.

was the scene of a MKULTRA-related death. Dr. Frank Olson, a scientist employed at Fort Detrick in Frederick, Maryland, jumped from a 10th-floor window of the hotel. Olson and several other government employees had ingested a quantity of LSD a week earlier to test its effects. The experiment resulted in a "bad trip" for Olson and, in an effort to counter the drug's effects, the scientist, accompanied by a CIA officer, sought psychiatric treatment in New York.

The circumstances of Olson's death and the MKULTRA program were not publicly disclosed until the mid-1970s. Congress responded by launching investigations of this program that had ended 10 years earlier. Despite the congressional reports and subsequent declassification of all surviving MKULTRA documents, the program remains the topic of speculation and lingering conspiracy theories six decades later.

■ 190. MAIL CENSORSHIP LESSONS FROM THE BRITISH

MAP II ▶ **Lyric spies:** Idlewild Airport (now John F. Kennedy International Airport), Queens

John F. Kennedy International Airport, known prior to 1963 as Idlewild International Airport or Idlewild Field, was the site of a secret CIA mail-opening operation that began in 1952, code-named SRPOINTER and later HTLINGUAL. Over two decades, the operation examined an estimated 215,000 pieces of mail from and to Soviet Bloc countries.

The targeted envelopes and packages were collected within a restricted area of Federal Building No. 111, known as the Jamaica Airmail Facility, adjoining Idlewild Airport. During the evening, a CIA team would photograph envelope exteriors with a Diebold camera, then select some for opening. One method of opening was to hold the envelope over a steaming tea kettle to soften the sealant, then slip a narrow stick under the flap and remove the letter. "Flaps and seals" specialists tested suspect letters and envelopes for secret writing, sought evidence of microdots, and evaluated Soviet censorship techniques. After the letters were tested and photographed, they were put back into their envelopes, resealed, and returned to the mails the following morning.

HTLINGUAL was, in essence, a continuation of an earlier joint British-FBI mail-opening program to detect and intercept covert communications of enemy spies. During World War II, the work was done at a British facility in the basement of Bermuda's Princess Hotel, today the Fairmont Hamilton Princess. The staff was composed primarily of women because they were judged better suited to the job requiring a high-level of fine motor skills.

■ 191. SPIES AND BEST-SELLING AUTHOR

MAP 7 ➤ **Roald Dahl residence:** 44 West 77th Street

Children's book author Roald Dahl wrote pro-British propaganda stories during World War II as a member of the BSC. After marrying actress Patricia Neal, the couple lived in this apartment on the Upper East Side.

Roald Dahl, beloved children's book author of *Charlie and the Chocolate Factory*, *James and the Giant Peach*, and many other stories was also a spy during World War II. Attached to the BSC as a liaison officer to the OSS, the future author made frequents trips to New York.

Following the war, Dahl devoted his time to writing and spent substantial time in New York City. His first New York address was the townhouse of a friend, Texas newspaper publisher Charles Marsh, on East 92nd Street, just off of Fifth Avenue. In July 1953, Dahl married future Academy Award–winning movie star Patricia Neal at Trinity Church (Broadway and Wall Street). The couple split their time between England and America, living in a series of New York apartments at 44 West 77th Street and 26 East 82nd Street.

One of Dahl's recollections of the early postwar years was a train ride with Ian Fleming, a fellow wartime British intelligence officer. When discussing their postwar plans, Fleming mentioned he was writing a novel about a fictional secret agent. Dahl, already an accomplished author, dismissed the idea and suggested Fleming "get a real job instead." Ignoring the advice, Fleming published *Casino Royale* in 1953, introducing James Bond, the world-famous fictional spy.

■ 192. THE PASSWORD IS ABRACADABRA

MAP 8 ➤ **John Mulholland residence:** 600 West 115th Street

John Mulholland, the most skilled sleight-of-hand magician of his generation and a virtuoso of close-up magic, began a six-year secret association with the CIA in 1953. Working from his office at 130 West 42nd Street

Magician and secret CIA contractor John Mulholland lived a stone's throw from the Columbia University campus in the Luxor apartment building.

and his home at 600 West 115th Street, Mulholland wrote two top-secret training manuals for the agency describing basic sleight-of-hand principles and practices, including the use of conceal-ments, misdirection, and clandes-tine signaling. Funded through the MKULTRA program, the manuals adapted the magician's stagecraft to tradecraft.

Although most of the CIA's MK-ULTRA materials were destroyed in 1973 by order of Director Richard Helms, the Mulholland manuals were somehow missed. They remained classified until 2003, 50 years after they were written, and were pub-lished in 2009 by HarperCollins as *The Official CIA Manual of Trickery and Deception*. By today's standards of performance magic, Mulholland's tech-niques are elementary, but the manuals offer a rare glimpse into the breadth of Cold War efforts to equip CIA officers with unconventional spy tools. Most enduring is Mulholland's underlying understanding that, in the words of for-mer acting DCI John McLaughlin, "Espionage and magic are kindred spirits."

■ 193. ISLAND OF SECRETS

MAP 12 ▶ **Plum Island Animal Disease Center:** Plum Island, New York

Plum Island lies in Gardiners Bay, east of Orient Point, off the eastern end of the North Fork coast of Long Island. Three miles long and one mile wide at its widest point, the government-owned island's 840 acres are dotted with more than 70 buildings, many dilapidated, that include the Plum Island Animal Dis-ease Center (PIADC).

Overseen by the Department of Homeland Security, the Plum Island Animal Disease Center plays a critical role in protecting the nation's livestock from infectious diseases.

One of the island's most mys-terious structures is Building 257, sometimes referred to as Lab 257, on the site of old Fort Terry. Building 257 and the newer Building 101 housed the US Army Chemical Corps anti-animal-biological-warfare testing programs from the 1950s to 1969. Building 101 continues to operate as the PIADC.

Plum Island has been linked to German scientist Erich Traub, who was brought to the United States after World War II as a "high-value intelligence target" during OPERATION PAPERCLIP, an American intelligence and scientific program to exploit German scientists' research and knowledge while denying their expertise to the USSR. A controversial and uncorroborated book published in 2004, *Lab 257: The Disturbing Story of the Government's Secret Germ Laboratory*, alleges that Traub provided information to the US Army Biological Warfare Headquarters in Fort Detrick that resulted in establishing an offshore germ-warfare animal disease lab on Plum Island.

Plum Island, once the site of a US Army biological warfare program, also gained fame as a potential vacation getaway for serial killer Hannibal Lecter in *Silence of the Lambs* and for a leading role in the Nelson DeMille thriller *Plum Island.*

Over the years Plum Island was at the center of accusations and conspiracy theories. Some attempted to link the island with nearby outbreaks of the Dutch duck plague virus, Lyme disease, and the West Nile virus. The US government asserts that no pathogen under study has ever escaped the island and once designated the property for possible sale. However, even 60 years after animal testing ended, questions of public safety persist. The property remains in government ownership pending additional environmental studies.

THE COLD WAR HEATS UP

(1960–1989)

The world did not anticipate the rapid collapse of the Soviet empire in the last decade of the 20th century. The political and economic decay that undermined the Soviet system was hardly evident in the successes of the USSR's intelligence services. At the time of the Soviet Union's collapse, the KGB and the GRU were running some of their most damaging penetrations of the US government, including FBI special agent Robert Hanssen and CIA officer Aldrich Ames.

As the appeal of Soviet communism after World War II diminished and the number of ideological spies who had been nurtured, seduced, and recruited by the NKVD in the 1930s and 1940s dwindled, the KGB and GRU, along with their surrogate services in Cuba and Czechoslovakia, changed tactics. New spies were often more motivated by offers of money, appeals to ego, satisfaction of greed, or extraction of revenge than ideology. For the Soviets, recruiting in the West frequently became a cash-and-carry business—exchanging dollars for documents. Advanced, proprietary Western technology became a major collection target, and miniaturized electronic devices for surveillance and covert communications added indispensable tools to the profession.

Expanding US military involvement in Vietnam met with domestic protests in New York, especially in the city's universities, presenting opportunities for foreign influence operations that fanned dissent. Soviet disinformation and active measures campaigns were launched to exacerbate policy and racial divisions in the American population. Wars and ethnic instability in the Middle East and Africa were cause for intelligence services from those regions to expand their presence in New York as the UN presented a platform to post spies and advance political agendas. China emerged as an international force with a corresponding intelligence reach following formal recognition by the United States. Increased numbers of Chinese diplomats and university students enabled an expansion of the country's intelligence presence.

Unchanged was the operational importance of New York to Cold War adversaries and new contenders for international prestige. The city became an international playground for spies of every country determined to advance their nation's interests. Through the early 1980s, as revelations of espionage and arrests of spies mounted, the American media dubbed 1985 "The Year of the Spy."

■ 194. MAFIA ASSASSINS

MAP 3 ➤ **OPERATION ZRRIFLE planning site:** Plaza Hotel, Fifth Avenue and Central Park South

On September 14, 1960, former FBI agent turned private investigator Robert Maheu, acting as CIA go-between, met former bootlegger and Chicago

The Plaza Hotel was the site of clandestine planning for an operation to assassinate Cuban dictator Fidel Castro with the help of organized crime. Code-named ZRRIFLE, the plot never materialized.

gangster John "Handsome Johnny" Roselli at the Plaza Hotel on Fifth Avenue and Central Park South. The purpose of the meeting was to explore the possibility of recruiting the Mafia to assassinate Cuban dictator Fidel Castro, his brother Raul, and their comrade Ernesto "Che" Guevara.

Following the initial discussion, the planning for the operation (code name ZRRIFLE) dragged on in various forms for three years before fizzling out in late 1963. When the plot was revealed in the mid-1970s, it became a catalyst for the 1976 Presidential Executive Order 11905 prohibiting any US government employee from planning or conducting assassination operations.

■ 195. MASTER-SPY NEGOTIATOR

MAP 10 ▶ **James B. Donovan residence:** 35 Prospect Park West, Brooklyn

James B. Donovan

Bronx-born James B. Donovan, a Fordham- and Harvard-educated lawyer, never expected to defend a Soviet spy. After Donovan entered the US Navy in 1943, he was assigned as legal counsel to the Office of Scientific Research and Development, where he handled matters associated with the Manhattan Project. By the war's end, he was a full commander, was awarded the Legion of Merit, and served as an assistant to Justice Robert H. Jackson during the Nuremberg trials.

Donovan returned to the private sector, working for the National Bureau of Casualty Underwriters before forming an insurance law practice as a founding partner of Watters, Cowen and Donovan. Unexpectedly, he reentered the espionage world in 1957 when the Brooklyn Bar Association appointed him to represent accused Soviet spy Rudolph Abel. The public-defender assignment brought threats and enmity from the public, particularly in response to his successful legal efforts to save the spy from a death sentence.

A few years later at the behest of the Department of Justice, Donovan acted as lead negotiator, along with CIA lawyer Milan C. Miskovsky, in the 1962 spy swap of Abel for U-2 pilot Francis Gary Powers, then imprisoned in the USSR. Among the earliest and most famous spy trades of the Cold War, the dramatic exchange took place on the Glienicke Bridge, between East and

James B. Donovan, the defense lawyer for Soviet spy Rudolph Abel, who later negotiated the release of Bay of Pigs prisoners in Cuba, lived in this Brooklyn apartment house at 35 Prospect Park West.

West Berlin. Donovan's 1964 book *Strangers on a Bridge: The Case of Colonel Abel and Francis Gary Powers*, was made into the Steven Spielberg movie *Bridge of Spies*.

Working pro bono with Miskovsky, Donovan also led negotiations to obtain the release in 1963 of hundreds of Cuban prisoners captured during the failed Bay of Pigs invasion. Their delicate negotiations with Fidel Castro required approximately a dozen trips to the island nation. The eventual deal traded prisoners for medicine, resulting in the release of 1,100 captives and allowing more than 9,000 of their family members to leave Cuba. Little known is that he also secured the release of three undercover CIA officers imprisoned since 1960. (Details of the three CIA officers' capture in Havana, imprisonment, and eventual release were made public for the first time in the authors' *Spycraft: The Secret History of the CIA's Spytechs, from Communism to Al-Qaeda*.) The CIA recognized Donovan's efforts by awarding him the Distinguished Intelligence Medal.

Throughout this period, Donovan lived at 35 Prospect Park West, Brooklyn, after previous residences in Bay Ridge and at 400 East 58th Street. As a public figure, Donovan failed in a run for the US Senate, though he served on the New York City Board of Education, including a term as its president. He was president of Pratt Institute from 1968 until his death in 1970 at age 53.

■ 196. THE GOVERNMENT'S CHIEF WHIP

MAP 3 ▶ **Great Northern Hotel:** 119 West 56th Street (today site of Le Parker Meridien)

Mariella Novotny (a.k.a. Stella Capes) was born in Czechoslovakia and claimed to be a niece of its former president. In the 1960s, she gained some notoriety as a striptease dancer in London, worked as a prostitute, and then captured worldwide headlines when linked to the John Profumo scandal. In *Thus Bad Begins*, author Javier Marías quotes Christine Keeler's description of Mariella: "She had a tiny waist that exaggerated her ample figure. She was a siren, a sexual athlete of Olympian proportions—she could do it all. I know. I saw her in action. She knew all the strange pleasures that were wanted and could deliver them."

In December 1960, Novotny traveled to New York City as a guest of British television producer Harry Alan Towers. She worked as a call girl from multiple New York apartments, including 300 East 46th Street, apartment 18-D; 54 East 83rd Street; and her favorite, the Great Northern Hotel, 119 West 56th Street. Reportedly through arrangements made by Stephen Ward, a principal figure in the Profumo affair, Novotny worked for a time as a courtesan at the Quorum Club in Washington, alongside suspected East German spy Ellen Rometsch. Novotny also purportedly met and partied with Robert Kennedy, John F. Kennedy, and other prominent American politicians.

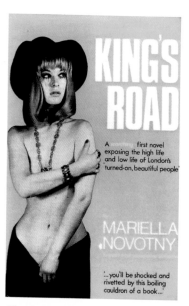

Although promoted as a tell-all about international spies and political scandal, Mariella Novotny's book revealed little.

On March 3, 1961, Novotny was arrested for soliciting while visiting Towers's apartment at 140 West 55th Street. Three days later Towers was arrested for violating the White Slave Traffic Act in a claim that he had brought her into the United States to work as a prostitute. After both were freed on bail, Novotny sailed back to the United Kingdom on the *Queen Mary* under the assumed name Mrs. R. Tyson. Towers fled to the USSR.

After US authorities alerted British immigration officers, Novotny was detained in the United Kingdom. She made a statement to the FBI that Towers was actually "a Soviet agent providing the Russians with information for the purposes of compromising certain prominent individuals." Novotny's "black book" was confiscated by the FBI, but charges against Towers and Novotny were eventually dropped.

Suspected spy Novotny was arrested at Harry Towers's apartment at 140 West 55th Street. Following her release on bail, she was mysteriously spirited out of the United States.

Novotny rejoined her friend Christine Keeler and returned to a life of party-girl at events hosted by Ward. So many prominent UK officials began attending their fetish/sadomasochistic parties that Novotny began referring to herself as "the government's chief whip." Through Ward, Keeler met Soviet naval attaché Yevgeny Ivanov and began a sexual relationship. Ward was rumored to be secretly working with MI5 to use Keeler to secure Ivanov's defection. Whether or not the MI5 connection was true, the matter became more convoluted when Keeler began a sexual relationship with John Profumo, the UK's Secretary of State for War. The security repercussions of the Ivanov-Keeler-Profumo imbroglio resulted in Ward's trial and suicide, Profumo's resignation from Parliament, and the fall of Prime Minister Harold Macmillan's government.

Towers later emerged relatively unscathed to become a film producer of dozens of largely B-movies that are cult classics today, such as *The Blood of Fu Manchu*, *Venus in Furs*, and *The House of 10,000 Dolls*. His film career lasted until his death in 2009.

■ 197. CUBAN HONEY TRAP

MAP 6 ➤ **Former Cuban mission to the UN:** 6 East 67th Street (now the permanent mission of the Slovak Republic to the UN)

Jennifer Miles exhibited an early taste for adventure. After growing up in South Africa, she toured the world on a tight budget, settled in Canada in the mid-1960s, and there, while recovering from an illness, fell in love

with the Cuban Revolution. Tales of Che Guevara and Fidel Castro prompted her to join pro-Cuban groups. She visited the tropical workers' paradise, met dignitaries, worked in the fields harvesting crops, and, in 1967, was recruited as an agent.

Tall, blonde, and strikingly attractive, Miles also possessed a captivating personality. She was given the code name MARY and instructed by Cuban intelligence service to secure a diplomatic job in Washington. Havana instructed her to develop contacts with influential persons and report on their vulnerabilities for potential recruitment as spies.

Jennifer Miles

The Cuban mission to the United States, once located at 6 East 67th Street, was a hotbed of espionage when occupied by the communist government.

FBI surveillance captured Jennifer Miles dining with her Cuban handlers in New York. The beautiful South African blonde was an almost irresistible honey trap.

Accordingly, Miles used her position as a clerk-typist at the South African embassy in Washington to secure invitations to diplomatic receptions and identify potential targets. Once she zeroed in on her prey, an invitation to her apartment and her charms in the bedroom proved too difficult for many men to resist. After a passionate assignation, pillow talk quickly turned to topics of interest to Havana.

Miles came to the attention of the FBI in mid-1969 when she filled a dead drop with a progress report near an apartment building on 82nd Street in Jackson Heights, Queens. A maintenance man discovered the material and reported his find to authorities. Given the personal information divulged in the report, the FBI identified Miles within 48 hours and placed her under surveillance. At first, agents could not identify the intelligence service for whom she was reporting, but four days later she was spotted dining at a bar-restaurant in Astoria, Queens, with her handler, a Cuban diplomat posted to the UN.

While Miles's Washington apartment was under surveillance, the FBI marveled at the number of male visitors she entertained. However, when she began entertaining White House staffers, the decision was made to terminate the operation, and she was arrested on October 4, 1970. At first refusing to cooperate, she eventually changed her mind and named her handlers, two diplomats working out of the Cuban mission to the UN, then located at 6 East 67th Street. Cuban counselor Rogelio Rodriguez Lopez and first secretary Orlando Prendes Gutierrez departed the United States five days later. Based in part on her cooperation with the FBI, Miles was allowed to return to South Africa.

■ 198. THE KGB SLEPT HERE

MAP 9 ▸ **A home for Soviet Spies:** 355 West 255th Street, Bronx

If you were a Soviet intelligence officer under diplomatic cover in New York during the Cold War, you most likely lived at an apartment compound in the Riverdale section of the Bronx at 355 West 255th Street. A 20-story, unadorned, concrete high-rise standing on a hill at the center of an impressively fenced compound provided living quarters and a social center for Soviet officials stationed in New York during the Cold War. Prior to the compound's construction, Soviet officials lived in hotels, such as the Excelsior at 45 West 81st Street and the Esplanade at 305 West End Avenue, now a senior residential facility. Both were targets of FBI eavesdropping operations under the code name MEGAHUT.

Not surprisingly, Cold War tensions made the Riverdale property a flash point in local politics. After occupying the compound in the 1970s, the Soviets battled neighbors, protesters, and the local zoning board as well as assaults that included gunshots and at least one bomb attack. In 1982, Bronx borough president Stanley Simon renamed the street Anatoly Shcharansky Square to show support for the jailed Russian dissident also known as Natan Sharansky. The small ceremony and new street sign at 255th Street set off a small diplomatic incident.

Higher-ranking officials were provided residences at the Soviets' UN mission, 136 East 67th Street, now the home of the Russian Federation's permanent mission to the UN, while the most privileged were given allowances for their own apartments. New York was considered a plum assignment, and at times as many as 300 Soviet intelligence officers under diplomatic cover lived throughout the city.

EXPLOITING SOCIAL TENSIONS

In an attempt to exploit racial and religious divisions among Americans, the KGB planned to launch OPERATION PANDORA in 1971. Conceived by the KGB's First Directorate, the plan called for the New York *rezidentura* to detonate an explosive device in "the Negro section of New York." It is unclear whether this meant Harlem or parts of Brooklyn or the Bronx, but the anonymous Moscow plotter suggested "one of the Negro colleges." The explosions would be followed by anonymous calls that blamed the terrorist act on the Jewish Defense League.

While the operation was never executed, that same year KGB chief Yuri Andropov approved the printing and distribution of racist pamphlets that looked as if they originated with the Jewish Defense League. Corresponding letters alleging Jewish atrocities against African Americans were sent to African American organizations. These racially themed plots were produced in the hopes of creating what the KGB called "mass disorders in New York."

■ 199. UNDISCLOSED PURPOSE

MAP 9 ▶ **House of intrigue:** 5437 Fieldston Road, Fieldston, Bronx

The 20-story residence in the Riverdale section of the Bronx at 355 West 255th Street opened for the families of Soviet diplomats in 1974. Soviet and Russian diplomatic facilities such as this frequently have sophisticated antennas installed on rooftops to intercept signals of government and commercial entities in their host countries. The electronic eavesdropping equipment is often camouflaged as ventilator pipes or enclosed in small rooftop sheds.

A small white house once stood in the now fenced and overgrown empty lot depicted here at 5437 Fieldston Road in the Riverdale section of the Bronx. In the background, the present-day Russian residence is seen adjacent to the site. Unconfirmed rumors suggested the house was a surveillance post owned by federal authorities to observe the Soviet compound.

The KGB's code name for the Riverdale rooftop intercept installation was FONAR. Tactical and strategic intercepts were handled separately. Intercepting tactical signals such as those from the police and the FBI were the responsibility of a section within the KGB *rezidentura* with the code name IMPULSE. Strategic signals were monitored by another *rezidentura* section, code-named ROCKET. Large satellite dishes on the lower level of the official compound enabled direct, secure communication with Moscow.

A privately owned house at 5437 Fieldston Road, next to the Riverdale compound, changed ownership several times during Soviet construction of the compound in the early 1970s. Eventually it was acquired by an unknown company, Van Courtland Realty. For decades afterward, although none of the local residents recalled anyone ever living in the house, someone regularly mowed the lawn, picked up the mail, and cleared circulars from the front doorstep. The general assumption of the neighbors was that the reclusive occupants were FBI agents who came and went largely unobserved and tended the location as an observation post for surveilling the Soviets next door.

In 2011, the property was purchased by the Talner Congregation Beth David, with a goal of redeveloping the property and building a synagogue. The house was demolished, and the site became an empty fenced lot.

■ 200. FAVORITE KGB SPY SITES

MAP 9 ➤ **David Marcus movie theater:** 3464 Jerome Avenue, Bronx (site now a post office)

When KGB major Vasili Mitrokhin defected to the West in the early 1990s, he brought with him a trove of notes meticulously copied during his three decades as a senior archivist for the Russian intelligence service. From those documents, Mitrokhin and University of Cambridge professor Christopher Andrew wrote *The Sword and the Shield*, revealing decades of Soviet intelligence secrets.

The sensational nature of the text obscured a small appendix titled "Some Favorite KGB Yavkas (Meeting Places) in the 1960s." Included are dozens of meeting locations in America's largest cities favored by Soviet intelligence, with New York City repeatedly mentioned as an operational center for secret meetings, called *treffs* by the KGB.

The KGB seemed to be particularly attracted to the Bronx, once a center of Russian émigrés. The David Marcus movie theater (originally the Tuxedo Theater) at 3464 Jerome Avenue, a favorite meeting place, is now the site of a post office. Another Bronx theater, the Earl Theatre, 58 East 161st Street, near Yankee Stadium and now a sports bar, was also a popular Soviet meeting place in the 1940s. The "restaurant Savarin" was almost certainly a reference to a defunct chain operated by the Union News Company, with locations scattered throughout the city. Other operational sites were the "display window" of "Wilma's Party Center," most likely a business that has since closed, while the Middletown Inn Restaurant, 3188 Middletown Road in the Bronx, no longer exists.

Many attributes that made businesses successful were also attractive for clandestine meeting sites. Multiple exits and entrances, heavy foot traffic on the street, and appeal to a wide-ranging demographic population served spies well. New York restaurants such as the defunct Bickford's cafeterias, Horn & Hardart Automats, and the more upscale Longchamps restaurant chain were also popular with Soviet spies.

Although Bickford's and the Automats are no longer available for espionage, the usefulness of popular, accessible eateries for spy meetings continued into the 21st century. Anna Chapman, one of 10 Russian

Now the site of a post office, this Bronx theater became a preferred meeting place for Soviet intelligence officers and their spies during the Cold War.

illegals arrested by the FBI in 2010, used Manhattan Starbucks locations for meetings, while Washington-based *illegal* Mikhail Semenko, who was apprehended in the same FBI operation, favored a casual Ruby Tuesday restaurant.

■ 201. THE JAMES BOND OF QUEENS

MAP II ➤ **Fresh Pond subway stop:** Fresh Pond Road near 67th Avenue, Queens

The arrest of Soviet intelligence officer Gennadi Zakharov at the Fresh Pond subway station precipitated a diplomatic flap between the United States and the USSR that was resolved by an eventual spy swap.

Double agent Leakh Bhoge parked at this neighborhood supermarket before walking several blocks to a clandestine rendezvous with a Soviet spy. The meeting was, in fact, staged and part of an elaborate FBI counterintelligence operation.

Leakh Bhoge, a Guyanese immigrant, was pursuing the American dream, attending Queens College and studying computer technology while living with his family at 140 Sheridan Avenue in the East New York section of Brooklyn. Then, in April 1983, another student gave him a tip about a part-time research job.

His employer would be a Soviet professor from "the Moscow Institute." Introduced under the name Genrick, the professor explained that the research consisted largely of photocopying specific articles from magazines and journals in college libraries. It was a classic recruitment approach and not particularly difficult work for Bhoge, but when he became suspicious of his employer's true motives, he contacted the FBI.

The FBI identified the professor as Gennadi Fyodorovich Zakharov, a physicist and scientific affairs officer at the United Nations Center for Science and Technology for Development who lived in a second-floor apartment at 6019 Tyndall Avenue in the Bronx. The Moscow Institute, along with the alias Genrick, were covers for a KGB operation that began with collection of open-source intelligence as part of the development process to eventually recruit the young Bhoge as a spy.

Bhoge agreed to continue the relationship, becoming a double agent under FBI direction. Code-named PLUMBER by the FBI and BIRGE by the KGB, Bhoge played the role for three years, meeting with FBI handlers at the now defunct

Bhoge, wired with a tape recorder, met Zakharov in a Queens park to collect incriminating evidence against the spy.

Hilltop Diner, 164-02 Union Turnpike in Fresh Meadows, Queens, and area fast-food restaurants and pizzerias.

Bhoge graduated from college—the first in his family to do so—and landed a job at a defense industry subcontractor. The company, H. G. Machine and Tool in Long Island City, Queens, manufactured parts for the Bendix Corporation and General Electric. From the KGB perspective, the long development process appeared to be paying off, and Zakharov offered to help Bhoge with graduate school expenses as well as suggested other firms where he could apply for jobs.

The end came on August 23, 1986. The FBI provided Bhoge with secret documents, supposedly pilfered from his Long Island City employer, to pass to Zakharov. Bhoge parked his car at the Finast supermarket (today a Stop & Shop) at 65th Street and Myrtle Avenue, Queens, and met Zakharov in a small park a few blocks away on Cypress Hills and Cooper Streets. Wired with a Nagra tape recorder, two 1-M5-007 transmitters, and four microphones, Bhoge walked with Zakharov first to the Central Bar on Central Avenue, where the pair split up. They met again on the platform of the Fresh Pond subway stop at Fresh Pond Road near 67th Avenue to exchange money for documents.

As Boghe handed the plain brown envelope to his Soviet handler, two FBI agents, who had been surveilling Zakharov and Bhoge, apprehended the 39-year-old KGB officer. After briefly resisting, Zakharov was arrested and held at the Metropolitan Corrections Center at 160 Park Row. A search of his Bronx apartment turned up an assortment of spy gear, including secret writing paper, chemicals used to develop secret writing, coded pads, and greeting cards along with other documents later found to contain microdots. Zakharov's UN employment did not afford him diplomatic immunity.

The Soviets retaliated. A week after Zakharov's arrest, Nicholas Daniloff, a *U.S. News & World Report* correspondent in Moscow, was apprehended while meeting a source who was said to have news clippings. At least eight KGB security officers emerged from a white van to tackle and subdue the reporter and took him to Lefortovo Prison. Soviet authorities condemned Daniloff as a spy while the US government termed the act a "seizure of a hostage."

Despite the uproar, within two weeks the respective governments agreed to release the two men to their respective embassies, though the charges remained in place. Talks regarding a possible summit between the Soviet premier and the US president dragged on throughout the month until a swap for the two men was finally arranged. Daniloff was put aboard a plane on September 29 with a stopover a Frankfurt. The next day, less than an hour before Daniloff's Pan American World Airways flight 61 touched down at Dulles International Airport near Washington, Zakharov boarded an Aeroflot plane in New York after pleading no contest in a Brooklyn courtroom.

The same day that the swap took place, US and Soviet leaders announced plans for a summit on October 11 and 12 in Reykjavík, Iceland.

■ 202. FROM PLATO'S RETREAT TO THE CIA

MAP 6 ➤ **Karl and Hana Koecher residence:** 50 East 89th Street

Playing the role of defectors from Czechoslovakia's repressive regime in 1965, Karl and Hana Koecher posed as passionate anticommunists when meeting with their new American friends. In fact, both were active *illegals* and intelligence officers of *the Státní Bezpečnost* (StB)—the Czechoslovakian intelligence service.

While Karl attended Columbia University, the couple resided at 50 East 89th Street in a luxury building with neighbors Mel Brooks, Anne Bancroft, and Tommy Tune. The Koechers were talented performers in their own right. When Ivan Lendl attempted to purchase an apartment in the building, they protested. The Czechoslovakian tennis champion was from a communist country, they claimed, and unworthy of living in the respectable building. Whether the couple's objection to Lendl was a security measure or simply aimed at reinforcing their cover is not known.

In New York, the Koechers built reputations as "swingers" by frequenting Plato's Retreat, a notorious sex club located in the Kenmore Hotel, 145 East 23rd Street, and then relocated to the Ansonia Hotel at 230 West 74th Street, and the Hellfire club, 28 Ninth Avenue. In a 1988 newspaper article, Ronald Kessler described Hana as "blonde and sexy . . . she looks like a movie star."

The couple's multipartner lifestyle enabled them to make contacts throughout a cross-section of society. They rubbed shoulders and other body parts with diplomats, military officers, and socialites with intelligence value or who could provide access to others who did.

Karl became a US citizen in 1971 and two years later was hired by the CIA as translator. The couple moved to Northern Virginia and continued their swingers' lifestyle, making contacts

Claiming to have escaped communist Czechoslovakia in 1965, communist spies Karl and Hana Koecher lived an American immigrant's dream in a high-rise in the Carnegie Hill section of Manhattan.

among senior military, political, and government employees. In the course of his CIA work, Karl acquired and passed information to the Czechoslovakian service and, by extension, to Soviet counterintelligence, which was able to identify Aleksandr Ogorodnik (code name TRIGON), a CIA agent in Moscow. Ogorodnik was arrested in 1977 and, while under KGB interrogation, committed suicide by taking a CIA-provided poison pill concealed in his pen.

The Koechers remained untouched until 1984, when Karl was arrested hours before boarding a flight to Switzerland. Hana was taken into custody as a material witness but not charged. Karl pleaded guilty to espionage on behalf of Czechoslovakia and was jailed in the United States. He was later swapped for Soviet dissident Natan Sharansky in February 1986 and returned with his wife to Prague.

■ 203. THE SPY WHO PLAYED OUT OF TUNE

MAP 3 ➤ **Steinway & Sons, Steinway Hall:** 109 West 57th Street (former location)

Operating as an *illegal*—a spy without protection of diplomatic status—is painstaking and risky work. Anatoli Rudenko (code name RYBAKOV, or FISHERMAN) was trained as a piano tuner by the KGB and sent to East Germany under the alias Heinz Walter August Feder. He then moved as a refugee in the early 1960s to the West, where he found employment

in a Steinway & Sons piano showroom in Hamburg. Next he relocated to London to adapt to an English-speaking society before finally coming to the United States.

In 1966, Rudenko arrived in New York on a tourist visa and applied for another job with Steinway & Sons, then located at 109 West 57th Street. With the help of the unwitting piano manufacturer, he acquired a work visa in 1967 and then an $80-a-week job. The counterfeit refugee had finally established a solid, if somewhat abbreviated, work history. To any neighbor or local store owner, he was just another hardworking New Yorker.

However, Rudenko must have displayed exceptional skills as a piano tuner because he was soon

Stately Steinway Hall, 109 West 57th Street, played a role in multiple intelligence operations. Anatoli Rudenko, a KGB *illegal*, worked there under cover of a piano tuner.

A ROCKEFELLER CONNECTION

Anatoli Rudenko was not the only Soviet *illegal* who attempted to establish contact with the Rockefeller family. In the early 1960s, Oleg Kalugin, an exchange student in New York and later a major general in the KGB, became friends with John Davison "Jay" Rockefeller IV, who later became governor of West Virginia, then a senator from that state. According to Kalugin, a chance meeting at a television studio led to an unlikely friendship despite profound political differences. The two maintained contact for a few years, but Rockefeller broke off the friendship when he entered politics.

servicing the instrument of renowned composer and concert pianist Vladimir Horowitz at 14 East 94th Street. Another client was three-time presidential candidate Nelson Rockefeller, then governor of New York, who had Rudenko service his piano at his Westchester County estate.

Rudenko's superiors seemed pleased with his progress, and he was considered to head a new *rezidentura* using the cover of a New York think tank. This operation would target single women at the United Nations who sought companionship. However, when "irregularities" and "suspicious behavior" were detected, Rudenko was summoned to Moscow in 1970. There he confessed to a secret marriage to a beautician during his time in Hamburg. She had accompanied him to America and knew he was a spy but believed it was for East Germany. Rudenko was also having an affair with a female accountant in Pennsylvania.

Both the secret marriage and affair represented serious security risks deemed untenable by Moscow. The KGB sought to minimize damage by having their wayward spy write seemingly heartfelt letters to each of the women, breaking off their relationships and instructing them not to look for him. According to *The Mitrokhin Archive: The KGB in Europe and the West*, by Christopher Andrew and Vasili Mitrokhin, this expensive *illegal* operation, which lasted more than a decade, resulted in two broken hearts, a colorful story, and little or no useful intelligence.

■ 204. FAKE NEWS: NOTHING NEW FOR THE KGB

MAP 6 ➤ **Susan Rosenstiel residence:** 5 East 80th Street

A successful Cold War–era fake news operation of KGB *dezinformatsiya*, or disinformation, was conducted against FBI chief J. Edgar Hoover. The long-term active-measures campaign to discredit Hoover by the KGB's Line A propaganda division involved a campaign of rumors and letter writing that the long-serving FBI director was gay and a cross-dresser.

Susan Rosenstiel, who once lived in luxury at 5 East 80th Street, later created an urban legend by accusing FBI director J. Edgar Hoover of cross-dressing. Soviet intelligence propagated her stories.

This effort was unwittingly helped along by Susan Rosenstiel, once a resident of 5 East 80th Street. Embittered by her divorce from Lewis Rosenstiel, a former bootlegger and founder of distillery giant Schenley Industries, she sought to retaliate against Hoover, believing he had intervened in her divorce settlement. The couple traveled in the same social circles as Hoover and then-prominent attorney Roy Cohn.

Rosenstiel peddled and retold a story for years that while attending parties at the Plaza Hotel in the late 1950s, she witnessed Hoover cross-dressing. She claimed he wore a feather boa and red dress that gave him the appearance of "an old flapper" and kept a wardrobe of a black dress, a wig, and lace stockings.

Hoover, according to Rosenstiel, thought himself unrecognizable in woman's garb and asked to be called Mary.

In 1993, journalist Anthony Summers's book *Official and Confidential: The Secret Life of J. Edgar Hoover* asserted that the Mafia blackmailed Hoover over his alleged cross-dressing and homosexuality. By then, Rosenstiel was all but forgotten and living in a modest residency hotel. According to multiple sources, Summers had paid Rosenstiel, a convicted perjurer, for her story.

Although Hoover was long dead, the Summers portrayal achieved an unwarranted level of acceptance. Despite multiple sources debunking the tale, the story stubbornly endures as both an urban legend and an example of a successful KGB *dezinformatsiya* operation.

■ 205. MIDNIGHT RECRUITMENT

MAP 8 ➤ **Grant's Tomb:** West 122nd Street and Riverside Drive

Lt. Gen. Dmitri Fedorovich Polyakov, a GRU officer, volunteered his services to the US government on August 9, 1961, during a cocktail party at the residence of Gen. Edward O'Neill, commander of the First United States Army, at Fort Jay on Governors Island.

On November 16, 1961, a second cocktail party was arranged at the O'Neill residence specifically so Polyakov, then working at the United Nations, could be introduced to FBI special agent John Mabey. Mabey then met secretly with

Dmitri Fedorovich Polyakov

Lt. Gen. Dmitri Polyakov, a Soviet military intelligence officer, lived at the Parc Cameron on West 86th Street when he volunteered to spy for the American government.

Polyakov was recruited during a midnight meeting at the General Grant National Memorial (a.k.a. Grant's Tomb).

Polyakov on November 23 at Columbus Circle, and from that meeting another encounter was scheduled at midnight at Grant's Tomb, West 122nd Street and Riverside Drive. There Polyakov formally agreed to work for the United States and was given the code name TOPHAT.

Polyakov was then living at the Parc Cameron, 41 West 86th Street. To monitor his comings and goings, the FBI established an observation post in a front-facing classroom at Hunter College, 695 Park Avenue, across the street from the Soviet mission, then located in the Percy R. Pyne House at 680 Park Avenue.

At the time of his recruitment, Polyakov was running a network of Soviet *illegals* in New York and used colored thumbtacks affixed to a sign outside of Tavern on the Green in Central Park to communicate with his network. He also made and retrieved clandestine drops at numerous places around the city. FBI records cite observing Polyakov picking up a drop under the original Kosciuszko Bridge, which spanned Newtown Creek and connected Greenpoint in Brooklyn to Maspeth in Queens. The 78-year old bridge was demolished and replaced in October 2017.

Through its long execution, the case required close coordination between the FBI and the CIA. Polyakov was handled by the FBI within the United States and by the CIA when in foreign locations. The information he provided established Polyakov as one of America's top spies before he quietly retired in Russia in the early

Spies found the area around the famous Tavern on the Green attractive for clandestine communications. An outdoor message board and a sign near the bridle path became useful signal sites. Thumbtacks, pinned inconspicuously and quickly to signs or posts, conveyed information about meetings and dead drops.

1980s. He had been betrayed to the GRU by FBI special agent Robert Hanssen in 1979, but without further corroboration the GRU took no action. However, five years later CIA turncoat Aldrich Ames reported the same information to the KGB, thereby confirming Hanssen's betrayal. The retired GRU general was arrested in 1986 and executed in 1988.

■ 206. THE AMBASSADOR WAS A SPY

MAP 6 ➤ **Arkady Shevchenko residence:** 160 East 65th Street, apt. 26D

Arkady Shevchenko was the highest-ranking Soviet official ever to defect to the United States. After joining the Ministry of Foreign Affairs in 1956, he rose to become an adviser to its director, Andrei Gromyko, and was appointed in 1973 to an undersecretary-general position at the United Nations. While his UN duties called for Shevchenko to fairly represent the interests of all member nations, his priority was clandestinely providing information and support to the USSR.

Ultimately Shevchenko's long exposure to Western countries convinced him the USSR was on the wrong path and that he was helpless to change its course by remaining loyal to the system. He secretly contacted the CIA in 1975, requesting political asylum. The CIA, for its part, saw greater value in having him remain in place to report on Soviet plans and intentions. Assigned the code name DYNAMITE, Shevchenko was regularly debriefed at a safe house on East 64th Street.

The United States rarely had a source with such in-depth knowledge of the inner workings of the Ministry of Foreign Affairs and its relationship with the KGB and the Soviet military. Despite the attention given US handlers to the security of the operation, Schevchenko sensed increased KGB surveillance of his movements and by 1978 came to believe the end was drawing near. His decision point came when he received an unexpected summons to return to Moscow for "consultations." Fearing the order was a ruse to have him arrested, Shevchenko activated the emergency escape plan given to

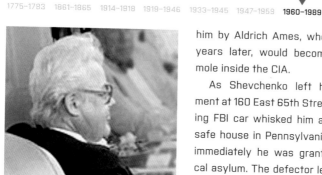

Arkady Shevchenko

UN undersecretary-general Arkady Shevchenko, the highest-ranking Soviet official to ever defect to the West to that time, lived in a high-rise apartment on East 65th Street while spying for the United States in the 1970s.

him by Aldrich Ames, who, several years later, would become a KGB mole inside the CIA.

As Shevchenko left his apartment at 160 East 65th Street, a waiting FBI car whisked him away to a safe house in Pennsylvania. Almost immediately he was granted political asylum. The defector left a note for his wife, Leongina, asking her to join him. Instead she contacted the KGB and was taken back to Moscow where she died of mysterious causes two months later.

Among the many charges Shevchenko hurled at the USSR in his 1985 memoir *Breaking with Moscow*, one has a contemporary ring. The disenchanted former ambassador described the Soviet Union as operating a gangster economy controlled by the KGB. Shevchenko lived in Bethesda, Maryland, until his death in February of 1998 at age 67.

■ 207. OPERATION LEMON AID

MAP 6 ▶ Permanent mission of the Russian Federation to the United Nations: 136 East 67th Street

In 1977, the FBI initiated an investigation of Soviet espionage activities conducted from the USSR's mission to the UN at 136 East 67th Street, today the permanent mission of the Russian Federation. The plan, code-named OPERATION LEMON AID, involved a dangle operation in which a controlled individual would pose as potential spy. Directed by the FBI, the double agent would report on Soviet tradecraft from initial assessment through development and recruitment.

The dangle, Arthur Lindberg, a lieutenant commander in the US Navy, was nearing retirement ostensibly with money problems, but he had access to classified antisubmarine warfare intelligence for which the Soviets would pay well. Using the code name ED, Lindberg was a double agent for the Naval Criminal Investigative Service and the FBI.

Valdik Enger

Rudolf Chernyayev

In August 1977, Lindberg made a trip on the Soviet cruise ship *Kazakhstan* from New York to Bermuda. When the ship docked, he passed a note offering to sell classified information for $20,000 to a ship's officer who, he believed, would deliver the offer to the KGB. Lindberg was later contacted by telephone by a Soviet intelligence officer using the cover name Jim.

This initial contact was followed by a steady stream of phone calls and letters to Lindberg. From them the FBI began to learn details of 1970s-era Soviet tradecraft. For example, covert messages and money were regularly passed to Lindberg at dead-drop sites in New Jersey Concealments were ordinary

Near the metal stairs on the southbound platform of the Metropark train station along the Garden State Parkway in Middlesex County, New Jersey, were wooden stairs (since collapsed) that served as a dead-drop site for the Soviets.

items such as cigarette packs, soda cans, orange juice cartons, a rubber hose from a household appliance, and magnetic key holders placed in phone booths. Instructions to Lindberg for finding the dead-drop sites were precise, as displayed in a message to ED on October 22, 1978.

After the FBI acquired sufficient information to make arrests, a trap was set on May 20, 1978. The FBI gave Lindberg five 35mm film canisters containing classified materials

Hello, Ed

Please, read this letter very attentively.
To-day, as I have already noticed we have a lot
of work to do: I)Receive your material. 2)Make
our first payment to you. As you understand
everything is prearranged and done with the
utmost security.The only thing for you to do is
to act as quickly & accurately as possible. So,
please, Strictly follow the instruction below and
it will be as easy as A, B, C.

  A. After readig this letter, scrutinizing map,
pictures & sketches (Enclosed.Your routes are
shown in green & places of operations in red.)
proceed Garden State pkwy (northbound).
Take exit I3I A and keeping always right enter
the parking lot in front of the "METROPARK STA-
TION".

  B. Park your car as shown at picture#I and go
to the EASTBOUND PLATFORM of the station.At the
east end of the platform there is a wooden stair,
Descending this stair drop your pack(with material) on the ground near the wooden pole of the
stair.(See picture #2.) After that go to your CAR
and immediately leave this area.Your material
will be picked up by us just in seconds.

  C. Again take Garden State pkwy(northbound).
Within 2 miles from exit I3IA enter the service
station (gas, telephone). By all means park your
car right behind TEXACO station as shown in oval
"C" at the map. There are 2 public phones outsid
the Texaco station. Wait here for my call.I call
you at 2.45p.m. and then (in case you are late)
at 3p.m., 3.I5p.m., 3.30p.m.. Here you'll get
further instructions to our next procedure.

                    Good luck,
                         Jim.

The operational instructions to double agent Arthur Lindberg from his Soviet handlers were specific but contained a unique mix of familiar Americanisms and odd syntax.

so the Soviets would be caught holding official secrets. Inside the trunk of Lindberg's car were two FBI special agents, while other agents hid near the drop site on Highview Drive, Woodbridge Township, New Jersey. Lindberg approached the site, stopped the car, picked up an empty Ann Page Bartlett Pears can, dropped the canisters into it, and drove off. Soon afterward, two KGB officers—Valdik Enger and Rudolf Chernyayev—were arrested as they cleared the dead drop. A third Soviet at the scene, Vladimir Zinyakin, had diplomatic immunity and was expelled from the United States.

Neither Chernyayev nor Enger had diplomatic immunity. They stood trial for espionage, were convicted in 1978, and sentenced to 50 years in prison. The following year the two were swapped for five Soviet dissidents in an exchange at New York's John F. Kennedy International Airport.

■ 208. UPPER EAST SIDE TRAITOR

MAP 5 ➤ **Aldrich Ames residence:** The Revere, 400 East 54th Street

Aldrich Ames

Before becoming a spy for the KGB, Aldrich Ames ran intelligence operations against Soviet diplomats in New York. He lived in this modest Upper East Side apartment building.

Before his treason led to the death or imprisonment of more than two dozen Soviets spying for the United States, CIA officer Aldrich Ames worked from an office in the Pan Am Building (now the Met Life Building) at 200 Park Avenue. At the time, Ames and his first wife, Nancy, lived in a one-bedroom apartment at the Revere, 400 East 54th Street. While in New York, Ames was involved with major CIA operations, including handling Sergey Fedorenko (code name PYRRHIC), a nuclear arms expert assigned to the USSR's UN delegation, and the 1978 defection of Arkady Shevchenko, then a UN undersecretary-general.

Despite these early operational successes, warning signs about Ames's suitability for the CIA appeared. He favored the Oyster Bar in Grand Central Station for what became excessive after-work drinking and once had his driver's license suspended for driving while intoxicated. On another occasion, he left his briefcase on the subway containing sensitive clandestine photos taken by Fedorenko. Ames told *The New York Times* in a 1994 interview that the first seeds of his treason were planted during his New York assignment.

In April 1985, several years after leaving New York, Ames volunteered to the KGB and was given the code name KOLOKO. During the following nine years as a mole inside the CIA, Ames exposed more than two dozen agents operating in the USSR, at least ten of whom were executed. By the date of his arrest in February 1994, he had received cash payments and deposits to an account in Moscow valued at a reported $4.6 million. His extra income financed a home in an upscale neighborhood in Arlington, Virginia, and a lavish lifestyle of expensive cars, jewelry, and clothing for himself, his wife, Rosario, and her mother. Convicted of espionage on April 28, 1994, Ames was sentenced to life without parole. Rosario Ames, who assisted and encouraged his treason, was sentenced to five years in prison.

■ 209. LIFE IN NEW YORK MADE HIM DO IT

MAP 3 ▶ **New York Public Library:** Wertheim Study, room 228, West 42nd Street and Fifth Avenue

Earl Edwin Pitts

Special Agent Earl Edwin Pitts joined the FBI in 1983 and was assigned to the FBI's New York field office in 1987. From the beginning, he struggled to live on an annual salary of $38,000 in one of America's most expensive cities. In an attempt to compensate, he made a 120-mile round-trip commute into Manhattan each day from his upstate residence in Newburgh, at 186 Temple Hill Road, apartment 22.

Seeking a solution to his money woes, Pitts wrote a letter to the Soviet mission to the UN offering to sell his services. A meeting was arranged in July 1987 in the law section of the New York Public Library Main Branch, West 42nd Street and Fifth Avenue. At the agreed-upon day and time, he first met with a Soviet officer, who then turned him over to Aleksandr Karpov, chief of Line KR, the counterintelligence component of the KGB's New York *rezidentura*.

The Wertheim Study is a private room in the New York Public Library Main Branch reserved for writers and researchers. Soon-to-be disgraced FBI special agent Earl Pitts reportedly met his Soviet contact in this area of the library.

Pitts had access to a wide range of sensitive and highly classified FBI operations. These included recruitment operations against Russian intelligence officers, double-agent operations, targeting operations, true identities of FBI human assets, operations against Russian *illegals*,

In the Main Branch of the New York Public Library, the KGB recruited an FBI special agent to spy for the USSR.

names of defectors, surveillance schedules of known meeting sites, internal policies, and procedures for surveillance of Russian intelligence officers. As an FBI counterintelligence agent himself, he could also confirm the FBI's identification, targeting, and reporting on known and suspected KGB intelligence officers in the New York City area.

From 1987 to 1992, Pitts passed secrets to his KGB handlers, receiving more than $224,000 in direct payments and a promise of $100,000 set aside for him as a reserve in Moscow. Pitts was identified as a spy in 1995 after his original KGB handler, Karpov, defected to the United States and agreed to help trap the FBI special agent. During the 16-month period Pitts was under investigation, his wife, also an FBI employee, independently reported her suspicions to her superiors that her husband was a spy.

After his arrest in late 1996, Pitts attempted to rationalize his actions in an interview with a reporter: "Life in New York City made me do it. It was expensive, dirty, and a lot of crime, a lot of people, very congested." Pitts was tried, convicted on June 27, 1997, and sentenced to 27 years in prison.

■ 210. GRAND CENTRAL TRADECRAFT

MAP 5 ➤ **Brush-pass tradecraft site:** Grand Central Terminal, Vanderbilt Avenue and East 42nd Street

Clandestine meetings with agents in denied areas—countries behind the Iron Curtain—presented particularly difficult operational problems

During the height of the Cold War, a CIA officer perfected a new style of clandestine brush passes in the crowded corridors of New York's Grand Central Terminal.

for CIA case officers during the Cold War. From Moscow to Prague to East Berlin, Soviet-trained counterintelligence officers were vigilant, suspicious, and seemingly omnipresent.

A pioneer in developing new tradecraft to defeat such pervasive security was a denied-area chief of station, Haviland Smith. After a Czechoslovakian agent feared leaving his package in a dead drop for any length of time, Smith reengineered the classic brief-encounter tradecraft technique called the "brush pass." As developed by Smith, the brush pass becomes a rapidly executed exchange of a package or document between two persons in a public place, done so quickly and naturally it is virtually undetectable.

Smith introduced elements of a magician's sleight-of-hand and misdirection into the maneuver, which he combined with careful site selection and precise choreography to conduct the exchange. Using the stairways and congestion of Grand Central Terminal at 15 Vanderbilt Avenue, he perfected the technique during the 1960s and introduced it to a Czechoslovakian agent along the corridor near a subway stairway in the Biltmore Hotel, now the Bank of America Plaza. Smith later demonstrated the new technique at a hotel in Washington where experienced CIA case officers were unable to detect the clandestine handoff. The revised technique was approved for field use.

■ 211. GUNRUNNER ON THE RUN

MAP 3 ➤ **Frank Terpil arrest site:** New York Hilton, 1335 Sixth Avenue

Former CIA officer Frank Terpil's career as gunrunner ended at the New York Hilton when he was arrested by NYPD detectives posing as Latin American revolutionaries. Terpil later jumped bail and lived in exile in Cuba.

Frank E. Terpil joined the CIA in 1965 and served as an officer in the Technical Services Division, the agency's gadget makers and procurers of special weapons and devices. Assigned to India in 1970, he enjoyed the good life, purchasing a Cadillac, renting a grand home in the Anand Niketan section of New Delhi, and acquiring a taste for gin and lime. His priority became finding a way to finance his lifestyle.

A solution Terpil hit upon involved currency trading. With the Indian rupee then overvalued in Afghanistan banks, Terpil could send rupees from India to Kabul, change the money into dollars, and bring the dollars back to New Delhi where they could be converted back to rupees at a nice profit. Terpil was fired when CIA superiors discovered his unauthorized entrepreneurial venture.

Unemployed and with an "unfavorable discharge," on his resume, Terpil moved to the Middle East, then met Libyan dictator Muammar Gaddafi on a trip to London. Gaddafi needed specialized weapons and explosives. In response, Terpil sensed an opportunity and used his contacts to procure weapons and more than 20 tons of plastic explosives for Gaddafi. He also recruited American mercenaries to help in supposedly "antiterrorist" operations, pocketing substantial profits from his Libyan deals.

In the late 1970s, Terpil performed similar functions for Ugandan dictator Idi Amin and, in turn, received the nickname *Waraki* (White Lightning). When

Amin's rule ended in March 1979, Terpil was at Entebbe Airport to load trunks of gold, and Amin, on the last flight out.

Terpil's gunrunning ended on December 22, 1979, in a suite at the New York Hilton Hotel. Two NYPD undercover detectives posing as Latin American revolutionaries paid him $56,000 as a deposit on a $2-million-dollar sale of 10,000 machine guns.

Terpil was arrested, granted bail, and immediately fled the United States. Included in the government's indictment were charges that he had delivered more than $135,000 worth of pistols, rifles, shotguns, sound suppressors, high-velocity ammunition, and voice-coding devices to the Ugandan mission to the United Nations at 336 East 45th Street.

Terpil was sentenced in absentia to 53 years in prison and lived the remainder of his life as an international fugitive. He spent several years in the Middle East before moving to Cuba. Castro's intelligence service gave Terpil the code name CURIEL (meaning GUINEA PIG) and used him in largely unsuccessful operations to entice US intelligence officers to defect. He died in a bungalow outside of Havana in March 2016.

■ 212. PRIEST, SPY, AND MARRIED WITH CHILDREN

MAP I ▶ **Father Mark Cheung's cover:** Church of the Transfiguration, 29 Mott Street

The Church of the Transfiguration, built in the early 1800s, unwittingly harbored Chinese spy Mark Cheung, who posed as a priest. After the arrest of retired CIA officer and Chinese spy Larry Wu Tai-Chin, Cheung immediately abandoned his cover and fled to China.

Larry Wu-Tai Chin's arrest in 1985 was a major embarrassment for the CIA. The retired analyst and translator had spied for communist China's Ministry for State Security (MSS) throughout his three-decade career at the agency. When confronted by the FBI, Chin, given the code name EAGLE CLAW, eventually admitted his contact with the Chinese communists but claimed he was only conducting personal shadow diplomacy to ease tensions between the United States and China.

At his trial, prosecutors argued that Chin was motivated by profit, not peace. Evidence showed he received hundreds of thousands of dollars for spying and used the money to buy rental properties and gamble in Las Vegas. The jury agreed with the prosecutors and found Chin guilty. In February 1986, the 63-year-old was sentenced to two life sentences and fines of more than $3 million. Two weeks later, Chin suffocated himself in a Virginia jail cell by securing a plastic trash bag tightly over his head with shoelaces.

Virtually lost in the Chin drama was the abrupt departure of a beloved New York Roman Catholic priest, Father Mark Cheung, from his position at Chinatown's Church of the Transfiguration, 25 Mott Street. Cheung became an assistant pastor in 1972 to the landmark church that sits on Five Points, once among the most crime-infested areas of New York. By 1985, he had become the parish administrator but vanished the day after Chin's arrest.

Secretly Cheung was an MSS intelligence officer operating under clerical cover. He was responsible for providing emergency covert communication and an escape route for Chin in the event of discovery. One phase of the plan was to be initiated by a meeting in a church confessional. Cheung's religious cover had been laboriously constructed over years with previous postings at churches throughout the South Pacific. When the FBI eventually tracked down Cheung in Hong Kong, the priest-spy refused to answer questions, then promptly disappeared into mainland China. Later was it discovered "Father Mark," as he was known in the parish, was actually married with children.

■ 213. LIVING THE AMERICAN DREAM

MAP 7 ➤ An *illegal's* **signal site:** Underpass at the 79th Street Boat Basin and Henry Hudson Parkway

Arriving in New York on a long-term assignment as a KGB *illegal*, Jack Barsky rented his first apartment at 201 West 77th Street.

Jack Barsky died at age 10 in September 1955 and is buried in Mount Lebanon Cemetery outside of Washington, DC.

Eighteen years later, Albert Dittrich, a 33-year-old East German chemist, was spotted and recruited by the KGB. Assigned the code name DIETER, he received months of intensive tradecraft training in East Berlin and Moscow to become a KGB *illegal* in America. The KGB planned to insert the young spy into America under an alias, then assume a different name, secure a US passport, and become one of its elite deep-cover spies.

For the assignment, Dittrich needed an American identity to enable him to obtain a Social Security

Barsky (indicated by the arrow) found employment as a programmer for an insurance company, a job that offered him access to American computer and software technology of interest to Soviet intelligence.

The wall beneath the overpass adjacent to the boat basin near West 79th Street served as a Barsky signal site. A chalk mark could convey information about dead drops and future meetings.

number and establish legal legitimacy. The identity of an American male who died as a child but would have been close to Dittrich's age was required to support a contrived profile for the Soviet spy. To create what the KGB called a "dead twin myth," Soviet intelligence officers made "cemetery walks" to spot graves of children who died at early ages. The KGB exploited the fact that death records in America and Canada were seldom reconciled with birth records and that information on tombstones could be used by Soviet spies.

Dittrich completed operational training in 1978, when the man who would become Jack Barsky departed for the United States under the alias of William Dyson, traveling as a Canadian national. He left a girlfriend and young son in East Germany, who were told he was being assigned to a top-secret space project inside the USSR. To protect his cover story, Dittrich prepared postdated letters the KGB periodically mailed to his family. Otherwise, he had no contact with his relatives, except brief reunions every two years when he returned to East Germany for debriefings.

Dittrich/Dyson first went to Belgrade and then to Rome, Mexico City, and Chicago. Upon arrival in the United States, the *illegal* had only $6,000 in cash and a photocopy of the birth certificate of the dead boy. He did everything else necessary to establish his identity as Jack Barsky on his own and took a bus to New York City. There his objective was to get close to President Jimmy Carter's national security adviser, Zbigniew Brzezinski.

Barsky later commented on how unprepared he was to live in America. Lifestyle training provided by the KGB was inadequate, incomplete, and often out of date. Though tasked with getting close to Brzezinski, he received no suggestions or training as to how that could be accomplished.

While his English was excellent, Barsky's cultural mannerisms for dealing with people were viewed as pushy, abrasive, and off-putting, even by New

York standards. He was admonished by some of his anti-Semitic KGB instructors to stay away from Jews despite the fact he was sent to a city with the largest Jewish population in the United States.

By contrast, Barsky's tradecraft training was well planned and thorough. To his instructors, he was known only as DIETER or BRUNO. He received one-on-one training from an experienced cadre of KGB Operative Technical instructors in sessions at safe houses in Berlin or his Moscow apartment. Like his identity, the mission of the spy-in-training was carefully guarded.

Among his KGB trainers, Barsky most respected the wisdom of Morris and Lona Cohen [Helen and Peter Kroger]. Both were former New Yorkers and part of Rudolf Abel's VOLUNTEER network of spies in the 1950s. The KGB pointed to the Cohens as two of its most successful agents. Barsky lived and trained with the Cohens for two weeks and later received weekly briefings from them on the challenges of living a double life in the West. The Cohens did not drink or become party animals. They were true believers in communism, were not spying for money, and successfully mastered their tradecraft. One tenant of Barsky's tradecraft was to avoid possessing any incriminating spy devices or equipment. While James Bond movies portray spy gadgets as essential for clandestine work, the opposite remains true. Should, for any reason, Barsky's person, home, or automobile be searched, he wanted nothing to be found that would betray his secret life. His only items of compromising spy gear were "one-time pads" filled with groups of seemingly random numbers used for deciphering secret messages and nondescript secret writing contact paper he kept at the back of a three-ring binder.

During 1979, his first year in New York City, Barsky lived in a low-cost residential hotel at 201 West 77th Street and devoted much of his time to building his cover legend. For employment, he became a bicycle messenger, crisscrossing the city to collect and deliver documents. Using his library card, Barsky obtained a membership card at the Museum of Natural History. With that, along with his forged birth certificate, he was able to get a driver's license. With a driver's license and birth certificate, he obtained a Social Security card. Holding him back in his work as an *illegal*, however, was his lack of a US passport, which he would need to travel internationally. That would be his ultimate identity prize.

Initially, Barsky performed basic intelligence collection. In every communication to the KGB, he profiled at least one new contact who might be recruited and provided analysis of some aspect of American life. While a student at Baruch College, 55 Lexington Avenue, from 1981 to 1984, he sent the KGB more than twenty profiles of left-leaning students for possible recruitment. Though he sought to avoid drawing attention, he graduated as the class valedictorian. Later, while employed as a programmer for the Metropolitan Life Insurance Company, he reported information on American computer technology to aid the Soviet Union's struggle to keep pace with Western computer advances.

Barsky received weekly instructions from the KGB through a series of random numbers broadcast from clandestine transmitters in Cuba, known as "numbers stations." The ciphered communications were picked up by a commercial Sony ICF-5900-W shortwave radio that he kept in his apartment. Although the transmissions were routinely intercepted by the NSA, only Barsky knew the designated time and frequency for his messages, and only his one-time pad could decipher the contents. When each page is used only once, then destroyed immediately, the encryption is unbreakable. He used the ICF for eight years before replacing it with a smaller Sony digital radio.

Barsky communicated to the KGB using traditional, proven tradecraft techniques such as secret writing, signal sites, and dead drops. Most of his communications to Moscow were monthly reports written in secret writing and sent to an accommodation address in West Berlin or Vienna. Later both European addresses were dropped and an address in Venezuela added. On two occasions when there was a large amount of information to convey, he photographed his written reports with a Canon AE-1 camera and passed the undeveloped 35mm film to his handler at a designated dead-drop site.

In his 10 years as an *illegal* in the United States, Barsky executed six dead-drop operations, conducted clandestine meetings in Vienna, Rome, Helsinki, and Paris, and used signal sites in New York to convey information to his handler.

One of Barsky's unusual assignments was to verify the location of Nikolai Khokhlov, a trained KGB assassin and defector to the West. In 1954, Khokhlov had gotten cold feet at the last minute before slipping radioactive thallium into the drink of Russian expatriate Georgi Sergeyevich Okolovich in Frankfurt. Khokhlov confessed his mission to the intended victim, then defected and was relocated in the United States. Barsky traveled to California, located Khokhlov, who was working as a professor at California State University, San Bernardino, and reported the information to his KGB handler. No harm befell Khokhlov, who died peacefully in 2007 in California.

In 1987, Barsky received an unexpected message from Moscow that he was being awarded the prestigious Order of the Red Banner and a $10,000 bonus. Rather than raising his spirits, the news had the opposite effect. He was already living in dread, expecting at the completion of his second five-year tour in New York City that he would be recalled to East Germany. Several years earlier, and unreported to the KGB, Barsky had married, fathered a child, and was living happily with his new family at 94-10 75th Street, Ozone Park, Queens. He could not contemplate leaving them behind to return to East Germany.

Faced with this reality, Barsky made the dangerous decision to quit spying, sever all contacts with the KGB, and remain in the United States. As a ploy, he sent a ciphered message to his handlers advising them that he had contracted HIV/AIDS, for which medical treatment was only available in the

US. He added that if left alone, he would remain quiet and not defect.

The KGB responded by threatening him. Failure to return, they said, meant death. Eventually, however, his offer was either accepted or the KGB was unable to extract him. Barsky, believing that this part of his life was over, attempted to erase all evidence of his links with the past. He destroyed his one-time pads and secret writing materials, then dropped his shortwave radio into the East River from the 59th Street Bridge, officially the Ed Koch Queensboro Bridge.

Barsky should have realized that the greater threat to his security arose not from discovery of his spy gear but through betrayal from the inside. Indeed, in 1992, following the collapse of the USSR, KGB archivist Vasili Mitrokhin defected to the United Kingdom.

Working from Mitrokhin's scrupulously detailed notes, FBI investigators identified a spy named DIETER living as Jack Barsky in the United States and placed him under surveillance in 1994.

By then, Barsky had moved to 437 Allegheny Road in Mount Bethel, Pennsylvania. FBI agents quietly occupied the house next door as an observation post. After three years, in May 1997, the FBI concluded Barsky was no longer actively spying and brought him in for questioning. The one-time spy chose to cooperate. In exchange for the accurate and detailed information he provided about KGB tradecraft, the Justice Department waived prosecution and assisted in legalizing his Jack Barsky identity. In 2014, the former *illegal* became a US citizen and finally received a US passport.

One of Barsky's dead-drop sites was a tree hollow (code name WOODY) in Inwood Hill Park.

Barsky's secret remained hidden until 2015 when it was publicly revealed in an exclusive story on *60 Minutes*. In 2017, Barsky released his memoir, *Deep Undercover: My Secret Life and Tangled Allegiances as a KGB Spy in America*.

Sony shortwave radios, such as Barsky's vintage ICF-5900, were often used by Soviet spies during the Cold War.

OPERATIONAL SITES AND INSTRUCTIONS GIVEN TO JACK BARSKY

The underpass at the West 79th Street Boat Basin and Henry Hudson Parkway: At the western entrance, the sidewalk makes a 90-degree turn and creates a dead zone that allowed the agent to leave a signal to his handler without being exposed. A horizontal chalk line by Barsky had one of two meanings: either "Arrived in the city" or "Received your radiogram."

Kissena Park, Flushing, Queens: This site of Barsky's first successful dead-drop operation in the United States involved an exposed lamppost in the park where a visible vertical chalk mark would signal the drop site was filled. The drop itself, a container disguised as a dented oil can, was 50 yards away at the edge of the park adjacent to a drainage grate. Inside the can, Barsky found $10,000 so carefully rolled and sealed in multiple layers of rubber and duct tape that it required more than an hour and a half to unwrap. The site on the western side of the park, once a grass field, is now tennis courts and baseball and soccer fields.

Elevated subway at 80th Street and Hudson Street, Queens: As an emergency signal, a red dot would be placed on the metal support beam at the northeastern corner of Liberty Avenue and 77th Street, next to the stairs leading up to the subway platform. If Barsky saw a red dot, it was the signal for "severe danger," and he was to activate his emergency procedure and leave the city.

Cloves Lake Park, Staten Island: Barsky's last scheduled dead drop in 1988 was to be on Staten Island. The package for him would be an oil can containing a passport and money for travel to Toronto and on to Moscow. The drop site was inside the heavily wooded park and adjacent to the roots of a large fallen tree. It was located to the right of a narrow, winding walkway, approximately 300 feet from the right edge of the park. Despite his best efforts to locate the oil can, Barsky never recovered it. Since his experience showed the KGB never failed to leave a package at a scheduled drop, it is possible the can is still somewhere in the woods.

Bronx River Parkway, Bronx: Barsky's stash of emergency documents was hidden near the Gun Hill Road subway station in the Bronx. He was required to walk north from the station on a small dirt path that ran through the middle of the 100-yard wide green belt between the Bronx River Parkway on the west and Bronx Boulevard on the east. On the western side of the path was a park bench where the documents were hidden beneath one of its legs on the left side.

Cunningham Park, Queens: A rock formation with the 1980s band name Styx written on one of the boulders was a drop site.

Inwood Hill Park: Barsky entered the southern tip of the park at Beak Street and followed the path uphill as it curved to the right. About 100 feet after the bend in the path, on the left side, stood a tree with a large hole at the bottom where the container was placed.

Van Cortlandt Park, Bronx: A hollow tree (not further described).

■ 214. SPYCRAFT LESSONS FROM A SOVIET *ILLEGAL*

MAP 7 ➤ **Surveillance detection route:** American Museum of Natural History, Central Park West at West 79th Street

Soviet *illegal* Jack Barsky was taught several clandestine techniques by the KGB to detect hostile surveillance. The long passageways, cavernous rooms, and elevators of the American Museum of Natural History, Central Park West and West 79th Street, were ideal for exposing surveillance and conducting brush passes. The numerous exits and classic escalators on multiple floors of major department stores such as Macy's, 151 West 34th Street, were useful for detecting anyone that may be following.

Barsky devised an emergency plan for escaping FBI surveillance if it ever became necessary. He planned to load his bicycle into the trunk of his car, drive to a park at the outer edge of the city, then bike to a subway station on the other side of the park. There he would lock and leave the bike on the street, continue by subway to an Upper Manhattan train station, where he would board another train to leave the New York City area. By executing the route, Barsky reasoned he would be able to detect any surveillant who attempted to follow him.

Barsky used "trapping" techniques to detect any indications that the FBI was searching his mail or residence. He mailed a letter to himself from a fictional address and left intact a small strip of the glue on the envelope's flap. He theorized that if the FBI steamed open the envelope to read its contents, they would completely reseal the flap before remailing it to him. Once the letter was finally received, Barsky could carefully open the envelope with a razor blade and observe if the flap was resealed or if the glue strip was intact.

To detect if his room had been searched, Barsky selected a lower drawer in a piece of office, bedroom, or living room furniture and left it open precisely four millimeters. The gap was measurable only from below and invisible during a routine inspection. Even a well-trained search team would be unlikely to spot the small difference, and after opening the drawer the searchers would likely close it completely. The small difference in the position of the drawer would also be undetectable in the before-and-after Polaroid photos FBI search teams routinely took of each room to be certain no visual indication of their presence was left.

Another technique to detect a search began by gluing one end of a small hair to the bottom of a drawer. Barsky affixed the other end of the hair to the frame of the furniture. Should the drawer be opened, one of the two ends would come loose, but this would likely be unnoticed by the search team.

■ 215. ALWAYS A NEW YORKER

MAP 12 ➤ **William Casey residence:** Mayknoll, 12 Glenwood Road, Roslyn Harbor, Long Island

The quintessential New Yorker, William Joseph Casey, who served as DCI from 1981 to 1987, was born in 1913 in the working-class neighborhood of Elmhurst, Queens. He attended New York Public Schools 13 and 89 there and, after the family moved to Bellmore, graduated from Baldwin High School, Baldwin, Long Island. The future DCI received his undergraduate degree at Fordham University and a law degree from St. John's University School of Law.

Casey first tasted espionage after joining the OSS during World War II as a protégé of William Donovan. Eventually Casey headed the London-based OSS Secret Intelligence Branch, which supported networks of agents in Europe. The branch sought volunteers from among Axis prisoners, provided clothing, documentation, and equipment, and then infiltrated them back into major German cities, such as Bremen, Munich, Stuttgart, and Berlin.

Following the war, Casey became a successful corporate lawyer while playing an active role in Republican Party politics. He cofounded the conservative think tank the Manhattan Institute and held appointed offices in the Richard Nixon and Gerald Ford administrations, including chairman of the Securities and Exchange Commission, undersecretary of state for Economic Affairs, and chairman of the Import-Export Bank. From 1976 through 1977, he was a member of the President's Foreign Intelligence Advisory Board. Casey served as campaign manager for presidential candidate Ronald Reagan in 1980 and in January 1981 was nominated to become Director of Central Intelligence. Although Casey would be CIA Director, the position was said to be a disappointment, as he wanted to become secretary of state.

With the support of President Reagan, Casey led an expansion of the CIA's capabilities and covert-action operations. Some of the latter, such as support of anti-Sandinista forces in Nicaragua and an arms-for-hostages operation, known as the Iran-Contra affair, were particularly controversial and generated extended battles with congressional intelligence-oversight committees.

Despite his years in Washington, Casey was known to quip, "You know the best thing about Washington? It's only an hour to New York." A brain tumor incapacitated Casey in December 1986 while he was serving as DCI, and he never returned to work. He died the following May and is buried in Cemetery of the Holy Rood, 111 Old Country Road, Westbury, Long Island.

■ 216. DIRECTOR OF CENTRAL INTELLIGENCE AT THE STRAND

MAP 4 ▶ **Strand Bookstore:** 828 Broadway

An author and voracious reader, DCI William Casey was a frequent visitor to the Strand Bookstore at 828 Broadway. The landmark independent bookstore has been a decades-long favorite among artists, writers, musicians and politicians, including former president Bill Clinton.

Casey made regular trips to the Strand, usually filling one or two of the store's trademark red-and-white shopping bags with books on each visit. According to Fred Bass, whose father founded the store in 1927, Casey was prone to losing his security detail while wandering through the aisles and once took a telephone call from President Reagan in the store's office. Calls from the Strand to inform Casey that special book orders had arrived for him were promptly connected to the DCI's seventh-floor office at CIA headquarters.

The landmark Strand Bookstore was a favorite haunt of CIA's DCI William Casey. A voracious reader, Casey departed with a shopping bag or two of books after each visit.

8

NEW THREATS AND OLD ADVERSARIES

(1990–2019)

The collapse of the Soviet Union did not diminish espionage activity in New York. Spies of all nationalities and political ideologies, as well as terrorists, continued to call the city home. The bombing of the North Tower of the World Trade Center in 1993, the attacks on the Twin Towers of the World Trade Center in 2001, and the foiled Times Square bombing of 2010 reflected the frightening nature of changing international conflict. New York, a target of terrorist attacks dating back to the Civil War, was now faced with the dangerous new threat of modern terrorism.

The arrest in 2010 of 10 Russian *illegals*—many of whom either lived in the city or were frequent visitors—created headlines and surprised many who thought the spy wars of the Cold War were over. Intelligence professionals, however, understood Russian intelligence operatives remained active and armed with the latest technology. The new-generation spies were young, well trained, and every bit as aggressive as their apparatchik predecessors.

Targets in New York broadened as intelligence services such as those of China, Cuba, France, Israel, Iran, and Russia retooled for post–Cold War collection of economic, technical, and political information. Cyber penetration of New York–based companies, media organizations, and US security services, enabled by new digital tools, made these targets vulnerable to espionage operations from distant locations. Using social media platforms, foreign services masquerading as American entities launched information campaigns that promoted divisive political agendas and encouraged social unrest. In the 21st century, technology created a new class of "agents of influence," potentially more effective than Soviet disinformation operations of the Cold War.

■ 217. DINNER SERVED BY A FUTURE SPYMASTER

MAP 11 ➤ **Scobee Diner:** 25229 Northern Boulevard, Little Neck, Queens (closed in 2010)

George Tenet

For more than seven decades, the Twentieth Century Diner, and later as the Scobee Diner (closed in 2010), was a landmark neighborhood eatery at 25229 Northern Boulevard, Little Neck, Queens. There George Tenet, director of Central Intelligence from 1997 to 2004, received an early education in hard work. The family-owned diner was sold in the early 1960s, but Tenet's father stayed on as chef, and America's future spymaster waited tables to earn money to buy his first car.

Tenet graduated from Benjamin N. Cardozo High School in Bayside, Queens, and earned degrees from Georgetown University in Washington, DC, and from Columbia University. Although he would eventually enter the closed-mouth intelligence profession, young George's reputation at the diner was that of a conversationalist who kept customers amused and returning. Among well-known patrons were the comedian Alan King and actor Telly Savalas.

■ 218. FIDEL'S SPIES

MAP 5 ➤ **Cuba's United Nations mission:** 315 Lexington Avenue

The unassuming building of the permanent mission of Cuba to the United Nations at 315 Lexington Avenue attracts little notice from neighbors or passersby but has a long history as an active center for espionage. The Cuban handler of Ana Belén Montes, a senior US Defense Intelligence

Agency analyst who spied for Cuba from 1985 until her arrest in September 2001, operated from the Lexington Avenue mission. Likewise, State Department official Walter Kendall Myers (code-named AGENT 202 by the Cubans) and his wife, Gwendolyn (AGENT 123), were directed for some of their nearly 30 years of spying by Cuban intelligence officers assigned to the mission and operating under diplomatic immunity.

MISION PERMANENTE DE CUBA

ANTE LAS NACIONES UNIDAS

PERMANENT MISSION OF CUBA TO THE U.N.

A small plaque at the front entrance of a building at 315 Lexington Avenue is the only indication that it houses the Cuban mission to the United Nations. Some of Cuba's most effective spies against the United States have been managed from here.

■ 219. SPIES WITH BADGES

MAP I ➤ **New York Police Department, Intelligence Division:** 250 Vesey Street

The NYPD increased its Intelligence Division capabilities following the 9/11 terrorist attacks.

Following the September 11, 2001, attacks on the World Trade Center, the NYPD redesigned the structure, operations, and culture of its Intelligence Division. The police commissioner created for the city an independent counterterrorism and intelligence capability. David Cohen, a former CIA Deputy Director for Operations (the CIA's top spymaster), was hired as Deputy Commissioner for Intelligence to lead the division.

Significant changes included:

- Measuring success: To change the culture, it was necessary for detectives to move away from a system that weighted success by the number of arrests. Instead, the Intelligence Division began to reward the recruitment and handling of long-term agents.

- Cyber unit: Added in 2002, this new component emphasized using the internet to detect and investigate radicalized terrorist agents before they could strike.

- Demographics and languages: A unit was created to help the Intelligence Division identify where terrorists might hide and to provide linguistic capabilities to understand and exploit raw intelligence.

- International program: In the fall of 2002, the Intelligence Division began sending detectives abroad to learn about terrorist tactics and plots developing overseas. The program eventually expanded to 11 major cities, including London, Quebec, and Paris.

- Civilian analysts: Dozens of analysts were added to mirror counterterrorism analytical units of the federal counter terrorism centers.

- Deep-undercover program: A group of younger officers in their twenties who were either born abroad or were first-generation Americans fluent in multiple languages were recruited to penetrate radical cells.

- Confidential informants: A team of detectives was trained to recruit, vet, and handle sources with access to terrorist operations and planning.

■ 220. SUSPICIOUS VIDEOGRAPHERS

MAP II ▶ **Iranian surveillance target:** Subway station, Roosevelt Avenue and 52nd Street, Queens

In 2003, a pair of Iranian diplomats were observed videotaping on the elevated subway station at Roosevelt Avenue and 52nd Street in Queens as the Manhattan-bound 7 train approached. It was 1:30 on a Sunday morning. Two uniformed police officers watched as the Iranians boarded the train and continued filming the tracks from the front of the subway car. As the train approached Court Square–23rd Street subway station, the cops moved in.

Iran's mission to the United Nations, at 622 Third Avenue, provides cover for the country's intelligence officers. When two Iranian nationals attached to the mission were caught clandestinely filming the New York City subway system, they claimed diplomatic immunity and were expelled from the country.

The men claimed they could not speak English, so a Farsi-speaking police officer interpreted. The pair identified themselves as diplomats assigned to Iran's UN mission and claimed diplomatic immunity. They also asserted they were returning from a party in Queens, but their camera contained only footage of subways. In accordance with their diplomatic status, the suspected spies were declared persona non grata and ordered out of the country.

The episode was not the first expulsion for suspicious filming of New York by Iranian diplomats. A similar incident occurred in 2002 when two other Iranians connected to the UN were expelled for videotaping landmarks, including the Statue of Liberty, the Brooklyn Bridge, and entrances to the tunnels leading to New Jersey.

More recently, Iran's government has been accused of using the Alavi Foundation, a nonprofit organization ostensibly devoted to charity work and promoting Islamic culture, as a front organization. A complaint filed by the US attorney for the Southern District of New York led to the seizure of Alavi's assets, including the Islamic Institute of New York, 55-11 Queens Boulevard, Woodside, Queens, the largest Shiite mosque in the city and the location most closely affiliated with Iran's UN mission.

■ 221. FOMENTING TERROR

MAP 10 ➤ **Blind Sheikh's mosque:** Al-Farooq Mosque, 552 Atlantic Avenue, Brooklyn

Before arriving in the United States, Islamic radical Omar Abdel-Rahman was jailed in Egypt for alleged involvement in the 1981 assassination of Egyptian president Anwar Sadat. Eventually acquitted of the crime but expelled from the country, he relocated to New York in 1990. The Blind Sheikh, as he became known, gathered a following of disaffected immigrants in the Al-Farooq Mosque at 552 Atlantic Avenue in Brooklyn.

On February 26, 1993, a rented truck packed with 1,300 pounds of explosives blew up on parking level B-2 of the North Tower of the New York World Trade Center, killing six people and injuring more than

A storefront mosque on Brooklyn's Atlantic Avenue was once led by Islamic radical Omar Abdel-Rahman. His message of hate influenced disaffected Muslims to attack the World Trade Center in 1993.

a thousand. Islamic militants Ramzi Yousef and Nidal Ayyad were among those implicated in the attack. The investigative trail of the two led back to Abdel-Rahman and discovery of plans to set off bombs in the Lincoln Tunnel, the Holland Tunnel, the United Nations complex, Federal Plaza, and the George Washington Bridge. Arrested in June 1993 with nine followers, Abdel-Rahman was convicted in 1996 of seditious conspiracy and sentenced to life imprisonment. His attorney, Lynne F. Stewart, was subsequently disbarred and convicted of providing material aid to terrorism by smuggling messages to the sheikh's militant followers after visiting her jailed client.

Despite Abdel-Rahman's conviction, the World Trade Center's Twin Towers remained an obsession for radical Islamic terrorists. On September 11, 2001, they struck again by flying airliners into each of the buildings. The Twin Towers collapsed along with collateral destruction to the World Trade Center's 47-story original Building 7 at 250 Greenwich Street, home to numerous government

tenants, including the Department of Defense, the New York City Department of Emergency Management, the Internal Revenue Service, the Securities and Exchange Commission, and the Secret Service. The Twin Towers are commemorated with a memorial at their previous location, while Building 7 was rebuilt in 2006 as a 52-floor office structure.

Abdel-Rahman died at age 77 at a federal prison medical center in North Carolina in 2017. His disgraced attorney, Stewart, had died just days earlier at age 78.

Omar Abdel-Rahman

■ 222. CHINA'S "PARLOR MAID"

MAP 4 ➤ **Katrina Leung residence:** 137 Chrystie Street

For a few years during childhood, Katrina Leung lived in New York at 137 Chrystie Street. The accused Chinese spy gained notoriety for affairs with two of her FBI handlers as well as for her alleged espionage.

Born in China, Katrina Leung (also known as Chen Wen Ying) immigrated to the United States in 1970 as a teenager. She lived with an uncle in an apartment at 137 Chrystie Street on the Lower East Side and attended Washington Irving High School, 40 Irving Place. Excelling at her studies, she received her undergraduate degree from Cornell University, then followed a new husband on to Chicago where she received an MBA from the University of Chicago.

Leung began working with the FBI in Los Angeles in the mid-1980s and was given the code name PARLOR MAID. Also known within the FBI as Bureau Source 410, she became a US citizen and reported on pro–mainland China groups in the Los Angeles area. But on business trips to China, she was allegedly recruited by the People's Republic of China's MSS. Code-named LUO by the Chinese, she reportedly increased the frequency of her China trips, contacts, and business dealings.

Suspicions about Leung were raised in the early 1990s after unreported contacts with Chinese intelligence were discovered. While living in Los Angeles in the 1980s, she had an affair with her primary FBI handler, and it was later revealed she also had an affair with a second FBI special agent. The damage was believed contained when her primary handler reported that based on his "thorough investigation," Leung's loyalty to the United States had been vetted. However, his investigative report omitted key details that showed she was operating under MSS control. Leung became the target in 2001 of a full FBI counterintelligence investigation and was arrested in 2003. She was accused of copying classified documents from her primary handler's briefcase and passing them to her Chinese case officer (code name MAO).

The case continued until 2005 when, despite evidence of espionage, a judge dismissed the charges after learning that a plea agreement between the government and the primary FBI special agent specified that he "could not share further information relating to the case with Leung or her counsel." Without the opportunity to depose the FBI agent as a witness, Leung would have been denied her right to a fair trial. The espionage charges were then dropped. Nevertheless, the loss of the classified information Leung allegedly passed to China is considered significant. As part of a plea agreement, Leung pleaded guilty to one count of lying to the FBI and a second count of filing a false federal tax form. She was sentenced to three years of probation, 100 hours of community service, and a $10,000 fine. She resides in California with her husband.

■ 223. TECHIE TURNS TRAITOR

MAP 10 ➤ **Kun Shan Chun residence:** 2953 Quentin Road, Brooklyn

The recruitment and handling of FBI employee Kun Shan Chun (a.k.a. Joey Chun) typified 21st-century Chinese espionage. Chun, a native of China and a naturalized US citizen, began working as an electronics technician for the FBI's New York field office, 26 Federal Plaza, in 1997. Assigned to the Computerized Central Monitoring Facility of the FBI's Technical Branch, he was granted a top-secret security clearance the following year.

Sometime in 2005, Chun and several of his relatives were approached by intelligence officers claiming to be affiliated with a company called Zhuhai Kolion Technology Company Ltd. In exchange for consulting and research on behalf of the firm, Chun, along with his relatives, received both cash and expense-paid travel.

Joey Chun, an FBI employee turned spy, lived on Quentin Road, a tree-lined street in the Marine Park section of Brooklyn.

By 2007, Chun was passing sensitive information to an unnamed official, presumably from one of China's intelligence services. Over the course of several years, he traveled to Hong Kong and mainland China at least nine times and made other trips to Canada, Thailand, Europe, Australia, and New Zealand.

Chun, who lived in Brooklyn at 2953 Quentin Road, fell under suspicion and became the target of an FBI investigation. In 2015, an undercover FBI agent, posing as a contractor, gained Chun's confidence and sufficient evidence for the spy to be arrested on March 16, 2016. According to the official report, during his time as a spy for China, Chun passed on information about the personnel structure of the FBI, the bureau's technological capabilities, its surveillance strategies, and categories of surveillance targets in New York City and elsewhere.

Chun confessed to spying, motivated primarily by money for himself and relatives. He pleaded guilty on August 1, 2016, and was sentenced to 24 months in prison and a $10,000 fine.

■ 224. THE NEARLY PERFECT SPY

MAP 7 ➤ **Flik's Video to Go:** 175 West 72nd Street (now closed)

Daood S. Gilani, who later changed his name to David Coleman Headley, operated Flik's Video to Go, a video rental business, with his Canadian wife at 175 West 72nd Street until its closure in 2008 amid complaints of false credit card charges. Secretly, however, Gilani, was a member of Pakistan's *Lashkar-e-Taiba* (LeT) Islamic militant group and performed the advance reconnaissance for the attacks in Mumbai, India, on November 26, 2008, that killed 164 people and wounded 308.

Daood S. Gilani (a.k.a. David Headley), seen here entering India to perform reconnaissance before the 2008 Mumbai attack

Prior to the attacks, Gilani, using his mother's maiden name of Headley, visited Mumbai five times to scout, photograph, and record the

GPS coordinates for the planned targets. Traveling in the persona of a Jewish American, Gilani was able to visit multiple countries without suspicion. He coordinated his itinerary with his Pakistani Inter-Services Intelligence handler, a Major Iqbal (later identified as Chaudhery Khan), and LeT terrorist Said Majeed (alias Sajid Mir). During the November 2008 attacks in Mumbai, Gilani monitored the events from a location in Pakistan. Afterward he returned to live with his second wife and four children in Chicago.

Gilani once owned and managed Flik's Video to Go, which once operated at 175 West 72nd Street, seen here after the business's closure amid complaints of falsified credit card charges.

In early 2009, Gilani returned to India to scout targets for another attack and then went to Copenhagen on a reconnaissance mission targeting the Danish newspaper *Jyllands-Posten*. LeT planned to behead the paper's publisher and its cartoonist because the newspaper had published cartoons depicting Muhammad as a terrorist. The operation's code name was MICKEY MOUSE.

During this trip Gilani came to the attention of the Danish Security and Intelligence Service as well as the United Kingdom's MI5. Because Gilani was an American, the FBI was alerted, and a case was opened with the code name of BLACK MEDALLION. The FBI arrested Gilani in October 2009 at Chicago's O'Hare Airport as he was boarding a flight to Philadelphia with onward connections to Pakistan. During questioning Gilani confessed to all his previous activities and cooperated with US authorities. At trial he pleaded guilty and was sentenced in 2013 to 35 years in prison.

■ 225. MONEY FOR ASSASSINS

MAP 5 ➤ **Payoneer Corporation:** 410 Park Avenue

There could be little doubt that well-trained and organized professionals killed Palestinian militant Mahmoud al-Mabhouh. In an operation reportedly code-named PLASMA SCREEN, al-Mabhouh was assassinated in his room at Dubai's luxury Al Bustan Hotel in January 2010. According to Dubai authorities, images of 27 members of the reconnaissance and hit squad were captured on closed-circuit television at the hotel and other locations before and after the attack. Who was behind the killing?

The heavily guarded Israeli consulate on Second Avenue served as the base for several high-profile Israeli spying operations against the United States during the 1980s.

A virtual office in this Park Avenue building served as headquarters for Payoneer, an internet-based financial services company. The firm is suspected of providing prepaid credit cards for the Israeli team that carried out the assassination of Palestinian militant Mahmoud al-Mabhouh in 2010.

One law-enforcement officer in Dubai said investigators were "99 percent certain the action was carried out by Israel's intelligence service, Mossad." This is hardly a surprising conclusion considering al-Mabhouh's history of organizing terrorist attacks against Israel.

But was there evidence of a New York City connection? Examination of financial and credit card records of the assassins led investigators to a New York company, Payoneer, with an address at 410 Park Avenue. Run by an Israeli named Yuval Tal, the firm provides prepaid debit MasterCards to companies to pay employee travel expenses or contractors. Investigators determined that 14 of the suspected assassins used prepaid Payoneer cards for hotel rooms and travel. Tal himself is reputed to have been a former member of Israeli special forces. When a journalist researching the story went to Payoneer's Park Avenue suite, he found only a virtual office that handled the phones and mail for hundreds of firms. The real Payoneer apparently is located at an undisclosed address.

Israeli intelligence operations in New York surfaced during the 1980s when Jonathan Jay Pollard, an employee of the US Naval Criminal Investigative Service, was recruited to spy for the Israeli Bureau of Scientific Relations (a.k.a. *ha-Lishka le-Kishrei Mada*, or LAKAM). As part of Israel's intelligence apparatus, LAKAM collected foreign scientific and technical intelligence and aggressively targeted potential agents, including US citizens. When Israeli Air Force colonel Aviem Sella, operating from the Israeli consulate at 800 Second Avenue under the cover of being a student of computer science at New York University, learned that Pollard was volunteering to cooperate, the American was recruited and assigned the code name THE HUNTING HORSE, meaning "someone who brings in good information that his superiors use to their own advantage."

Sella later handed Pollard off to another Israeli case officer, Yosef Yagur, who also worked out of the Second Avenue consulate. Pollard smuggled hundreds of thousands of pages of classified information from his office to his handlers in return for jewelry, trips, and a $2,500 monthly stipend. Arrested in 1985, Pollard pleaded guilty to espionage and received a life sentence. LAKAM was disbanded in 1986, and Israel formally acknowledged Pollard as its spy in 1998. Repeated petitioning of the US government by Israel for Pollard's release was rejected prior to his parole in 2015.

Yagur also ran other American agents from New York, such as Ben-Ami Kadish, who worked without compensation from 1979 to 1985 for Israeli intelligence. Kadish passed secret technical information on F-15 fighter jets, the Patriot missile system, and nuclear weapons. When arrested in 2008, the 85-year-old Kadish pleaded guilty and declared he spied "for the benefit of Israel." In deference to his age, the spy received a $50,000 fine but no prison time. An Israeli consulate official dismissed the matter saying, "This is an old case which occurred over 25 years ago, and all aspects of it are part of the past."

■ 226. A NEW GENERATION OF RUSSIAN *ILLEGALS*

MAP I ▶ **Anna Chapman residence:** 20 Exchange Place

The FBI arrest of 10 Russian intelligence officers in June 2010 made international headlines. All were *illegals* and part of a long-running operation of the *Sluzhba Vneshney Razvedki* (SVR), the successor to the KGB's First Directorate. Those involved lived in major US population centers—Boston, New York, New Jersey, Northern Virginia, and Seattle. The reaction to the arrests, both in the American media and among the public, was more a

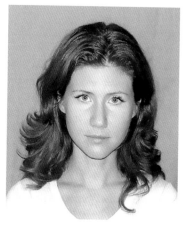

Anna Chapman

Mikhail A. Vasenkov

Mikhail Kutsik

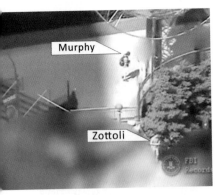

Spies such as Vladimir Guryev and Mikhail Kutsik, previously unknown to each other (and identified in the photo by their aliases), used recognition signals and a verbal parole to meet near landmarks such as the globe at Columbus Circle.

sense of amusement than alarm, as if the episode was a chapter from a classic Cold War novel. The Russian Foreign Ministry's response replayed boilerplate denial: "These actions [arrests by the FBI] are unfounded and pursue unseemly goals. We don't understand the reasons which prompted the US Department of Justice to make a public statement in the spirit of Cold War–era spy stories."

New York City and its surrounding areas were the hub for the operation that ran for more than a decade. Clandestine meetings for transferring cash, supplies, and information occurred at sites from downtown Brooklyn to the globe sculpture outside the Trump International Hotel and Tower at 1 Central Park West as well as the adjoining Columbus Circle.

Vicky Peláez, a US citizen originally from Peru, and Mikhail A. Vasenkov, living under the alias of Juan Lazaro at 17 Clifton Avenue in Yonkers since 1985, commuted into New York City for their cover jobs. Peláez, previously a well-known television reporter in Peru, once described as "the most aggressive journalist on TV," wrote columns critical of American policy for the left-leaning Spanish-language paper *El Diario La Prensa*, now located on the 18th floor of 1 MetroTech Center, Brooklyn. A self-described "journalist and anthropologist," Vasenkov taught as an adjunct professor for a single semester at Baruch College. In 2006, he retired from the SVR after an intelligence career of three decades.

Vladimir and Lidiya Guryev, using the aliases Richard and Cynthia Murphy, lived in Montclair, New Jersey, in a $481,000 house paid for by their Moscow controllers. Lidiya commuted into the city for a job as a vice president of a small wealth-management firm, Morea Financial Services, at 120 Broadway. In the United States since the mid-1990s, Lidiya had earned degrees from New York University and an MBA from Columbia Business School. Vladimir, playing the role of a house husband, met with his handlers in New York City as well as abroad and transferred money and spy gear to another *illegal*

couple, Mikhail Kutsik and Natalia Pereverzeva (a.k.a. Michael Zottoli and Patricia Mills). On March 7, 2010, Guryev passed an updated laptop, money, and encrypted flash media cards to Kutsik at the now defunct Tillie's Coffee shop at 248 Dekalb Avenue in Brooklyn's Fort Greene neighborhood.

Russian *illegals* Vladimir Guryev ("Richard Murphy") and Christopher Metsos are photographed by FBI surveillance while meeting in Sunnyside, Queens.

Anna Chapman (born Anna Vasil'evna Kushchenko), the youngest of the intelligence officers, used multiple sites, including a Starbucks on West 47th Street and Eighth Avenue and the Barnes and Noble Bookstore at 97 Warren Street in Tribeca, to communicate with her Russian handlers through special software on her laptop. Of the 10 *illegals*, media attention focused on the photogenic Chapman, who lived in a fashionable Financial District highrise at 20 Exchange Place, where she hung photos of Marilyn Monroe, Frank Sinatra, and Audrey Hepburn on her apartment's walls. The 28-year-old redhead established her business cover as an internet real estate entrepreneur.

Originally headquarters for the City Bank Farmers Trust Company, this 57-story art deco masterpiece was home to Russian *illegal* Chapman.

Chapman led a high-flying lifestyle. She carried a $2,300 Wi-Fi–enabled Chanel bag when posing for society photographer Patrick McMullan and mingled with celebrities at private parties. She frequented trendy nightspots and maintained updated profiles on Facebook and LinkedIn. Just prior to her meeting with an FBI undercover agent in the Starbucks at 10 Hanover Place and subsequent arrest on June 27, 2010, at the NYPD's First Precinct, 16 Ericsson Place, she named herself CEO of a start-up company, Property Finder LLC. She also purchased the website www.NYCrentals.com.

However, Chapman's tradecraft was flawed. When she purchased a burner cell phone at a Verizon store in downtown Brooklyn, she listed her

The Starbucks on Hanover Square was where Chapman met an undercover FBI counterintelligence agent posing as a Russian intelligence officer.

name and address on the contract as Irine Kutsov, 99 Fake Street. She tossed the contract, with an address that could have been borrowed from an episode of *The Simpsons*, and other paperwork from the store into a nearby trash can. The FBI picked it up.

Once London tabloids obtained semi-nude photographs of Chapman courtesy of her British ex-husband (now deceased), she became internationally known as the "hot spy." Compared to the other nine low-key Russian spies, she projected the glamour of a Hollywood-scripted secret agent. During her six months in the United States, Chapman demonstrated that the effectiveness of "sexpionage" endures, as she seduced influential men for possible recruitment by her intelligence service. Accounts of Chapman's Bond Girl–meets–*Sex and the City* story obscured the seriousness of a national security threat posed by the Moscow-directed spy network. A senior FBI counterintelligence official predicted that "within six months Anna Chapman would have been the most dangerous Russian spy in America."

After the 10 were returned to Russia as part of spy swap in July 2010, Chapman evolved into a national hero with her own television show, *Secrets of the World with Anna Chapman*. Her provocative poses graced the pages of *Maxim* magazine, and she paraded the catwalk during Fashion Week in Moscow, accidentally dropping the real pistol she carried as a prop. The Russian intelligence failure inadvertently produced a pop culture star and youthful new image for the SVR, as Chapman appeared a world apart from the dour Soviet Cold War spies whose sole public recognition might be a colorless commemorative postage stamp.

Image-conscious Russian president Vladimir Putin seized the opportunity to minimize the importance of the 10 intelligence officers and underplay the significance of their arrests. Appearing on *Larry King Live* on December 1, 2010, Putin admitted they were spies but asserted they would have become operational only "in crisis periods, say, in case of a breakup of the diplomatic relations." In other words, the 10 may have been spies but as "sleeper agents" posed no immediate security threat to the United States.

The reality was otherwise. Contrary to press narratives, the *illegals* were dedicated SVR officers. Their level of tradecraft sophistication and success in developing access to influential members of America's financial and political community were marks of professionals. Except for Chapman and another young officer, Mikhail Semenko, all were seasoned intelligence officers. An encrypted memo from Moscow to the Murphys, intercepted by the FBI, clarified their mission: "You were sent to USA for long-term service trip. Your education, bank accounts, car, house etc.—all these serve one goal: fulfill your main mission, i.e. to search and develop ties in policymaking circles in the United States and send [intelligence reports] to the Center."

The decade-long FBI operation that exposed the Russian spies, code-named GHOST STORIES, involved hundreds of agents and thousands of hours of manpower prior to the June 2010 arrests. The investigation uncovered a sophisticated and far-ranging intelligence operation that integrated traditional tradecraft with the latest advancements in communication technology. The Russian spies used private ad hoc wireless networks to burst data from laptops to mobile units, executed "flash passes" in train stations to exchange money, and communicated over the internet through encrypted messages embedded with stenanography in benign images such as flowers.

The FBI management of the GHOST STORIES operation required leadership, vision, discipline, security, patience, and perseverance. The ripples from the arrests spread to expose additional SVR *illegals* in other parts of the world, and the case stands as one of the FBI's greatest counterintelligence successes.

■ 227. TARGETING THE GRAY LADY

MAP 3 ➤ *The New York Times*: 242 West 41st Street

In September 2012, Chinese hackers reportedly penetrated the computer network of *The New York Times*, 242 West 41st Street, and stole the corporate passwords of every employee. For approximately four months, with assistance from an outside consulting firm, the *Times* monitored and tracked the cyberattack. The Chinese seemed to maintain business hours, logging on at around 8:00 a.m. Beijing time, then working through a typical business day.

When the computer network of *The New York Times* was compromised in 2012, all clues pointed to Chinese hackers. The newspapers assigned reporters to cover the episode.

The attackers eventually focused on the paper's Shanghai bureau chief, David Barboza, as well as a previous bureau chief, downloading documents from their corporate accounts. Motivation for the attack appears to have been

NEW THREATS AND OLD ADVERSARIES

a series of reports that detailed the billion-dollar fortune amassed by relatives of China's prime minister at the time, Wen Jiabao, and his allegedly illegal business practices. Although China suspected a spy or network of spies was feeding Barboza information, the journalist maintained his reporting was actually based on publicly available sources such as China's State Administration for Industry and Commerce.

China's hackers also targeted another American news organization that reported on corruption among Chinese officials. In 2013, Bloomberg News confirmed to the *Times* that unsuccessful attacks were launched against its networks after publishing reports on wealth accumulated by relatives of Xi Jinping, then China's vice president. In the wake of the *Times* report, the *Washington Post* and the *Wall Street Journal* also reported cyberattacks from China.

Official denials followed. "Chinese laws prohibit any action including hacking that damages Internet security," China's Ministry of National Defense said in a statement. "To accuse the Chinese military of launching cyberattacks without solid proof is unprofessional and baseless." China's Foreign Ministry spokesman, Hong Lei said, "The competent Chinese authorities have already issued a clear response to the groundless accusations made by *The New York Times*." Hong added, "To arbitrarily assert and to conclude without hard evidence that China participated in such hacking attacks is totally irresponsible. China is also a victim of hacking attacks. Chinese laws clearly forbid hacking attacks, and we hope relevant parties takes [*sic*] a responsible attitude on this issue."

■ 228. A PRESIDENT AVOIDS THE WALDORF

MAP 5 ➤ Waldorf Astoria: 301 Park Avenue

President Barack Obama ended a long-time presidential tradition of staying at the Waldorf Astoria, 301 Park Avenue, when in New York to address the 2015 United Nations General Assembly. Obama's decision to change hotels was likely not because of poor room service in the Presidential Suite but rather related to its new owner, China's Anbang Insurance Group. The Chinese company, which bought the hotel for a reported $1.95 billion in 2014, was itself taken over by the Chinese government in February 2018.

The magnificent Waldorf Astoria Hotel became a security concern for the US government following its purchase by a Beijing-based insurance company.

Before China's government assumed control of Anbang, however, US officials concluded that information and personnel security of US officials staying at the hotel could not be assured. All guest rooms, meeting rooms, offices, telephones, internet service, and Wi-Fi could potentially be monitored on-site or remotely by the new Chinese owners. Compromise of personal possessions of guests and visitors to the hotel, including their smartphones and computers, was a related threat.

China's intelligence service was at the time accused of hacking into US government and defense company computers to access policy

President Barack Obama stayed at the Lotte New York Palace Hotel on Madison Avenue instead of the Waldorf Astoria after the latter came under Chinese ownership.

and technological secrets. For the president and his entourage, a stay at the Chinese-owned New York landmark might appear to be inviting problems that could become more politically controversial than simply abandoning a tradition.

The Waldorf is no stranger to espionage. Since opening in 1931, the 2,200 room, 47-story hotel has hosted numerous spies among its guests. These included the Third Reich's Gerhard Alois Westrick and British double agent Duško Popov. While spying for the United States in the late 1970s, Arkady Shevchenko, then a United Nations undersecretary-general, met with his handlers at the Waldorf.

The immediate issue of whether American presidents would stay at the Waldorf became moot in 2017 when Anbang Insurance Group closed the hotel for renovations. The company said a majority of the rooms would be converted to luxury condos.

As for President Obama, he chose in 2015 to stay at the Lotte New York Palace, 455 Madison Avenue. Its ownership by a South Korean company was not a problem for the White House.

■ 229. SPIES IN SUITS AND TIES

MAP 9 ▶ **Evgeny Buryakov residence:** 5833 Liebig Avenue, Bronx

The FBI broke up a Russian spy ring in New York City in January 2015 that was targeting confidential US stock market and economic data, including classified information on expected sanctions to be

Evgeny Buryakov

Evgeny Buryakov, an SVR officer under cover as a banker, lived in this modest house in the Bronx.

imposed on Russian banks. Central to the case was Russian intelligence officer Evgeny Buryakov (code name ZHENYA), whose cover was being deputy representative of Vnesheconombank (VEB), 777 Third Avenue, suite 29-B.

Buryakov, who lived at 5833 Liebig Avenue in the Bronx, worked with two other Russian spies. Igor Sporyshev of 428 West 259th Street, the Bronx, was a trade representative at the Russian Federation to New York, and Victor Podobnyy, was an attaché in the permanent mission of the Russian Federation to the United States, 136 East 67th Street. All three were officers of the SVR's Directorate ER, which focused on gathering economic secrets about US trade and commerce.

Podobnyy and Sporyshev attempted to recruit agents in New York, including college students, as intelligence sources for Russia. Among Sporyshev's roles was that of a cutout who passed intelligence requirements from Moscow to Buryakov. Along with Podobnyy, he was responsible for reviewing and forwarding Buryakov's intelligence reports back to the SVR.

The FBI revealed that Buryakov used coded messages to communicate with his fellow SVR officers for more than four dozen meetings. Buryakov also relied upon traditional clandestine tradecraft techniques such as brush passes to hand off written notes in a bag or magazine to Sporyshev in outdoor settings. The SVR believed face-to-face meetings outdoors were less risky than indoor meetings that might be monitored by FBI listening devices.

Uncharacteristic of their otherwise professional-level tradecraft, Buryakov and Sporyshev sometimes used double-talk in phone conversations, with phrases such as "need to meet to transfer tickets," in an amateurish attempt to mislead anyone eavesdropping on their calls. FBI files noted the two men were never seen "attending, or discussing in any detail, events that would typically require tickets."

Buryakov's residence had a particular advantage for the spy that was not immediately obvious. Located only a few blocks from the Russian embassy's residential compound in Riverdale, between Mosholu Avenue and Fieldston Road near 255th Street, Buryakov's Bronx address offered direct line-of-sight to the upper stories of the 20-story Russian apartment building. Using an infrared or other covert optical system, Buryakov could securely communicate with personnel at the living quarters while avoiding any suspicious in-person contacts with other suspected SVR spies under possible FBI surveillance.

Following Buryakov's arrest on January 26, 2015, Sporyshev and Podobnyy took advantage of their diplomatic immunity and departed the country. Buryakov pleaded not guilty in his first court appearance but later changed his plea to guilty in exchange for a reduced sentence of 30 months in prison. He was released in March 2017 and deported to Russia six days later.

■ 230. MYSTERIOUS DEATH ON THE UPPER EAST SIDE

MAP 6 ➤ **Russian consulate:** 9 East 91st Street

Sergei Krivov, the Russian consular deputy commander in New York City, appeared to have died of blunt force trauma at the diplomatic mission on East 91st Street. Later the cause of death was announced as a heart attack.

Early on the morning of November 8, 2016, a body was found lying outside the Russian consulate in New York City. To bystanders it appeared a man had fallen from the building, but Russian officials insisted the victim, Sergei Krivov, had died from a heart attack, not a fall.

Suspicious, the NYPD began investigating. Krivov's listed address, 11 East 90th Street, was a support building for the Smithsonian's Cooper-Hewitt design museum, not a residence. Further, in what seemed a strange coincidence, the address was only one block from the Russian consulate at 9 East 91st Street. Consulate officials could not explain the discrepancy.

Krivov was actually a consular deputy commander, cover for his work as an operative technical officer for the SVR. His responsibilities included protecting the consulate against sabotage and secret intrusion, preventing bugs from being planted, and thwarting any attempted eavesdropping.

In this capacity, Krivov would have access to the consulate's *rezidentura* and *referentura*, the top-secret cipher area where Russian diplomatic and intelligence service communications are received and transmitted. Inside the *referentura's* vault-like enclosure, Russian diplomatic bags containing classified information are prepared to be hand-carried by couriers on Aeroflot flights between Moscow and New York City. Krivov would also have played a major role in the physical protection of all classified spaces and performed monthly inspections of the *referentura* and *rezidentura* to confirm that no technical penetrations had occurred.

No official explanation of the inconsistencies surrounding Krivov's death was ever offered, and suspicions about the true circumstances remain unaddressed.

■ 231. RUSSIAN DIPLOMACY A DANGEROUS JOB

MAP 6 ▶ Permanent Mission of the Russian Federation to the United Nations: 136 East 67th Street

Known as a base for espionage operations, the permanent mission of the Russian Federation to the United Nations on East 67th Street may have also been a murder scene. Mysterious circumstances surrounding the death of Russian ambassador Vitaly Churkin have yet to be satisfactorily explained.

In the suspicion-shrouded world of Russian foreign affairs, serving as a diplomat or intelligence officer can lower life expectancy. In less than four months from November 2016 to February 2017, death from assassination or more ambiguous causes came unexpectedly to two senior Russian officials in New York and another six in other countries.

Mikhail Lesin, 57, a former media adviser to Russian president Vladimir Putin, was found dead in a Washington, DC, hotel room on November 5, 2015. A coroner's report stated he died from blunt force trauma.

On November 8, 2016, Sergei Krivov, 63, the Russian consular deputy commander in New York City, died of blunt-force trauma. When his body was discovered, he appeared to have fallen from the top floor of the Russian consulate at 9 East 91st Street. The cause of death was later said to be a heart attack.

Andrey Karlov, 62, Russia's ambassador to Turkey, was assassinated by nine shots fired by an off-duty policeman on December 20, 2016, in Ankara.

Petr Polshikov, 63, the Russian Foreign Ministry's chief adviser on Latin America, was reportedly shot dead in his Moscow apartment bedroom on December 20, 2016.

Roman Skrylnikov, in his mid-50s and posted at the Russian consulate in Kazakhstan, was found dead by his driver on December 26, 2016, reportedly from a heart attack.

Oleg Erovinkin, a 61-year-old former KGB and FSB general who was suspected of helping the former MI6 spy Christopher Steele compile a dossier on presidential candidate Donald Trump, was found dead in his car in Moscow by an apparent heart attack on December 26, 2016.

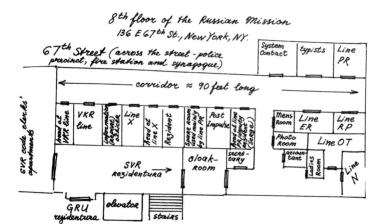

8th floor of the Russian Mission
136 E 67th St., New York, NY.

The SVR *rezidentura* (intelligence station) as it appeared in the 1990s, sketched by Russian defector Col. Sergei Tretyakov, was located on the 8th floor inside the Soviet mission to the United Nations.

Andrey Malanin, 55, head of the consular department at the Russian embassy in Athens, reportedly died under "natural circumstances" in his apartment in Athens on January 8, 2017.

Alexander Kadakin, 67, the Russian ambassador to India, died of "natural causes" on January 26, 2017.

Vitaly Churkin, Russian ambassador in the Russian Federation mission to the UN, 136 East 67th Street, died unexpectedly on February 20, 2017. With no history of health problems, the 64-year-old ambassador suddenly fell ill and died before he reached the hospital. Rumors persisted that he suffered a heart attack, but the New York City medical examiner said the death "required more study." Later the examiner's office refused to release its findings and asserted that the death certificate was protected by diplomatic immunity.

> **"Any fool can commit a murder, but it takes an artist to commit a good natural death."**
>
> **—Cold War–era KGB quip**

Finally, on March 4, 2018, Sergei Skripal, 66, a former Russian military intelligence officer, and his daughter, Yulia, were poisoned in Salisbury, England. Skripal was serving a lengthy prison sentence in Russia before his release in July 2010 as part of a spy exchange for 10 Russian *illegals* in the United States. Although the Skripals survived, a British woman died after being exposed to poisoned material believed to have been used in the Skripal attack. The British government formally accused the Russian Federation of carrying out the attack using the nerve agent Novichok.

■ 232. LUXURY LONG ISLAND SPY DACHAS

MAP 12 ➤ **Killenworth:** Off Dosoris Lane, Glen Cove, Long Island
Norwich House (renamed the Elmcroft Estate): Off Mill River Road, Upper Brookville, Oyster Bay, Long Island

The Russian government maintained two Long Island estates as recreational compounds for its diplomatic personnel stationed at the United Nations. Both estates rankled local residents because the Russians enjoyed nearby beaches and services but paid no local property taxes under their diplomatic status. The properties also played lesser-known roles as platforms for advanced electronic eavesdropping systems targeting New York City communications.

The 40-acre, 49-room Killenworth estate in Glen Cove, Long Island, was constructed in 1912 and acquired by the Soviet Union in 1951 for $49,000. The highest-ranking Soviet official to defect to the West, Arkady Shevchenko, revealed the property's secret role in the 1980s: "All the top floors . . . are full of sophisticated equipment . . . to intercept all conversations of anything which is going on. . . . At least 15 or 17 technicians were working . . . to do this job." He further explained, "Their eavesdropping equipment occupied so much space, in fact, that one of the two large unused greenhouses had been commandeered to store it. These quarters were off limits to other personnel."

The second location was the grand 14-acre Norwich House estate in Upper Brookville, a village within the town of Oyster Bay, Long Island. Once

The Russian government's 40-acre Oyster Bay compound, known as Killenworth, featured a sophisticated signals intercept capability. The US government seized the facility in December 2016.

owned by a New York governor, it was purchased by the Soviets in 1952 for $80,000. At the time of the acquisition, the house itself was described as a 36-room mansion with outdoor and indoor pools and billiard and sun rooms. The local press cited a neighbor's report years later that the upper floor of the house across from the Oyster Bay compound, 105 Mill River Road, was an FBI observation post, with cameras and listening devices mounted in the trees to surveil the site.

On December 27, 2017, the US government informed the Russian government that both properties on Long Island, and a third property in Centreville, Maryland, were known centers of espionage against the United States. As such, they were to be immediately closed. Concurrently 35 Russian intelligence officers and their families were declared persona non grata and expelled from the US. The potentially confrontational move was a response to the harassment of US diplomats in Moscow and a pattern of cyber aggression that included suspected Russian intrusions into the computer systems of the Democratic National Committee and the hacking of social media sites.

■ 233. SPY CATCHERS

MAP I ➤ **FBI New York field office:** Jacob K. Javits Building, 26 Federal Plaza

The Federal Bureau of Investigation's history in New York dates to 1910. Two years after the FBI was established in Washington, the New York office opened in the Old Post Office Building, the site of what is now City Hall Park. Over the next four decades, the office moved to 15 Park Row, to the Sub-Treasury Building on Wall Street, to 370 Lexington Avenue, to the Foley Square Courthouse, to 290 Broadway in 1952, and then to 201 East 69th Street in 1956. Since 1980, the FBI's New York field office has been in the Jacob K. Javits Federal Building, 26 Federal Plaza. From this location, the FBI's largest field office led the investigations and arrests of some of the most damaging spies, spy rings, and terrorists in American history.

With interconnected world communications and instantly shared information, the challenges faced by

Dubbed the "Ant Hill," the Jacob K. Javits Federal Building houses multiple government agencies, bureaus, and departments, including the FBI's largest field office. From here, FBI agents have broken some of the most widely publicized espionage cases in America.

A memorial on the site of New York's World Trade buildings commemorates victims of the 9-11 attack on America and honors the courage of the responders.

security and counterintelligence services have both multiplied and diffused. Some spies of the past seem almost quaint. Espionage, crime, and terrorist operations have access to much of the same technology as governments. Enormous amounts of money generated by transnational criminal organizations as well as from sponsoring governments pour into clever global financial labyrinths for laundering. Thumb-sized USB flash drives with 32- and 64-gigabit storage can hold huge volumes of sensitive data. The breach of seemingly secure institutions can be equally devastating through recruitment of a well-placed agent or by a planned, or careless, single click on an e-mail link. The most dangerous spy may no longer be a New York resident but a bot created by a distant hacker safe from the immediate physical reach of the FBI.

Today terrorists, transnational criminal organizations, and spies continue their clandestine activities targeting the city's political, creative, and economic power structures. Armed with the latest technology and as aggressive as their historic predecessors, they pose a range of threats broader than those seen by law enforcement of past generations. In the city that is said to never sleep, silent wars of espionage, fought in the shadows, never end.

APPENDIX:
SPY SITES MAPS

Readers should note that the locations depicted on the maps are approximate and may not represent the precise address of a site. If visiting or looking for a specific site, please refer to the text for the complete address.

To the best of the authors' information, as of press time the addresses cited in the book are accurate. The physical appearance of many sites may have changed since the location was last used for spy activity. Ownership, redevelopment, and business changes have and will continue to occur. Particularly for private residences, we urge readers to respect the privacy of occupants and owners.

MAP 1:

■ MANHATTAN

➤ **Financial District, Tribeca, Soho, Chinatown, and Little Italy**

south tip of Manhattan, west of Bowery and St. James Place, south of Houston Street

1. **Nathan Hale statue** (2)
   City Hall Park at Broadway, Park Row and Chambers Street

4. **America's first attack submarine** (5)
   West Side of the Battery in Lower Manhattan

5. **James Rivington publishing house** (6)
   Northeast corner of Wall Street and Broadway
   (site redeveloped)

6. **Culper spy ring headquarters** (7)
   Peck Slip, east side of street near Pearl Street
   (site redeveloped)

7. **Mulligan brothers store** (9)
   23 Queen Street (now Pine Street)

9. **Fraunces Tavern** (12)
   54 Pearl Street

10. **Kennedy Mansion** (13)
    1 Broadway

12. **Benedict Arnold residence** (16)
    5 Broadway

13. **John Jay birthplace** (17)
    66 Pearl Street

15. **Rhinelander Sugar House prison site** (19)
    1 Centre Street

16. **Sugar House Prison** (20)
    34 and 36 Liberty Street (then called Crown Street)

21. **Winthrop Hilton printing plant** (27)
    11 Spruce Street

22. **Pauline Cushman residence** (28)
Astor House Hotel, west side of Broadway between Vesey and Barclay Streets

23. **P. T. Barnum's American Museum** (29)
Broadway and Ann Street

25. **Astor House Hotel** (31)
West side of Broadway between Vesey and Barclay Streets

29. **Office for German sabotage operations** (38)
60 Broadway

31. **Carl Ruroede office** (41)
Maritime Building, 8 Bridge Street (replaced by skyscraper), opposite Alexander Hamilton US Customs House

35. **G. Amsinck and Company** (48)
6 Hanover Street (site redeveloped)

37. **US Secret Service** (51)
Alexander Hamilton US Custom House, 1 Bowling Green

40. **Labor's National Peace Council offices** (56)
55 Liberty Street

43. **World War I British consulate** (61)
44 Whitehall Street

44. *New York Evening Mail* **offices** (61)
34 Park Row

45. **George Bacon cover office** (62)
Central Powers War Films Exchange, 150 Nassau Street

46. **Office of Naval Intelligence, World War I branch office** (64)
14 Wall Street

49. **American Protective League headquarters** (67)
32 Nassau Street

53. **German cover office** (74)
60 Wall Street (site redeveloped)

MAP 1: continued

■ MANHATTAN

➤ **Financial District, Tribeca, Soho, Chinatown, and Little Italy**

south tip of Manhattan, west of Bowery and St. James Place, south of Houston Street

56. **Suspected surveillance site** (76)
20 Broad Street (site redeveloped)

63. **Bureau of Investigation** (86)
15 Park Row (now the Park Row Building)

65. **House of Morgan** (89)
23 Wall Street, corner of Wall and Broad Streets

96. **International Development Company** (126)
19 Rector Street

139. **German consulate** (181)
Whitehall Building, 17 Battery Place

145. **Mob boss headquarters** (189)
Meyer's Hotel, 119 South Street

146. **First headquarters of the Manhattan Project** (191)
Arthur Levitt State Office Building, 270 Broadway

164. **Central Intelligence Group field office** (212)
39 Broadway

183. **Morris and Jack Childs brush-pass site** (241)
11 Broadway, 9th floor

185. **Information Department of Cable and Radio Censorship** (243)
90 Church Street

212. **Father Mark Cheung's cover** (280)
Church of the Transfiguration, 29 Mott Street

219. **New York Police Department, Intelligence Division** (293)
250 Vesey Street

226. **Anna Chapman residence** (301)
20 Exchange Place

233. **FBI New York field office** (313)
Jacob K. Javits Building, 26 Federal Plaza

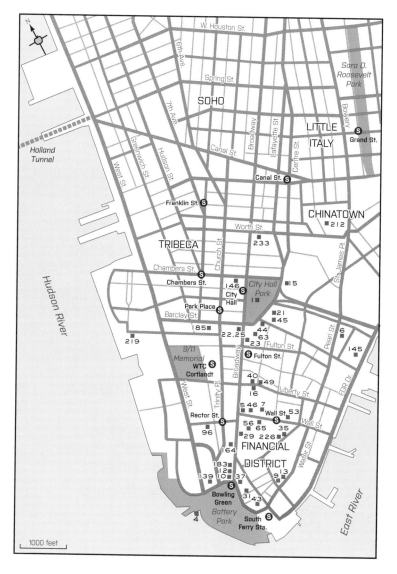

MAP 2:

■ MANHATTAN

➤ West Village and Chelsea

north of Houston Street, west of Fifth Avenue, and south of 34th Street

17. **Old Grapevine Tavern** (24)
West 11th Street and Sixth Avenue (site redeveloped)

30. **Martha Held "residence"** (39)
123 West 15th Street

32. **Safe house** (42)
123 West 15th Street

47A. **Agnes Smedley residence** (65)
2 Bank Street

47B. **Agnes Smedley residence** (65)
156 Waverly Place

61. **James A. Farley Post Office Building** (84)
Eighth Avenue and West 33rd Street

76. **Sergei Konenkov residence and studio** (101)
37 West 8th Street

93. **Elizabeth Bentley apartment** (123)
58 Barrow Street

141. **Astor family office** (183)
23 West 26th Street

143. **OPERATION PASTORIUS safe house** (185)
Governor Clinton Hotel (now Stewart Hotel), 371 Seventh Avenue at West 31st Street

187. **National Committee for Free Europe Inc. headquarters** (246)
Empire State Building, 350 Fifth Avenue, room 301

189. **Secret drug-testing apartment** (249)
81 Bedford Street

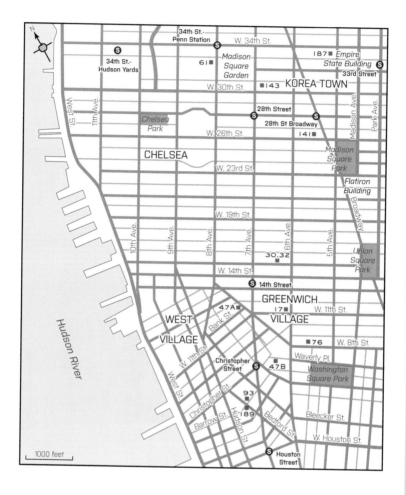

MAP 3:

■ MANHATTAN

➤ Garment District, Midtown West, Hell's Kitchen

north of 34th Street, west of Fifth Avenue, and south of 59th Street

20. **New York Crystal Palace (26)**
Bryant Park, West 42nd Street between Fifth and Sixth Avenues

38. **New York Yacht Club (54)**
37 West 44th Street

66. **World's Tower Building (90)**
110 West 40th Street

71. **Taft Hotel (now The Michelangelo) (96)**
152 West 51st Street

72. **Luxor Baths (96)**
121 West 46th Street

74. **Itzhak Akhmerov hat shop (99)**
19 West 57th Street (since redeveloped)

75. **Leon Theremin residence (100)**
37 West 54th Street

80. **American Women's Association (107)**
353 West 57th Street

81. **Alexander Orlov residence (108)**
Wellington Hotel, 871 Seventh Avenue

95. **Artkino Pictures (126)**
723 Seventh Avenue

99. **Tempus Import Company (130)**
119 West 57th Street

106. **Horn & Hardart Automat (140)**
1391 Broadway (now a drugstore)

MAP 3: continued

■ MANHATTAN

➤ **Garment District, Midtown West, Hell's Kitchen**

north of 34th Street, west of Fifth Avenue, and south
of 59th Street

188. **Museum of Modern Art** (247)
11 West 53rd Street

194. **OPERATION ZRRIFLE planning site** (256)
Plaza Hotel, Fifth Avenue and Central Park South

196. **Great Northern Hotel** (258)
119 West 56th Street (today site of Le Parker Meridien)

203. **Steinway & Sons, Steinway Hall** (268)
109 West 57th Street (former location)

209. **New York Public Library** (277)
Wertheim Study, room 228, West 42nd Street and Fifth Avenue

211. **Frank Terpil arrest site** (279)
New York Hilton, 1335 Sixth Avenue

227. *The New York Times* (305)
242 West 41st Street

MAP 4:

■ MANHATTAN

➤ **Lower East Side, East Village, and Gramercy Park**

east of Bowery and Fifth Avenue, north of Brooklyn Bridge, to shore of East River, south of 23rd Street

47. **Agnes Smedley residence** (65)
16th East 9th Street

48. **John Held Jr. residence** (67)
151 East 19th Street

64. **Union of Russian Workers** (87)
133 East 15th Street

67. **Union Square** (92)
Broadway at East 14th Street

68. **Daily Worker** (93)
35 East 12th Street

70. **Isaiah Oggins residence** (94)
308 East 18th Street

82. **Commercial cover** (110)
Phantom Red Cosmetics, 67 Fifth Avenue (site redeveloped)

85. **George Mink mail drop** (112)
26 East 10th Street, apt. 5-F

86. **Socialist Workers Party headquarters** (114)
116 University Place (now redeveloped)

104. **Julius and Ethel Rosenberg residence** (137)
10 Monroe Street, apt. GE-11

105. **David Greenglass residence** (138)
265 Rivington Street

108. **GRU station at the Raven Electric Company** (142)
889 Broadway

112. **Edwin Emerson residence** (150)
215 East 15th Street

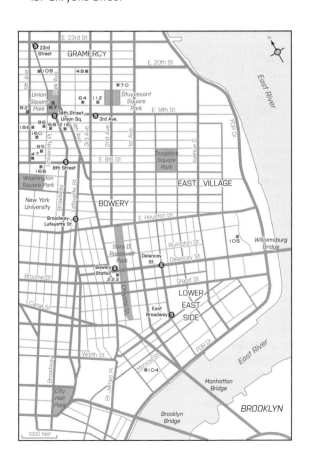

MAP 5:

■ MANHATTAN

➤ Kip's Bay, Murray Hill, and Midtown East

north of 23rd Street, east from Fifth Avenue, to shore of East River, south of 59th Street

2. **Mary Lindley Murray commemorative plaque** [3]
Southwest corner of East 35th Street and Park Avenue

18. **George H. Sharpe residence** [24]
31 East 39th Street [site redeveloped]

28. **American Black Chamber** [36]
141 East 37th Street

50. **Maria de Victorica dead-drop site** [70]
Pew 30, St. Patrick's Cathedral, Fifth Avenue and East 50th Street

57. **69th Regiment Armory** [78]
68 Lexington Avenue between East 25th and 26th Streets

77. **Mail-drop address** [102]
121 Madison Avenue [at East 30th Street]

92. **Arthur Adams residence** [121]
Peter Cooper Hotel [now The Tuscany St. Giles Hotel], 120 East 39th Street

111. *Amerasia* **offices** [146]
225 Fifth Avenue, 11th floor

124. **Texaco headquarters** [165]
Chrysler Building, 405 Lexington Avenue

129. **St. Regis Hotel** [171]
2 East 55th Street

MAP 5: continued

■ MANHATTAN

➤ **Kip's Bay, Murray Hill, and Midtown East**

north of 23rd Street, east from Fifth Avenue, to shore of East River, south of 59th Street

225. **Payoneer Corporation** (299)
     410 Park Avenue

228. **Waldorf Astoria** (306)
     301 Park Avenue

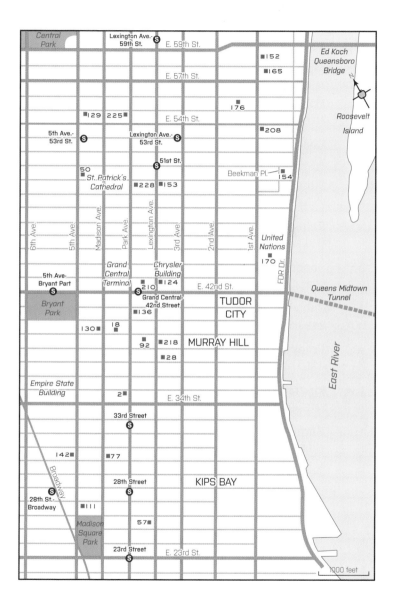

MAP 6:

■ MANHATTAN

➤ **Upper East Side, and Yorkville**

north of 59th Street, south of 110th Street

58.   **Marlborough Churchill residence** (79)
40 East 83rd Street

62.   **Charles Nott residence** (85)
151 East 61st Street

73.   **FBI observation post** (97)
Pierre Hotel, 2 East 61st Street (opposite Russian consulate)

87.   **Robert Sheldon Harte residence** (114)
1148 Fifth Avenue

91.   **Jacob Epstein residence** (119)
958 Madison Avenue

94.   **John Hazard Reynolds residence** (125)
825 Fifth Avenue

97.   **Ernest Hemingway apartment** (127)
1 East 62nd Street

114.   **Ignatz Griebl residence and office** (152)
56 East 87th Street

116.   **German American Bund headquarters** (155)
178 East 85th Street at Third Avenue

117.   **Gerhard Kunze residence** (156)
211 East 87th Street (site redeveloped)

122.   **FBI secret residence** (164)
53 East 93rd Street

123.   **Lilly Stein residence** (164)
780 Madison Avenue

MAP 6: continued

■ MANHATTAN

➤ Upper East Side, and Yorkville

north of 59th Street, south of 110th Street

204. **Susan Rosenstiel residence** (269)
5 East 80th Street

206. **Arkady Shevchenko residence** (272)
160 East 65th Street, apt. 26D

207. **Permanent mission of the Russian Federation to the United Nations** (273)
136 East 67th Street

230. **Russian consulate** (309)
9 East 91st Street

231. **Permanent mission of the Russian Federation to the United Nations** (310)
136 East 67th Street

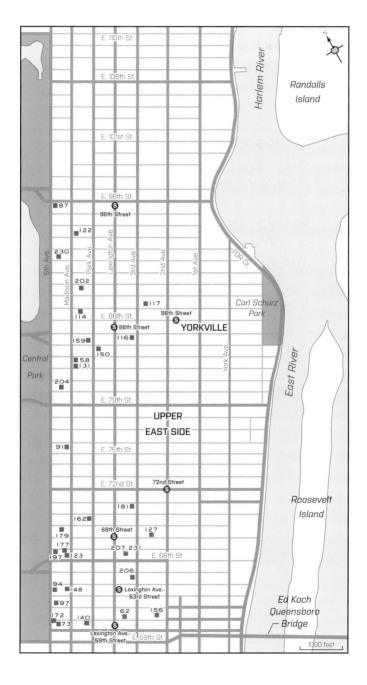

MAP 7:

◼ MANHATTAN

➤ Upper West Side and Central Park

north of 59th Street, south of 110th Street

36. **Sidney Reilly residence** [49]
260 Riverside Drive

100. **The Majestic** [131]
115 Central Park West

101. **Boris Morros residence** [132]
50 Riverside Drive

102. **Vasily Zarubin residence** [134]
2788 Broadway, apt. 4-A

103. **J. Robert Oppenheimer childhood home** [135]
155 Riverside Drive

109. **Klaus Fuchs residence** [144]
128 West 77th Street

115. **Kate Moog residence** [153]
276 Riverside Drive

120. **Frederick Joubert Duquesne residence** [160]
24 West 76th Street

157. **Central Park** [203]
Fifth Avenue, Eighth Avenue, 59th Street, and 110th Street

161. **Robert Ryan apartment** [206]
The Dakota, 1 West 72nd Street

166. **Harry Dexter White residence** [214]
334 West 86th Street

169. **Valentin Gubitchev residence** [219]
64 West 108th Street, apt. 3-A

191. **Roald Dahl residence** [251]
44 West 77th Street

213. **An *illegal's* signal site** (281)
Underpass at the 79th Street Boat Basin and Henry Hudson
Parkway

214. **Surveillance detection route** (287)
American Museum of Natural History, Central Park West at West
79th Street

224. **Flik's Video to Go** (298)
175 West 72nd Street (now closed)

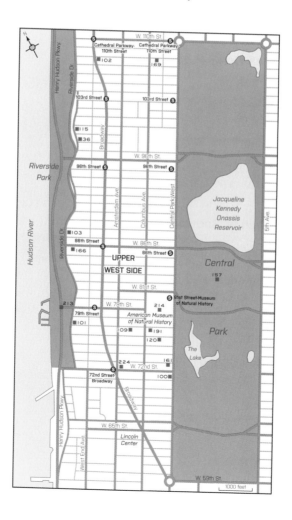

MAP 8:

■ MANHATTAN

➤ **Morningside Heights, Harlem, and Washington Heights**

north 110th Street and south of George Washington Bridge

3. **Columbia University mathematics building** (4)
2990 Broadway, between West 117th and 118th Streets

11. **Alexander Hamilton residence** (14)
Hamilton Grange National Memorial, 414 West 141st Street
between St. Nicholas Avenue and Hamilton Terrace

33. **George Fuchs residence** (44)
630 West 139th Street

48. **John Held Jr. residence** (67)
736 Riverside Drive

52. **Chandra Chakravarty residence** (73)
364 West 120th Street

54. **American Geographical Society** (75)
3755 Broadway

60. **Crescent Theatre** (83)
36–38 West 135th Street (site redeveloped)

98. **Michael Borislavsky murder site** (129)
St. Nicholas Terrace side of the Covent of the Sacred Heart,
West 133rd Street and Convent Avenue

107. **Theodore Hall family home** (140)
725 West 172nd Street

144. **Simon Koedel residence** (187)
660 Riverside Drive

151. **Moe Berg birthplace** (198)
East 121st Street (exact address unknown—approximately
at East 121st Street and Lexington Avenue)

178. **Christina Krotkova residence** (234)
561 West 141st Street, apt. 78

192. **John Mulholland residence** (251)
600 West 115th Street

205. **Grant's Tomb** (270)
West 122nd Street and Riverside Drive

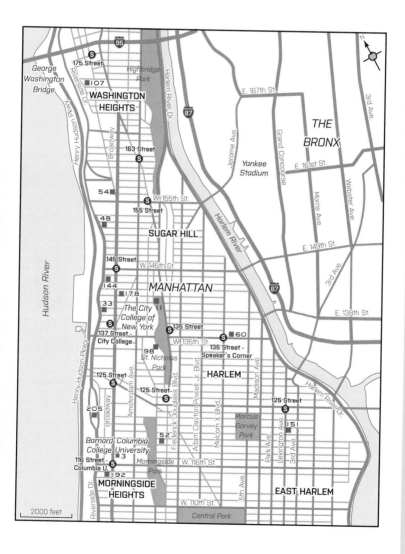

MAP 9:

▪ MANHATTAN, THE BRONX, AND WESTCHESTER COUNTY

➤ **Inwood, the Bronx, and Scarsdale**

north of George Washington Bridge, off the island into the Bronx and points north

24. **Former Mary Elizabeth Bowser memorial site** (30)
Old West Farms Soldiers' Cemetery, Bryant Avenue and East 180th Street, Bronx

59. **Leon Trotsky residence** (82)
1522 Vyse Avenue near East 172nd Street, Bronx

84. **Walter Krivitsky apartment** (111)
36 West Gun Hill Road, Bronx

119. **Wilhelm Grote studio** (159)
946 East 181st Street, Bronx (site redeveloped)

125. **Gerhard Westrick residence** (167)
188 Mamaroneck Road, Scarsdale

198. **A home for Soviet Spies** (262)
355 West 255th Street, Bronx

199. **House of intrigue** (263)
5437 Fieldston Road, Fieldston, Bronx

200. **David Marcus movie theater** (264)
3464 Jerome Avenue, Bronx (site now a post office)

229. **Evgeny Buryakov residence** (307)
5833 Liebig Avenue, Bronx

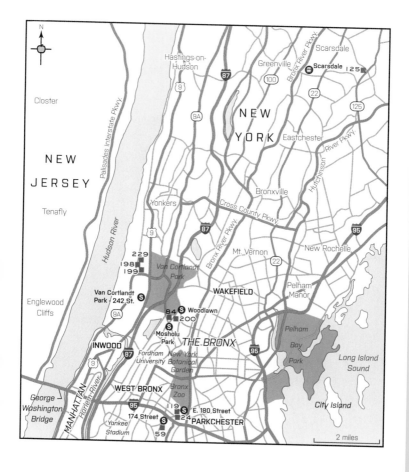

MAP 10:

■ BROOKLYN AND GOVERNORS ISLAND

14. **Fort Greene Park** (18)
Between Myrtle and Dekalb Avenues and between St. Edwards and Cumberland Streets, Brooklyn

19. **John Yates Beall execution site** (25)
Castle Williams on Governors Island

55. **Nolan Park** (76)
Governors Island

78. **RKO Prospect Theatre** (104)
327 9th Street, Brooklyn (today condos and Steve's 9th Street Market)

88. **Safe house for murderers** (115)
881 Washington Avenue, Brooklyn

89. **Sylvia Ageloff residence** (116)
50 Livingston Street, Brooklyn

90. **Hotel Pierrepont** (118)
55 Pierrepont Street, between Henry and Hicks Streets, Brooklyn (building remains on rehabilitated site of St. Charles Jubilee Senior Center of Brooklyn)

126. **Boys High School** (168)
832 Marcy Avenue, Brooklyn

158. **Lord Haw Haw childhood residence** (203)
1377 Herkimer Street, Brooklyn

173. **Yevgeni Brik childhood residence** (224)
1119 Foster Avenue, Brooklyn

174. **Rudolph Abel studio** (225)
252 Fulton Street, Brooklyn (site redeveloped)

175. **Reino Häyhänen residence** (229)
3403 Foster Avenue, East Flatbush, Brooklyn

180A. **Weisband jewelry store** (236)
8016 Third Avenue, Brooklyn

180B. **Weisband jewelry store** (236)
8320 Fifth Avenue, Brooklyn

195. **James B. Donovan residence** (257)
35 Prospect Park West, Brooklyn

221. **Blind Sheikh's mosque** (295)
Al-Farooq Mosque, 552 Atlantic Avenue, Brooklyn

223. **Kun Shan Chun residence** (297)
2953 Quentin Road, Brooklyn

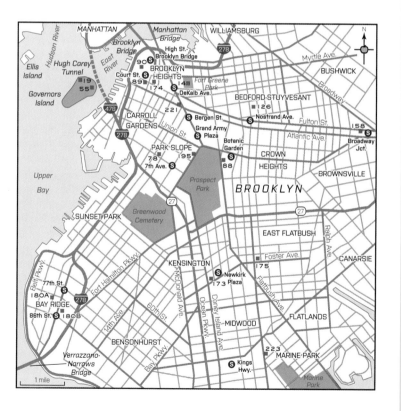

MAP 11:

QUEENS

51. **Despina Storch grave (72)**
Mount Olivet Cemetery, 65-40 Grand Avenue, Maspeth, Queens

69. **J. Peters residence (93)**
83-46 118th Street, Queens

79. **Victor Perlo residence (105)**
72-15 37th Avenue, Queens (sometimes listed as Long Island)

83. **Samuel Dickstein burial site (110)**
Union Field Cemetery, 82-11 Cypress Avenue, Queens

110. **Harry Gold meeting site (145)**
Newsstand (no longer exists) beneath the 90th Street Station at Elmhurst Avenue, Queens

163. **Ralph Bunche residence (209)**
115-24 Grosvenor Road, Queens

190. **Lyric spies (250)**
Idlewild Airport (now John F. Kennedy International Airport), Queens

201. **Fresh Pond subway stop (265)**
Fresh Pond Road near 67th Avenue, Queens

217. **Scobee Diner (292)**
25229 Northern Boulevard, Little Neck, Queens (closed in 2010)

220. **Iranian surveillance target (294)**
Subway station, Roosevelt Avenue and 52nd Street, Queens

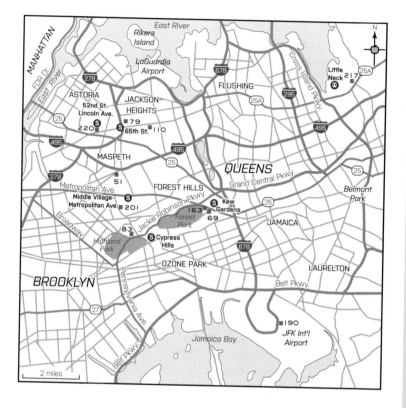

MAP 12:

■ LONG ISLAND

8.   **Abraham Woodhull grave** [10]
Setauket Presbyterian Church cemetery, 5 Caroline Avenue, Setauket, Long Island

26.   **Wardenclyffe Tower** [34]
5 Randall Road, Shoreham, Long Island (only base remains)

27.   **Telefunken transmission tower** [35]
North of the railroad tracks, west of Cherry Avenue, West Sayville, Long Island (only remnants of tower remain)

113.   **William Lonkowski and Senta de Wanger residence** [151]
83 Lincoln Boulevard, Hempstead, Long Island

118.   **Long Island Nazi camp** [157]
Intersection of Mill Road and German Boulevard, Yaphank, Long Island (private side road)

121.   **Secret radio transmitter** [161]
28 Bankside Drive North, Centerport, Long Island

147.   **Secret transmitter site** [193]
408 North Side Road, Wading River, Long Island

193.   **Plum Island Animal Disease Center** [252]
Plum Island, New York

215.   **William Casey residence** [288]
Mayknoll, 12 Glenwood Road, Roslyn Harbor, Long Island

232.   **Killenworth** [312]
Off Dosoris Lane, Glen Cove, Long Island

232.   **Norwich House** [312]
Off Mill River Road, Upper Brookville, Oyster Bay, Long Island

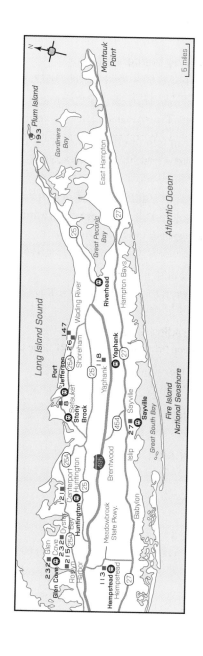

MAP 13:

◼ NEW JERSEY

34. **Robert Fay residence** (45)
    28 50th Street, Weehawken, New Jersey

39. **New Jersey Agricultural Chemical Company** (55)
    1133 Clinton Street, Hoboken, New Jersey (site redeveloped)

41. **Black Tom Island commemorative plaque** (58)
    Foot of Morris Pesin Drive in Liberty State Park, Jersey City, New Jersey

42. **Memorial at Vest Pocket Park, former site of Canadian Car and Foundry Company** (59)
    213 Clay Avenue, Lyndhurst, New Jersey

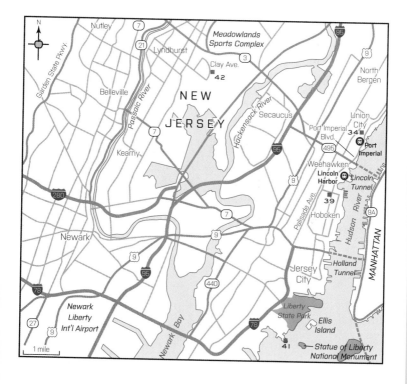

SELECTED BIBLIOGRAPHY

Andrew, Christopher, and Oleg Gordievsky. *KGB: The Inside Story of Its Foreign Operations from Lenin to Gorbachev*. New York: HarperCollins, 1990.

Andrew, Christopher, and Vasili Mitrokhin. *The Mitrokhin Archive: The KGB in Europe and the West*. New York: Penguin, 1999.

————. *The Sword and the Shield: The Mitrokhin Archive and the Secret History of the KGB*. New York: Basic Books, 1999.

Bakeless, John. *Turncoats, Traitors and Heroes: Espionage in the American Revolution*. Cambridge, MA: Da Capo Press, 1998.

Baker, Robert K. *Rezident: The Espionage Odyssey of Soviet General Vasily Zarubin*. Bloomington, IN: iUniverse, 2015.

Barron, John. *KGB: The Secret Work of Soviet Secret Agents*. New York: Reader's Digest Press / E. P. Dutton, 1974.

Bernikow, Louise. *Abel*. New York: Trident, 1970.

Bigger, Philip J. *The Negotiator: The Life and Career of James B. Donovan*. Bethlehem, PA: Lehigh University Press, 2006.

Blass, Bill. *Bare Blass*. New York: HarperCollins, 2003.

Blum, Howard. *Dark Invasion: 1915: Germany's Secret War and the Hunt for the First Terrorist Cell in America*. New York: HarperCollins, 2014.

Bradley, Mark A. *A Very Principled Boy: The Life of Duncan Lee, Red Spy and Cold Warrior*. New York: Basic Books, 2014.

Brown, Anthony C. *Bodyguard of Lies: The Extraordinary True Story behind D-Day*. New York: Harper & Row, 1975.

————. *The Last Hero: Wild Bill Donovan*. New York: Times Books, 1982.

Clarke, Samuel Clarke. *Memoir of Gen. William Hull*. Boston: D. Clapp & son, printers, 1893.

Cohan-Solal, Annie. *Leo and His Circle: The Life of Leo Castelli*. New York: Knopf, 2010.

Conant, Jennet. *The Irregulars: Roald Dahl and the British Spy Ring in Wartime Washington*. New York: Simon & Schuster, 2008.

Conradi, Peter. *Hitler's Piano Player: The Rise and Fall of Ernst Hanfstaengl, Confidant of Hitler, Ally of FDR*. Cambridge, MA: Da Capo Press, 2006.

Cook, Andrew. *Ace of Spies: The True Story of Sidney Reilly*. Stroud, UK: History Press, 2005.

Coward, Noel. *The Letters of Noel Coward*. Edited by Barry Day. New York: Knopf, 2007.

Daigler, Kenneth A. *Spies, Patriots, and Traitors: American Intelligence in the Revolutionary War*. Washington, DC: Georgetown University Press, 2014.

Downes, Donald C. *The Scarlet Thread: Adventures in Wartime Espionage*. London: Derek Verschoyle, 1953.

Earley, Pete. *Comrade J: The Untold Secrets of Russia's Master Spy in America after the End of the Cold War*. New York: Penguin, 2008.

Farago, Ladislas. *A Game of Foxes: The Untold Story of German Espionage in the United States and Great Britain during World War II*. New York: David McKay Company, Inc., 1971.

Feiffer, Jules. *Backing into Forward: A Memoir*. New York: Doubleday, 2010.

Gage, Beverly. *The Day Wall Street Exploded: A Story of America in the First Age of Terror*. New York: Oxford University Press, 2010.

Gazur, Edward. *Alexander Orlov: The FBI's KGB General*. New York: Carroll & Graf Publishers, 2002.

Grose, Peter. *Gentleman Spy: The Life of Allen Dulles*. New York: Houghton Mifflin, 1994.

Gross, Michael. *740 Park: The Story of the World's Richest Apartment Building*. New York: Broadway Books, 2006.

Harris, Charles H., and Louis R. Sadler. *The Archaeologist Was a Spy: Syvanus G. Morley and the Office of Naval Intelligence*. Albuquerque: University of New Mexico Press, 2009.

Haynes, John Earl, and Harvey Klehr. *Early Cold War Spies: The Espionage Trials that Shaped American Politics*. New York: Cambridge University Press, 2006.

Hersh, Burton. *Old Boys: The American Elite and the Origins of the CIA*. New York: Charles Scribner's Sons, 1992.

Herzberg, Bob. *The FBI and the Movies: A History of the Bureau on Screen and behind the Scenes in Hollywood*. Jefferson, NC: McFarland, 2006.

Holmes, Colin. *Searching for Lord Haw-Haw: The Political Lives of William Joyce*. Abingdon, UK: Routledge, 2015.

Horan, James D. *The Pinkertons: The Detective Dynasty That Made History*. New York: Bonanza Books, 1967.

Hyde, Montgomery. *Room 3603: The Incredible True Story of Secret Intelligence during World War II*. New York: Lyons Press, 2001.

Hyman, Harriet. *Robert E. Sherwood: The Playwright in Peace and War*. Amherst: University of Massachusetts Press, 2007.

Isaacson, Walter. *Einstein: His Life and Universe*. New York: Simon & Schuster, 2007.

Isaacson, Walter, and Evan Thomas. *The Wise Men: Six Friends and the World They Made*. New York: Simon & Schuster, 1986.

Jackson, Kenneth T., ed. *The Encyclopedia of New York City*. New Haven, CT: Yale University Press, 1995.

Kahn, David. *The Codebreakers: The Story of Secret Writing*. New York: Macmillan, 1967.

———. *Hitler's Spies: German Military Intelligence in World War II*. Cambridge, MA: Da Capo Press, 2000.

Kalugin, Oleg, and Fen Montaigne. *The First Directorate: My 32 Years in Intelligence and Espionage Against the West*. New York: St. Martin's Press, 1994.

Kodosky, Robert J. *Psychological Operations American Style: The Joint United States Public Affairs Office, Vietnam and Beyond*. Guilford, CT: Lexington Books, 2007.

Lathrop, Charles E. *The Literary Spy: The Ultimate Source for Quotations on Espionage & Intelligence*. New Haven, CT: Yale University Press, 2004.

Loftis, Larry. *Into the Lion's Mouth: The True Story of Dusko Popov: World War II Spy, Patriot, and the Real-Life Inspiration for James Bond*. New York: Dutton Caliber, 2016.

Lycett, Andrew. *Ian Fleming: The Man Behind James Bond*. Atlanta: Turner Publishing, 1996.

Macintyre, Ben. *A Spy Among Friends: Kim Philby and the Great Betrayal*. New York: Broadway Books, 2014.

Macrakis, Kristie. *Prisoners, Lovers, and Spies: The Story of Invisible Ink from Herodotus to al-Qaeda*. New Haven, CT: Yale University Press, 2015.

McCrum, Robert. *Wodehouse: A Life*. New York: W. W. Norton, 2005.

Melton, H. Keith, and Robert Wallace. *The Official CIA Manual of Trickery and Deception*. New York: HarperCollins, 2009.

Morgan, Ted. *A Covert Life: Jay Lovestone, Communist, Anti-Communist, and Spymaster*. New York: Random House, 1999.

Morros, Boris. *My Ten Years as a Counterspy*. New York: Viking, 1959.

Nash, Jay Robert. *Spies: A Narrative Encyclopedia of Dirty Tricks and Double Dealing from Biblical Times to Today*. New York: M. Evans and Company, Inc., 1997.

Persico, Joseph E. *Roosevelt's Secret War: FDR and World War II Espionage*. New York: Random House, 2001.

Phillips, Timothy. *The Secret Twenties: British Intelligence, the Russians and the Jazz Age*. New York: Granta Books, 2017.

Pinkerton, Allan. *History and Evidence of the Passage of Abraham Lincoln from Harrisburg, Pa., to Washington, D.C., on the 22d and 23d of February, 1861*. 1861. Reprint, Ithaca, NY: Cornell University Library, 2009.

Polmar, Norman, and Thomas B. Allen. *Spy Book: The Encyclopedia of Espionage*. New York: Random House, 1997.

Popov, Dusko. *Spy/Counterspy: The Autobiography of Dusko Popov.* New York: Grosset & Dunlap, 1974.

Price, Ruth. *The Lives of Agnes Smedley.* New York: Oxford University Press, 2005.

Reppetto, Thomas A. *Battleground New York City: Countering Spies, Saboteurs, and Terrorists since 1861.* Washington, DC: Potomac Books, 2012.

Reynolds, Nicholas. *Writer, Sailor, Soldier, Spy: Ernest Hemingway's Secret Adventures, 1935–1961.* New York: William Morrow, 2017.

Rintelen, Franz von. *The Dark Invader: Wartime Reminiscences of a German Naval Intelligence Officer.* Abingdon, UK: Routledge, 2016.

Romerstein, Herbert, and Eric Breindel. *The Venona Secrets: The Definitive Exposé of Soviet Espionage in America.* Washington, DC: Regnery History, 2014.

Saunders, Frances S. *Who Paid the Piper: CIA and the Cultural Cold War.* New York: New Press, 2013.

Shevchenko, Arkady N. *Breaking with Moscow.* New York: Knopf, 1985.

Stashower, Daniel. *The Hour of Peril: The Secret Plot to Murder Lincoln before the Civil War.* New York: Minotaur Books, 2013.

Stephenson, William Samuel. *British Security Coordination: The Secret History of British Intelligence in the Americas, 1940–1945.* New York: Fromm International, 1999.

Stevenson, William. *A Man Called Intrepid: The Incredible WWII Narrative of the Hero Whose Spy Network and Secret Diplomacy Changed the Course of History.* New York: Harcourt Brace Jovanovich, 1976.

Sulick, Michael J. *American Spies: Espionage against the United States from the Cold War to the Present.* Washington, DC: Georgetown University Press, 2013.

———. *Spying in America: Espionage from the Revolutionary War to the Dawn of the Cold War.* Washington, DC: Georgetown University Press, 2012.

Trahair, R. C. S., and Robert L. Rober. *Encyclopedia of Cold War Espionage, Spies, and Secret Operations.* New York: Enigma Books, 2012.

Troy, Thomas. *Donovan and the CIA: A History of the Establishment of the Central Intelligence Agency.* McLean, VA: Central Intelligence Agency, 2000.

Tsarev, Oleg, and John Costello. *Deadly Illusions: The KGB Orlov Dossier Reveals Stalin's Master Spy.* New York: Crown, 1993.

Tunney, Thomas. *Throttled! The Detection of the German and Anarchist Bomb Plotters.* Boston: Small Maynard, 1919.

Vaughan, Hal. *FDR's 12 Apostles: The Spies Who Paved the Way for the Invasion of North Africa.* Guilford, CT: Lyons Press, 2006.

Wallace, Robert, H. Keith Melton, and Henry R. Schlesinger. *Spycraft: The Secret History of the CIA Spytechs, from Communism to Al-Qaeda.* New York: Dutton, 2008.

Waller, Douglas. *Wild Bill Donovan: The Spymaster Who Created the OSS and Modern American Espionage.* New York: Free Press, 2011.

Weinstein, Allen, and Alexander Vassiliev. *The Haunted Wood: Soviet Espionage in America—The Stalin Era.* New York: Modern Library, 1999.

West, Nigel. *MI6: British Secret Intelligence Service Operations 1909-1945.* New York: Random House, 1983.

————. *Spycraft Secrets: An Espionage A–Z.* Stroud, UK: History Press, 2017.

White, Norval, Elliot Willensky, and Fran Leadon. *AIA Guide to New York City.* New York: Oxford University Press, 2010.

Yardley, Herbert O. *The American Black Chamber.* Indianapolis: Bobbs-Merrill, 1931.

ILLUSTRATION CREDITS

All images and photographs are property of the authors except as noted below (with page numbers):

Albert D. Richardson: Albert D. Richardson (31).

Alsandro, Wikimedia Commons: Museum of Modern Art (247).

Americasroof, Wikipedia: Steinway Hall (268).

Archive of American Art: Luis Arenal (115).

Asher Brown Durand, Wikimedia Commons: André arrest (13).

Aude, Wikipedia Commons: Information Department of Cable and Radio Censorship (244).

Australian War Memorial / standingwellback.com, Wiki permissions: German incendiary device (55).

Beyond My Ken, Wikimedia Commons: Pierre Hotel (98).

Bibliothèque Nationale de France: Ho Chi Minh (83).

Brooklyn Public Library, Brooklyn Collection: Pierrepont Hotel (119).

Bundesarchiv, Bild 102-13486 / CC-BY-SA 3.0, Wiki permissions: Heinrich Albert (51).

Bureau of Civil Aviation Security of India: Daood S. Gilani (298).

Central Intelligence Agency: George Tenet (292).

City of New York Collection: Hamburg-America Line building (52).

Chris Weitz: John Weitz (207).

David Mink: George Mink (112).

Family of James Donovan: James B. Donovan (257).

Federal Bureau of Investigation: Robert Fay (45); Maria de Victorica scarf (70); Gaik Ovakimian (98); Itzhak Akhmerov (99); Jacob Golos (123); Vasily Zarubin (134); David Greenglass (138); Ruth Greenglass (139); David Greenglass implosion diagram (139); Theodore Hall (141); Klaus Fuchs badge (144); Carl Alfred Reuper (159); Frederick Duquesne (160); William Sebold spy house (162); Axel Wheeler-Hill (162); Josef Klein (163); Lilly Stein (164); Kurt Frederick Ludwig (180); Ludwig spy ring (181); Duško Popov passport photo (182); Ernest Peter Burger (186); George John Dasch (186); Lucky Luciano (189); Alger Hiss (217); Valentin Gubitchev (219); Judith Coplon (220); Robert Hanssen (222); Abel dead-drop site (228); Abel dead-drop site (228); Morris Childs (241); Jennifer Miles (260); Jennifer Miles surveillance photo (261); Valdik Enger (274); Rudolf Chernyayev (274); "Hello, Ed" letter (275); Aldrich Ames (276); Earl Edwin Pitts (277); Anna Chapman (301); Mikhail A. Vasenkov (301); Mikhail Kutsik (302); Columbus Circle (302); Guryev and Metsos surveillance photo (303); Hanover Square Starbucks surveillance photo (304).

Gary Kern: Victor A. Kravchenko book cover (235).

Ghost Army Legacy Project: Bill Blass (208).

Harper's Weekly: Confederate plot against New York City (29).

Henry R. Schlesinger: Mary Lindley Murray plaque (3); Peck Slip (7); Mulligan vault (9); Alexander Hamilton grave (15); Prison Ship Martyrs' Monument (18); Rhinelander Sugar House window (20); George Fuchs residence (44); Peninsula Hotel (50); New York Yacht Club (54); Labor's National Peace Council (57); 14 Wall Street (65); Agnes Smedley Bank Street apartment (66); Agnes Smedley Waverly Place residence (66); John Held apartment (67); St. Patrick's Cathedral pew (72); American Geographical Society (75); 69th Regiment Armory (78); Donovan Sutton Place residence (78); Leon Trotsky residence (82); Leon Trotsky workplace (83); Charles Cooper Nott Jr. residence (85); 225 Fifth Avenue, Brooklyn (86); 15 Park Row (87); Union of Russian Workers (88); Wall Street shrapnel damage (89); World's Tower Building (91); *Daily Worker* headquarters (93); J. Peters residence (94); Isaiah Oggins residence (95); Taft Hotel (96); 121 Madison Avenue (103); Radio City Music Hall (103); Victor Perlo residence (106); Wellington Hotel (108); Walter Krivitsky residence (112); 235 East 13th Street (113); SWP headquarters (114); Robert Sheldon Harte residence (114); Luis Arenal residence (116); Mark Zborowski residence (117); Jacob Epstein residence (120); Fanny McPeek residence (120); Keynote Records (121); Elizabeth Bentley residence (124); 212 Fifth Avenue (125); Artkino (126); Ernest Hemingway residence (128); Michael Borislavsky residence (129); Martha Dodd and Alfred Stern residence (132); Boris Morros residence (133); Simón Bolívar statue (133); Vasily Zarubin residence (135); Julius and Ethel Rosenberg residence (137); Theodore Hall residence (141); Anatoly Yatskov residence (142); 889 Broadway (143); elevated train platform Elmhurst (145); 225 Fifth Avenue (146); Edwin Emerson residence (150); Ignatz Griebl residence (153); 178 East 85th Street (155); 206 East 85th Street (159); Frederick Duquesne residence (160); Knickerbocker Hotel (161); 55 East 93rd Street (164); Hunter College (169); Robert E. Sherwood residence (172); Vichy French operations building (178); Duško Popov home (182); Astor family office (183); Hotel Martinique (187); Stewart Hotel (187); Simon Koedel home (188); Baker and Williams warehouses (191); Woolworth Building (192); Pupin Hall (192); Schermerhorn Hall (193); Shinran Shonin statue (193); Velvalee Dickinson doll shop (195); Park Central Hotel (196); Marlene Dietrich home (196); Julia Child home (199); Belmont Plaza Hotel (199); Kenmore Hotel (200); 21 Club (201); Ernest Cuneo residence (201); Allen Dulles residence (202); William Joyce birthplace (204); P. G.

Wodehouse residence (205); Hotel Van Rensselaer (206); John Weitz residence (207); Bill Blass residence (208); CIG offices (212); Louise Page-Morris residence (214); Harry Dexter White residence (214); Laurence Duggan death scene (216); Grand Hyatt Hotel (217); Chambers meeting site (218); Percy R. Pyne House (221); Robert Hanssen residence (222); American Trading Organization (222); Pierre Hotel (223); Pratt Mansion site (223); Yevgeni Brik residence (224); Hotel Latham (226); Rudolph Abel apartment (227); Reino Häyhänen signal site (230); Reino Häyhänen residence (230); Sutton-East Hotel (232); Everard Turkish Baths (232); Michael Whitney Straight residence (233); Office of War Information (234); Victor Kravchenko residence (236); William Weisband residence (237); Weisband family jewelry store (238); Harry Winston Inc. (240); Childs meeting site (241); J. M. Kaplan Fund building (245); Radio Free Europe (246); Bedford Street apartment (249); Hotel Pennsylvania (250); Roald Dahl residence (251); John Mulholland residence (252); Plaza Hotel (256); James B. Donovan residence (258); Mariella Novotny arrest site (259); Former location Cuban mission (261); Fieldston Road site (263); David Marcus theater site (264); Gennadi Zakharov arrest site (265); Gennadi Zakharov parking site (265); Gennadi Zakharov meeting site (266); Karl and Hana Koecher residence (267); Susan Rosenstiel residence (270); Dmitri Polyakov residence (271); Tavern on the Green (272); Arkady Shevchenko residence (273); Arthur Lindberg dead-drop site (274); Wertheim Study (277); New York Public Library (278); Grand Central Terminal (278); Frank Terpil arrest site (279); Church of the Transfiguration (280); Jack Barsky residence (281); 79th Street Boat Basin (282); Strand Bookstore (289); NYPD Intelligence Division (293); Iranian mission to UN (294); Blind Sheikh mosque (295); Katrina Leung residence (296); Joey Chun residence (298); Flik's Video to Go site (299); Israeli consulate (300); Payoneer headquarters (300); Anna Chapman residence (303); Waldorf Astoria Hotel (306) Lotte New York Palace Hotel (307); Evgeny Buryakov residence (308); Russian consulate (309); Russian mission to UN (310).

Maxwell Arthur Schlesinger: Martha Held German safe house (40).

William Walker Schlesinger: Nathan Hale plaque (2); 141 East 37th St. (37); Sidney Reilly residence (50); Theremin workshop (100); J. Robert Oppenheimer residence (136); Kate Moog residence (154); 780 Madison Avenue (165); Brooklyn's Boys High School (168); BSC headquarters (175); Ralph Bunche Park (209); Aldrich Ames residence (276); Cuban mission plaque (293); *New York Times* (305).

Jack Barsky: Jack Barsky at MetLife (282).

Jim Henderson, Wikipedia: Castle Williams (25).

John F. Kennedy Presidential Library and Museum, Ernest Hemingway Photographic Collection: Hemingway Visa (128).

Joyce Turiskylie: Inwood Park dead-drop site (285).

Kai Pilger, Wikimedia Commons: 30 Rockefeller Center (170).

Library of Congress: Fraunces Tavern (12); John Jay (17); George H. Sharpe (24); Pauline Cushman (28); Johann Henrich von Bernstorff (38); Karl Boy-Ed (48); Franz von Rintelen (54); Kurt Jahnke (58); Spencer Fayette Eddy (64); Waldorf Astoria Hotel (71); Dennis Nolan (76); Brig. Gen. Marlborough Churchill (79); Farley Post Office Building (84); A. Mitchell Palmer (87); Wall Street bombing (89); Ludwig Martens (90); J. Peters before HUAC (93); Whittaker Chambers (104); Samuel Dickstein (111); Elizabeth Bentley (123); Lauchlin Currie (127); Martha Dodd and Alfred Stern (131); march on East 86th Street (155); William Sebold surveillance (162); Chrysler Building

(166); Gene Tunney (177); Whitehall Building (181); Vincent Astor (184); Fulton Fish Market (190); Meyer's Hotel (190); Hotel Astor (190); the Dakota (206); Rudolph Abel woodblock concealment (227); John V. Grombach (242); Killenworth (312).

Michael Holley, Wikipedia: Confederate currency (27).

Moving Picture World (August 1916): Mena Edwards (40).

National Archives and Records Administration: Benedict Arnold (16); Haym Salomon (20); Horst von der Goltz (42); Pumpkin Papers film canisters (105); Anatoly Yatskov (142); William Joyce (204); Robert Fay residence (46); Walter L. Schultz garage (47); Robert Fay saboteur's kit (46); Robert Fay disguise (47); Lehigh Valley Railroad pier (58); Kingsland, New Jersey, explosion (60); George Vaux Bacon (63); slacker raid (69); Maria de Victorica (70); Carl von Rodiger (71); Despina Davidovitch Storch (72); Wolf von Igel (74); mail bomb (85); Harry Gold (145); Edwin Emerson (150); Gerhard Kunze (156).

National Baseball Hall of Fame Library Cooperstown, New York: Moe Berg (198).

National Park Service: Hamilton Grange (15); Grant's tomb (271).

National Security Agency: Herbert O. Yardley (36).

New York City Department of Parks and Recreation: Nathan Hale statue (2).

New York City Historical Society: Royal Gazette (6).

New York City Municipal Records: Camp Siegfried swastika (157); Camp Siegfried street sign (158).

New York Public Library: Kennedy Mansion (13); Old Grapevine Tavern (24).

New York Times (1902): *New York Evening Mail* building (62).

Noel Coward Archive Trust: Noel Coward (179).

Peter Earley: Dmitri Polyakov (271).

Peter Earley / Col. Sergi Tretyakov: *Rezidentura* sketch (311).

Photograph © Bruce M. White: Einstein sculpture (102).

Postcard: Camp Siegfried flags (158).

Raymond Batvinis: Benson House (194).

Raynham Hall Museum: Raynham Hall (10).

Robin S. Oggins: Isaiah Oggins (95).

St. Regis New York: St. Regis Hotel (171).

US Department of Agriculture: Plum Island Animal Disease Center (252); Plum Island (253).

US Department of State: Ridgway Knight (174).

US Naval History and Heritage Command: USS *Corsair* (184).

US Signal Corps: William Donovan (78).

Wikipedia: Battle of Harlem Heights (4); Tesla Tower (34); Telefuncken transmission tower (35), Agnes Smedley (65); Alexander Orlov (108); P. G. Wodehouse (204); Omar Abdel-Rahman (296); Jacob K. Javits Federal Building (313).

Wikipedia Commons: Rhinelander Sugar House Prison (19); Horst von der Goltz (43).

William Oliver Stevens, *A History of Sea Power*: *Turtle* diagram (5).

INDEX

Page numbers in italics refer to photos and illustrations.

O

ABOUT THE AUTHORS

H. KEITH MELTON is the owner of the world's largest private collection of espionage artifacts, an intelligence historian, and the author of several intelligence-related books, including *Ultimate Spy: Inside the Secret World of Espionage*, and the coauthor of *Spycraft: The Secret History of the CIA's Spytechs, from Communism to Al-Qaeda*; *The Official CIA Manual of Trickery and Deception*; *Spy Sites of Philadelphia*; and *Spy Sites of Washington, DC*.

ROBERT WALLACE is a retired senior intelligence officer. He has written several other intelligence-related books with H. Keith Melton, including *Spy Sites of Washington, DC*. He is also coauthor, with Paul A. Newman and Jack Bick, of *Nine from the Ninth*, a collection of essays about the Vietnam War.

HENRY R. SCHLESINGER is a New York–based writer who has collaborated previously with the authors on several books, including *Spy Sites of Washington, DC* and *Spycraft*.